ENCYCLOPEDIA OF CONTEMPORARY AMERICAN SOCIAL ISSUES

ENCYCLOPEDIA OF CONTEMPORARY AMERICAN SOCIAL ISSUES

VOLUME 1
BUSINESS AND ECONOMY

Michael Shally-Jensen, Editor

ABC-CLIO

Santa Barbara, California • Denver, Colorado • Oxford, England

Library of Congress Cataloging-in-Publication Data

Encyclopedia of contemporary American social issues / Michael Shally-Jensen, editor.
    v. ; cm.
    Includes bibliographical references and index.
    Contents: Vol. 1: business and economy — Vol. 2: criminal justice — Vol. 3: family and society — Vol. 4: environment, science, and technology.
    ISBN 978-0-313-39204-7 (set : alk. paper) — ISBN 978-0-313-39205-4 (set ebook)
  1. United States—Social conditions—Encyclopedias.   2. United States—Economic conditions—Encyclopedias.   3. United States—Politics and government—Encyclopedias.
I. Shally-Jensen, Michael.
    HN59.2.E343 2011
    306.0973—dc22   2010041517

ISBN: 978-0-313-39204-7
EISBN: 978-0-313-39205-4

15 14 13 12 11   1 2 3 4 5

This book is also available on the WorldWideWeb as an eBook.
Visit www.abc-clio.com for details.

ABC-CLIO, LLC
130 Cremona Drive, P.O. Box 1911
Santa Barbara, California 93116-1911

This book is printed on acid-free paper ∞

Manufactured in the United States of America

Contents

VOLUME 2: CRIMINAL JUSTICE

VOLUME 3: FAMILY AND SOCIETY

VOLUME 4: ENVIRONMENT, SCIENCE, AND TECHNOLOGY

Preface

The growing prominence of news, information, and commentary of all kinds, and in every medium, has unfortunately not always been matched by a deepening or a widening of consumers' understanding of the issues at hand. In this era of tweets and peeks (information and video clips), of blogging and befogging (electronic opining), people of all stripes are under increased pressure to make snap judgments about matters about which they may know little. The fact that so many of the issues of the day—corporate misdoings, criminal violence, the condition of the schools, environmental disasters—touch the lives of so many Americans suggests that awareness of them at *any* level is a good thing. At some point, however, one needs to move beyond the news feeds and sound bites and begin to appreciate current issues for the complex matters that they are. This is precisely what the *Encyclopedia of Contemporary American Social Issues* is designed to do.

As with other works of its kind, the present encyclopedia is intended to serve as a bridge between the knowledge of experts and the knowledge of those new to the subjects it covers. We present here, then, scholarly research on a broad array of social issues in a format that is accessible and interesting, yet informative. The contributors have taken care with both the quality of their prose and the accuracy of their facts, the aim being to produce entries that are clear, accurate, and thorough. Contributors and editors alike have paid attention to the language of the entries to ensure that they are written in an intelligible style without losing sight of the terms and conventions employed by scholars writing within their disciplines. Thus, readers will find here thoughtful introductions to some of the most pressing issues currently confronting American society.

Scope

The *Encyclopedia of Contemporary American Social Issues* is divided into four volumes: (1) Business and Economy; (2) Criminal Justice; (3) Family and Society; and (4) Environment, Science, and Technology. Within each volume, the entries are arranged in alphabetical order. There are just over 200 entries in the encyclopedia, the essays ranging in length from about 1,500 words to more than 8,000. Each essay discusses a contemporary issue and ends with suggestions for further reading.

The first problem in compiling an encyclopedia of this type, of course, is determining what constitutes a social issue. It would seem a common enough term about whose meaning there is general consensus. Still, the matter bears a quick review. The *American Heritage Dictionary* defines an issue as:

a. a point or matter of discussion, debate, or dispute;
b. a matter of public concern;
c. a misgiving, objection, or complaint;
d. the essential point, crux.

In other words, not only a matter of public debate or discussion but also a point of concern or matter about which there are misgivings or objections. Included in the mix, moreover, is the idea of a neat summary or something boiled down to its essentials.

In the present encyclopedia, readers will find entries reflecting these varied senses of the term *issue*. There are entries, for example, such as "Health Care," "Oil Drilling," and "Gun Control" whose subjects one often hears debated in public forums. On the other hand, there are entries such as "Globalization," "Sprawl," and "Social Justice" whose subjects are rather harder to identify as clear-cut matters for public debate and seem more like general areas of concern. Of course, more than the general public, it is scholars who routinely examine the ins and outs of various subjects; and for scholars there is little doubt that globalization and the like are key issues requiring careful description and analysis. Fortunately for readers of this encyclopedia, included here are the considered opinions of some 170 scholars and professionals from a variety of different fields, all of whom were asked to lay out "the essential points" for lay readers.

No encyclopedia can encompass the complete spectrum of issues within the contemporary United States. The question of what to include and what to omit is one that has vexed us from the start. The best strategy, we found, was to keep constantly in mind the readers who turn to a work like the *Encyclopedia of Contemporary American Social Issues,* whether in a school or college library or in a public library reference center. We recognize that reference works like this serve a range of purposes for the reader, from gleaning facts to preparing a research paper or introducing oneself to a subject in order to appreciate where it fits within the world at large. In the end, as editors who have been around school curricula and have worked in library reference publishing for many years, we followed our own counsel in deciding upon the contents of this work. We do so knowing that we cannot satisfy all readers; we hope, however, that we have satisfied the majority of those in need of the kind of information presented here.

Although the emphasis is on *contemporary* social issues, the entries generally situate their topics in historical context and present arguments from a variety of perspectives. Readers are thus able to gain an understanding of how a particular issue has developed and the efforts that have been made in the past—including in the most recent times—to address it. Thus, perennial issues such as taxes, education, and immigration are examined in their latest permutations, and newer developments such as cloning, identity theft, and media violence are discussed in terms of both their antecedents and the conversations currently surrounding them. If there is any trend to be noted with respect to contemporary American social issues, it might only be that with each step forward comes the likelihood of further steps yet to be negotiated. We get from point A to point B only by making good use of our democratic heritage and anticipating the prospect of multiple voices or multiple intermediary steps. The *Encyclopedia of Contemporary American Social Issues* reflects that fact and advances the idea that it is useful to know where and how a question first arose before attempting to answer it or move it forward in the public agenda.

There is an established tradition in sociology that focuses on "social problems" and the many means by which these problems can be and have been researched and analyzed. Always something of an eclectic enterprise, and drawing on the collective wisdom of social scientists working in a variety of different fields (including criminology, demography, anthropology, policy studies, and political economy), in recent years the social problems tradition has widened its range still further to include questions about the environment, corporations, the media, gender politics, and even science and technology. It is this expanded version of the sociological traditional that the present encyclopedia takes as its animating vision. Encompassed herein are all of the above fields and more. We welcome the expansion and see it as linked to the broader meaning of the term *social issues*.

The four volumes assembled here—Business and Economy; Criminal Justice; Family and Society; and Environment, Science, and Technology—have benefited from work done earlier by others, work hereby democratically brought forward and expanded in scope. Specifically, we have drawn upon a series of books published previously by Greenwood Press and entitled *Battleground*. Key entries from that series have been updated, revised, rewritten, and in some cases replaced through the efforts of either the original authors or experienced editors knowledgeable in the applicable fields. In addition, some two dozen entries appear here for the first time, the aim being to ensure that issues emerging in the last few years receive the attention they deserve. Among this latter group of entries are "Bank Bailouts," "Cybercrime," "Consumer Credit and Household Debt," and "Airport and Aviation Security."

Acknowledgments

It is to the contributors, then, that I, personally, owe the greatest debt of gratitude. Without their patience and understanding, their expertise and professionalism, this work would not have been possible. An associate editor, Debra Schwartz, and development editor Anne Thompson provided invaluable service in the preparation of entries for publication, and the assistance of Scott Fincher in this regard is happily acknowledged as well. Acquisitions editor Sandy Towers, with whom I first worked in conceiving the project, proved a valuable friend and professional asset throughout the process. Also present from the beginning was Holly Heinzer, whom I thank for her support. Many thanks, too, to the production staffs at both ABC-CLIO and Apex CoVantage for their invaluable assistance in helping to refine the text and set up the volumes for publication. I am grateful to Jeff Dixon for handling the graphics.

—Michael Shally-Jensen

A

ADVERTISING AND THE INVASION OF PRIVACY

Phylis M. Mansfield and Michael Shally-Jensen

Networked Selling

Selling has gone social. Advertisers can now rely on consumers and their interests in locating bargains and evaluating shopping experiences to promote the advertisers' products. Most of us have had experience with a Web site such as Amazon.com, for example, where one's purchases are instantly calibrated in terms of other like-minded consumers' purchases and a targeted list of additional "recommendations" is presented for consideration. That was an early application of networked selling. Today, there are many more such "apps" and services, and with each new one consumers are asked to reveal ever more information about themselves, their personal preferences, and their buying habits. Using the smart-phone application Shopkick, for example, consumers are provided with advice on where to find bargains in local retail stores and can earn points, or credits toward purchases, merely by visiting a store—their presence is automatically recorded by an on-site Shopkick tracking device (Clifford 2010). Additional points can be earned by entering a dressing room to try on goods or by using one's phone to scan barcodes on items being promoted in the store. Shoppers also can invite friends to visit (thus earning more points) or share their shopping experiences through links to Facebook and Twitter (two popular social networking services). Swipely, another social shopping service, allows consumers to publish their purchases online merely by swiping their credit or debit cards at the time of purchase. Other users of the service may then comment on those purchases or, as Swipely's motto puts it, "turn purchases into conversations." The idea is that by sharing and rating their buys and bargains, users will be able to discover new shops, restaurants, and products and find daily bargains (PBN Staff 2010).

In doing so, however, what used to be private information—how one spends one's money—becomes a public conversation. Obviously, not everyone will be attracted to these types of services, but Swipely, Shopkick, and a growing number of others seek to tap into a trend, particularly among young people, toward increased willingness to share the details of one's life with others as part of a digitally connected social network. The trend is clearly present and growing, but as of mid-2010 it represented but a small portion of the advertising industry's overall efforts to win buyers and influence shoppers.

Advertising in the Movies

In the 2006 comedy film *Talladega Nights: The Ballad of Ricky Bobby*, viewers probably were not too surprised to see the obvious pitches for NASCAR, Sprint, Wonder Bread, and Power Ade as the story unfolded. In fact, the advertising connection between the movie and products continued into the retail environment, as grocery stores began to sell NASCAR-branded hotdogs and other Talladega-branded merchandise—a phenomenon known as branded entertainment. Sports events, particularly auto racing, have long been associated with corporate sponsorships, which have grown to be an acceptable part of the experience. However, is the blitz of products as props or part of the story line in a movie an invasion of the customer's privacy? Consumers pay to be entertained by a movie, not to be exposed to a two-hour-long commercial.

Corporate sponsorship through product placements in movies, TV shows, and video games has become an increasingly prevalent method of promotion. Global spending on paid product placement promotion increased by 42 percent in 2005 and by another 39 percent in 2006. It declined by a few percentage points for the first time in its history in 2009, owing to the global economic recession. The United States is the world's fastest growing market in the phenomenon, estimated to have generated nearly $4 billion in 2009. Companies have found that this method of promotion is more precise in reaching their targeted audiences than regular television advertising since technology has allowed customers to stream ad-free or "ad-lite" versions of shows online or skip over TV commercials by using the TiVo digital system.

Movie executives have embraced the use of product placement and branded entertainment as a means to bolster their movie budgets and offset costs before the film is ever introduced to the public. One of the most profitable product placement agreements was in the 2002 movie *Minority Report*, starring Tom Cruise. Corporate sponsors paid close to $25 million in product placement fees for their products, representing one-fourth of the movie's total budget. Even the plot itself deals with the business of advertising. In the film, the character played by Tom Cruise walks through a shopping mall bombarded by holograph advertising messages as he passes each store. In the movie, this

AD SPENDING BY MEDIA

Media	Expenditure
Newspapers	$25.1 billion
Consumer magazines	$28.9 billion
Internet*	$9.7 billion
Network TV	$26.7 billion
Cable TV	$18.9 billion
Radio	$9.5 billion
Outdoor**	$3.9 billion
Spot TV (by station)	$10.7 billion
Branded entertainment**	$22.3 billion

*Does not include paid search advertising.
**Includes product placement, event sponsorship/marketing, advertising games, and webisodes.
Source: AdAge, June 22, 2009; Product Placement News, March 28, 2008.

was a scene from the future year 2054, but today's technology has increased the many ways that marketers are getting to their prospective customers. The future is already here in the world of advertising.

Searching for the Customer

Advertisers have used many forms of media to get their messages to potential customers over the years. Spending on advertising through radio, magazines, newspapers, and outdoor media (billboards) all peaked in the mid-1940s with the advent of television. Until 1994, newspapers were the largest ad medium. In 2009, television was the largest medium (including network, cable, and local), with magazines a distant second. While marketers are looking to other technologies to communicate to their customers—for example, mobile media (smart phones and other handheld devices)—the majority of media buys are still for the older types of media. One reason for this may be that costs to place ads on radio, on TV, in newspapers, or on billboards are higher than those for the Internet or other forms of direct marketing, and the returns may be better, or at any rate more predictable.

The cost issue may also be the reason companies are looking for other ways to reach their target audiences. One of these ways is for advertisers to show regular 30- and 60-second commercials in movie theaters before the featured movie begins. Advertisers look to this venue for two primary reasons: (1) they are able to reach a specific target segment with their ads, and (2) they have a captive audience. It is easier for a company to determine who is watching a certain genre movie than it is to target who is watching a television program, and it is likely that the viewer is not going to switch to another station on the remote or TiVo the ad. An additional benefit to the advertiser is the effectiveness of this medium. Research shows that the audience retains the information in an ad shown in a movie theater better than in one provided by television or other media. Cinema advertising has grown almost 40 percent in the last five years and is expected to double to over $1 billion by 2011.

Another fast-growing method for targeting specific audiences and delivering advertising is through radio signal tracking. When radios are tuned in, they not only receive signals, they also transmit them. Technology allows companies to pick up radio signals from passing cars, determining what station the occupants are listening to. Although the technology was first used to measure consumers' actual listening habits of various radio stations, it is now being used for a more interactive purpose. MobilTrak, a company specializing in this technology, can pick up radio signals and give retail businesses specific data about the type of radio stations that the passing traffic is listening to. While a radio station can claim that it is the number one station in the market, it may be number one on the east side of town but not on the west. MobilTrak can help retailers target their advertising buys more specifically, so that they can place their commercials on the specific stations that are most popular in their geographical area.

This type of technology is also being used in outdoor advertising, where radio signals from passing traffic help to determine the specific ads that are on billboards. With the advent of multiple-ad billboards, where the ads change frequently through computer panels, several companies can share the cost of a single location. These electronic billboards can be set to change and show a new commercial every few seconds. However, with radio signal tracking, the ads change depending on the average demographic driving by at the time, determined by which radio stations they have tuned in. If the majority of the drivers are listening to a country station, the ad might be for a local truck dealer; however, if most of the drivers are listening to a public radio station, the ad might be for the local symphony.

Reaching the Customer by Phone

The idea of tracking specific customers as they pass by is not limited to radio signal technology. Marketers realize that people are spending more time on the Internet and cell phones than watching television, and so they are finding ways to develop commercials that get to the customer on these types of devices. Nearly 300 million consumers in the United States own mobile phones, providing a viable format for reaching large numbers of potential customers. In the film *Minority Report,* the character played by Tom Cruise is bombarded by holographic messages as he walks by stores. Today, the technology exists (based on the Global Positioning System, or GPS) that allows retailers to text message commercial ads as customers walk through a mall. They can identify specific customers and send a message about new items that are in the store or about specific items that are on special that day. Marketers can also send commercials to cell phone screens. Many companies are revising the usual television ads and formatting them for the smaller screen. For now, it does not appear that consumers are offended by the ads; however, as more companies engage in this type of promotion, the public's attitude may change. The trend for mobile marketing is expected to grow significantly in the next few years.

Technology Enables New Methods

Technology has also enabled marketers to target their customers more specifically. For several years, personalized ads have run in magazines that are targeted to specific subscribers. Ads are included in magazines with the individual's name imprinted on the page, making the ad not only more personal but also more recognizable, therefore increasing the likelihood that the individual will read the message. This same type of technology is now being used to print special commercial messages on bank statements. Companies like Chase and Wells Fargo have been foregoing the usual mail inserts and instead have been imprinting personalized messages in the statements, through print and online. The messages typically are for other products that the companies offer or related products in which consumers may have an interest, like a financial planning seminar. However, in the future, these specialized ads could be for other companies' products and services.

Older technologies have also been employed for new purposes. In some larger retail outlets, managers use video cameras to track shoppers' movements and observe their buying habits. Companies such as Envirosell specialize in providing retailers with this service, supplying trained personnel to monitor the cameras and analyze the results. In some cases, the cameras have been used to monitor the behavior of floor salespersons— for example, to see whether they approach customers in a specified amount of time. Privacy advocates, such as those belonging to Consumers Against Supermarket Privacy Invasion and Numbering, find the practice to be a clear violation of individual privacy rights (Rosenbloom 2010).

Some Alternative Forms of Advertising

Whether enabled by technology, a spark from a creative advertiser's mind, or just plain common sense, there are many new, alternative means for the world of advertising to reach the potential customer.

The company marketing Purell hand sanitizer invented a new campaign that would reach potential customers in doctors' offices ("Purell" 2006). The company placed bright yellow, two-by-three-inch stickers on the top right corners of the magazines in a doctor's office waiting room. The stickers read "Caution" in large type: "How many patients have coughed on this" or "gently sneezed on this" or "Exposing patients to more than germs," all pointing to the need for Purell hand sanitizer. The ads further suggested that hand washing was not enough—that a hand sanitizer was necessary to kill the germs.

Another unique form of advertising was reported by National Public Radio; US Airways was planning to begin placing advertising for other companies on its air sickness bags. Seeing the blank space on the bags, a clever marketer felt that it would be able to bring some needed cash to the airline's bottom line.

Other companies have found blank space on city sidewalks, street posts, and even trees. Called *wild posting,* companies spray paint ads on sidewalks and street posts. Although the practice is illegal, the fines imposed on the companies are a fraction of what legitimate advertising would cost. In 2006, Reebok painted over 200 mini billboards on the sidewalks of Manhattan. Their fine was $11,000 in cleanup costs; however, if they had placed the same ads on 200 phone booths during the same period, it would have cost over $400,000. Old Navy found blank space on the trees along one Manhattan street and tied Old Navy logos on them (McLaren 2007).

On the golf course, many of the conveniences offered to golfers are also media for advertising messages. GPS screens mounted on golf carts offer several services: golfers can place orders at the clubhouse restaurant so that they can be ready when the game is over or keep electronic scores and compare themselves to other golfers. The screens also provide space for advertising, which can be tailored to the specific hole the cart is approaching. Additionally, ads have been placed in the bottom of each hole on a golf course so that when the player picks up the ball, the ad is seen. The golf course is an attractive medium to marketers due to the demographics of the players. It is estimated that there are 27 million golfers in the United States, a number that continues to grow—perhaps at a more exaggerated rate, with the number of baby boomers who will be retiring in the next decade. The players tend to be men (85 percent), own their own homes (80 percent), well educated (47 percent are college graduates), and have an average household income of over $100,000 (Prentice 2006).

Perhaps the most invasive form of alternative advertising is following consumers into public bathrooms. Initially, the ads were in the form of posters, primarily on the

CUSTOMER PREFERENCES IN ADVERTISING

Prefer Marketing That

is short and to the point.	43%
I can choose to see when it is convenient for me.	33%
provides information about price discounts or special deals.	29%
is customized to fit my specific needs and interests.	29%

Source: "2005 Marketing Receptivity Study by Yankelovich Partners, Inc." Chapel Hill, NC: American Association of Advertising Agencies, April 2005.

back of stall doors and above the urinals. However, they have gone to new locations to reach the captive customer. Companies are placing ads on urinal mats in men's rooms, and, while not every company relishes the idea of men urinating on their logo, there are many that do. In fact, urinal mats are big business in bar bathrooms, and bathroom advertising is currently the fastest growing form of indoor advertising. In addition to the urinal mat are audio ads delivered via talking toilet paper dispensers, interactive poster ads that will emit a fragrance sample when pressed, and digital screens placed in the floor right in front of the toilet. All of these media are designed to reach a captive audience and can be tailored to fit the demographic of the audience. Ads can be placed in men's or women's rooms and can be targeted to the age group likely to be customers. Most interactive bathroom advertising is in the restrooms of nightclubs, bars, and restaurant-bar combinations.

When Is It Too Much?

While consumers have grown to expect advertising messages to appear through various forms of media, the proliferation of ads and the means by which marketers reach us could have negative consequences. At some point, consumers may say "enough." Consider a couple who have traveled out of town to attend a friend's wedding. After checking in, they retire to their hotel room and see the message light blinking on the phone. Expecting to retrieve their messages, they first hear a 30-second commercial for the restaurant down the street. Later, they go to dinner, maybe in that same restaurant. The man excuses himself to go to the restroom and, while relieving himself, reads an advertisement printed on a urinal mat. But our couple's exposure to commercial messaging does not stop here. When they get to their friend's wedding, they find that corporate sponsors have been invited to the wedding. The food is sponsored by a local restaurant, which has imprinted its logo and ad on the wedding tableware. The florist has a mobile billboard located just inside the reception hall, and the photographer's business cards are located at each table setting. The wedding has become a promotional event.

From the Marketer's Point of View

While there are many critics of advertising, the fact that our culture is exposed to advertising is a sign of an open society. Additionally, research suggests that the public actually *likes* advertising—but prefers that it be less obtrusive and on a time schedule that they select (see the sidebar "Customer Preferences in Advertising"). Marketers consider advertising to be a form of free speech and a part of doing business in a capitalistic society. Additionally, advertising is necessary for informing the public about the many products that are offered for sale. Gone are the days when Henry Ford offered his car only in black. Today, improvements in industrialization processes and technology have made it possible to offer a proliferation of products that can

CUSTOMER ATTITUDES TOWARD ADVERTISING

I am constantly bombarded with too much advertising.	65%
Advertising exposure is out of control.	61%
Advertising is much more negative than just a few years ago.	60%
I avoid buying products that overwhelm me with advertising and marketing.	54%
I am interested in products and services that would help skip or block marketing.	69%

Source: "2005 Marketing Receptivity Study by Yankelovich Partners, Inc." Chapel Hill, NC: American Association of Advertising Agencies, April 2005.

be tailored to every need. No longer does a customer go to the store to simply buy toothpaste; he is now met with a number of choices that even a decade ago was not thought to be possible. One can buy toothpaste made by Aim, Aquafresh, Colgate, or Crest, in paste or gel, and in flavors of mint, cinnamon, or orange; moreover, one has choices for sensitive teeth, tartar control, whitening, cavity prevention, and so on. The average supermarket in the United States offers approximately 33,000 products to choose from. It is estimated that every year there are an additional 25,000 new consumer products offered for sale; some are truly new products, and some are modifications of existing ones. However, the majority of these new products fail—as many as 90 percent of them in some industries—which keeps down the total number in stores at any given time. To cut through the product offering clutter, marketers feel the need to get the word out to their customers and inform them of the product's benefits, both tangible and intangible.

However, marketers also know that there is a saturation point for advertising, a point at which any additional expenditures are wasted on the customer. This saturation point differs by industry, type of product, content of the ad, and other variables, but it can be calculated for the specific ad and product. The question is, at what point does the customer become saturated by advertising in general? It is difficult for marketers to calculate this saturation point due to the number of products, ads, and media by which we are exposed to advertising every day. The number of messages each of us is exposed to every day is estimated to be as high as 3,500. However, it is suggested that we can only process and recall about 1 percent of them (Kitcatt 2006).

Will marketers continue to search for new methods to reach their targeted audiences? Will consumers grow weary of the onslaught of advertising or, worse, grow indifferent? At what point does it all become overkill?

See also **Marketing to Children; Marketing to Women and Girls; Sex and Advertising; Internet (vol. 4)**

Further Reading

Berger, Arthur, *Ads, Fads, and Consumer Culture,* 3d ed. Lanham, MD: Rowman & Littlefield, 2007.

Clifford, Stephanie, "Aisle by Aisle, an App That Pushes Bargains." *New York Times* (August 17, 2010).

Consumers against Supermarket Privacy Invasion and Numbering. http://www.nocards.org

Kirkpatrick, Jerry, *In Defense of Advertising: Arguments from Reason, Ethical Egoism, and Laissez-Faire Capitalism.* Claremont, CA: TLJ Books, 2007.

Kitcatt, Paul, "Be Heard—Speak Softly." *Marketing* (July 12, 2006): 24.

McLaren, Carrie, *As Advertisers Race to Cover Every Available Surface, Are They Driving Us Insane?* 2007. http://www.stayfreemagazine.org/archives/18/adcreep.html

PBN Staff, "Swipely Goes Live to U.S. Consumers as a Way to Share Purchase Experiences." *Providence Business News* (August 18, 2010).

Prentice, Kathy, *Fore! The Latest on Golf Course Ads.* 2006. http://www.medialifemagazine.com/news2003/jan03/jan06/1_mon/news5monday.html

Purell: Guerilla Marketing in the Doctor's Office. 2006. http://www.caffeine marketing.com/guerilla-marketing/purell-guerilla-marketing-in-the-doctors-office

Ries, Al, and Laura Ries, *The Rise of PR and the Fall of Advertising.* New York: Collins, 2002.

Rosenbloom, Stephanie, "In Bid to Sway Sales, Cameras Follow Shoppers." *New York Times* (March 19, 2010).

Schwartz, Barry, *The Paradox of Choice: Why More Is Less.* New York: HarperCollins, 2004.

Stanford, Eleanor, *Advertising: Introducing Issues with Opposing Viewpoints.* San Diego: Greenhaven Press, 2007.

Wilkins, Lee, and Clifford G. Christians, eds., *The Handbook of Mass Media Ethics.* New York: Routledge, 2009.

AFFIRMATIVE ACTION

William M. Sturkey

Affirmative action is the practice of preferential hiring for minorities to ensure that employees in businesses represent population demographics. In the American business world, there is a growing debate about whether affirmative action is effective, or even necessary. This article will concentrate on the history of the affirmative action concept in the United States and illustrate the arguments on each side of the affirmative action debate.

How and Why Did Affirmative Action Begin?

Affirmative action began largely as a result of the African American civil rights movement of the 1950s and 1960s. The first person to use the term *affirmative action* was President John F. Kennedy. His goal was to use affirmative action to ensure that the demographics of federally funded positions represented the nation's racial demographics more proportionately. With the passage of the 1964 Civil Rights Act, eight months after Kennedy was assassinated, affirmative action began to spread to realms outside of government. Title VI of the act stated that "no person…shall, on the ground of race, color, or national origin, be excluded from participation in, be denied the benefits of, or be subjected to discrimination under any program or activity receiving Federal financial assistance." Title VII laid out exemptions to this law, stating that, under special circumstances, gender, religion, or national origin could be used as a basis for employee selection. This was the beginning of the type of preferential hiring that we now refer to as affirmative action.

FIVE MYTHS ABOUT AFFIRMATIVE ACTION

1. *Affirmative action only benefits African Americans.* Affirmative action is designed for, and applied to, all minority groups, including white women.
2. *Over the last 30 years, affirmative action has clearly leveled the playing field for minority groups.* According to one study, although blacks represent approximately 12 percent of the U.S. population, they make up less than 5 percent of the management ranks and considerably less than 1 percent of senior executives (Brief et al. 2002). The disparity is prevalent among gender, too. Women who work full-time throughout the year earn approximately 78 percent as much as men (Stolberg 2009).
3. *Affirmative action costs a lot of white workers their jobs.* According to the U.S. government, there are fewer than 2 million unemployed African Americans and more than 100 million employed whites. Considering that affirmative action policies extend to only qualified job applicants, if every unemployed, and qualified, African American took the place of a white worker, less than 1 percent of whites would be affected ("Ten Myths" n.d.).
4. *Affirmative action gives preference to women and people of color based only on their race.* No one is ever hired or accepted strictly based on skin color. This practice is prohibited by law.
5. *Once an affirmative action candidate is hired, she has a job for life, no matter how poor her performance.* The terms of performance in the workplace are the same for minorities as they are for white men. Often, minorities are expected to contribute more to the workplace than white men due to stereotypes that all minorities in business are hired due to affirmative action.

Other myths surrounding affirmative action are that it was developed as a means to end poverty within certain social groups and that it was designed to make amends for slavery or similar economic hardships placed on various minority groups throughout the history of the United States. It was designed to open the door to a certain minority group's ability to obtain a foothold in workplaces from which they had consistently been excluded.

Kennedy's successor, Lyndon B. Johnson, was the first to use the term affirmative action in legislation. In Executive Order No. 11,246 (1965), Johnson required federal contractors to use affirmative action to ensure that applicants are employed and that employees are treated during employment, without regard to race, creed, color, or national origin. Johnson also wanted to extend Title VII into realms outside government-financed jobs.

Johnson's affirmative action was designed to implement institutional change so that American organizations could comply with the Civil Rights Act. The need for this change was based on the following assumptions: (1) white men comprise the overwhelming majority of the mainstream business workforce. Providing moral and legislative assistance to underrepresented minorities is the only way to create a more equal space in the business place. (2) The United States, as the so-called land of opportunity, has enough economic space for all its citizens. (3) Especially after the Civil Rights Act, the government assured itself, and the citizens of the United States, that public policy was the proper mechanism to bring about equality of opportunity. (4) Racial prejudice exists in the workplace, and it adversely affects the business and academic worlds' hiring of minorities. (5) Social and legal coercion is necessary to bring about desired change.

One of the most common misconceptions of affirmative action is that it sanctions quotas based on race or some other essential group category such as gender. It does not. This was affirmed in 1978 when the U.S. Supreme Court, in *Regents of the University of California v. Bakke,* ruled that racial quotas for college admissions violated the Fourteenth Amendment's equal protection clause, unless they were used to remedy discriminatory practices by the institution in the past. In *Bakke,* white applicant Allan P. Bakke argued that his application to the University of California, Davis's Medical School was denied due to the university's use of quotas to admit a specific number of minority students to the medical school each year. In its highly fractious decision, the Supreme Court ruled that Bakke's application was rejected because of the quota and ruled quotas unlawful. Muddying the waters, however, was Justice Powell's *diversity rationale* in the majority decision. The diversity rationale posited that ethnic and racial diversity can be one of many factors for attaining a heterogeneous student body in places of higher education. Thus, while *Bakke* struck down sharp quotas, the case created a compelling government interest in diversity.

How Is Affirmative Action Implemented?

Affirmative action requires companies to perform an analysis of minority employment, establish goals to create a more demographically representative workforce, and develop plans to recruit and employ minority employees. For most companies that have effective programs, affirmative action extends beyond hiring practices to include maintaining a diverse workforce, periodic evaluations of the affirmative action program, educating and sensitizing employees concerning affirmative action policies, and providing a work environment and management practices that support equal opportunity in all terms and conditions of employment. Many of the biggest companies in the United States today have departments and legal staffs dedicated entirely to ensuring diversity in the workplace.

A multitude of problems inhibit or complicate the enforcement of affirmative action. The bulk of these problems include issues surrounding practices common to the modern business world, stereotypes, and employee preferences. Most of these problems

LEGAL HISTORY OF DIVERSITY IN THE AMERICAN PUBLIC SPHERE

Equal Pay Act of 1963
- Requires that men and women workers receive equal pay for work requiring equal skill, effort, and responsibility, and performed under similar working conditions.

Civil Rights Act of 1964
- Title VI states that "no person...shall, on the ground of race, color, or national origin, be excluded from participation in, be denied the benefits of, or be subjected to discrimination under any program or activity receiving Federal financial assistance."
- Title VII laid out exemptions to this law, stating that, under special circumstances, gender, religion, or national origin could be used as basis for employee selection.
- Executive Order No. 11,246 (1965) stated that "the head of each executive department and agency shall establish and maintain a positive program of equal employment opportunity for all civilian employees and applicants for employment within his jurisdiction in accordance with the policy set forth in Section 101."

1978, *Regents of the University of California v. Bakke*
- The U.S. Supreme Court decided that any strictly racial quota system supported by the government violated the Fourteenth Amendment and the Civil Rights Act of 1964.

1980, *Fullilove v. Klutznik*
- The Supreme Court upheld a federal law mandating that 15 percent of public works funds be set aside for qualified minority contractors.

1986, *Wygant v. Jackson Board of Education*
- The Court ruled against a school board whose policy it was to lay off nonminority teachers first, before laying off minority teachers.

1995, *Adarand Constructors v. Peña*
- The Court called for "strict scrutiny" to be applied to cases in which past discrimination is alleged, and it required affirmative action programs to be "narrowly tailored" to address specific issues at hand, not broad trends.

1997, California's Proposition 209

- California passed legislation that banned all affirmative action programs in the state.

2003, *Gratz and Hamacher/Grutter v. The Regents of the University of Michigan*

- The Supreme Court upheld the University of Michigan's law school admissions policy, which considered race as a factor.

2009, *Ricci v. DeStefano*

- The Court ruled that (non-minority) firefighters in New Haven, Connecticut, were justified in claiming reverse discrimination. The city had thrown out the results of advancement exams because it feared the results would prevent a sufficient number of minority candidates from advancing.

are extremely hard to investigate and often involve serious issues, such as personal relationships or job loss, that make the problem even more complicated.

One of the biggest problems facing U.S. companies today is how to handle affirmative action when downsizing. What role should affirmative action play when deciding who is expendable during downsizing? Rarely do companies plan downsizing strategies that include consideration of workforce diversity. When deciding who to downsize, employers have a great number of factors to consider. These factors include race, gender, seniority, tenure with the company, rank, and personal relationships. There is no standard way of dealing with downsizing because each situation, and each employer, is different. Juggling the aforementioned factors while paying attention to the levels of merit between employees now competing for jobs can become incredibly complicated and pressured.

Perhaps the most widespread problem facing effective affirmative action practices today is also the hardest to identify and fix and is the most complicated. This problem is commonly referred to as the *good old boy factor*. The good old boy factor involves nepotism, the employment of friends and family over those who may be more qualified for certain positions. The basic problem behind this type of employment is that the employer's family and close personal friends most often share the same ethnic background as the employer, thus limiting diversity in certain realms of employment. Ironically, although not termed this, the good old boy factor is, for all effective purposes, a form of affirmative action. However, this type of affirmative action does not require any amount of education, experience, competence, or overall job qualifications for employment. The way to handle this problem is to change the employment practices and values of the highest ranking executives in a company. However, because they are the highest ranking executives, they may not have anyone to whom they answer, and their immediate subordinates are often people hired due to their relationships as well. In reality, white men have been hired for years, and continue to be hired, due to racial and personal preferences.

THE GOOD OLD BOY FACTOR

The career of former Federal Emergency Management Agency (FEMA) director Michael Brown is an example of the good old boy factor at work. Before taking over FEMA, Brown was the judges and stewards commissioner for the International Arabian Horse Association (IAHA), from 1989 to 2001. Brown resigned his $100,000-a-year post in 2001 amid scandal. Brown left the IAHA so financially depleted that the organization was forced to merge with the Arabian Horse Registry of America and has since ceased to exist.

Shortly after his dismissal, Brown joined FEMA as general counsel, under the guidance of then FEMA director Joe Allbaugh, who ran President George W. Bush's 2000 election campaign. When Allbaugh resigned in 2003, Brown, with Allbaugh's recommendation, became the new head of FEMA, with an annual salary of $148,000.

When Hurricane Katrina hit the city of New Orleans on August 29, 2005, it quickly became one of the most horrific natural disasters to ever affect the United States. The storm killed more than 400 people, displaced approximately one million Gulf Coast residents, cost nearly 400,000 jobs, and caused as much as $200 billion in damage (*Katrina* 2005). While the storm was obviously beyond human control, the U.S. government, specifically FEMA and Brown, received criticism from across the globe pertaining to its slow response to the storm. Democratic and Republican politicians criticized FEMA and called for Brown's immediate dismissal. Brown was forced to resign on September 12, 2005, after a significant tragedy in U.S. history.

On September 9, 2005, *Time* magazine reported that it had found false claims in Brown's biography on the FEMA Web site. The biography exaggerated previous emergency experience, lied about a teaching award and job status at Central State University, and fabricated a role with the organization known as the Oklahoma Christian Home. Another member of the press, Michelle Malkin (2005), stated that Brown was a "worthless sack of bones.... And I don't care if he has 'Bush appointee' stamped on his forehead or a GOP elephant tattooed to his backside. Brown's clueless public comments after landfall are reason enough to give him the boot...and he should never have been there in the first place." Columnist Russ Baker (2006) wrote that "Michael Brown will forever remain the poster child for federal incompetence" and "it makes absolutely no sense that Michael Brown should have been holding any major government post." So why did this happen?

The answer is the good old boy factor. Mike Brown and Joe Allbaugh were college roommates and had been friends for decades. Allbaugh served on George Bush's administration while Bush was the governor of Texas and ran his 2000 presidential campaign. Allbaugh appointed Brown director of FEMA after his resignation from the post, despite Brown reportedly having few supporters within the organization. Instead of relying on credentials, President Bush and long-time political ally Joe Allbaugh hired one of Allbaugh's old friends, who, despite a misleading résumé and an apparent display of incompetence at his last job, had similar political interests. This is an example of good old boy affirmative action. Mike Brown received his job because of his long-time friendship with the administration, while other potential FEMA administrators were passed over. Good old boy hiring occurs in the business world all the time, and many believe that it is a key factor in inhibiting the objectives of affirmative action.

The Argument against Affirmative Action

Since its inception, affirmative action has constantly faced harsh critics who would like to see the process changed, altered, or disbanded altogether. The critics of affirmative action claim that the practice actually creates unequal hiring practices; is impractical; is unfair to those who, they claim, lose jobs due to the practice; and is even unfair to those who gain employment because they may not be able to do the work. One of the most common misconceptions about those who are against affirmative action is that they are all white conservative men. However, many minorities, even liberal ones, are also opposed to affirmative action, if not as a concept, then to the way it is implemented in the U.S. system. This section will outline some of the major arguments against affirmative action as it is generally applied in the United States today.

The most prevalent argument against affirmative action is that the practice creates reverse discrimination. Those who argue this stance point to Title VI of the 1964 Civil Rights Act, which was designed to prevent exclusion of minority groups based on race, religion, sex, or national origin. Those who claim reverse discrimination when arguing against affirmative action claim that white men are now victims of discrimination due to their race and sex.

One of the biggest changes in U.S. society over the past 40 years has been the cultural and judicial insistence on civil rights for every citizen. The most famous impetus for this sociological development was the civil rights movement of the 1950s and 1960s, which produced wide gains in the public sphere for African Americans. Included in these gains was the Civil Rights Act of 1964, which outlawed discrimination in public realms such as education, housing, and hiring practices. To many Americans, the treatment that African Americans experienced in this nation until this act was passed was unacceptable and unfair. By enacting the Civil Rights Act of 1964, President Lyndon B. Johnson created, in many citizens' eyes, an equal playing ground for African Americans. To them, affirmative action went beyond the means and goals of the Civil Rights Act of 1964 and was excessive because discrimination was now outlawed by the federal government, and African Americans would be on equal footing with whites.

Furthermore, many argue that affirmative action is unfair because those who lose, supposedly the white majority, and those who gain, supposedly all minority groups, are not all victims of the historical process that created past inequalities. They ask, why should contemporary whites have to pay for the inequalities created by past generations before they were born? At the same time, they ask, why should minorities, specifically African Americans, benefit from the socioeconomically subordinate positions their ancestors held in society? In essence, why should whites pay for discrimination that took place before they were born, and why should contemporary African Americans benefit from the suffering of their ancestors, which they have never experienced?

One of the most common arguments against affirmative action that comes from minority leaders is that affirmative action turns people into victims. When expecting the government to take care of minorities and give them preferential treatment, individuals tend to act as if the government owes them something. Some do not consider this progress because it tends to alienate historically underprivileged minority groups from mainstream society.

Another part of this argument is that affirmative action taints minorities in the workplace. When minorities are hired for high-level positions, it is automatically assumed that they received their jobs due to affirmative action. This argument basically claims that individual accomplishments by people from minority groups are virtually impossible because of the cloud created by affirmative action. That cloud, they argue, often leads to assumptions that every minority person in the workplace is there because he or she is a minority and that this person took the job of a white man. This creates stereotypes and ineffective working environments because many minority employees may not be taken seriously.

There are many arguments against affirmative action as we know it today. The arguments are made from various viewpoints and from various political, racial, and economic groups. The opponents of affirmative action are many, and their arguments are multifaceted, with conflicting views prevalent even among would-be allies against this practice.

The arguments for affirmative action are somewhat different and have changed over the course of this practice. As a new type of anti–affirmative action ideology has developed, affirmative action advocates have answered the challenge.

The Argument for Affirmative Action

The historical origins of the argument for affirmative action are obvious. Throughout U.S. history, white men have dominated nearly every aspect of the social landscape. Affirmative action was developed in tandem with civil rights advancements to open more fully opportunities for minority citizens. The arguments supporting affirmative action have now taken the form of debunking myths and exposing truths that indicate problems and misconceptions in the arguments opposing affirmative action.

The biggest and most obvious argument in support of affirmative action challenges the notion of reverse discrimination and beliefs that job markets are closed to whites when competing with minorities. Proponents of affirmative action are quick to point out that, even though minority groups have achieved great gains, they are still underrepresented in the workforce, specifically in white-collar jobs. For example, African Americans and Latinos make up approximately 22 percent of the U.S. labor force. In comparison, they make up only 9 percent of U.S. doctors, 6 percent of lawyers, 7 percent of college professors, and less than 4 percent of scientists (Jackson 1996). Proponents of affirmative action are quick to point out that the labor force does not mirror an equal employment system. The number of age-eligible employees does not correlate to the percentage employed. If the system was equal, then employment figures should not be as lopsided as they are.

This argument also suggests that the Civil Rights Act of 1964 did not solve the United States' racial issues; it simply hid them. After the Civil Rights Act of 1964, and even today, African American and Latin American U.S. citizens are proportionately poorer than their white counterparts. The Civil Rights Act of 1964 opened spaces in the public sphere, but it did not provide concrete economic or financial means for success among minority groups.

Affirmative action backers also argue that diversity is good for society as a whole. Owing to the hiring, promotion, and economic advancement of minorities, diversity has started to seep into more realms of American life. In essence, diversity is becoming more mainstream than it was in the past. Because of this increased diversity, prejudices held about various minority groups have become less prevalent. Partially due to mainstream diversity, the United States is becoming more culturally affluent and accepting. Prejudice is no longer acceptable in most realms of U.S. society, and affirmative action offices and practices create environments in which diversity is accepted, learned, and experienced.

Pro–affirmative action advocates also argue that affirmative action has helped foster the development of minority role models as more and more minorities enter professional and political positions. Furthermore, their entry has led to the development of a raised consciousness among the American citizenry about issues such as racism, rape, immigration, and poverty that before were invisible to mainstream U.S. society.

Affirmative action advocates argue that, contrary to popular opinion, affirmative action is still necessary. The research being done by advocates shows very clearly that there is still a major discrepancy between the United States' population demographics and its social and economic characteristics. This discrepancy is most prevalent in the workplace and education, where affirmative action has been used the most. Not only do the advocates back their claims of inequality, they show how, in many ways, minorities in this country are hardly better off than they were when affirmative action was first implemented. They argue that affirmative action measures should be increased because of a lack of effectiveness and because of the token affirmative action that many firms use today. For all effective purposes, token affirmative action is affirmative action with quotas. In token affirmative action, the quota usually equals one. Companies will hire a token minority and appoint him or her to a public position to eliminate any doubts concerning the organization's diversity. It is often the case that beyond these token appointments, minority groups are underrepresented in all other sectors of the organization.

Affirmative action advocates have also argued that affirmative action is good for all people involved because it increases workplace diversity and expands traditional ideas. It not only helps individuals obtain positions previously unavailable to them, but it also helps create a broader sense of the world within individuals and within organizations. In essence, it forces people to broaden their horizons.

Conclusion

Affirmative action has become a very controversial topic. Opponents suggest that affirmative action causes reverse discrimination that hurts white men and, in fact, is detrimental to minorities who are placed because of it. Furthermore, they believe that the practice of affirmative action contradicts the basic civil rights guaranteed by the Constitution. Advocates believe that discrimination still exists and that affirmative action gives minorities a chance to work, which affects every aspect of their lives. The debate will continue until minorities are represented in every job class and type.

See also **Glass Ceiling; Immigrant Workers**

Further Reading

Anderson, Terry H., *The Pursuit of Fairness: A History of Affirmative Action*. New York: Oxford University Press, 2004.

Baker, Russ, *Unholy Trinity: Katrina, Allbaugh and Brown*. 2006. http://www.russbaker.com/The%20Real%20News%20Project%20-%20Unholy%20Trinity%20Katrina,%20Allbaugh%20and%20Brown.htm

Brief, Arthur P., et al., "Beyond Good Intentions: The Next Steps toward Racial Equality in the American Workplace." In *HRM Reality*, ed. W. R. Nord and L. A. Krefting. Upper Saddle River, NJ: Prentice Hall, 2002.

Dobbin, Frank, *Inventing Equal Opportunity*. Princeton, NJ: Princeton University Press, 2009.

Jackson, J. L., "People of Color Need Affirmative Action." In *Affirmative Action*, ed. A. E. Sadler. San Diego: Greenhaven Press, 1996.

Katrina Numbers Illustrate Storm's Toll. 2005. http://www.planetark.com/dailynewsstory.cfm/newsid/32446/story.htm

Katznelson, Ira, *When Affirmative Action Was White: An Untold History of Racial Inequality in Twentieth-Century America*. New York: W. W. Norton, 2005.

Kellough, J. Edward, *Understanding Affirmative Action: Politics, Discrimination, and the Search for Justice*. Washington, DC: Georgetown University Press, 2006.

Malkin, Michelle, *Not Another Damned Commission*. 2005. http://michellemalkin.com/archives/003492.htm

Stolberg, Sheryl Gay, "Obama Signs Equal Pay Legislation." *New York Times* (January 29, 2009).

"Ten Myths about Affirmative Action." Understanding Prejudice. http://www.understandingprejudice.org/readroom/articles/affirm.htm

B

BANK BAILOUTS

Elizabeth A. Nowicki

A "bank bailout" occurs when a regulatory or government authority provides assistance to a bank that is failing and on the path to insolvency. In a bank bailout, either a regulatory or government authority provides the funds needed for the bailout, or the authority orchestrates assistance of the failing bank by private parties, essentially rescuing or assisting a bank that would otherwise fail and go bankrupt. The people who have deposited their money with the bank (depositors) are otherwise likely to lose all of the money they thought they were depositing for safekeeping.

Bank bailouts are conducted in one of two ways: Either a bank that is on the verge of insolvency is prevented from failing by an infusion of capital that helps the bank continue in operation, or the failing bank is allowed to fail but the party providing the bailout helps the bank liquidate and guarantees repayment to the depositors.

In recent U.S. history, major bank bailouts have only occurred at four distinct times:

- 1930s: many banks were bailed out after the stock market crash of 1929.
- 1984: bailout of Continental Illinois National Bank, then the nation's seventh largest bank.
- 1985–1999: approximately 1,043 savings and loan institutions were bailed out.
- 2008–2009: bailouts included Bear Stearns, Fannie Mae and Freddie Mac, Lehman Brothers, AIG, Citigroup, and Bank of America.

Bank bailouts in the United States are controversial, in part because they come at a cost to taxpayers, they represent failure in an industry populated by highly paid executives, and they implicate what economists refer to as a "moral hazard problem," meaning that some believe that bailing out banks creates an incentive for bank managers to behave in a risky manner, since they know that their banks will be bailed out if their banks run into financial trouble. Yet bank bailouts have an emotional appeal, in part because bailouts of major banks are often preceded by urgent clamors that the failing bank needs to be assisted because it is "too big to fail." The too-big-to-fail theory posits that, if a large bank is allowed to fail, there could be catastrophic ripple effects in the economy, as parties with whom the bank was dealing will lose money on transactions or deposits they had with the failed bank, such that these other banks will be compromised and will not be able to continue robust lending to businesses, such that businesses will not be able to expand or will need to lay off employees, and unemployed consumers will then cut back on purchases, such that demand for goods and services will decrease, which will result in businesses laying off more employees, and a vicious and devastating economic cycle will be created.

That said, bailouts generate populist anger, and, in his first state of the union address, during the beginning of the 2008 bank bailouts, President Barack Obama noted that "if there's one thing that has unified Democrats and Republicans—and everybody in between—it's that we all hated the bank bailout. I hated it." Still, the president observed that the bailouts were "necessary," much like a root canal.

History of Bank Bailouts

The modern history of bank bailouts in the United States began in the 1930s, after the stock market crash of 1929. When the stock market began crashing, large numbers of people began withdrawing their money from banks. This compromised the ability of banks to pay depositors who wanted to withdraw their money, since banks only keep a limited amount of cash on hand, instead maintaining the rest of their money in less liquid assets such as investments and insurance. The inability of banks to immediately pay every depositor who wanted to withdraw her money raised concerns about whether banks would be able to repay all of their depositors, which led to panicked "bank runs." In order to repay depositors, banks needed to liquidate assets, but, given the declining economic climate, banks were forced to sell assets at gravely depressed prices. Therefore, many banks were unable to raise enough cash to pay all of their depositors, and some banks became insolvent. Fear of insolvency exacerbated the bank runs, which put an even greater strain on the available cash remaining and forced even more asset sales, which further depressed the prices at which assets could be sold by banks, such that bank runs became contagious and accelerated the failure of banks that had run out of money.

The Federal Reserve, which was created by legislation passed in 1913, had the authority to provide assistance to troubled banks, but its mandate extended only to member banks, which did not include the majority of the smaller failing banks. Moreover, the Federal Reserve would only make temporary loans on good collateral, which banks failing in the midst of the Great Depression did not have. Bank failures soared, with 2,294 occurring in 1931 (Kennedy 1973, 1), and almost 13 percent of the nation's remaining banks suspending operations by 1933 (Meltzer 2003, 402n153).

Overall, the economic climate was dismal: the stock market had crashed, so many investors lost everything. Moreover, banks were failing such that depositors were losing their remaining savings, borrowing money was nearly impossible, and bank runs were commonplace. Pervasive panic and a crisis of public confidence compounded the problems. Therefore, the government decided to act.

In 1932, the government established the Reconstruction Finance Corporation (RFC) to help distressed banks, and, in 1933, the Emergency Banking Act of 1933 authorized the RFC to bail out banks directly by purchasing preferred stock from distressed banks to infuse new capital into these banks, backed by the United States Treasury. The RFC purchased roughly $782 million in bank preferred stock and $343 million in bank bonds, resulting in the bailout of nearly 6,800 banks. The RFC ceased operations in 1953, but the Federal Deposit Insurance Corporation (FDIC), an independent agency of the federal government established by the Banking Act of 1933, continued to exist and conduct bank bailouts.

The FDIC was created in order to address the public confidence crisis that led to the catastrophic bank runs after the stock market crash of 1929 and to prevent future confidence crises. The FDIC preserves public confidence by insuring deposits in banks to eliminate depositor worries about losing deposits and by monitoring and addressing both systemic risk and deposit-related risk. The FDIC is funded by insurance premiums that banks pay for deposit insurance and from earnings on investments in U.S. Treasury securities. The Federal Deposit Insurance Act of 1950 gave the FDIC the power to bail out a failing bank if that bank was judged essential to the community.

After the bank bailouts in the 1930s, the next major bank bailout was in May 1984, when the FDIC bailed out the Continental Illinois National Bank and Trust Company (Continental Illinois), the seventh largest bank in the United States as measured by deposits. Continental Illinois was struck a fatal blow in part due to bad loans compounded by a bank run, and bank regulators intervened because of a concern that grave damage could be done to the banking system as a whole otherwise. Specifically, many other banks had invested heavily in Continental Illinois, and regulators feared that if Continental Illinois were allowed to fail, banks that lost their investments in Continental Illinois would then fail, with a grievous public confidence impact that would lead to economic disaster (Federal Deposit Insurance Corporation 1997, 250–251). Therefore, the FDIC provided over $4 billion in various forms of assistance to Continental Illinois.

The savings and loan bailout in the 1980s was next. Savings and loans financial institutions (S&Ls) were financial institutions that specialized in residential lending and home mortgages (White 1991, 82–89). They took in money from depositors to whom they then paid high interest rates, and they lent out that deposited money to home buyers needing mortgages. S&Ls began failing in the 1980s as real estate markets began to soften. The value of the assets secured by the mortgages fell, and the S&Ls' ability to pay depositors disappeared. A wave of S&L failures exhausted the available funds in the government-established industry insurance organization, the Federal Savings and Loan Insurance Corporation (FSLIC), which functioned much like the FDIC.

Concerned about how the collapse of the S&L market might undermine the economy, Congress authorized the creation of a new agency, the Resolution Trust Corporation (RTC), to bail out the S&Ls by way of bailing out the FSLIC so that the FSLIC could repay S&L depositors. The RTC, as created by the 1989 Financial Institutions Reform, Recovery, and Enforcement Act, oversaw the sale of assets of failed S&Ls and repayment of S&L depositors. From 1986 to 1995, over 1,000 S&Ls with assets of more than $500 billion failed, costing an estimated $153 billion in bailout money, $124 billion of which came from U.S. taxpayers (Curry and Shibut 2000, 33).

The next major bank bailouts began in 2008, when the U.S. banking system experienced a liquidity crisis (Congressional Oversight Panel 2009, 4–6), banks began failing, and some feared that the economy was being destabilized. Although the precise cause of the banking crisis is still under debate, as described below, the response that followed included massive bank bailouts coupled with a related legislative overhaul.

The Recent Financial Crisis and Bank Bailouts

The bank bailouts that began in 2008 were part of what some viewed then and continue to regard as the worst financial crisis since the Great Depression. The cracks in the U.S. economy infrastructure that led to the crisis and the bailouts started to show in 2006 and 2007, however. Specifically, until approximately 2006, the U.S. housing market experienced what some would call a "bubble." Driven by subprime lending—lending to borrowers who traditionally had been viewed as undesirable due to, for example, having little or no money available as a deposit—and facilitated by securitization and derivative financial products, housing prices escalated as housing borrowing and sales skyrocketed (Congressional Oversight Panel 2009, *supra* note 9, at 8). Housing prices increased at an average of 12 percent per year from 1999 to 2006 (Congressional Oversight Panel 2009, *supra* note 9, at 8).

In 2006, however, housing prices began a modest decline that spiraled into a double-digit percentage decline by 2008 (Congressional Oversight Panel 2009, *supra* note 9, at 8). This led to a rash of mortgage defaults by subprime borrowers and a spate of home foreclosure sales by banks, and banks found themselves unable to sell at a price high enough to recoup what they had lent. Foreclosure sales accelerated the decline of real estate prices, and a dismal financial free fall eclipsed the beginning of 2008. The carnage from this lending and housing implosion was magnified by widespread use of derivatives and securitization products by banks; therefore, even financial institutions that did not hold mortgages but held instead, for example, credit default swaps or other mortgage-related derivative products suffered from the market decline as well (Congressional Oversight Panel 2009, *supra* note 9, at 9).

The first major bank bailout in 2008 was that of Bear Stearns, the fifth largest U.S. investment bank and the leading trader of mortgage-backed bonds. In early 2008, Bear Stearns reported that it was highly exposed to the unstable subprime mortgage market. Alarmed, Bear Stearns clients withdrew their funds from Bear Stearns, and within three days in March 2008, Bear Stearns's available capital fell by 90 percent (Ritholtz 2009, 187). This prompted Federal Reserve and Treasury officials to try to arrange for a bailout of Bear Stearns. The bailout resulted in JPMorgan Chase buying Bear Stearns upon the agreement of the Federal Reserve Bank of New York to guarantee $29 million in Bear Stearns's riskiest assets, which led to reported losses of billions of dollars for the Federal Reserve Bank within months of participating in this bailout.

Shortly thereafter, Lehman Brothers, another banking behemoth, began to fail. While many clamored for a bailout for Lehman Brothers, it was instead allowed to fail completely and file for bankruptcy in September 2008, after the Federal Reserve and the Treasury made clear that they hoped never again to need to rescue a bank the way they rescued Bear Stearns (Ritholtz 2009, 190–192).

Lehman's failure spurred fears that other big banks and financial institutions would soon fail and the entire economy would be destabilized. Concern focused on American International Group (AIG), the world's largest insurer. AIG was deeply involved in the international derivatives market, and, in September 2008, as it became clear that many of AIG's investments were tied to failing mortgage-related assets, regulators decided that the world's largest insurer and a key participant in the international derivatives market must not be allowed to fail, because its failure could have far-reaching economic effects.

The Federal Reserve System is the central bank of the United States, and it was founded in 1913 by Congress to provide a more stable, safer monetary and financial system. It has four general categories of duties: influencing monetary and credit conditions in order to stabilize the economy, supervising and regulating banking institutions, containing systemic risk, and providing financial services to depository institutions and the U.S. government, among others. The chairman of the Federal Reserve oversees the seven-person board of governors of the Federal Reserve. The chairman and the board are appointed by the president. The secretary of the Treasury is appointed by the president and is the federal government's chief financial officer. The secretary, among other things, advises the president on tax and financial policy, oversees currency manufacturing, manages public debt, and serves on boards such as the Social Security Fund, the Medicare Fund, and the International Monetary Fund.

The Federal Reserve and Treasury purchased a majority stake in AIG stock for $68 billion, thereby providing much-needed capital to AIG, and the government continued to make additional loans and purchases of stock so that, by March 2009, the government had infused roughly $175 billion into AIG (Ritholtz 2009, 208).

September 2008 also saw the government takeover and bailout of the Federal National Mortgage Association (Fannie Mae) and Federal Home Loan Mortgage Association (Freddie Mac). These two government-sponsored enterprises (GSEs) had been established by Congress to participate in the mortgage market and foster the accessibility of home loans. As the subprime mortgage market deteriorated, Fannie Mae and Freddie Mac became financially compromised, and Congress adopted legislation to provide for the government takeover of both GSEs in addition to the Federal Reserve infusing well over $100 billion into the GSEs.

Also in 2008, Citigroup, a Wall Street titan that had combined commercial banking with investment banking and a brokerage house, became a focus of concern. Citigroup held billions of dollars in mortgage-related securities whose value plummeted as the housing and mortgage markets crashed. The Treasury and Federal Reserve refused to risk a fatal blow to the already precarious banking system by allowing the largest financial institution on Wall Street to fail, so a complex deal valued at hundreds of billions of dollars to stabilize Citigroup was struck (Ritholtz 2009, 217).

The Citigroup bailout and later bailouts (including bailouts in the automotive industry) were a product of legislation—the Emergency Economic Stabilization Act (EESA)—hastily adopted on October 3, 2008, in the wake of the expanding financial crisis. EESA established the Troubled Assets Relief Program (TARP)—the bailout program. The program authorized the secretary of the Treasury, in consultation with the chairman of the Federal Reserve, to purchase up to $700 billion in "troubled assets," such as subprime mortgage-based securities, in order to promote financial market stability by removing toxic assets from the banks' balance sheets.

By the end of 2009, the Treasury had disbursed over $350 billion under TARP (General Accounting Office 2009). For example, pursuant to TARP, the FDIC, Treasury, and Federal Reserve entered into an agreement with Bank of America in January 2009 to purchase $20 billion in preferred stock from Bank of America and provide protection against loss for approximately $118 billion in assets. Banks that participated in TARP or received bailouts pursuant to TARP included some of the biggest and previously strongest banks, such as Citigroup, JPMorgan Chase, Wells Fargo, Bank of America, Goldman Sachs, and Morgan Stanley, and the top nine participants in TARP represent 55 percent of all U.S. bank assets.

Conclusion

Bank bailouts are not a new phenomenon, but the massive bailouts in 2008 and 2009 have forced both politicians and bankers to revisit the necessity of bailouts, the advisability of bailouts in general, and the reasons why, in less than a century, the United

States has needed two massive rounds of bank bailouts. Is there a way to restructure the banking system to avoid the need for bailouts? What would have happened if no bailouts were provided in the 1930s and in 2008–2009? Would the billions of dollars spent on bank bailouts be better spent on a different facet of banking?

These are some of the obvious questions raised by reflecting on the major bank bailouts in recent U.S. history. It remains to be seen whether the common themes underlying these bailouts repeat again or whether valuable lessons can be learned from reflecting on these bailouts and finding ways to avoid the need for bailouts in the future.

See also **Financial Regulation; Government Subsidies**

Further Reading

Black, William K., *The Best Way to Rob a Bank Is to Own One: How Corporate Executives and Politicians Looted the S&L Industry.* Austin: University of Texas Press, 2005.

Calavita, Kitty, Henry N. Pontell, and Robert H. Tillman, *Big Money Crime: Fraud and Politics in the Savings and Loan Crisis.* Berkeley: University of California Press, 1997.

Congressional Oversight Panel, *December Oversight Report: Taking Stock: What Has the Troubled Asset Relief Program Achieved?* December 9, 2009. http://cop.senate.gov/documents/cop-120909-report.pdf

Curry, Timothy, and Lynn Shibut, "The Cost of the Savings and Loan Crisis: Truth and Consequences." *FDIC Banking Review* (December 2000).

Federal Deposit Insurance Corporation, "Continental Illinois and 'Too Big to Fail.'" In *History of the Eighties—Lessons for the Future.* Vol. 1, *An Examination of the Banking Crises of the 1980s and Early 1990s.* Washington, DC: FDIC Division of Research and Statistics, 1997. http://fdic.gov/bank/historical/history/235_258.pdf

Federal Deposit Insurance Corporation, "The S&L Crisis: A Chrono-Bibliography." 2002. http://www.fdic.gov/bank/historical/s&l/

General Accounting Office, *Troubled Asset Relief Program: One Year Later, Actions Are Needed to Address Remaining Transparency and Accountability Challenges—Highlights.* October 2009. Washington, DC: GAO-10–16.

Kennedy, Susan Estabrook, *The Banking Crisis of 1933.* Lexington: University Press of Kentucky, 1973.

Lewis, Michael, *The Big Short: Inside the Doomsday Machine.* New York: W. W. Norton, 2010.

Meltzer, Allan H., *A History of the Federal Reserve.* Vol. 1, *1913–1951.* Chicago: University of Chicago Press, 2003.

Olson, James S., *Saving Capitalism: The Reconstruction Finance Corporation and the New Deal, 1933–1940.* Princeton, NJ: Princeton University Press, 1988.

Ritholtz, Barry, *Bailout Nation: How Greed and Easy Money Corrupted Wall Street and Shook the World Economy.* Hoboken, NJ: John Wiley, 2009.

Stern, Gary H., and Ron J. Feldman, *Too Big to Fail: The Hazards of Bank Bailouts.* Washington, DC: Brookings Institution Press, 2004.

White, Lawrence J., *The S&L Debacle: Public Policy Lessons for Bank and Thrift Regulation.* New York: Oxford University Press, 1991.

Woelfel, Charles J., *Encyclopedia of Banking and Finance,* 10th ed. Chicago: Probus, 1994.

C

CONGLOMERATION AND MEDIA MONOPOLIES

William M. Kunz

Conglomeration poses a range of issues for citizens and consumers. Does the presence of prominent news outlets in multinational conglomerates influence the coverage of contentious social and political issues? What effect does industry concentration have on media content—motion pictures, television programs, music, and so on? Does the loss of diversity in ownership result in the replication of money-making formulas that promote a corporate ethos at the expense of original ideas? Overall, does consolidation make it impossible or at least improbable for independent voices and viewpoints to reach citizens and consumers? These are just a few of the questions that surround the ownership controversy.

The focal point in the battle over media conglomeration is the concentration of prominent news and entertainment firms in a handful of corporations. Free market advocates argue that centralized ownership is necessary if companies are to remain profitable. They point to the explosion in the number of programming outlets, arguing that consolidation has not restricted the variety of media content. But opponents contend that conglomeration eliminates alternative viewpoints and empowers corporate media to promote dominant ideas and frame public discussion and debate.

Defining Conglomeration

Conglomeration is the process through which distinct companies come under common ownership within a single corporation. There are two different models of conglomeration, and prominent media firms fall within each of them. The traditional definition of conglomeration involves the grouping of wide-ranging, unrelated businesses from various industrial sectors. This model involves unrelated diversification, which is the expansion into industries that are not related to the core business of a conglomerate. The General Electric acquisition of NBC in 1986 is a classic example of this type. A second model of conglomeration builds through related diversification, which involves the acquisition of firms that are connected to the core business in critical areas. The evolution of Viacom is an example of this form. Cable television was Viacom's core business in the 1980s, with ownership of MTV, Nickelodeon, and Showtime, before it expanded into motion pictures and broadcast television with the acquisitions of Paramount Pictures in 1994 and CBS in 2000.

Monopolies

Conglomeration is one factor that leads to concentration, and ultimate consolidation results in monopolies. That structure exists when there is just a single seller of a given product in a market. True monopolies have traditionally been most common in the newspaper business. Countless cities have just one daily, like Atlanta's *Journal-Constitution*. More recently, cable systems operators have been subject to similar criticism. Far more common, however, are media markets that are oligopolies, which feature a few

CONGLOMERATION AND THE LOSS OF LOCALISM

The headlines about conglomeration are often written when studios and networks combine, but less discussed is the potential impact at the local level. Local ownership of newspapers was once common, but as newspaper chains expanded, local ownership became rare and the number of cities with multiple dailies declined. The nature of local television and radio ownership also changed, as Congress and the Federal Communications Commission (FCC) relaxed one-to-a-market rules and allowed groups to reach a higher percentage of households nationwide. These changes transformed the marketplace with massive station groups and less local ownership, and more appear to be on the horizon. In 2003, the FCC voted to relax its prohibition on the cross-ownership of newspapers and television stations in the same market. The justification was the numerical increase in the number of available outlets, including the Internet. The firestorm that followed made clear that there was not universal agreement, and courts blocked their implementation, but the FCC started down a similar path in 2006. By the end of the decade, corporate control of multiple media outlets within local markets had generally increased, raising questions about information democracy. In a few cases, for example, complaints were made regarding cable companies that were allegedly blocking ads by their competitors. Such disputes (for example, between Verizon and Cablevision in 2009), usually faded after the company named in the complaint publicly denounced the practice and demonstrated access to its medium or services by competitors.

giant sellers of a product with each having a significant share of the market. In the mid-2000s, for example, four global giants—Universal Music, Sony BMG, Warner Music, and EMI Group—accounted for over 80 percent of music sales in the United States and worldwide. Some use the phrase *media monopolies* to describe the small collection of corporations that are dominant in various media markets.

Issues of Ownership and Control

One of the battle lines in the debate over conglomeration is whether ownership and control matters. From a free market perspective, ownership of a firm is not a concern unless combinations create market structures that lead to anticompetitive conditions. The Sherman Antitrust Act was enacted in 1890 to address such behavior in the United States, and it has shaped media markets. In 1938, the federal government launched a decade-long legal battle with the Hollywood studios, accusing the majors of "combining and conspiring" to "monopolize the production, distribution and exhibition of motion pictures." When the same corporation owns production studios as well as the theaters that show the movies it makes, the control of production, distribution, and exhibition could effectively close out competition. The so-called Paramount consent decrees, a series of agreements between the government and studios, prohibited anticompetitive behavior and forced the "divorcement" of production and distribution from exhibition. Free market advocates argue that this is as far as the government should delve into the marketplace.

The question is whether the nature of media products raises more significant concerns and demands additional government action. The attention to such issues has shifted over time as new ideas and ideologies come to the fore. In 1966, International Telephone and Telegraph (ITT) attempted to acquire the ABC television network, and despite claims that the network would remain independent, the Department of Justice and others questioned the impact ITT's international operations might have on ABC News and blocked the merger. Two decades later, the regulatory climate was altogether different, and there was little opposition to the combination of General Electric and NBC, although the issues were very similar. Much the same could be said of the 2007 purchase of Dow Jones, publisher of the *Wall Street Journal,* by News Corp., owner of the Fox Broadcasting Company. There was a vocal minority opposed to the sale, but the transaction went through unhindered.

The focus on ownership and control hinges, in part, on the potential impact of media content. Mark Fowler, chair of the Federal Communications Commission (FCC) in the 1980s, once stated that a television is nothing more than a "toaster with pictures." This, in turn, meant that the government could treat television the same as other industries. Scholar Douglas Kellner, however, argues that television assumes a critical role in the "structuring of contemporary identity and shaping thought and behavior." In his view, television has undertaken functions once ascribed to "myth and ritual," including "integrating individuals into the social order, celebrating dominant values," and "offering models of thought, behavior, and gender for imitation." From this perspective, media play a significant role in society and conglomeration becomes a far more serious issue.

Types of Conglomeration

There are multiple incentives for conglomeration. The expansion into diversified businesses creates opportunities for growth and allows a conglomerate to cushion the impact of downturns in core business sectors. General Electric is often cited as the model of a diversified conglomerate, and its collection of businesses makes it, among other things, a military contractor and designer of nuclear power plants. For much of its life under General Electric, NBC Universal has contributed less than 10 percent of the total revenue of the parent company. Yet, with a number of news outlets, NBC might be thought of as more important to the parent company in helping shape public debate over contentious issues, such as militarism and energy production, through NBC News, MSNBC, and CNBC. In 1987, for example, less than a year after the meltdown of the nuclear reactor in Chernobyl, NBC News aired an hour-long show titled "Nuclear Power: In France It Works."

Even so, in a weak economy, business is business—which is perhaps why General Electric decided to sell a controlling interest (51 percent) in NBC to the Comcast cable company in 2009. The latter sale raises a host of additional questions concerning media consolidation, such as: What is the potential for loss of free network television content? What is the likelihood of price hikes for consumers of cable services? Does the sale foster or further limit media competition? And what of the matter of "information democracy"?

Synergy

As the NBC sale demonstrates, the practice of related diversification is increasingly common in media industries. This practice allows a conglomerate to build upon a strong business through the diversification into areas that are close to the core. This can create synergies that enable it to increase revenues and decrease costs through the common management of multiple businesses. This is evident in the conglomeration of media assets in corporations such as the Walt Disney Company, Time Warner Inc., and News Corp. motion picture production and distribution remain important contributors to the Disney bottom line, for example, but the most successful unit in Disney is the Media Networks division, which includes both ABC and ESPN. Disney's corporate expansion into related fields proved to be quite lucrative.

Horizontal and vertical integration are defining characteristics in media consolidation since the 1980s. With horizontal integration, firms acquire additional business units at the same level of production, distribution, or exhibition. Such consolidation enables

THE CONGLOMERATION OF MICKEY MOUSE

The transformation of the Walt Disney Company from a struggling studio operating in the shadow of its related theme parks into a sprawling corporation provides one of the clearest examples of conglomeration. The first step was the creation of production units to develop a diversified slate of films. In 1983, combined domestic and foreign box office receipts for its motion pictures totaled $82.5 million. A decade later, the filmed entertainment division of Disney generated $3.67 billion in revenue. The diversification into related businesses was the next and most significant step. The biggest headlines came in 1996 with the acquisition of Capital Cities/ABC Inc. This created vertical integration between ABC and the production units within Disney, links that were most evident a decade later when three shows from Touchstone Television, *Lost*, *Desperate Housewives*, and *Grey's Anatomy*, fueled a resurgence of the network. That merger also included ESPN, which became the most lucrative unit in the Disney empire. In 2004, the diversified conglomerate generated over $30 billion in revenue, 20 times what it did in 1984. Two years later, it purchased Pixar Animation Studios, and in 2009 it bought Marvel enterprises, bringing the likes of Spiderman and the Fantastic Four under the Disney umbrella.

conglomerates to extend their control and maximize economies of scale through the use of shared resources. With vertical integration, firms acquire additional business units at different points in the process. This allows them to control the supply and cost of essential materials and enables them to rationalize production and increase their control over the market.

Using vertical and horizontal integration, media conglomerates gain far greater control over the marketplace, but such economic strategies limit market access for independent producers and distributors. This is most evident in the motion picture and television industries. Independent film distributors were prominent in the late 1980s, but a decade later the major conglomerates had swallowed most of these firms and large theater chains had overtaken small movie houses. By 1997, six corporations accounted for over 92 percent of box office revenue, and the blockbuster and the multiplex came to define the American moviegoing experience. The same pattern is evident with prime-time television. As networks exerted greater control over television production, fewer programs originated from outside of conglomerates focused on financial control and less-risky programs became appealing. Numerous versions of profitable formulas multiply in seemingly endless spin-offs, as the dearth of original, innovative television productions become more evident.

These practices extend to foreign markets as well, and the impact of Hollywood on indigenous production is a long-standing concern. The U.S. government promotes the export of media products across borders, and one of the justifications for the relaxation of ownership restrictions at home is the argument that the media conglomerates need to be massive to succeed overseas. This contributes to a general mindset that firms that do not grow through mergers and acquisitions will be swallowed. Ted Turner's pursuit of both broadcast networks and motion picture studios before Turner Broadcasting became part of Time Warner in 1996 is testament to this way of thinking. Turner summarized the goal in simple terms: "The only way for media companies to survive is to own everything up and down the media chain....Big media today wants to own the faucet, pipeline, water, and the reservoir. The rain clouds come next."

Changes in the Nature of Conglomeration

The change in the corporate control of the three major broadcast networks—ABC, CBS, and NBC—illustrates how conglomeration transformed media assets since the 1980s. In 1985, two of the networks were still linked to the individuals who created them—ABC and Leonard Goldenson and CBS and William Paley—while NBC remained in the hands of the corporation that launched its radio network in the 1920s, RCA. At that time, the networks remained the core businesses of their corporate parents, and the news divisions supported the public interest mandate that came with broadcast licenses. In 2005, all three shared ownership with a major motion picture studio—ABC and Walt Disney, CBS and Paramount Pictures, and NBC and Universal Pictures—and the news divisions were important revenue centers. (CBS and Paramount later became separate.) These combinations raise various concerns, not the least of which is the coverage of the conglomerates themselves. Michael Eisner once put it in simple terms: he did not want ABC News covering developments at Disney.

Not all combinations prove to be successful, and some argue that modern conglomerates are too unwieldy to react to changes in the marketplace. The most notable failure is the merger of America Online and Time Warner in 2001. The melding of old media and new media did not reap the promised rewards, and AOL was dropped from the corporate letterhead in 2003. But it was not just the size of Time Warner that was its undoing, as pundits point to various problems. And some changes are more cosmetic. In 2006, Viacom split its assets into two corporations, Viacom Inc. and CBS Corp., but Sumner Redstone remained in control of both of them, so ownership and control did not change hands. The rationale for the split was not the size of the conglomerate but the price of Viacom stock, with Redstone and others contending that the true value of the motion picture and cable television assets would be realized after the split from the slower-growing broadcast interests.

Conglomeration: Multiplicity or Diversity

When Ben Bagdikian published the first edition of *The Media Monopoly* in 1983, he estimated that ownership of most of the major media was consolidated in 50 national and multinational conglomerates. When he published *The New Media Monopoly* two decades later, Bagdikian concluded that the number had dwindled to just five. The degree of conglomeration in media industries is evident across the board. In 1985, there were six major motion picture studios and three major broadcast television networks, and nine different conglomerates controlled one of each. In 2005, the number of broadcast networks had doubled with the addition of Fox, The WB, and UPN, but the number of corporations that owned a studio or network had dwindled to just six. Those corporations—Disney, NBC Universal, News Corp., Sony, Time Warner, and Viacom—also held an ownership interest in over 75 percent of the cable and satellite channels with over 60 million subscribers, as well as the most prominent premium movie channels, HBO and Showtime.

Therein rests an important battleground in this debate. Since the 1980s, Congress and the FCC relaxed ownership rules based on the argument that increases in outlets rendered such regulations needless interference in the marketplace. When the FCC announced the relaxation of various rules in 2003, chair Michael Powell argued that the "explosion of new media outlets" demanded change so the commission did not "perpetuate the graying rules of a bygone black and white era." There is little question that the number of outlets has increased. Less certain is whether this growth resulted in more independent voices and diverse viewpoints. The FCC under President Barack Obama has not made any significant departures from prior practice.

Central to this debate is the distinction between multiplicity and diversity, since it is possible to increase the number of available outlets without a parallel expansion in the range of ideas and values in the public commons. The rise of cable news services, for example, diluted the influence of the broadcast network news divisions and created the impression of abundance. This could be quite significant, since the dissemination of news and information from diverse and antagonistic sources is considered a pillar of self-government in democratic societies. When one traces the ownership and control of the cable news services, however, the promised excess is nowhere to be found. The five prominent cable news services—CNN, HLN (formerly CNN Headline News), CNBC, MSNBC, and Fox News Channel—are all part of major media conglomerates, as are the broadcast networks. These are far from diverse and antagonistic sources of news and information, although Fox has emerged as sympathetic to the conservative political viewpoint, and MSNBC has emerged as sympathetic to the liberal point of view. As a pair of opposites of sorts, the two organizations raise the question of objectivity in the news—or, to put it differently, of media bias. Thus does the debate on media conglomeration continue to rage and likely will do so in the foreseeable future.

See also **Intellectual Property Rights; Interest Groups and Lobbying**

Further Reading

Bagdikian, Ben, *The New Media Monopoly*. Boston: Beacon Press, 2004.

Chester, Jeff, *Digital Destiny: New Media and the Future of Democracy*. New York: New Press, 2007.

Croteau, David, and William Hoynes, *The Business of Media: Corporate Media and the Public Interest,* 2d ed. Thousand Oaks, CA: Pine Forge Press, 2006.

Herman, Edward S., and Noam Chomsky, *Manufacturing Consent: The Political Economy of the Mass Media.* New York: Pantheon Books, 1988.

Kellner, Douglas, *Television and the Crisis in Democracy.* Boulder, CO: Westview Press, 1990.

Kunz, William M., *Culture Conglomerates: Consolidation in the Motion Picture and Television Industries.* Boulder, CO: Rowman & Littlefield, 2007.

McChesney, Robert, *The Problem of the Media: U.S. Communication Politics in the Twenty-First Century.* New York: Monthly Review Press, 2004.

Turner, Ted, "Break Up This Band." *Washington Monthly* (July/August 2004): 33–44.

Wasko, Janet, *How Hollywood Works.* Thousand Oaks. CA: Sage, 2003.

CONSUMER CREDIT AND HOUSEHOLD DEBT

Robert D. Manning and Anita C. Butera

The use of consumer credit has become an increasingly important feature of the U.S. postindustrial economy in general and household financial management in particular. In fact, the recent economic boom of the mid-2000s was primarily fueled by consumer spending that was financed by soaring levels of household borrowing. Although the Great Recession of 2008–2010 has generated intense debate over indolent consumption financed by household debt, Lendol Calder (2001) sagely cautions that each generation has issued moralistic warnings against increasing dependence on consumer credit. And they have typically resonated during major economic downturns in the 19th and 20th centuries—most notably the Great Depression of the 1930s.

Background

Historically, the American debate over credit and debt has been shaped by Puritan sociocultural values that regulated appropriate moral behavior in the personal/social/household sphere (Manning 2000). The uniquely American response, as guided by the Weberian notion of the *geist* or "spirit of capitalism," reinforced household thrift in the social realm by rewarding self-discipline and hard work in the economic realm through reinvestment of household wealth in economic enterprises (Weber 1905). For example, Calvinism promoted material asceticism whereby hard work and frugality were valued over leisure and consumption. The ability to resist indolent material desires and thus demonstrate one's worthiness for salvation in the afterlife was confirmed through the accumulation of wealth. The more frugal the lifestyle and commitment to self-denial, then the more household assets that could be publically revealed as virtuous evidence of appropriate moral conduct. Indeed, Ben Franklin's moralistic prescription that "a penny saved is a penny earned" is firmly embedded in American culture as universal wisdom for personal success. Ultimately, the Protestant work ethic has contributed to the emergence of a national American entrepreneurial culture that promotes "good" debt while increasing personal wealth and discourages "bad" debt that merely satisfies consumptive wants and desires.

The use and dependence on credit has varied over time. In rural agricultural areas, for example, farmers routinely rely on business and personal credit during the planting and growing seasons, which is then repaid with proceeds from the harvest. Social attitudes encouraged borrowing for costly equipment like a mechanical thresher or a multipurpose tractor because they were "good" debts: business investments that increased labor productivity and economic self-sufficiency. Similarly, buying a sewing machine on credit was viewed as a prudent investment since it reduced household expenditures on store-bought clothes and could generate supplemental income by taking in seamstress work. Even local merchants were relatively stingy with their self-financed "open book" credit. By cultivating consumer loyalty, they had to balance greater store sales that encouraged responsible consumption while limiting household debt to manageable risk levels for maintaining adequate store inventories. Hence, from the late 19th through the mid-20th century, banks prioritized the lending of relatively scarce credit to economically productive activities. In the process, this policy imposed greater social control over discretionary household expenditures and leisure activities as they were more closely regulated by the religious and community norms of the period.

Today, the responsible use of consumer credit is as important as the prudent management of household income. Although Americans have assumed much higher levels of debt to maintain their families, the social dichotomy of good versus bad debt still persists. For instance, a home mortgage is perceived as a good debt since it satisfies an important household need while accumulating a substantial future asset. Student loans are generally viewed as good human capital investments since higher education enhances occupational mobility and income growth. Of course, even good debt can lead to financial distress, such as when housing prices exceed family resources or costly terms of adjustable-rate mortgages greatly exceed the financial gains of home ownership. Accordingly, borrowing for expensive college or vocational training programs may be bad debt by consigning the borrower to many years of debt servitude. This may result from circumstances outside of the borrowers' control, such as deteriorating macroeconomic conditions (recession) or declining demand for specific occupational skills due to outsourcing (software engineers).

Bank Loans and Household Debt in Postwar United States

The post–World War II growth in household consumer debt has been shaped by supply—changing bank underwriting standards—and demand—higher material standard of living financed by easy access to consumer credit. In terms of the former, the national system of community banks was more risk averse in its loan approval process.

Traditionally, bank lending was based on the three Cs of consumer loan underwriting: character, collateral, and capacity. That is, the likelihood that the borrower would repay the loan (character), whether the borrower had sufficient assets to satisfy the loan in case of default (collateral), and whether the borrower possessed adequate income to repay the new loan based on existing household debts and expenses (capacity). These more stringent bank underwriting standards meant that loans were repaid over a shorter period of time (e.g., three-year auto loans), which accelerated the accumulation of household assets and collateral and thus reduced lender risk. Furthermore, loan applications were often rejected due to relatively high monthly payments and the inability to defer payments one to two years, as is common today. As a result, community banks enforced local standards of financial responsibility until they became absorbed by national banks during the merger and acquisition frenzy of the 1990s and 2000s.

Until the early 1980s, state usury laws restricted risk-based pricing policies, which offer high interest rate loans to less creditworthy consumers, while unsecured bank credit cards were not generally profitable and thus limited to higher-income/low-risk customers They were offered primarily as a convenience to the banks' best customers or to cement consumer loyalty with specific retailers through private issue cards such as Sears and Montgomery Ward (Manning 2000). In fact, consumer credit cards were barely profitable until after the 1981–1982 recession. Furthermore, the rapid growth of the U.S. manufacturing economy and its high levels of unionization in the 1950s and 1960s led to increasing real wages and expansion of the U.S. middle class, with high saving rates even in one-income households. For most Americans, household debt was limited primarily to low-cost mortgage (20- to 25-year fixed) and auto (one car) loans; higher education was affordable and generally self-financed. And interest payments on consumer loans were tax deductible until 1990. The 1986 Tax Reform Act featured a 4-year phased out period for deducting consumer loan finance charges, including credit cards and autos. A tax loophole that allowed home equity loans to retain their tax deductible status is responsible for their explosive growth in the 1990s and 2000s.

The consumer lending revolution took off after the 1981–1982 recession, as banking deregulation and international competitive pressures contributed to the profound transformation of U.S. society—from an industrial manufacturing to a postindustrial consumer economy. This enormous economic stress, which included the loss of millions of blue-collar manufacturing jobs, contributed to the sharp increase in demand for consumer credit among middle- and working-class families. This financial situation was exacerbated by the long-term decline in real wages beginning in the late 1970s. Furthermore, with high inflation in the late 1970s and early 1980s, peaking at over 15 percent annually, consumer borrowing became a prudent strategy as falling real wages were counterbalanced by the declining cost of borrowing. With the end of state usury laws and low inflation by 1984 (under 5 percent), the rising consumer demand and real cost of borrowing led to a dramatic shift in lending to less creditworthy households as

WHAT HAPPENED TO CONSUMER USURY LAWS?

In 1978, federal usury laws were essentially eliminated with the landmark U.S. Supreme Court decision *Marquette National Bank of Minneapolis v. First of Omaha Service Corp.* (439 U.S. 299). This ruling invalidated state antiusury laws that regulated consumer interest rates against nationally chartered banks that are headquartered in other states. Only the Office of the Comptroller of the Currency, through its enforcement of laws enacted by the U.S. Congress, can impose such restrictions on national banks. This resulted in the exodus of major banks to states without the restrictions, such as South Dakota and Delaware. The deregulation of interest rates was followed by the 1996 U.S. Supreme Court decision *Smiley v. Citibank* (517 U.S. 735), which effectively ended state limits on credit card penalty fees. Penalty and service fees now pervade the industry and are its third largest revenue stream following consumer interest and merchant fees. As a result, federal pre-emption has become the guiding principle of bank regulation and shifted authority from the individual states to the U.S. Congress.

With the extraordinary consolidation of the U.S. banking industry over the last three decades, the top three credit card companies (Citibank, Chase, Bank of America) control nearly two-thirds of the credit card market (Manning 2009),and state usury laws apply to a very small fraction of total consumer loans, primarily offered by state chartered banks and other nonbank financial institutions. The exception is federally chartered credit unions whose interest rates are capped at 18 percent. The result has been soaring finance rates and fees—even with the effective interest rate or cost of funds charged to major banks at near zero in 2010. Although more stringent federal credit card regulations were enacted with the 2010 CARD Act, efforts to mandate new federal interest rate limits were soundly defeated by the U.S. Congress in spring 2010.

strategically guided by risk-based pricing policies (Evans and Schmalensee 2005; Manning 2000; Nocera 1994).

As banks invested in new technological efficiencies, including automatic teller machines (ATMs) and credit card processing systems, they began pursuing greater profit opportunities by marketing to less-creditworthy groups (students, working poor, senior citizens, immigrants, handicapped) and then increasing household debt levels. Not surprisingly, by dramatically reducing loan underwriting standards, consumer lines of credit and household debt levels soared. For example, consumer credit card debt jumped from $70 billion in 1982 to nearly $960 billion in 2008, while the national household savings rate fell from nearly 10 percent to about–1 percent. By the mid-1990s, an extraordinary pattern emerged: U.S. bankruptcy filings nearly doubled while unemployment rates fell sharply. Between 1994 and 1998, consumer bankruptcies soared from 780,000 to 1.4 million (79.5 percent) while national unemployment dropped from 6 percent to about 4.2 percent (–30 percent). This pattern is shown in Figure 1. For the first time, the deregulated banking industry, with its diluted underwriting standards, had increased the

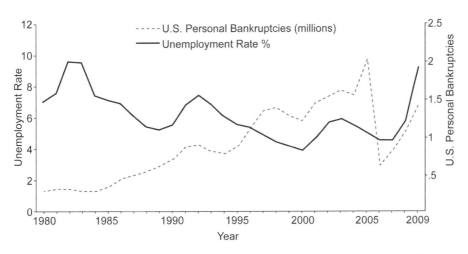

Figure 1. U.S. Personal Bankruptcy Filings and National Unemployment Rates, 1980–2009

amount and cost of household debt beyond the capacity of millions of families to repay their loans. The situation has been exacerbated by greater job insecurity, rising cost of housing, soaring health-related expenses, climbing cost of higher education, and low household saving rates. As a result, unexpected social and financial emergencies have pushed millions of responsible Americans over the edge of financial solvency (Manning 2000, 2005; Sullivan, Warren, and Westbrook 2000; Warren and Tyagi 2003).

Undeniably, the dependence of U.S. households on consumer credit and debt exploded over the last decade. For instance, between 1990 and 1999, total household debt increased from about $3.3 trillion to $6 trillion. As the U.S. Federal Reserve exercised its monetary policy power by sharply reducing the cost and increasing access to consumer credit, the U.S. economy surged, feasting on unprecedented levels of debt-based household consumption (Baker 2009; Zandi 2009; Fleckenstein and Sheehan 2008). From the onset of the 1999 recession to the peak of the bubble period in 2008, U.S. household debt jumped to over $12 trillion—an extraordinary increase of $6 trillion! More striking is the composition of this growth in debt. Americans were seduced to assume unprecedented levels of "good" mortgage debt—from $4.2 trillion in 1999 to almost $10.4 trillion in 2008. Similarly, credit card debt surged from $611 billion in 1999 to $958 billion in 2008 (U.S. Federal Reserve Board 2009). (See Figure 2.) Admittedly, over $400 billion in credit card debt and even more for other consumer purchases (autos, boats, all-terrain vehicles, vacations, college tuition) are included in these mortgage statistics due to the ease of refinancing during this period. Incredibly, the average U.S. household's indebtedness, as measured by its share of household disposable income, has jumped from 86 percent in 1989 to more than 140 percent today (Mischel, Bernstein, and Shierholz 2009).

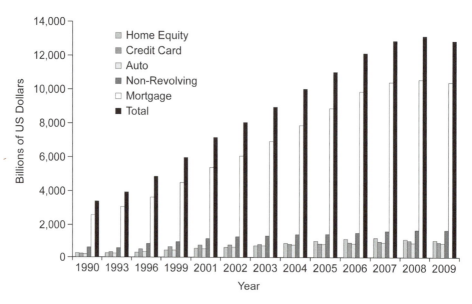

Figure 2. Household Consumer Debt by Category, 1990–2009 (nominal dollars)

The U.S. Economy on Steroids: How We Got Here

Unlike the past three business cycle recessions (1981–1982, 1990–1991, 2001), the on-going 2008–2010 consumer-led recession is distinguished by unprecedented levels of household debt, declining family income, and sharply reduced household wealth (see Figure 3). Indeed, in the aftermath of these previous recessions, real household income increased significantly (18.5 percent)—from $41,724 in 1981 to $49,455 in 2001—whereas it declined slightly (–1.1 percent) to $48,931 in 2008. Similarly, hous-ing prices rose during the last two recessions (5.6 percent in 1990–1991 and 6.3 percent in 2001), whereas they fell at least 12 percent in 2008 and over 10 percent in 2009.

Overall, U.S. economic recoveries during this 20-year period were largely financed by employment growth, increased real income, and increased household debt. Significantly, revolving (credit card) debt jumped much more rapidly than home mortgage debt dur-ing the 1980s and 1990s. For example, after adjusting for inflation, average revolving household debt jumped from $3,500 in 1981 to $6,700 in 1991 and then to $16,100 in 2001, while average mortgage debt jumped from $29,200 in 1981 to $42,500 in 1991 and then to $60,600 in 2001. With soaring housing prices, weakening loan underwriting standards, and easy home equity extraction, the U.S. housing bubble period (2001–2006) witnessed the dramatic growth of mortgage debt and plummeting home asset values; average home owner equity fell from 70 percent in 1980 to 38 percent in 2009. In real 2008 dollars, average household mortgage debt soared from $60,600 in 2001 to $94,500 in 2008, while revolving debt increased marginally over the same period, from $16,100 to $16,300. Between 2001 and 2006, it is estimated that over $350 billion in credit card debt was paid off through mortgage refinancings and home equity loans.

HAVE AMERICANS LEARNED A COSTLY LESSON ABOUT CONSUMER DEBT?

Since the 1981–1982 recession, outstanding revolving U.S. consumer debt (98 percent credit cards) jumped from about $70 billion to over $958 billion in 2008. By the spring of 2010, the year-long decline in household credit card debt led media pundits to declare that the U.S. spending binge was over and that Americans had learned a costly lesson from the easy credit period. That is, Americans were returning to their prudent spending patterns and paying down their costly consumer debt. Overall, credit card debt fell nearly $130 billion, from $958 billion at the end of 2008 to $830 billion in summer of 2010. Also, the household saving rate rose from about–1.0 percent in 2008 to over 4.5 percent in 2010.

The assertion that Americans are undergoing a profound behavior change in their spending patterns belies the economic reality of the current recession. Americans are concerned and cautious about their economic situation, but there is inadequate information to reach a definitive conclusion. With soaring bankruptcy rates (over 3.1 million in 2008–2009) and few home equity loan options, most of this decline in credit card debt is due to bankruptcy discharge and loan defaults rather than paying down consumer debt balances. In fact, over $100 billion in credit card debt was discharged through the U.S. bankruptcy courts in 2008 and 2009; over $75 billion is expected in 2010. Also, millions of Americans are in the process of home foreclosure. By not making housing payments, they are able to remit monthly payments on their credit cards and auto loans. Millions will default on these loans when they have to resume making housing payments over the next two to three years. Furthermore, sharply reduced credit lines have prevented millions of Americans from increasing their household expenditures and outstanding debt. Between 2007 and 2010, total outstanding lines of revolving credit plummeted from $5.5 trillion to $2.7 trillion. Of course, those with low levels of debt experienced the smallest reductions, while those with high levels of debt experience the greatest reductions. Hence, it is premature to conclude that Americans have fundamentally changed their attitudes toward credit and debt. If consumers continue their restrained borrowing preferences after banks relax their lending requirements, then there may be evidence to support a major change in Americans' attitudes toward credit and debt.

The U.S. economy experienced a precariously fragile yet incredibly robust economic expansion over 2001–2006 that was based on unsustainable access to global capital for financing consumer credit. Indeed, as the household consumer savings rate dropped from over 8 percent in the mid-1980s to near zero at the end of the 1990s, residential housing values soared to extraordinary heights; average housing prices slowly rose from about $45,000 in 1950 to $101,000 in 1990 and then soared to nearly $150,000 in 2000 before peaking at about $222,000 in 2006. The accelerated velocity of the real estate roller coaster ride is illustrated in Table 1. With more stringent underwriting standards,

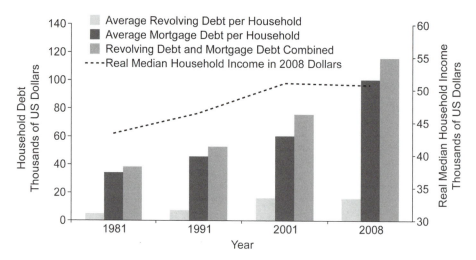

Figure 3. Average Household Debt versus Median Household Income in Current and Past Recessions (in 2008 Dollars)

TABLE 1. Median Sale Prices of Residential Houses

Year	National	Washington DC	New York City	Los Angeles
1940	30,600			
1950	44,600			
1960	58,600			
1970	65,300			
1980	93,400			
1990	101,100			
2000*	119,600	165,000	250,000	234,000
2005	219,000	425,800	445,200	529,000
2006	221,900	431,000	469,300	584,000
2007	219,000	430,800	469,700	589,200
2008	201,000	343,400	445,400	402,100
2009**	173,500	306,200	375,000	345,100

Source: National Association of Realtors, Quarterly Survey, http://www.realtor.org/research/research/metroprice; 1940–2000 data from U.S. Census Bureau Decennial Survey (in 2000 dollars), http://www.census.gov/hhes/www/housing/census/historic/values.html
*2000 metro house prices are estimated based on relevant periodical articles from that year.
**2009 prices are third quarter data.

including income verification and size of down payments, the average sales price of residential homes fell below the rate of inflation in the 1980s, rose from $93,400 to $101,100 in 1990, and then gained momentum with diluted lending standards in the 1990s, jumping nearly 50 percent to $149,600 in 2000.

It is the five-year bubble period (2001–2005) that witnesses the sharp upward acceleration in average sale prices—nearly 50 percent to $219,000 in 2005—followed by an abrupt stagnation in sale prices in 2006 (about 1 percent increase) and then a 22 percent decline over the next three years to $173,500. More striking is the regional variation in the U.S. real estate market. On the West Coast, average sales prices in Los Angeles soared from $234,000 in 2000 to $584,000 in 2006 and then plummeted to $345,000 in 2009. On the East Coast, average sales prices in New York City jumped from $250,000 in 2000 to $469,000 in 2006 and dropped to $375,000 in 2009. In the nation's capital, prices more than doubled in this five-year period, from $165,000 to $431,000, and then fell to $306,000 in 2009. Housing prices are expected to register further declines over the next three to four years, depending upon the level of public price support, willingness of lenders to write down mortgage principal to near market values, and job growth in specific regions of the country.

As federally subsidized general service entities (GSEs), the mortgage lenders Fannie Mae and Freddie Mac diluted their underwriting standards in order to expand their market share through the widespread packaging and resale of loans through asset-backed securities (controlling over $5 trillion of the $10 trillion residential mortgage market in 2008), U.S. home ownership rates reached a historic high of almost 69 percent in 2007. In the process, the sizzling U.S. housing market created an enormous increase in "paper" asset wealth for middle-class Americans that fueled the dramatic growth of unsecured lines of credit that underlies the second credit card bubble. The massive increase in United States consumer debt—from almost $8 trillion in 2001 to

SUBPRIME MORTGAGES AND U.S. FINANCIAL SYSTEM MELTDOWN

A distinguishing feature of the 2008–2010 recession is the central role of the U.S. housing market collapse. On the supply side, sharply diluted underwriting standards kept real estate prices soaring, which attracted a record number of speculative investors. Why invest in risky stock markets when you can make huge returns on borrowed money? To keep the real estate engine fully lubricated, it required new groups of home owners who were increasingly less creditworthy. The rise of subprime mortgages simply meant that borrowers could not qualify for traditional government-insured loans such as FHA mortgages.

In marketing the American dream of home ownership, real estate agents and brokers made bigger commissions by selling larger loans. The key was to qualify consumers for the home mortgage, which often included an inflated property appraisal, and then sell the loan via brokers to major Wall Street investment banking units. Surprisingly, a wide range of comparatively risky mortgage loans were created and approved by bank regulators that were impossible for millions of consumers to afford. These included 2/28 and 3/27 adjustable-rate mortgages that often started at 1–2 percent APR and jumped to

(continued)

(*continued*)

over 9–10 percent APR after the two- or three-year introductory period, five-year interest-only mortgages, "no doc" or unverified financial information loans, and pick-a-payment loans that permitted negative amortization. Of course, the inability to save for a down payment was not a major problem and even loan closing costs could be financed and added to the mortgage. So, while low-income and largely urban minorities became the first casualties of the subprime catastrophe, it was primarily due to their lack of financial resources and their acceptance of the worst borrowing terms rather than irresponsible money management. Middle- and upper-income households also took subprime mortgages, but they tended to have more financial resources and thus were able to prolong the foreclosure process through the late 2000s.

On the demand side, major Wall Street investment firms were buying, packaging, and reselling these subprime mortgages via asset-backed securities (ABS) that were sold to institutional investors (banks, insurance companies, mutual funds) throughout the United States and around the world. Major bond rating agencies like Moody's and Fitch were seduced by lucrative Wall Street consulting agreements and fueled the global sale of these securitized mortgages by certifying them as investment grade, which enabled the securities to be insured. Wall Street investment firms such as Goldman Sachs purchased billions of dollars of subprime mortgages, packaged and sold them as investment-grade securities, and then bought hedge insurance from companies like AIG (bailed out by the U.S. government with over $183 billion and counting) that essentially bet that the mortgages would not be paid—and they received billions in insurance payments. Other mortgage-backed securities were even riskier, featuring specific strips of the subprime mortgage. For example, the riskiest securities included the first 10 percent of the subprime mortgage, the next riskiest was the next 20 percent, with the least risky being the lowest strips.

As long as the housing bubble was inflating, the riskiest securities outperformed all other ABS products since the liquidation value of the homes at least satisfied the value of the mortgages. Why invest in 8 percent ABS products when the 15 percent ABS products appeared to be very low risk? Of course, when the housing bubble burst, the riskiest mortgage-backed securities immediately became worthless. As investors sought to mitigate their losses, they incentivized their mortgage servicers to accelerate foreclosure proceedings in the hope of recovering some economic value. This created a domino effect that exacerbated the fall in home sale prices and further increased their investment losses. In an attempt to stabilize the housing market, the U.S. Congress provided over $200 billion to home mortgage finance giants Fannie Mae and Freddie Mac to purchase delinquent mortgages. Together with government programs that offer lower interest rates but without principal reductions, the current housing market has reached a soft floor that will result in at least 4 million to 5 million foreclosures over the next three years. This means that the subprime mortgage catastrophe will continue, with the cost eventually exceeding a trillion dollars. It is for this reason that the U.S. Congress enacted more stringent regulations and oversight of Wall Street as specified in the 2010 Dodd-Frank Wall Street Reform and Consumer Protection Act.

nearly $13 trillion in 2008—was increasingly financed by foreign investors; the U.S. share of global savings peaked at nearly 65 percent in 2005 and had already fallen below 50 percent in 2008, as countries with balance-of-trade surpluses redirected their liquidity to national economic stimulus projects.

Furthermore, both consumer mortgage and credit card loans increasingly featured adjustable-rate terms in the 2000s that have stretched household debt capacity to its limits; monthly minimum payments continue to rise, whereas the value of household assets continues to fall. Today, with the virtual disappearance of home equity loans and the sharp cutback in bank card lines of credit, the collapse of the double financial bubble has left most U.S. households maxed out on their credit, with debt levels that they cannot possibly repay in full given the current trends of declining household income and wealth. Additionally, the rising debt service of U.S. households has dramatically reduced consumer discretionary spending. This rippled throughout the United States and global economies in 2008 and 2009. In the process, it triggered sharp reductions in macroeconomic growth and rising unemployment rates (combined unemployed and underemployed at nearly 25 percent in the United States) that are the primary forces shaping the ongoing consumer-led recession in the United States. As a result, with over 2.3 million foreclosures in 2008, millions of Americans are confronting the stark reality that they may lose their homes and even their jobs in the early 2010s. An estimated 5 to 7 million homes are expected to enter into foreclosure proceedings over the next three years.

Conclusion: After the Double Financial Bubble

Like an athlete on steroids, the U.S. economy was not nearly as powerful as it seemed in the mid-2000s as it bulked up on cheap financial "boosters" from major trade partners such as China, Japan, and Middle East oil producers. With their enormous trade surpluses with the United States, which underlies their huge dollar-denominated currency reserves, these "bankers of necessity" were happy to supply low-cost loan "fixes" as long as it kept the U.S. consumer society addicted to its massive volume of imported goods and services (Baker 2009; Fleckenstein and Sheehan 2008; Schechter 2007). For example, China purchased the mortgage-backed securities that fueled the housing boom in order to provide compliant U.S. consumers with building materials (e.g., cheap sheetrock), interior furnishings, electronics and appliances, and clothing and other personal items. As long as inexpensive credit was easily available in the United States, then Americans were able to refinance and leverage their skyrocketing home values through ever lower interest rates (Muolo and Padilla 2010; Zandi 2009; Schechter 2008). This meant that while real U.S. wages continued to decline in the 2000s, Americans believed that they actually were better off economically due to impressive stock market (401(k)) and home equity gains (Mishel, Bernstein, and Shierholz 2009; Leicht and Fitzgerald 2007; Manning 2005).

As the financial steroids began to wear off, the U.S. financial system abruptly collapsed in September 2008, and the resulting institutional paralysis left the nation in shock and the economy in turmoil (Zandi 2009; Baker 2009; Schechter 2008). Like the poststeroids athlete, the United States is struggling to recover its former glory while its economic foundation and financial infrastructure remain perilously debilitated. Furthermore, after the bubble burst, overleveraged households now must pay down their record consumer debts almost exclusively from salaries and wages that continue to fall while millions of Americans are unable to find gainful employment. No wonder that record bankruptcy rates are expected over the next three to four years. With the lack of available credit, moreover, the pendulum of the market has swung in the opposite direction as asset sale prices do not necessarily reflect intrinsic value since fewer people can qualify for loans. Shockingly, commercial and residential real estate is often sold at below its replacement cost—that is, homes and office buildings can be purchased for less than it costs to build them! Together with the glut of houses on the market, these are the key reasons that the construction and real estate industries will not recover in the near term. And, since it is unlikely that real household income will reverse its long-term slide in the near future, the timing of the next upswing in the residential real estate market is crucial to restoring consumer confidence as well as augmenting shrinking family incomes. These factors both underlie the depth of the current recession and the policy prescriptions for restoring the health of the U.S. economy.

See also **Bank Bailouts; Debt, Deficits, and the Economy; Financial Regulation; Trade Deficits (and Surpluses)**

Further Reading

Baker, Dean, *Plunder and Blunder: The Rise and Fall of the Bubble Economy.* New York: Polipoint Press, 2009.

Barber, Benjamin R., *Consumed: How Markets Corrupt Children, Infantilize Adults, and Swallow Citizens Whole.* New York: W. W. Norton, 2007.

Calder, Lendol, *Financing the American Dream: A Cultural History of Consumer Credit.* Princeton, NJ: Princeton University Press, 2001.

Cohen, Lizabeth, *A Consumers' Republic: The Politics of Mass Consumption in Postwar America.* New York: Vintage, 2004.

Evans, David, and Richard Schmalensee, *Paying with Plastic: The Digital Revolution in Buying and Borrowing,* 2d ed. Cambridge, MA: MIT Press, 2005.

Fleckenstein, William, and Frederick Sheehan, *Greenspan's Bubbles: The Age of Ignorance at the Federal Reserve.* New York: McGraw-Hill, 2008.

Leicht, Kevin T., and Scott Fitzgerald, *Post-Industrial Peasants: The Illusion of Middle Class Prosperity.* New York: Worth, 2007.

Mann, Ronald J., *Charging Ahead: The Growth and Regulation of Payment Card Markets around the World.* New York: Cambridge University Press, 2007.

Manning, Robert D., *Credit Card Nation: America's Dangerous Addiction to Credit.* New York: Basic Books, 2000.

Manning, Robert D., *Living with Debt: A Life Stage Analysis of Changing Attitudes and Behaviors.* Charlotte, NC: Lending Tree.com, 2005.

Manning, Robert D., "The Evolution of Credit Cards." *Credit Union Magazine* (October 2009): 35–38.

Mishel, Lawrence, Jared Bernstein, and Heidi Shierholz, *State of Working America, 2008/2009.* Ithaca, NY: Cornell University Press, 2009.

Muolo, Paul, and Mathew Padilla, *Chain of Blame: How Wall Street Caused the Mortgage and Credit Crisis.* New York: John Wiley, 2010.

Nocera, Joseph, *A Piece of the Action: When the Middle-Class Joined the Money Class.* New York: Simon & Schuster, 1994.

PEW Health Group, *Still Waiting: Unfair or Deceptive Credit Card Practices Continue as Americans Wait for New Reforms to Take Effect.* Washington, DC: Pew Charitable Trusts, 2009.

Schechter, Danny, *In Debt We Trust: America before the Bubble Burst.* Film. DisInformation Films, 2007. http://www.Indebtwetrust.org

Schechter, Danny, *Plunder: Investigating Our Economic Calamity and the Subprime Scandal.* New York: Cosimo Books, 2008.

Sullivan, Teresa A., Elizabeth Warren, and Jay L. Westbrook, *The Fragile Middle Class: Americans in Debt.* New Haven, CT: Yale University Press, 2000.

U.S. Federal Reserve Board, Consumer Credit and Household Debt Statistical Releases. 2009. http://www.creditcardnation.com/trends.html

Warren, Elizabeth, and Amelia Warren Tyagi, *The Two-Income Trap: Why Middle-Class Parents Are Going Broke.* New York: Basic Books, 2003.

Weber, Max, *The Protestant Ethic and the Sprit of Capitalism.* London: Unwin Hyman, 1905.

Zandi, Mark, *Financial Shock: A 360° Look at the Subprime Mortgage Implosion, and How to Avoid the Next Financial Crisis.* Upper Saddle River, NJ: FT Press, 2009.

CORPORATE GOVERNANCE

Ashutosh Deshmukh

Corporate governance refers to the way a corporation is managed, administered, and controlled by the various stakeholders. The stakeholders such as the shareholders, boards of directors, and managers run the corporation and shape and execute the strategies and day-to-day operations. The other stakeholders such as employees, customers, suppliers, regulators, and society at large are also interested in proper management of the corporation. The objectives of good corporate governance include economic efficiency and maximization of shareholder value and may include other goals as assigned by the regulators and the society.

The term *corporate governance* appeared in 1981, and the topic has become a subject of intense research, especially in the last decade. However, even with such a focus, no single definition of corporate governance suffices to serve the purposes of all stakeholders. Corporate governance has been in part defined by various regulations and in part by the human element involved in operationalizing the term. In order to achieve the objectives of good corporate governance the shareholders, boards of directors, and managers need to be honest, trustworthy, and respectful of the letter and spirit of the law. Sometimes demands of the various stakeholders can conflict, giving rise to complex and thorny ethical dilemmas. Thus, the topic is of interest to all of us.

Why Corporate Governance Is Important

To understand the importance of corporate governance, we must first understand the nature of a corporation and the far-reaching influence wielded by today's corporations. The corporate form for conducting business has gained international popularity. Why? The simple reason is that a corporate form of business offers *limited liability* to the owners of a corporation. For example, if the owners put $100 in the corporation (buy shares) and the corporation goes bankrupt, then the owners lose only $100. However, if the business is run as a sole proprietorship (single owner) or as a partnership, then the owner(s) can be responsible for all debts incurred by the company and may even lose personal assets such as a house or car. This legal protection offered by the limited liability concept results in risk taking and innovation. Today's corporations are owned by thousands of investors who pool their money and delegate the running of the company to professional managers. The people invest and the managers manage, and, if both are successful, everyone reaps the rewards. Some legal scholars have put the idea of corporate form at par with industrialization as a force that helped drive the explosive growth of business and commerce.

However, because owners generally have no direct hand in running a corporation, there is a possibility of mismanagement by the managers; in other words, bad corporate governance can ruin the investors. This is often referred to as an agency problem. What is to stop the managers (agents) from running the company for their own benefit (to the detriment of owners)? This question becomes even more urgent if we scrutinize today's global corporation. Presently, in the United States and across the world, the economic landscape is dominated by global corporations; many of them rival governments in terms of their budgets and power. Any major mistake by the mangers of such a corporation can affect the economies of nations as well as the lives of the common people. The world faced a major economic crisis in 2008–2009 when U.S. banking and investment firms used faulty models in measuring risks in the housing market. As this article is being written, the ecosystem of the Gulf of Mexico is being threatened because of mishaps with offshore oil drilling. The livelihoods of millions of people are at stake.

TABLE 1. History of Legislation to Prevent Corporate Mismanagement and Fraud

Legislation	Reason
Owens-Glass Act of 1913: This act provides rules for financial reporting and reserve requirements for banks.	This act was enacted due to bank failures caused by inadequate or nonexistent reserves.
Glass-Stegall Act of 1933: This act separated commercial and investment banking.	There was a conflict of interest in banks that conducted commercial and investment operations, which resulted in massive banking frauds.
Securities Act of 1933: This act requires disclosure of all important information before securities (shares) are registered.	Shares were issued by many corporations that provided false and misleading information to the public.
Securities Exchange Act of 1934: This act requires that all companies listed on stock exchanges file quarterly and annual audit reports with the Securities and Exchange Commission.	Many corporations issued unaudited fraudulent financial reports and manipulated their stock price for the benefit of the top management.
Investment Company Act of 1940: This act established financial responsibilities for directors and trustees of investment companies (the companies that invest in stock markets). It also made disclosure of financial and managerial structure mandatory.	Investment companies abused the funds provided by the investors by investing in related companies and manipulating prices.
Foreign Corrupt Practices Act of 1977: This act made proper design, maintenance, and documentation of internal control systems a requirement for U.S. companies.	U.S. corporations were bribing foreign officials for business and also made banned political contributions in the United States.
FIDCA Improvement Act of 1991: This act mandated reports by the managers on internal controls and also compliance with the federal laws.	There was a massive failure of savings and loan institutions due to fraud and conflict of interest among officers and directors.
Private Securities Litigation Reform Act of 1995: This act requires auditors and lawyers to inform the Securities and Exchange Commission of any allegations of wrongdoing (including financial wrongdoing) by the corporation.	This act is intended to prevent frivolous litigation against public companies.
Sarbanes-Oxley Act of 2002: This act strengthens various aspects of corporate governance.	This act was prompted by a series of corporate frauds and failures that involved blue-chip companies in the United States.

(continued)

TABLE 1. (*continued*)

Legislation	Reason
Dodd-Frank Wall Street Reform and Consumer Protection Act of 2010: This legislation is aimed primarily at the banking and investment industry; it seeks to make trading in derivatives and other securities more transparent and protect consumers from corporate fraud and mismanagement.	This legislation came in the wake of the 2008–2009 recession, which was caused in part by high-risk and often faulty investment products—primarily mortgage-backed securities—sold by Wall Street firms.

Mechanisms of Corporate Governance

The corporate form of business has been abused by managers many times, and a host of laws have been passed as a result. In the United States, each corporation must follow state incorporation laws in forming, running, and dissolving a corporation. Such laws stipulate basic governance structures to protect the interests of the shareholders. Additionally, many other laws have been instituted over the years to foster proper management of corporations. The history of these laws, passed long before corporate governance became a major topic of interest, were designed to prevent mismanagement and fraud by the managers. They can make fascinating reading. The stock market crash of 1929 was partly caused by management fraud or lax corporate governance. Consequently, Congress passed the Securities Act of 1933 and the Securities Exchange Act of 1934. This history repeated itself in 2002, when a host of blue-chip companies that had been certified by their auditors and endorsed by Wall Street were exposed as giant frauds, causing bankruptcies. As a result, the Sarbanes-Oxley Act of 2002 was passed. These laws have directly or indirectly attempted to bolster good corporate governance.

The commonly accepted mechanisms of corporate governance are as follows:

1. **Board of directors:** The directors are elected by the shareholders to protect the interests of the shareholders. The directors meet regularly in board meetings and have the power to appoint, remove, and fix the compensation of the top executives. The independent and outside directors are invaluable in monitoring the top management and assessing progress of the corporation.

2. **Checks and balances:** The power inside the company is carefully distributed across various positions. For example, the chief financial officer (CFO) is responsible for preparing the financial results of the corporation, the chief information officer is responsible for information technology infrastructure, and the chief executive officer (CEO) provides overall leadership to the company. Such separation of powers is carried down to the lowest levels of the corporation. There is also a carefully designed system of internal controls to ensure reliable financial reporting, increase operating efficiency, and maintain

proper compliance with laws and regulations. Such arrangements prevent one person from committing fraud or damaging the corporation through errors of judgment.

3. **External auditors:** Every public corporation is legally obligated to get its financial accounts audited by external auditors. The external auditors have professional responsibilities and are not under the control of top management or the board of directors.

4. **Executive compensation:** The board of directors designs the compensation for the top management in such a way that the interests of the top management and those of shareholders will be the same. Thus, top managers' actions, even though arising from the profit motive, will benefit the shareholders. Good compensation schemes, however, are notoriously difficult to design and often result in unintended consequences.

There are also external forces at work—such as employees, media, financial analysts, and creditors—all of whom may demand good governance and financial transparency. Governmental regulations, as noted above, likewise play a vital role in promoting good corporate governance.

Why Mechanisms of Corporate Governance Fail

The myriad mechanisms of corporate governance are not always enough. Human ingenuity, greed, systemic failure of the markets, and new business innovations can outstrip carefully designed controls. Moreover, accountants who deliver financial reports play a significant role in corporate governance. The performance of top management and of the corporation as a whole is measured by such financial reports. The financial reporting rules in the United States (and in the rest of the world) are flexible and can be interpreted in a variety of ways. These rules can be manipulated—by means of legal stratagems (loopholes) or even by illegal and unethical means—and cause lasting damage to the corporation.

Let us look at a few reasons for the failure of available control mechanisms. First, top management can collude and operate over and above the internal controls of the corporation for management's own profit. Such unethical behavior generally results in fraudulent financial reporting involving manipulating the accounting data used by the company. Often the external auditors of the company are either complicit in the fraud or choose to ignore it. Eventually, the fraud comes to light and frequently the company goes bankrupt. Second, top management can take excessive risks in the business. Since the bulk of the capital is provided by shareholders, top managers can take risks that they would not otherwise take if their own money were involved. For example, the economic crisis that affected the United States and the rest of the world in 2008–2009 partly resulted from financial instruments that hid the risk of lending money to people who did not have the ability to pay it back. Such risks ended up enriching a handful of managers and corporations but caused trillions of dollars in losses to the nation's economy. Third, a large corporation can have thousands of shareholders, and most of the shareholders have little time or inclination to study financial reports, attend shareholder meetings, or take an active part in corporate governance. Finally, the top managers control information about the company. Even a vigilant board of directors and a strong body of external auditors can be misled by top managers, if the latter desire to do so.

As a result of these factors, we see in the United States and elsewhere periodic scandals and great swings and crashes in the stock market. In extreme cases, recessions set in, dragging down the national economy. The popular outrage that accompanies such events often forces governments to introduce further regulations. As of this writing (mid-2010), lawmakers in Congress and members of the Obama administration are crafting legislation designed to bolster the nation's financial regulations. It is expected, however, that the new regulations will complement rather than undo or rewrite the Sarbanes-Oxley Act, which remains the most far-reaching law on the books regarding corporate governance.

The Sarbanes-Oxley Act

In 2000, as the stock market nose-dived and the Internet bubble burst, there was a general discontent among the investors regarding corporate governance. The following year saw a succession of corporate scandals that shocked the public. The biggest fraud involved a company called Enron. This company, based in Houston, Texas, dealt in electricity, natural gas, paper, and communications and claimed revenues of approximately $100 billion. At the time, the company employed approximately 20,000 people and was considered one of the most innovative companies in the nation. The performance of Enron was revealed to be a fraud, however—sustained by accounting gimmicks and not business fundamentals. The company went bankrupt in 2001, and investors and employees sustained billions of dollars in losses. Enron's external auditor, Arthur Andersen, a leading accounting firm, also went bankrupt. Other similar scandals involving such companies as WorldCom, Tyco, and Adelphia further fueled public outrage.

Because of Enron and other scandals, Congress took steps that resulted in the Sarbanes-Oxley Act. The act is named after its sponsors, Senator Paul Sarbanes (D-MD) and Representative Michael Oxley (R-OH), and was overwhelmingly approved by both congressional houses. This act contains 11 titles (sections) that deal with various aspects of corporate governance. These include, for example, the responsibilities of the managers, the independence of the auditors, and requirements for financial disclosure. The act also shifted responsibility for setting auditing rules and standards from the private sector (the American Institute of Certified Public Accountants) to the public sector (Public Company Accounting Oversight Board). The major provisions of the act that affect corporate governance are summarized below.

TABLE 2. Time Line for Sarbanes-Oxley Act of 2002

Time	Event
2000	The stock market begins to cool off.
2001	Enron scandal comes to light; billions of dollars of market value vanish.
2002	Many well-known corporations such as AOL, Adelphia, Global Crossing, Kmart, Lucent Technologies, Merck, Tyco International, and Waste Management are found to be culpable of committing fraud.
June 15, 2002	Arthur Andersen, the Enron auditing firm, is indicted and criminally convicted.
July 9, 2002	President George Bush gives a speech about accounting scandals.
July 21, 2002	WorldCom files for bankruptcy—the largest corporate bankruptcy ever; a major financial fraud underlies the demise of the company.
July 30, 2002	The Sarbanes-Oxley Act is passed.

Responsibilities of the Board of Directors

As mentioned earlier, shareholders appoint the members of the board of directors. The board is supposed to protect the interests of the shareholders. In the real world, the CEO often chooses board members from among friends and acquaintances, to the detriment of shareholders' interests. In an attempt to remedy this cronyism, Sarbanes-Oxley contains provisions to strengthen the independence of the members of the board of directors from management. The act mandates that the audit committee (a committee of directors that deals with financial matters) of the board of directors should have people who do not serve (and get money from) the company in any other capacity and should not work for a subsidiary of the company. The audit committee also needs to keep track of complaints received regarding financial improprieties and problems with the internal controls. If necessary, the audit committee can hire independent counsel to investigate critical matters.

Responsibilities of the Managers

Sarbanes-Oxley imposed a number of key responsibilities, obligations, and prohibitions on senior management, including certification of the accuracy of financial reports, creation of the internal control reports, and restrictions on personal loans and stock sales. The act also stipulates heavier penalties for criminal behavior.

Public corporations are required to issue an annual report containing financial statements, management discussion of operating results, and the auditor's report.

TABLE 3. Section 404: A Four-Letter Word?

(a) Rules Required	The Commission shall prescribe rules requiring each annual report required by section 13(a) or 15(d) of the Securities Exchange Act of 1934 (15 U.S.C. 78m or 78o(d)) to contain an internal control report, which shall— (1) State the responsibility of management for establishing and maintaining an adequate internal control structure and procedures for financial reporting; and (2) Contain an assessment, as of the end of the most recent fiscal year of the issuer, or the effectiveness of the internal control structure and procedures of the issuer for financial reporting.
(b) Internal Control Evaluation and Reporting	With respect to the internal control assessment required by subsection (a), each registered public accounting firm that prepares or issues the audit report for the issuer shall attest to, and report on, the assessment made by the management of the issuer. An attestation made under this subsection shall be made in accordance with standards for attestation engagements issued or adopted by the Board. Any such attestation shall not be the subject of a separate engagement.

Source: Institute of Internal Auditors, "Sarbanes-Oxley Section 404: A Guide for Managers." Altamonte Springs, FL: Institute of Internal Auditors, 2008.

Sarbanes-Oxley now requires the CEO and the CFO to certify that the financial reports accurately reflect the company's real performance. In the past, top executives accused of fraud often pleaded ignorance of accounting matters and tried to shift the blame onto accountants. This certification closes such loopholes.

The managers are also required to issue an internal control report with each annual report (Section 404). The internal control report states that establishing and maintaining internal controls is the responsibility of the management. It also assesses the existing internal control system strengths and weaknesses. The external auditors then attest to the veracity of that report. The auditors cannot check every transaction in the company since modern corporations have trillions of transactions; rather, they rely on internal controls to evaluate the financial position of the company. If the top management is negligent in establishing and enforcing internal controls, audits are ineffective. The internal controls report, as it is issued by top management, compels management to pay attention to internal controls. Section 404 is the most contentious aspect of the Sarbanes-Oxley Act because of its requirement to implement, document, and test internal controls—a procedure that can be very expensive, especially in larger organizations.

Sarbanes-Oxley also bans corporations from offering personal loans to their executive officers and directors. For example, former WorldCom CEO, Bernard Ebbers, received an approximately $300 million personal loan from the company. Many such instances of personal loans came to light in 2001–2002. Sarbanes-Oxley put an end to that practice.

Many top managers are granted stock options or stock in the company. Since top managers have better information about the company than the average member of the public, they can time the sale of stock to reap maximum profits. Sarbanes-Oxley does not ban this kind of insider trading (except under certain conditions), but it does require that such sales be reported quickly for the benefit of all investors. Compensation for CEOs and CFOs is similarly required to be disclosed publicly. Such disclosure had been required prior to Sarbanes-Oxley, but now the information is easier to find and more transparent. Additionally, top managers are required to return any bonuses awarded for financial performance that later were found to be based on faulty accounting.

Criminal and civil penalties for violation of securities laws and misstatement of financial data are made more severe under the law. In the past, laws dealing with financial fraud were rather lenient and courts tended to award light sentences. Sarbanes-Oxley provides long jail sentences and stiff fines for any managers who knowingly and willfully misstate financial data.

Responsibilities of the Auditors

The auditors are expected to be independent from their clients. In the past, auditing contracts were awarded on the basis of friendships and business relationships, which compromised the auditor's independence. Independence is the cornerstone of any effective audit, and Sarbanes-Oxley contains many provisions to strengthen the auditor's independence.

Auditors are banned from providing other fee-based services that could lead to a conflict of interest and undermine their independence. Before Sarbanes-Oxley, auditors were allowed to provide certain consulting services such as advice for hiring personnel, internal auditing, and designing financial information systems. Sarbanes-Oxley provides a long list of services that can no longer be performed by auditors. Such a ban is designed to prevent business relationships between the auditor and the client. It is believed that these other, possibly more profitable, contracts compromise auditors' independence and undermine their willingness to adhere strictly to auditing standards.

The act contains other provisions to preserve independence of the auditor. The audit partner supervising the audit should be rotated every five years, which is meant to encourage professional (as opposed to personal) relationships between the partner and top management. Furthermore, a person employed by an audit firm is barred from assuming a top managerial position with the client company for at least one year after leaving the auditing firm. This provision prevents what used to be called a revolving door between the audit firm and the client. Finally, the newly established Public Company Accounting Oversight Board has the power to investigate auditing firms and penalize them for noncompliance with the law.

Responsibilities of the Securities and Exchange Commission (SEC)

The SEC is a federal agency whose duties include administration of the Sarbanes-Oxley Act. The SEC has been granted additional powers and an expanded budget to supervise compliance with the act. The SEC can:

1. Set standards of professional conduct for lawyers who practice before the SEC,
2. Prohibit a person from serving as a director or an officer of a public company, and
3. Freeze payments to officers or managers of the company if it suspects that securities laws have been violated.

These provisions in Sarbanes-Oxley seem to be straightforward and appropriate for proper corporate conduct. However, the enactment and implementation of the provisions have raised a host of ethical and operational questions.

Consequences of Sarbanes-Oxley

The Sarbanes-Oxley Act raised a firestorm of controversy upon its passage, and certain of its aspects continue to be debated. The objections against the act are philosophical and operational in nature. Romano (2005) raises a compelling philosophical argument against Sarbanes-Oxley. Romano argues that Sarbanes-Oxley demands substantive corporate governance mandates. This means that the act specifies how a business should be conducted and is thus intrusive in nature. The earlier laws required complete disclosure of all information but not directives on how to conduct business. The author argues, after evaluating the academic literature, that such a far-reaching law is not required. Gifford and Howe (2004) argue that such government mandates are detrimental to business because they do not allow more efficient and effective private-sector solutions to bubble up. Similarly, the operational objections against Sarbanes-Oxley refer to excessive compliance costs, the possibility of outsourcing and offshoring accounting jobs, smaller public companies going private to avoid the rigors of Section 404, foreign companies delisting themselves from the U.S. stock exchanges, and the costs of new accounting infrastructure, among other issues.

Much research has taken place regarding the costs and benefits of Sarbanes-Oxley over the last few years. The results, though not conclusive, provide us with some understanding of the consequences of the Sarbanes-Oxley Act. The research is ongoing and has not resolved issues conclusively. The results are summarized below.

Costs

The philosophical issues surrounding the passage show no sign of abating. Romano (2009) argues that Sarbanes-Oxley remains a hurried piece of legislation, a response to a financial crisis. The legislation is flawed and will continue to cause problems for businesses. Butler and Ribstein (2006) suggest that individual investors are better off diversifying their investments. The Sarbanes-Oxley Act, however, imposes costs on all companies, depressing earnings and stock prices for the entire market. The specific findings of various studies are as follows:

1. Compliance costs (costs related to Section 404) have increased due to the passage of Sarbanes-Oxley Act. These costs include direct costs such as training of employees, time spent by executives in dealing with compliance, and purchasing of hardware and software as well as indirect costs such as loss in productivity due to resources being diverted to comply with the Sarbanes-Oxley Act. The SEC's Advisory Committee estimated that the costs for compliance ranged from 0.06 percent of revenues for companies with revenues greater than $5 billion to 2.6 percent for companies having revenues of less than $100 million. There are many other, varying estimates of costs.

2. Costs increased rapidly immediately after the act was passed. Compliance costs began to rise slowly and then showed some decline as companies became more skilled in complying with the act and also made the needed infrastructure investments.

3. Audit costs initially increased rapidly, but, as time has gone by, auditors have become more efficient and audit fees have remained flat or decreased slightly.

4. There is some evidence that some public companies have gone private to avoid complying with Sarbanes-Oxley. Moreover, some private companies have decided not to go public for the same reason.

5. The market value of smaller public firms has been negatively affected by the act. However, the SEC is providing additional guidance and time to help the smaller firms.

6. The insurance premiums for directors serving on the board have gone up. The composition of the directors is now more tilted toward lawyers, financial experts, and retired (as opposed to current) executives. Director pay and total costs have significantly increased.

Benefits

The benefits of compliance, as compared to the costs, are somewhat more diffuse, long term, and harder to quantify. Michael Oxley, for example, asks: "How can you measure the value of knowing that company books are sounder than they were before?" He adds that these costs are really investments for the future. Moody's, a credit rating firm, believes that companies are strengthening their accounting controls and investing in infrastructure required to support quality financial reporting. Bradford, Taylor, and

Brazel (2010) argue that compliance with the act has helped corporations to achieve strategic goals and analyze performance more effectively and efficiently. The specific findings of various studies can be summarized as follows:

1. Some experts believe that the act has helped restore investor confidence in the integrity of financial statements. Some empirical research suggests that Section 404 may reduce the opportunity for intentional or unintentional accounting errors and improve the quality of reported earnings.
2. Section 404 reports allow the investors to assess risks more accurately and can affect the firm's cost of equity. Companies that improve their controls lower their borrowing costs.
3. A survey carried out by the Institute of Management Accountants indicated that both public and nonpublic companies have improved processes, expanded employee job responsibilities, eliminated duplicate activities, and automated manual controls due to compliance with the act. Interestingly, nonpublic companies reaped more benefits due to the compliance.
4. Compliance with the act may help companies in getting dismissals, a favorable result, in securities fraud class-action cases.
5. The boards of directors, especially the audit committees, are far more independent and responsive to shareholders than they were in the pre–Sarbanes-Oxley era.
6. A paper issued by the Institute of Internal Auditors (Rittenberg and Miller 2005) suggests that internal controls in corporations have improved and their financial statements are viewed as more reliable.

The Economic Crisis of 2008–2009

Sarbanes-Oxley is the latest salvo in an ongoing war against poor corporate governance, mismanagement, and fraud. The act required that many aspects of corporate governance, which were earlier left to management's discretion, conform to the new legal mandates. Many powerful forces—for example, global corporations, top managers, big accounting firms, politicians, and lobbyists—bring forward complaints whenever new accounting rules and regulations are set. These groups have competing agendas and motives, which, moreover, do not necessarily coincide with the public interest. Occasionally, however, momentous events, such as a series of corporate frauds and bankruptcies, converge to create the need for sweeping legislation.

The economic crisis of 2008–2009 has, in many respects, overshadowed the Sarbanes-Oxley debate. This latest crisis is similar to but worse than the one seen in 2001–2002. The losses due to speculation in mortgage-backed securities can be measured in the trillions of dollars, and the human costs in terms of jobs, savings, pensions, state and local governments, and so on are greater still. The crisis presents a host of new legal, ethical, and regulatory issues. Yet many of the provisions of Sarbanes-Oxley, such as requiring due diligence, preventing conflict of interest, and adhering to basic fiduciary responsibilities, remain relevant to the current situation. Thus, the chances that Sarbanes-Oxley will be rolled back seem remote. As noted, the Obama administration has given strong signals that additional legislation is on the way.

It is clear that the new regulations are aimed primarily at the financial and banking industry. The draft of the act proposes reforms to meet five key objectives (Department of the Treasury n.d.):

1. Promote robust supervision and regulation of financial firms,
2. Establish comprehensive supervision and regulation of the financial markets,
3. Protect consumers and investors from financial abuse,
4. Improve tools for managing financial crisis, and
5. Raise international regulatory standards and improve international cooperation.

To achieve these objectives, various measures have been proposed—for example, creation of a Financial Services Oversight Council, granting additional powers to the Federal Reserve, establishing a national bank supervisor, enhancing regulation of the securities market and derivatives (which lay at the heart of the problem), and implementing higher standards for the providers of consumer financial products. There is discussion, too, of not relying on corporate disclosure but rather providing mandates on running and managing a business. The ensuing legislation will likely share many features with Sarbanes-Oxley and will likely cause considerable controversy and debate.

Conclusion

The cycle of corporate wrongdoing and government regulation goes on. As people increasingly look to the stock market for investments and put their hard-earned savings in the market, it becomes ever more imperative that these markets remain transparent, properly regulated, and compliant with the rules of the game. Regulations such as Sarbanes-Oxley or the most recent financial regulatory reform bill have, of course, both advantages and disadvantages. There are ideological and philosophical issues that need to be drawn out, defined, and discussed. Even when enacted, it is difficult to properly evaluate these regulations or perform straightforward cost/benefit analyses. Thus it seems that the perpetual chase between the law and the outlaws will continue for some time.

See also **Bank Bailouts; Corporate Tax Shelters; Financial Regulation; Corporate Crime (vol. 2)**

Further Reading

Akhigbe, A., A. Martin, and M. Newman, "Risk Shifts Following Sarbanes-Oxley: Influences of Disclosure and Governance." *Financial Review* 43 (2008): 383–401.

Alkhafaji, A., "Corporate Governance: The Evolution of the Sarbanes-Oxley Act and Its Impact on Corporate America." *Competitive Review: An International Business Journal* 17, no. 3 (2007): 193–202.

Anandarajan, A., G. Kleinman, and D. Palmon, "Auditor Independence Revisited: The Effects of SOX on Auditor Independence." *International Journal of Disclosure and Governance* 5, no. 2 (2008): 112–126.

Ashbaugh-Skaife, H., D. Collins, W. Kinney, and R. LaFond, "The Effect of SOX Internal Control Deficiencies on Firm Risk and Cost of Equity." *Journal of Accounting Research* 47, no. 1 (2009): 1–43.

Baynes, L., "Just Pucker and Blow? An Analysis of Corporate Whistleblowers, the Duty of Care, the Duty of Loyalty, and the Sarbanes-Oxley Act." *St. John's Law Review* 76, no. 4 (2002): 875–896.

Bhagat, S., B. Bolton, and R. Romano, "The Promise and Peril of Corporate Governance Indices." *Columbia Law Review* 108, no. 8 (2008): 1803–1882.

Bradford, M., E. Taylor, and J. Brazel, "Beyond Compliance: The Value of SOX." *Strategic Finance* (May 2010): 48–53.

Butler, H., and L. Ribstein, *The Sarbanes-Oxley Debacle: What We've Learned: How to Fix It.* Washington, DC: AEI Press, 2006.

Chang, H., G. Fernando, and W. Liao, "Sarbanes-Oxley Act, Perceived Earnings Quality and Cost of Capital." *Review of Accounting and Finance* 8, no. 3 (2009): 216–231.

Department of the Treasury, *Financial Regulatory Reform: A New Foundation: Rebuilding Financial Supervision and Regulation.* Washington, DC: Department of the Treasury, n.d.

Gifford, R., and H. Howe, "Regulation and Unintended Consequence: Thought on Sarbanes-Oxley." *CPA Journal* 74, no. 6 (2004): 6–10.

Jung, K., "How Will the Current Economic Crisis Change Corporate Management?" *SERI Quarterly* (October 2009): 63–72.

Marshall, J., and E. Heffes, "Is Sarbanes-Oxley Working? Study Suggests It Is." *Financial Executive* 24, no. 1 (2008): 10.

Mason, M., and J. O'Mahony, "Post-Traditional Corporate Governance." *Journal of Corporate Citizenship* (Autumn 2008): 31–44.

Mishra, S., "Counting Progress: The State of Boards Five Years after Sarbanes-Oxley." *Corporate Governance Advisor* 16, no. 1 (2008): 12–20.

Petra, S., and G. Lukatos, "The Sarbanes-Oxley Act of 2000: A Five-Year Retrospective." *Corporate Governance* 9, no. 2 (2009): 120–132.

Rezaee, Z., *Corporate Governance Post-Sarbanes-Oxley: Regulations, Requirements, and Integrated Processes.* New York: John Wiley, 2007.

Rittenberg, L., and P. Miller, *Sarbanes-Oxley Section 404: Looking at the Benefits.* Altamonte, FL: IIA Research Foundation, 2005.

Romano, R., "The Sarbanes-Oxley Act and the Making of Quack Corporate Governance." *Yale Law Journal* 114, no. 7 (2005): 1521–1611.

Romano, R., "Does the Sarbanes-Oxley Act Have a Future?" *Yale Journal of Regulation* 26, no. 2 (2009): 229–342.

Sherman, S., and V. Chambers, "SOX as Safeguard and Signal: The Impact of Sarbanes-Oxley Act of 2002 on US Corporations' Choice to List Abroad." *Multinational Business Review* 17, no. 3 (2009): 163–178.

Stovall, D., "SOX Compliance: Cost and Value." *Business Review* 11, no 2 (2008): 107–113.

CORPORATE TAX SHELTERS

Keith C. Farrell

A fundamental objective of the federal tax law is to raise revenues to cover the cost of government operations. Ordinarily, Congress will set annual budgets, based on anticipated revenues, to plan expenditures and create a balanced budget. Until recently, the last balanced budget was in 1969. Beginning in 1970, there were 28 straight years of deficits. The budget was again balanced from 1998 through 2001, but, since 2002, the federal budget has run at a deficit—in fact, the largest in the nation's history.

The internal revenue code (IRC) comprises numerous code sections, complete with abrupt twists and sudden stops. It has been a complaint of U.S. taxpayers that the tax code is too complicated, often defying logic. Even trained professionals can be baffled by the complexity of a tax return. Recently, the Internal Revenue Service (IRS), the governmental body charged with collecting taxes and auditing tax returns for compliance, has stated that its mission is to simplify the tax code. However, ask any tax professional, and he or she will tell you that, to date, simplifying the tax code has seemingly resulted in three additional binders of tax code.

The IRS distributes more than 650 types of tax forms, schedules, and instructions (Hoffman et al. 2009). That being said, there often is a reason behind every oddity that occurs in the tax code, whether it is an economic, social, or political reason. An example is how the federal government has tried to encourage charitable giving to nonprofit organizations. An individual's ability to deduct charitable contributions from his or her taxes is a social practice that Congress has encouraged through tax deductions. Another example is research and development credits, which are given to encourage organizations to develop innovative ideas and processes.

Background

During the thriving 1990s, business in the United States was growing at unprecedented levels, breaking many corporate earning records. Between 1988 and 1998, corporate revenues grew 127 percent, from $292.5 billion to $666.4 billion. The surge also had a positive impact on the U.S. Treasury. Throughout this time period, reported corporate taxable income increased by 99 percent, or from $94.5 billion to $188.7 billion (Crenshaw 1999). So why did corporate taxes not keep pace with corporate revenues? Experts say that this was due to the emergence of complicated tax shelter plans.

VARIOUS REASONS FOR TAX CODE

Social

Home mortgage deduction.

Encourage society to purchase homes by subsidizing the interest cost.

Charitable contribution deduction.

Encourage society to give to charities.

Adoption tax credit.

Encourage and help subsidize adoptions.

Retirement plans (IRA, 401(k), etc.).

Create means to save and encourage retirement planning.

Hope and Lifetime Learning credits.

Encourage students to attend higher educational institutions by subsidizing a part of the cost.

Economic

Section 179.

Allows for an immediate write-off of an asset rather than depreciating it over a period of time. This allows a company to recoup its investment faster.

The Selection.

Allows small corporations to avoid double taxation.

Political

Tax incentives for farmers.

Special income averaging and depreciation methods for the farming industry.

Oil and gas exploration.

Expense drilling and development costs immediately rather than capitalizing and amortizing over a period of time.

Other

Dividend received deduction.

Grants relief to corporations from triple taxation of income and dividends.

Like-kind exchange.

Allows for the deferral of tax on capital gain transactions that occur from trading property and not receiving cash.

Natural disasters.

Usually involve charitable contribution incentives for donations to charities. Often adjust tax-filing dates to assist and encourage compliance. Examples are 9/11 and Hurricane Katrina.

During the 1990s, a peculiar situation developed where, by strict application of the IRC, tax professionals were able to create paper losses that a corporation would be able to use to offset income. This strange phenomenon caught the eye of the IRS in the late 1990s as it began discover the flourishing industry of marketed tax planning packages that enabled corporations to lower their total taxable income and, ultimately, pay less in taxes. In 1999, Stanford law professor Joseph Bankman projected the cost to the U.S. Treasury to be at $10 billion (Stratton 1999). It is reasonable to expect the current cost to have grown greater since that time.

Total corporate taxes paid as a percentage of the entire amount of taxes collected by the IRS have fallen significantly over the past two decades as corporations have found and exploited loopholes in the IRC. These loopholes allow them to reduce their total tax bill, usually by concealing revenues or accumulating additional expenses. For example, a corporation is taxed on its net income, which is generally calculated by taking total revenues received less total expenses incurred to generate the income. By lowering revenues or amassing additional expenses, you can lower your net income and, effectively, your total tax due. These loopholes manipulate the IRC in ways that were never intended by Congress. Tax sheltering methods can be legitimate or illegitimate.

HOW DID THE TAX SHELTER INDUSTRY START?

In the 1990s, during a period of startling corporate growth, it became a strategy of tax departments in many large companies to find solutions to lower the tax liability that would be due on substantial taxable income. Managers aggressively reviewed their budgets for ways to lower cost, and no expense was bypassed. It seemed logical that if all expenses listed on an income statement were fair game, then tax expense would eventually become a focus for cost-conscious managers.

The industry was not started by the invention of tax shelters; corporate managers did not seek out accountants' and lawyers' advice on how to shelter income, but the industry really started with accounting and law firms creating tax shelter plans and promoting them to their high–net worth individuals and corporations with substantial taxable income. It was during this period that many companies' best tax professionals were recruited by large accounting firms for their technical expertise.

The incentive was the ability to earn higher incomes by designing and marketing these tax shelter plans (Rostain 2006). There were penalties in place—20 percent of money received for implementing the tax shelter—but many firms had feasibility studies performed that proved that the profits created far exceeded the penalties that could be incurred. These marketed tax shelters would create sizeable tax write-offs and, consequently, bring in substantial fees for their implementation. It may cost $200,000 to purchase the services required to set up and execute these schemes, but if they save the company $2 million in taxes, it is worth the expense.

Naturally, there are two sides to this debate. On one hand, if a given transaction follows the letter of the law, then how can it be considered abusive or unethical? Conversely, it is justifiable to deem transactions that contain no economic gain, aside from lowering an entity's tax liability, as fraudulent tax reporting?

What Is a Tax Shelter?

There is no clear definition that characterizes all tax shelters. The purpose of a tax shelter is "to reduce or eliminate the tax liability for the tax shelter user" (Committee on Governmental Affairs 2005, 1). The definition of a tax shelter would include both legitimate and illegitimate actions. The controversy centers on what is considered tax planning and what is considered abusive tax sheltering.

There are many instances written into the IRC that allow a company to structure a transaction that will reduce the tax liability of the organization. It is reasonable for a person to plan his or her affairs so as to achieve the lowest tax liability. Judge Learned Hand is cited as saying, "There is not even a patriotic duty to increase one's taxes" (*Gregory v. Helvering* 1934). It is reasonable to believe that if these taxpayers follow the IRC, they should be rewarded for their proper planning and work. For years, tax minimization tactics have been used and have afforded taxpayers the ability to properly plan transactions to achieve the least tax consequences. However, it should be noted that these minimization tactics have been done using acceptable, practical procedures. The argument next focuses on whether these transactions ordinarily contain substance and motivation on some economic level to justify performing the transaction.

Abusive tax shelters can be categorized as financial mechanisms with the sole purpose of creating losses to deduct for tax purposes (Smith 2004). These complex transactions produce significant tax benefits in ways that were never intended by the tax code. These benefits were never expected by the underlying tax logic in effect and, in essence, are transactions used only to avoid or evade tax liability.

Since there is no firm differentiation between legitimate and illegitimate tax planning, it is hard to tell where the line is. A working definition of an abusive tax shelter is a "corporate transaction involving energetic paper shuffling aimed at having favorable tax consequences along with no, or next to no, economic consequences other than the tax consequences" (Shaviro 2004, 11). The purpose of these types of transactions is to create transactions that will generate tax losses that can be offset against other taxable income. There is no economic sense to these transactions except to generate these losses and reduce the total tax liability.

At its core, the IRS is the agency exclusively responsible for detecting any transaction with the sole purpose of eliminating or avoiding taxes. The IRS, through audits of filed returns, and the U.S. Treasury have begun to spot and publish legal regulations on transactions they consider abusive. These mandates warn taxpayers that use of such listed transactions may lead to an audit and assessment of back taxes, interest, and penalties for using an illegal tax shelter.

The IRS requires that, under certain circumstances certain transactions be reported and disclosed to the IRS as potentially illegal tax shelter transactions. A listed transaction is one that the IRS has determined to have a potential for tax avoidance or evasion. In addition, transactions that are similar in their purpose to the listed transactions require similar disclosure. The IRS uses several distinctive judicial doctrines to determine whether a transaction is legitimate or abusive in nature.

Why Tax Shelters Are Harmful

When enacting changes to the tax code, Congress is often directed by the concept of revenue neutrality. Revenue neutrality is the idea that new legislation will neither increase nor decrease the net revenues produced under existing laws and regulations. In other words, the total revenues raised after new tax laws are passed should be consistent with revenues generated under the prior tax laws. One taxpayer will experience a decrease in tax liability, however, at another taxpayer's expense.

When corporations engage in illegitimate tax sheltering schemes, they, in essence, steal from the U.S. Treasury. Over the years, billions of tax dollars have been lost. Recently, the IRS and Congress have taken a firm position with legislation to impede tax shelters that have been identified. It is estimated that legislation to prohibit certain shelter transactions, specifically lease-in lease-out shelters and liquidating real estate investment trust transactions, have saved taxpayers $10.2 and $34 billion, respectively (Summers 2000).

When corporate taxpayers do not pay their respective tax liabilities, the result is lower revenues for the U.S. Treasury, which ultimately causes or escalates a government's deficit. Congress, the U.S. Treasury, and individual U.S. taxpayers are dependent on corporations paying their fair share of the tax bill to maintain government operations. Shortages in tax revenues can make fiscal planning difficult when budgeted income falls short of what was anticipated and pledged for various governmental programs.

To maintain tax revenue collections, Congress has only a couple of options: raise corporate taxes or raise individual taxes. Buried deep in the corporate tax shelter controversy is their effect on individual taxpayers. A side effect of a corporation engaging in fraudulent tax practices is that the federal government redistributes the tax burden, ordinarily, back onto the remaining taxpayers, who would otherwise enjoy a tax reduction. To say it differently, the rest of the population picks up the tab for the use of abusive corporate tax shelters.

Why Tax Shelters Can Be Beneficial

In the 1980s, President Ronald Reagan cut corporate tax rates as part of his monetary policy. The United States was a leader worldwide in lowering its tax burdens on

AN EXAMPLE OF A TAX SHELTER TRANSACTION

A corporate taxpayer agrees to purchase property from a foreign entity for $101 in exchange for $1 cash and a 10-year interest payment–only loan of $100 at 10 percent. The corporation will be required to make annual payments of $10 on the loan for interest. Subsequently, the foreign entity leases the property back from the corporation to use during the period for $10 per year. At the end of the 10-year period, when the balance on the loan is due, the corporation will sell the asset back to the entity for $100, thus retiring the debt to the foreign entity.

What is the benefit of this transaction for the corporation? The $10 lease revenue received negates the $10 annual interest expense, allowing the corporation to operate this transaction without cost. In addition, it will receive additional depreciation expense over the 10 years it owns the asset. Foreign assets that are used for these types of transactions typically involve governmental infrastructure—for example, water and sewer systems. These assets have no value to a U.S. corporation and would never be abandoned by the foreign government entities from which they are purchased. This is a good example of a transaction that has no economic purpose and is solely performed to reduce tax liability (Smith 2004).

It is important to note why transaction schemes like the aforementioned are difficult for the IRS to contest. The purchase of assets and claiming depreciation is allowable under the current IRC and is altogether different from not reporting income that is received from an individual's side business. It is more difficult to disallow a deduction that is in compliance with the tax code than to substantiate the omission of earned income as a violation of the IRC.

corporations as a way to facilitate economic growth, and, during the mid-1980s, the United States' tax rates were the lowest around the world. However, this started a sequence of events where many industrialized countries around the world began cutting their tax rates by an average of 30 percent in response, according to the Organisation for Economic Co-operation and Development (OECD), a group of 30 countries that works to address economic and social issues.

Twenty-five years later, many counties around the globe have surpassed the United States in its tax-cutting policies. Federal and state corporate taxes average 39.3 percent, approximately 10 percentage points higher than the OECD average ("Let's Make a Deal" 2005). To look at it from a different angle, a corporation in the United States has Uncle Sam as more than a one-third shareholder.

Indeed, of the 30 wealthiest countries in the world, the United States now levies one of the highest corporate income tax rates on its businesses (along with Japan, Canada, Germany, and Spain). In 1996, these 30 countries' average corporate tax rate was 38–30 percent that in the mid-2000s. Overall, global corporate tax rates fell over 20 percent during this time period (Edwards and Mitchell 2008). Although U.S.

individual tax rates decreased during this time period, corporate tax rates have remained unchanged.

Furthermore, the effects tax rates have on U.S. businesses go beyond cutting the tax piece of the profits out of a corporation's net income. The world has become a global marketplace, where executives and managers compete against not only their rivals next door but on the other side of the world. Higher corporate tax rates place U.S. companies at a competitive disadvantage when compared to their foreign counterparts. Higher tax rates produce increased pressure to maintain or lower costs.

Imagine two identical corporations located in the United States and Ireland. Ireland's corporate tax rate is 12.5 percent. These two companies have the same gross sales and administrative costs and, with all other factors being the same, report the same net income. However, the corporation in Ireland is allowed to keep an additional 27.5 percent of its income in comparison to the one located in the United States (40 percent versus 12.5 percent tax rates). This additional income can be used for additional research and development costs, higher employee wages, or greater dividend payouts for stockholders. To gain greater market share, the Irish corporation is better situated to compete on price and can still produce the same net income after taxes as the U.S. corporation with lower prices.

Having one of the highest tax rates in the world is self-defeating because it encourages U.S. corporations to engage in questionable tax practices as a means of staying competitive globally. Many legal and accounting firms are hired primarily for the purpose of creating arrangements that enable the company to pay little or no tax. With real tax benefits achieved by moving operations to countries like the Cayman Islands, Bermuda, and other international tax havens, many CEOs and boards of directors feel that it is their duty to get involved with these practices.

Solutions to Abusive Corporate Tax Shelters

With high tax rates versus foreign competitors, a potential solution would be to lower the corporate tax rate imposed on U.S. corporations. If a primary reason to engage in questionable tax practices is to become more competitive versus global competition, a tax rate that is more in line with other similar industrial countries could alleviate the pressure that causes corporation managers to investigate these practices. A lower flat tax rate for all industries could not only benefit corporations, but also their employees, who would work for more competitive organizations. A result would be more jobs and job security. In addition, with the need for tax shelters removed, decreasing the use of phony transactions and bringing into the United States income that was held offshore would create a windfall of revenue for the U.S. Treasury.

When President Reagan first initiated corporate tax cuts as part of the Tax Reform Act of 1985, other countries responded by lowering their tax rates. It is reasonable to expect this same activity to occur again should the United States lower its corporate tax rates, but it probably cannot afford to lower them much more. Only a tax-free situation would ensure that corporations would not find motivation to investigate tax shelter activities.

Another option, the one preferred by President Barack Obama, would be to require that a corporation's *book income* be equal to its *tax income*. Corporations are allowed to maintain two sets of books: book and tax. Book income is what is reported to shareholders, while tax income is what is reported to the IRS for taxation purposes. Many transactions deductible for book purposes are not deductible for tax and vice versa. An example of this is the depreciation expense. Differing methods are required to be used when computing depreciation expenses for book and tax purposes. Generally, tax depreciation allows you to write off the value of an asset much quicker than book. This generates a higher book income and a lower tax income. These types of differences occur quite frequently because book and tax income do not agree.

This encourages managers to perform transactions that show a lower tax income, and therefore a lower tax liability, while still reporting the higher book income to the shareholders. In other words, they are able to realize the best of both worlds. To remedy this problem, making tax income equal to book income would once again deter tax departments from creating loopholes in the tax code designed specifically to maintain book income but lower tax income. The Obama administration has sought to apply this strategy to companies operating out of the Cayman Islands. The administration also worked with the government of Switzerland to revise its tax laws in order to allow the U.S. government to levy taxes on certain U.S. holders of Swiss bank accounts.

Conclusion

Embedded in the IRC are numerous tax-planning possibilities for taxpayers. Many corporations have taken tax planning a step too far, infringing on what may be out of bounds in the field of tax planning. Arguments can be made on both sides of the debate as to why corporations should or should not engage in such activities, but the fundamental reason that abusive tax sheltering is detrimental is its redistribution of the tax burden. In addition, tax-sheltering methods should be considered abusive and rejected in their entirety when they offer a benefit that is inconsistent with the purpose of the tax code.

See also **Corporate Governance; Debt, Deficits, and the Economy; Financial Regulation**

Further Reading

Committee on Governmental Affairs, *The Role of Professional Firms in the U.S. Tax Shelter Industry.* Washington, DC: U.S. Government Printing Office, 2005.

Crenshaw, Albert B., "When Shelters Aren't Aboveboard: IRS, Hill Step Up Efforts as Improper Deals to Help Firms Cut Taxes Rise." *Washington Post* (November 23, 1999): E01.

Edwards, Chris, and Daniel J. Mitchell, *Global Tax Revolution: The Rise of Tax Competition and the Battle to Defend It.* Washington, DC: Cato Institute, 2008.

Gregory v. Helvering, 69 F.2d 809, 810 (2nd Cir. 1934), aff'd, 293 U.S. 465 (1935).

Hoffman, William H., et al., *South-Western Federal Taxation: Corporations, Partnerships, Estates and Trusts.* Belmont, CA: Thomson South-Western, 2009.

"Let's Make a Deal." *Wall Street Journal* (December 28, 2005): A14.

Rostain, Tanina, "Sheltering Lawyers: The Organized Tax Bar and the Tax Shelter Industry." *Yale Journal on Regulation* 23 (2006): 77.

Shaviro, Daniel N., *Corporate Tax Shelters in a Global Economy.* Washington, DC: AEI Press, 2004.

Slemrod, Joel, *Taxing Ourselves: A Citizen's Guide to the Debate over Taxes,* 4th ed. Cambridge, MA: MIT Press, 2008.

Smith, Hedrick, *Tax Me If You Can.* Documentary. Boston: PBS (a Frontline coproduction with Hendrick Smith Productions), 2004.

Stratton, Sherly, "Treasury Responds to Critics of Corporate Tax Shelter Proposals." *Tax Notes* 84 (1999): 17.

Summers, Lawrence H., *Tackling the Growth of Corporate Tax Shelters.* Washington, DC: Office of Public Affairs, Department of the Treasury, 2000.

D

DEBT, DEFICITS, AND THE ECONOMY

John J. Seater

When conversation turns to the economy, one of the most popular topics of discussion is the government deficit. Newspaper columnists, TV pundits, and, of course, politicians never tire of talking about the size of the deficit and what it means for the economy. Big deficits are considered bad—except that back in the 1950s and 1960s, they often were considered good. Big deficits depress the economy because they drive up interest rates—except that back in the 1950s and 1960s, the usual argument was that deficits stimulated the economy by encouraging people to spend more. So which is it: Are deficits good or bad? Do they depress or stimulate the economy? To answer those questions, we have to answer a more fundamental question: Exactly what *is* the government deficit? Once we know that, we can proceed to the more interesting questions of how deficits affect the economy and whether they are good or bad.

Debt and Deficits: What Are They?

The deficit is the addition to the outstanding stock of government debt, so to understand what the deficit is, we first have to understand what government debt is. The government undertakes many activities, from national defense to providing medical insurance. To pay for them, the government usually collects taxes. Sometimes, though, the government prefers to postpone collecting part of the taxes it needs and instead borrows funds by selling government bonds to the public. Those bonds, just like a corporate bond, represent a loan the government has taken out and eventually will repay. The person

TYPES OF GOVERNMENT DEBT

Governments issue several types of debt, which can be classified in various ways. One classification is by the type of government that issued the debt. In the United States, the main divisions are federal, state, and local debt; local debt can be divided further by type of locality, such as county or city. A second classification of government debt is by maturity at the time of issue. When we talk about a 10-year bond or a 30-year bond, we are talking about the length of time between the date when the bond was first issued and the date on which the principal will be repaid. Federal debt is divided into three convenient maturity categories. Treasury *bills* have initial maturities of 1 year or less (three-month bills, year bills, etc.); Treasury *notes* have initial maturities of between 1 and 10 years; and Treasury *bonds* have initial maturities longer than 10 years. State and local government securities generally are just called bonds, irrespective of the initial maturity. A *perpetuity* is a bond with an infinite maturity, which means the principal is never repaid and interest payments are made forever. The British government once issued some perpetuities, calling them consols.

A third way of classifying government securities is by the source of the revenue to repay them. *General obligation bonds* will be repaid with revenue collected by taxing the public; *revenue bonds* will be repaid with revenue collected from specific user fees, such as bridge or highway tolls. This way of classifying debt is used only for state and local debt.

who buys a government bond hands over money to the government and in return gets a bond stating the amount of the loan (the principal or face value of the loan), the interest rate that will be paid on the loan, and the date when the principal will be repaid (the maturity date of the loan). The money paid to the government by the buyer of the bond is that person's loan to the government, and the bond is the contract stating the terms of the loan. The government debt is the total amount of bonds that the government has issued but not yet repaid.

Whenever current government expenditure exceeds tax revenue, the government borrows the difference by selling new bonds to the public. In such a situation, the government budget is said to be in deficit. The amount of new debt issued in a given period of time (such as a calendar year) constitutes the deficit for that period. In contrast, when expenditure is less than tax revenue, the government budget is in surplus. At any time, the deficit is the negative of the surplus and vice versa.

How Much Government Debt Is There?

At the end of 2009, there was about $12.3 trillion of federal debt outstanding. Of that, 43 percent ($5.3 trillion) was held by federal agencies and trust funds, which means that the government owed almost half the debt to itself. Such internal debt is only a bookkeeping device for tracking the flows of funds within the federal government. An accurate analogy would be a household in which one child borrowed money from a sibling. That kind of intrafamily debt has no bearing on the family's net indebtedness and is ignored by credit rating agencies, banks, credit card companies, and so forth. The situation with respect to intragovernment debt is exactly the same: as far as the economy is concerned, the debt doesn't exist. It has no implications at all for the economy or public welfare. Unfortunately, popular discussions of the debt frequently fail to distinguish between internal and external government debt and thus overstate the relevant number, which is the amount of federal debt held by private investors. At the end of 2009, that amount was about $7 trillion. State and local governments also issue debt, and they have about $2.4 trillion in outstanding debt, most of which was held by private investors. Thus, the total amount of privately held government debt was about $9.4 trillion at the end of 2009.

Until about the mid-1980s, government debt as a fraction of gross domestic product (GDP) of the U.S. economy was not especially large except during wars and immediately after them. At the end of the Second World War, for example, outstanding federal debt alone (i.e., ignoring state and local debt) was slightly larger than GDP, and then it fell substantially over the next two or three decades. The federal government always has issued debt to cover part of the abnormally high level of government purchases during wars and then paid off the wartime debt in the following peacetime. By using debt to finance unusually high purchases during wars, the government avoids large fluctuations in tax rates, which would have adverse effects on economic activity. Since the mid-1980s and especially since the end of 2008, government debt has grown substantially relative to GDP. That growth is unusual because it resembles wartime debt behavior but has occurred in the absence of any major war. At the end of 2009, U.S. GDP was about $14.3 trillion, so the ratio of total, privately held outstanding government debt to GDP was about 76 percent. That is still below the debt-to-GDP ratio at the end of 1945, but it is growing unusually fast and, unlike during a war, is accompanied by no expectation of reduced future government expenditure to lead to a retirement of the debt without increases in tax rates. Note that the focus here is restricted to privately held federal, state, and local debt because that is the debt that matters to taxpayers and the economy in general. The figure usually seen in the news refers only to federal debt but includes debt held by federal agencies as well as by private individuals. Total outstanding federal debt at the end of 2009 was $12.3 trillion, equal to 86 percent of 2009's GDP of $14.3 trillion.

The foregoing numbers on the amount of outstanding government debt are the numbers one would see reported in the newspaper. They must be adjusted before they can be used to discuss the effect of debt on the economy.

The most important adjustment is for inflation. The *nominal* value of a bond is the price in dollars that it would fetch on the open market. The *real* value of that same bond is the number of units of output that it can buy. If DVD movies cost $20 each, then the real value of a $200 bond is 10 DVD movies. In other words, if you sell your bond, you will receive in return enough cash to buy 10 DVDs. If, however, the prices of all goods double, so that DVDs now cost $40 each, then the bond's cash value now buys only 5 DVDs. The bond's nominal value is unchanged by inflation and remains at $200. Its real value, however, is changed. Real values are what matter because what people care about is how many goods their paper assets can buy. That is precisely what the real value of a bond measures. Adjusting official debt and deficit figures for inflation can change the measurement of the debt's size by a substantial amount. In 1947, for example, official federal government statistics report a surplus of $6.6 billion. However, inflation that year was almost 15 percent. That inflation reduced the value of outstanding debt by about $11.4 billion. That reduction was equivalent to an additional surplus because it reduced the real value of what the federal government owed its creditors. The true surplus, therefore, was about $18 billion, nearly three times as high as the official figure. Another example is the decade of the 1970s, when the official federal deficit was positive every year but the inflation-corrected deficit was negative (that is, there was a real surplus) in exactly half those years.

Another adjustment is for changes in interest rates. The value of outstanding debt changes as market interest rates change. To see what is involved, suppose that you buy a one-year $10,000 Treasury bill (equivalently, you make a loan of $10,000 to the federal government) at 10:00 A.M. The bond carries an interest rate of 10 percent, which means you will be paid $1,000 in interest when the bond matures one year from now. At 11:00 A.M., the Federal Reserve announces a change in monetary policy that causes one-year interest rates to fall to 9 percent. Your bond now is worth more than when you bought it an hour ago because you could now sell the bond to someone else for more than $10,000. The reason is that anyone who wants to lend $10,000 for one year now will find that new bonds pay only 9 percent, meaning an interest payment in one year of $900. Your bond, however, has a 10 percent rate locked in and will pay $1,000 interest for sure. That makes your bond's market value higher than its par value of $10,000. These kinds of changes happen continually, day in and day out. As a result, the market value of the outstanding government debt fluctuates from day to day even if there is no inflation and even if the government issues no new debt and retires no outstanding debt. The market value of outstanding debt will be greater than the par value if interest rates have fallen on average since the debt was issued and will be smaller than the par value if rates have risen. The difference between par and market value of the outstanding debt is typically a few percentage points. Unfortunately, market values for the total outstanding government debt are not readily available. Governments do not report them, and newspaper reports rarely mention them.

The Economic Effects of Government Debt

To see how government debt may affect the economy, we need to understand how government debt affects the flow of net income to the people lending to it. When the government borrows, it promises to repay the lender. To make those repayments, the government ultimately will have to raise extra taxes, beyond what it needs to pay for its other activities. The economic effect of government debt depends heavily on how taxpayers perceive those future taxes. Perceptions are difficult to measure, and neither economists nor others understand exactly how people form their perceptions. As a result, economists still disagree on the economic effect of government debt.

A simple example will help illustrate the situation. Suppose the government buys $1 trillion worth of goods and services every year and pays for them entirely by collecting taxes. The government's budget is balanced because revenue equals expenditure. Suppose that the government decides to change the way it finances its expenditures but does not change the amount being spent. In the first year, the government reduces taxes by $100 billion and replaces the lost revenue by selling $100 billion worth of bonds that mature in one year and carry an interest rate of 10 percent a year. In the second year, the bonds mature, and the government pays the $100 billion principal and the $10 billion of interest. Taxes in the first year are $100 billion lower (the government is running a deficit), but in the second year taxes are $110 billion higher (the government is running a surplus). How does this rearrangement of the timing of tax collections affect people? In the first year, people give the same total amount of revenue to the government as they did when they paid only taxes, but now $100 billion of the total payment is in the form of a loan that will be repaid in the second year with an extra $10 billion in interest. On this account, people may feel richer because they seem to be paying less in total taxes over the two periods. This year, they pay $900 billion in taxes and $100 billion in loans for the same $1 trillion total that they were paying before the government decided to issue debt. Next year, however, it seems they will be better off than before. They will pay $1 trillion in taxes, but they will receive $110 billion in repayment of their first-year loan. Their net payment in the second year will be only $890 billion. This seems like a good deal, but unfortunately it won't turn out that way. When the second year arrives, people will find that their net payment is $1 trillion, just as if the debt never had been issued. Why is that? To pay the $110 billion in principal and interest, the government must come up with an extra $110 billion in revenue, so it must raise taxes by that amount. Those extra taxes exactly cancel the payment of the principal and interest! The government gives with one hand and takes away with the other. The net result is that people do not really get back the $100 billion they lent the government or the $10 billion in interest on it, and the loan is equivalent to having paid the $100 billion in taxes in the first year. The same result holds from any maturity of debt, whether it is a 1-year bond, as in the previous example, a 10-year bond, or even a perpetuity.

Note, by the way, that the government cannot beat the mathematics by refinancing old debt with new debt. If the government tried to repay existing debt, including the interest on it, by issuing new debt, the amount of debt would grow at the rate of interest. In our example, in the second year, the government owes $110 billion in principal and interest on the debt issued in the first year. The government could raise the revenue by issuing $110 billion in new debt. It then would have to pay $121 billion in principal and interest in the third year ($110 billion in principal and $11 billion in interest, assuming the interest rate stays at 10 percent for simplicity). Thus, the debt would grow by 10 percent every year that the government issued new debt to repay the old debt. The problem is that interest rates generally exceed the growth rate of the economy, so, in

WHAT DEBT IS THE RISKIEST?

There is an inconsistency in popular discussions of government debt compared to other types of debt. Corporations and households both issue debt (that is, borrow money). Corporate debt outstanding was about $7.3 trillion at the end of 2009, about $2 trillion less than the amount of privately held government debt. Household debt is larger. In 2009, households' total debt stood at $13.4 trillion, 43 percent larger than the privately held government debt.

Commentators regularly express concern that government debt represents a risk to the economy, once in a while express similar concerns about household debt, and virtually never mention corporate debt. In fact, household and corporate debt can represent an economic risk in some rather rare circumstances, but government debt virtually never represents such a risk. In a deep recession, debtors may become unable to repay their debts and be forced to default on them. That, in turn, can make financial institutions insolvent and lead to a collapse of the financial system. Such a mechanism seems to have been the reason the recession of 1929 became the Great Depression of 1932. Deflation made existing debt increasingly costly to repay, leading to widespread defaults on debt. The banking system came under great pressure and eventually collapsed with the banking panic of 1932.

This sort of thing happened from time to time up through the Great Depression but has not happened since, largely because of regulatory changes and an improved understanding by the Federal Reserve System of how to conduct monetary policy in the face of such circumstances. Such a collapse may nearly have happened in the financial turmoil of late 2008, when the market for collateralized debt obligations (CDOs) fell apart. CDOs were a new type of instrument that fell outside the regulatory structure that had worked so well since the Great Depression. Their emergence combined with other changes in the financial industry, such as the rise in importance of the housing lenders Fannie Mae and Freddie Mac, which also were outside the post-Depression regulatory structure. Strong action by the Federal Reserve System prevented a deflation that could have caused a repetition of the asset market crash that started the Great Depression.

In contrast, default by any level of government in the United States has been exceedingly rare, and the federal government has never defaulted on its debt obligations. However, the unprecedented peacetime rise in the amount of outstanding federal debt in 2009 and 2010 has raised concerns—unresolved at the time of this writing—about the government's ability to repay its debt.

finite time, the government would reach a point where it was issuing debt equal in value to the entire gross domestic product of the economy. After that, it would not be able to issue any new debt because the government would be promising to repay more than could possibly be available to it, and the scheme would come to an end.

Two major factors determine how government debt affects the economy. One is the kind of taxes the government uses to collect revenue, and the other is the way that people perceive the future taxes implied by current debt. It is easiest to start with people's perceptions in a simple case and then move on to the more complicated case that actually confronts us.

Suppose for a moment that taxes are very simple. In particular, suppose that the government uses what are called lump-sum taxes to finance everything it does. A lump-sum tax is one whose amount is independent of anything the taxpayer does. For example, a taxpayer could draw a number out of a hat, and that would be his tax, irrespective of whether he was rich or poor. Actual taxes are more complicated, usually being based on income, consumption, or some form of wealth. The taxpayer has some influence over how much of those kinds of taxes she pays because she can control how much income, spending, and wealth she has. For the moment, though, concentrate on the simple, even if unrealistic, case of a lump-sum tax. In that simple case, government debt is unlikely to have any significant effect on the economy. People generally try to estimate their future income, and, of course, what they care about is their income after taxes. That means that, in effect, they try to estimate their future taxes. As we have seen already, any government debt issued today implies extra taxes at some time in the future. If people are aware of that fact, then they will know that any reduction in today's taxes brought about by the government issuing new debt is going to be offset by more taxes in the future. The example above showed that the offset is exact. The question is whether people recognize at least approximately that the offset is exact. If they do, then bond finance is equivalent to tax finance, as the example above showed. In that case, government debt has no effect on anything important—a property known as Ricardian equivalence after David Ricardo, the economist who first discussed it. If people do not foresee all the future taxes implied by government debt, then they feel wealthier when the debt is issued but poorer in the future, when, unexpectedly, they have to pay higher taxes to finance the principal and interest payments. They then are likely to increase their consumption expenditure today and perhaps work less today. In the future, when the inevitable taxes arrive, they will have to reduce their consumption and increase their work effort. So if people do not correctly perceive the future taxes implied by current debt, they will alter their economic behavior when debt is issued or retired and thus affect the economy.

The situation becomes more complicated when we extend our examination to include the fact that taxes are not lump sum. Taxes in the real world take some fraction of the tax base, which is the thing taxed—income for an income tax, consumption purchases for a sales tax, and so on. To keep the discussion simple, restrict the story to an income tax by supposing that that is the only kind of tax the government uses. The principles are the same for other taxes, so nothing important is lost by this simplification. The problem with taxes that are not lump sum, such as an income tax, is that they have positive *marginal tax rates*. The marginal tax rate is the fraction that you must pay in tax on the next dollar of income that you earn. A proportional income tax, for example, levies a fixed tax rate on your income, no matter how high or low your income is. If the marginal rate were 20 percent, then you would pay 20 cents on every dollar that you earn, whether you earn $10,000 or $10,000,000. Everybody would pay exactly 20 percent of their income in taxes. This is the so-called flat tax. Some state governments levy that kind of income tax. A graduated or progressive income tax is one whose tax rate rises with the income of the taxpayer. The federal income tax is that type of tax. Somebody earning $20,000 has a marginal tax rate of 15 percent, so if he earns another dollar, he will pay 15 cents of it to the federal government in tax. In contrast, someone earning $200,000 has a marginal rate of 35 percent and will pay in tax 35 cents of the next dollar she earns. For our purposes, it is sufficient to consider a proportional income tax, with the same marginal tax rate for everyone.

The important thing about marginal tax rates is that they affect people's economic behavior. People's choices depend on the tax rate they face. Think of someone trying to decide whether to work an extra hour. Suppose he earns $30 an hour. If there were no tax, then one more hour of work will earn him $30, pure and simple. If, in contrast, he is in the 15 percent tax bracket, he will get to keep only 85 percent of his extra $30 dollars, which is $25.50. The other $4.50 goes to the government as tax. Thus, the effective return to working another hour is not the stated $30 but the after-tax earning of $25.50. It is less attractive to work an hour for $25.50 than for $30, so fewer people would decide to work when there is a tax compared to when there isn't. The same reasoning holds for investment. People will be less likely to make the next investment (buying a new machine for their machine shop, for example), because the return on that investment is reduced by the tax.

So what does this all have to do with government debt? Remember that debt rearranges taxes over time. It therefore also rearranges the incentive effects associated with those taxes. For example, if the government reduces taxes today by issuing debt, in reality the taxes it reduces will be income taxes, not lump-sum taxes. Thus, by issuing debt, the government will reduce the disincentive effects of taxes today and increase them tomorrow. As a result, the government will affect the timing of people's economic decisions. The effects of rearranging disincentive effects over time get to be quite complicated, but the important thing for this discussion is that, precisely because debt does rearrange taxes and their disincentive effects over time, it has real effects on the economy. The situation becomes even more complicated if people cannot figure out exactly what the new timing will be after debt is issued. No one really knows when the government will collect the taxes to repay a new 30-year bond. It may decide to retire the bond early, or it may decide after 30 years to replace it with another bond, say a 5-year note, thus postponing the repayment by 5 years. In the face of such uncertainty, figuring out exactly what the incentive effects will be can become extremely complicated.

Unfortunately, there is no reliable way to discover people's expectations about taxes, so we have to use statistical methods to learn the effect of government debt on the economy. Even though economists have been studying this issue for nearly 40 years, they have not yet reached a consensus. Statistical measures of the effect of debt on economic activity are straightforward in principle but difficult to carry out in practice. Overall, though, the evidence is that debt's effects are not strong. Some of the evidence even favors Ricardian equivalence (no effect of debt at all) as a close approximation. For example, Figure 1 shows two plots. One is the federal deficit as a share of GDP, and the other is the real interest rate on three-month Treasury bills. There is no obvious relation between the two series, and the correlation between them is a virtually nonexistent negative 1 percent.

A related issue here is the desirability of deliberately using deficits to influence the path of the economy. Under full equivalence of deficit and tax finance, no such thing can be done, of course, because deficits do not affect anything important. Under incomplete equivalence, though, deficits do have effects, as we have just seen. Therefore,

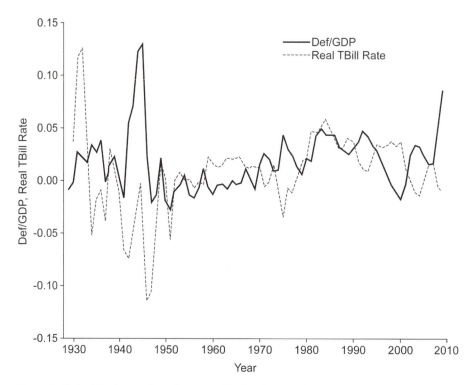

Figure 1. Federal Deficit to Gross Domestic Product Ratio and the Real Interest Rate on Three-Month Treasury Bills (Congressional Budget Office, President's Council of Economic Advisers)

it might seem desirable to run up deficits in recessions to encourage people to spend more and run up surpluses in booms to restrain spending. The problem is that these seemingly desirable effects arise for undesirable reasons: the taxes distort choices, and, on top of that, people may fail to perceive the effects of future taxes implied by deficits. Any such misperception means that deficits have effects in part because they fool people into thinking they suddenly have become wealthier (and conversely for surpluses). Is it desirable to influence the path of the economy by using a policy that is effective because it deliberately misleads the public? Such a proposition seems difficult to justify. Another problem is that any desirable effects are accompanied by other effects that might not be deemed desirable. When equivalence is incomplete, changing the stock of debt outstanding also changes the interest rate in the same direction. In particular, running a deficit in a recession would raise interest rates, which would reduce investment and economic growth, which in turn would reduce output in the future. Thus, using deficits to stimulate the economy now to ameliorate a recession comes at the cost of reducing output later. Whether that is a good exchange is not obvious and requires justification.

See also **Bank Bailouts; Consumer Credit and Household Debt; Corporate Tax Shelters; Financial Regulation; Income Tax, Personal; Trade Deficits (and Surpluses); War and the Economy**

Further Reading

Gordon, John Steele, *Hamilton's Blessing: The Extraordinary Life and Times of Our National Debt.* New York: Walker, 2010.

Kelly, Robert E., *The National Debt of the United States, 1914–2008.* Jefferson, NC: McFarland, 2008.

Morgan, Iwan W., *The Age of Deficits: Presidents and Unbalanced Budgets from Jimmy Carter to George W. Bush.* Lawrence: University Press of Kansas, 2009.

Wright, Robert E., *One Nation under Debt: Hamilton, Jefferson, and the History of What We Owe.* New York: McGraw-Hill, 2008.

Yarrow, Andrew L., *Forgive Us Our Debts: The Intergenerational Dangers of Fiscal Irresponsibility.* New Haven, CT: Yale University Press, 2008.

DUMPING OF IMPORTS

Thomas Grennes

Dumping is selling an imported product for less in the United States than the seller charges for a comparable product in the seller's own domestic market. This kind of activity is illegal in the United States, even if it does not reduce competition. Antidumping is part of a broader set of laws that deal with so-called unfair trade practices. Antidumping laws can allow the U.S. government to impose taxes, called tariffs, on foreign-made products that have been found to have been dumped. Additional tariffs, called safeguards, can temporarily be imposed to offset surges in imports of a particular product.

Who Dumps?

Dumping has been illegal in the United States since 1921, but dumping cases have become more common in recent decades. More antidumping tariffs are now imposed globally in a single year than were imposed over the entire period of 1947 to 1970 (Blonigen and Prusa 2003). U.S. firms that compete with imports are the main beneficiaries, and they are also the main political proponents of antidumping law. High tariffs against dumping are a way to circumvent the limits on tariff levels agreed to by members of the World Trade Organization.

All buyers of imports and close domestic substitutes are harmed by antidumping laws. U.S. antidumping law applies to all trading partners, including its North American Free Trade Association partners, Canada and Mexico. Some of the more controversial cases have involved Canadian and Mexican products. The basic U.S. antidumping law was amended in 2000 by the Continued Dumping and Subsidy Offset Act, better known as the Byrd Amendment. The Byrd Amendment was found to violate the rules of the World Trade Organization regarding protectionism, and it was repealed by Congress in January 2006.

In the early experience with antidumping, U.S. firms were the most frequent filers of complaints. Over time, Canada, the European Union, and Australia became more frequent filers, and, by the late 1980s, these four traders accounted for more than 90 percent of antidumping cases filed in the world.

Recently, firms in other countries have become more frequent complainers, and since 2000, the four traditional filers accounted for only 33 percent of the cases. China and India have become more frequent filers, and since 2000, India has filed more cases than any other country. U.S. firms that were once the most frequent complainers about dumping have become some of the most frequent targets of antidumping cases. The United States is the world's largest trading nation, and its economic size influences the number of cases in which U.S. firms are involved. When data are adjusted for the volume of a country's trade, the prominence of U.S. firms is reduced.

East Asian countries—especially China, South Korea, and Taiwan—have been the most common targets of antidumping cases. The U.S. steel industry has generated more antidumping complaints than any other industry. These cases have pitted domestic steel producers against important steel-using firms. Steel users have organized a lobby, claiming that tariffs have destroyed more jobs in steel-using firms than they have saved in steel-producing firms. Other prominent dumping cases in the United States involved Canadian lumber, cement from Mexico, wooden furniture from China, and chemicals and electrical products.

THE BYRD AMENDMENT

The Byrd Amendment allows firms that file antidumping cases to receive the revenue from the tariffs imposed on import companies found guilty of dumping. Thus, the victim is rewarded twice by (1) reducing competition it faces from imports and (2) receiving tariff revenue. The United States has been the only country to resort to this unusual practice, and it was challenged immediately by other member countries in the World Trade Organization (WTO). The WTO ruled in 2000 that the amendment violated the rules of the WTO, and it authorized other WTO members to retaliate against the United States by imposing tariffs against U.S. exports. After the U.S. Congress refused to change the law, the European Union, Canada, and Japan imposed large tariffs against U.S. exports in 2005. Finally, in January 2006, Congress repealed the law but insisted on continuing payments to U.S. firms through 2007. Foreign sanctions against U.S. exports remained in place.

Some strange developments have occurred under the Byrd Amendment. In the case of wooden bedroom furniture dumped by Chinese firms, some U.S. furniture companies have been simultaneously paying tariffs on furniture they import and sell in the United States and receiving payments from complaints they filed under the Byrd Amendment against dumping of furniture.

Enforcing Antidumping

How is the U.S. antidumping law administered? U.S. firms claiming to be harmed by dumping can initiate action by filing a complaint with the U.S. Department of Commerce (DOC) against specific foreign dumpers. As the result of an investigation, the DOC has ruled in favor of dumping in 94 percent of recent cases filed. In determining whether the price charged in the United States is too low, the DOC rarely compares the price charged in the United States with a price charged in the supplier's home market. Instead, the DOC makes its own estimate of cost of production in the supplier's market. In effect, dumping in the United States becomes pricing below cost of production as estimated by the DOC.

If the DOC rules in favor of dumping, the case moves to the U.S. International Trade Commission (USITC) to determine whether U.S. producers were harmed by dumping. The USITC has found injury in 83 percent of recent cases. In assessing injury, the USITC staff is guided by a peculiar asymmetry in the law. The USITC is asked to estimate the damage done to U.S. producers by dumping, but it is not allowed to take into account the gain to U.S. buyers from paying lower prices for products affected by dumping. If harm is found, the USITC estimates the amount of dumping and recommends a remedy to the president. It is usually a tariff whose level is related to the dumping amount, and it is imposed for an indefinite period against firms guilty of dumping. The tariff is retroactive to the day the dumping complaint was filed. Consequently, imports from accused firms often stop before cases are resolved. On the basis of the high percentage of successful cases, U.S. firms competing with imports have a strong incentive to complain about imports.

Impacts

What are the economic effects of the U.S. antidumping law? Domestic producers gain in the same way they gain from any tariff. Competition from imports is reduced, and domestic producers can charge a higher price for their products. Foreign suppliers who are not accused of dumping and do not face the dumping tariff also gain from the reduction in competition.

Consider the example of steel. Say that antidumping tariffs are imposed on certain foreign steel producers. All steel producers in the United States and foreign steel suppliers not subject to antidumping tariffs gain from antidumping tariffs. Because of reduced competition, domestic producers are able to raise their steel prices. Since both domestic steel and imported steel are more expensive, all buyers of steel in the United States are harmed by antidumping laws. Since the United States is a net importer of steel, the total value of losses to buyers of steel exceeds the gains to domestic steel producers. Many of the steel buyers are businesses that use steel in their own production, and an association of steel users has become a vocal opponent of steel tariffs in recent years.

Similar impacts occur from other antidumping examples. In the case of Canadian lumber, antidumping has increased the cost of a key component of housing. In the Mexican cement case, antidumping restrictions magnified shortages of cement following the hurricanes that hit the Gulf Coast in 2005. For all antidumping cases combined, losses to U.S. buyers have exceeded gains to domestic producers by an estimated $2 billion to $4 billion per year. Antidumping has become one of the costliest forms of trade protection for the United States and for the world as a whole (Blonigen and Prusa 2003).

Justification

If antidumping laws are harmful for the nation, are they merely special interest legislation for U.S. producers, or can they be justified in some other way? One possible rationale is that antidumping prevents foreign companies from achieving monopoly power in the U.S. market. It has been suggested that foreign dumpers might charge low prices to drive all U.S. rivals out of business. Without rivals, they would then raise prices to monopoly levels. However, this argument has two weaknesses. First, if the predatory firm succeeds in destroying all current rivals, it has no way of blocking entry by new firms once it raises its price. Second, real-world cases of monopoly achieved by this strategy are extremely rare. If the goal is to prevent lower prices for foreign-made products from leading to monopoly control, there is no reason to have a special law against foreign firms. Antitrust laws, which are laws against monopolies, could be enforced equally against both domestic and foreign companies who might acquire monopoly power.

There is an additional practical argument against the U.S. antidumping law. The administration of the law is said to be systematically biased toward finding dumping, even when there is none. Lindsey and Ikenson (2003) have constructed examples in which the DOC procedures produce prices in the United States that appear to be lower than in the supplying foreign country, even when the true prices are identical in the two countries. They conclude that the antidumping law is just a standard form of protectionism.

Dumping Reform

Short of completely repealing the U.S. antidumping law, are there ways to reform the law that would better serve producers, consumers, and society in general? First, the antidumping law could be modified to make it consistent with general antitrust policy. In that case, price differences would not be illegal unless they also increased the monopoly power of the dumping firm. For example, if a South Korean firm is one supplier of imported steel among many, lower prices charged by that firm would not necessarily be illegal. Its illegality would be judged in terms of its contribution to monopoly power in the U.S. market for steel. Retailers who offer discounts to students and senior citizens do not violate domestic antitrust law, even though they charge different prices for the same product. Price differences by foreign firms could be judged by the same standard as price differences by domestic firms.

A second reform would allow the DOC and USITC to estimate the consumer gains from dumping and compare them with domestic producer losses. Instead of evaluating exclusively the losses and harm to domestic producers, the agencies would evaluate dumping in terms of the general public interest of both buyers and sellers of products. By this broader standard, dumping that harms U.S. producers but provides greater benefits to U.S. buyers would not be illegal.

A third reform is to reduce barriers faced by U.S. exporters, especially in countries that charge different prices for their products in their home and foreign markets. Dumping can only occur if buyers in the lower-price market are prevented from reselling the product in the higher-price market. If Korean firms tried to dump steel in the United States, and buyers could resell the cheap steel in Korea, their scheme would not be profitable, and an antidumping case would not be necessary. Thus, negotiating to reduce trade barriers facing exports from the United States would discourage dumping in the United States.

Antidumping laws and all laws that protect producers against unfair trade practices face the possibility of penalizing perfectly legitimate behavior by sellers. Is it unfair to invent a new and better product that harms producers of traditional products? Was it unfair to introduce automobiles, which replaced horses and buggies, or computers, which replaced typewriters? The new competition from automobiles and computers must have appeared to be unfair to the traditional producers, and they were definitely harmed. Candle makers may have considered natural sunlight to be unfair competition, and sellers of irrigation equipment may consider rainfall to be an unfair rival. However, if all practices that harm traditional producers are judged to be unfair and illegal, consumers will not be served, and there will be no economic growth.

See also **Foreign Direct Investment; Trade Deficits (and Surpluses)**

Further Reading

Blonigen, Bruce, and Thomas Prusa, "Anti-Dumping." In *Handbook of International Trade,* ed. E. K. Choi and J. Harrigan. Malden, MA: Blackwell, 2003.

Campbell, Doug, "Trade Wars." *Regional Focus* (Spring 2006): 20–23.

Drope, Jeffrey, and Wendy L. Hansen, "Anti-Dumping's Happy Birthday?" *World Economy* 29 (2006): 459–472.

Hufbauer, Gary Clyde, et al., *U.S.-China Trade Disputes: Rising Tide, Rising Stakes.* Washington, DC: Institute for International Economics, 2006.

Lindsey, Brik, and Daniel Ikenson, *Anti-Dumping Exposed: The Devilish Details of Unfair Trade Law.* Washington, DC: CATO Institute, 2003.

U.S. Tariff Commission, *Information Concerning Dumping and Unfair Competition in the United States and Canada's Anti-Dumping Law.* Washington, DC: USTC, 2009.

E

ELECTION CAMPAIGN FINANCE

Ruth Ann Strickland

Campaign finance costs associated with running for political office have historically evoked concern. Most political candidates rely heavily on fundraising for travel, public appearances, support staff, and mass media advertising. Unless they have independent wealth, they must raise monies from individual, business, nonprofit, and other organizational sources. Jesse Unruh, speaker of California's state assembly from 1922 until 1987, said money is "the mother's milk of politics." Many would argue today that this has been true since the inception of the U.S. electoral process.

Historical Background

As early as 1905, heavy corporate financing prompted Theodore Roosevelt to propose that candidates for federal office be required to disclose campaign finances and be prohibited from receiving corporate contributions. In 1907, Congress passed the Tillman Act, which prohibited candidates for federal office from receiving corporate contributions; and later, in 1910, Congress passed the Federal Campaign Disclosure Law, which required candidates for federal office to disclose sources of campaign financing (Farrar-Myers and Dwyre 2008, 8).

Owing to embarrassing incidents such as the Teapot Dome scandal and corruption in President Warren G. Harding's campaign of 1920, Congress passed the Federal Corrupt Practices Act, which required congressional candidates to disclose campaign receipts and expenditures. In 1939 and 1940, the Hatch Acts prohibited political parties from soliciting campaign contributions and other support from federal employees. Because of the Hatch Acts, federal employees, until 1993, could not participate in political fundraising. In 1947, Congress passed the Taft-Hartley Act, which permanently made it illegal for labor unions to financially contribute to federal candidates for office.

Because so many campaign finance laws were ineffective and hard to enforce, Congress passed the Federal Election Campaign Act (FECA) of 1971. Replacing the old Corrupt Practices Act of 1925, the new law set limits on candidates' spending on communications media, established limits on financial contributions to candidates, and required disclosure of financial contributions made by political committees and individuals greater than $10, as well as disclosure by candidates and contributors and expenditures greater than $100. Revelations made after President Richard M. Nixon's resignation and funding illegalities in his 1972 reelection campaign catapulted election campaign financing back into the limelight and prompted Congress to amend FECA. In 1974, Congress established spending limits for presidential and congressional candidates and for national political parties in party primaries, general elections, and runoff elections. The new FECA set contribution limits on individuals, political action committees, and political parties and provided for voluntary public financing of presidential elections. FECA of 1974 established the Federal Election Commission to implement campaign finance law provisions (Cooper 2000, 259).

In 1976, the U.S. Supreme Court in *Buckley v. Valeo* (1976) declared some FECA provisions unconstitutional, primarily those dealing with campaign spending limits. The Court held that limits on campaign expenditures unreasonably restricted the free speech rights of corporations. *Buckley v. Valeo* allowed limits on campaign contributions on the rationale that this proviso would reduce actual corruption or the appearance of corruption in the electoral process. At the same time, it struck down limits on campaign expenditures saying that free speech permits candidates to spend as much as they choose (Farrar-Myers and Dwyre 2008, 13). After *Buckley v. Valeo*, an intense debate began over the question: Does money equal speech? Critics of the *Buckley* ruling say it allows giant corporations and wealthy individuals to overwhelm and drown out the voices of ordinary citizens; corporations, in essence, have a larger voice (or "more speech") than those who can make only small contributions (Cooper 2000, 260). On the other hand, the *Buckley* ruling is also criticized by free speech advocates who say that neither contributions nor expenditures should be limited, because this generally limits political discourse. Justices Antony Kennedy and Clarence Thomas have advocated overturning *Buckley* for these reasons (Farrar-Myers 2005, 48–50).

Congress amended FECA again in 1976 and 1979 to elaborate on "hard money" versus "soft money" and to ease up on contribution and expenditure disclosure requirements. Because candidates and political action committees voiced concerns over FECA's detailed reporting requirements, calling them burdensome and redundant, Congress sought to streamline and simplify reporting requirements. Voter registration efforts and get-out-the-vote campaigns were exempted from the contribution and expenditure limits applied to hard money contributions to candidates. Although Congress did not create the hard/soft-money distinction, it specified that party committees could use hard dollars only toward contributions to party candidates or coordinated spending ceilings. The eased provisions gave state and local political parties a greater role to play in federal elections, as soft money contributions could be used to fund party activities if not the actual campaigns of candidates for office (Corrado 2005, 28–30).

Recent Years

Triggering events in the 1996 and 2000 presidential elections prepared Congress for another run at campaign finance reform. In 1996, Democratic fundraising practices, such as the "selling" of access to the White House, raised serious questions. In the 2000 election, both parties saw an increase in soft money contributions and the rise of issue-advocacy electioneering in which soft money is used to promote (primarily through media slots) issues that are near and dear to candidates while not endorsing the candidates themselves. The practice made many believe that the current campaign finance regulatory structure was ineffective. U.S. Senator John McCain (R-Arizona), in his run for the presidency in 2000, focused much of his time arguing for campaign finance reform and reducing the role of big money in U.S. politics (Cooper 2000). After dropping out of the 2000 presidential campaign, McCain returned to the U.S. Senate and joined forces with Senator Russ Feingold (D-Wisconsin), Representative Christopher Shays (R-Connecticut), and Representative Marty Meehan (D-Massachusetts) to close loopholes in the campaign finance system. Their efforts culminated in the first major campaign finance reform in over 30 years—the Bipartisan Campaign Reform Act (BCRA). Senator McCain argued that a ban on soft money was necessary to end corruption in U.S. politics.

In 2002, the BCRA became law. The major provisions of this law prohibited national party committees from accepting or spending soft money. This provision, particularly unpopular with the national party elites, sought to exercise control of so-called party-building contributions from labor unions, corporations, and individuals that had in fact been used for campaign electioneering purposes. It further limited state and local parties, telling them that they could not spend money in federal electioneering but instead could focus on get-out-the-vote and voter registration drives. National, state, and local parties also could not ask for or contribute money to nonprofit organizations (which in turn engage in advocacy without endorsing any candidate's election or directly subsidizing federal candidates' campaigns). The following hard money contribution limits were instated:

- individual contributions for House and Senate campaigns: $2,000, indexed to grow with inflation;

- total aggregate contribution limits for individuals: $95,000, with $37,500 to candidates and $57,500 to political parties and political action committees;
- political action committees: $5,000 per candidate per election with an additional $15,000 to a national party committee and $5,000 combined to state and local party committees.

Moreover, broadcast, cable, or satellite communications that target federal candidates for office or show their likeness in their district or state media outlets (known as electioneering communications) were banned from being issued or shown within 60 days of a general election or 30 days of a primary. In addition, unions and corporations were prohibited from directly contributing to electioneering communications and could only pay for such advertising through hard money or through PACs. Similarly, nonprofit organizations and 527s could only pay for these types of advertisements through PACs (Jost 2002, 974). Also included is a "millionaires' provision" that permits candidates facing independently wealthy opponents to accept up to $6,000 per election from individual contributors (Jost 2002, 976–977).

The BCRA has sparked not only heated debate and controversy but also a lot of litigation. One controversy—the growth of 527 organizations—put a lot of pressure on the Federal Election Commission (FEC). These 527s are political committees that raised and spent unlimited amounts of money on issue advertisement, polling, and get-out-the-vote drives. They claimed tax-exempt status under section 527 of the Internal Revenue Service Code and did not register as political committees with the FEC. These 527 groups, which existed prior to BCRA, did not have to identify donors, nor did they have to disclose how much they raised or how the money was spent. They grew by leaps and bounds after the BCRA's passage. Senator McCain and other campaign finance reformers pressured the FEC to do something about these groups. In the 2004 presidential election alone, the 527s spent nearly $400 million. Not only did they spend huge sums of money, but they have paid for attack ads in hundreds of television markets, and no one can pinpoint the sources of the funds due to the loophole that exempted them from the BCRA provisions (Munger 2006).

In addition to the controversy over 527s, many observers questioned whether it was constitutional to ban soft money spending by national political parties and to regulate funds raised by corporations, unions, and advocacy groups for electioneering purposes. Opponents argued that these restrictions violated free speech and limited political discourse. Shortly after BCRA was signed into law, U.S. Senator Mitch McConnell (R-Kentucky), then the Senate majority whip, took the Federal Election Commission to court, claiming that the BCRA unconstitutionally infringed on the free speech rights of advocacy groups such as the National Rifle Association. Initially in 2003, the U.S. Supreme Court in *McConnell v. Federal Election Commission* upheld the electioneering communications provisions and the soft money regulations (Ciglar 2005, 71). In 2003, the Court favored the BCRA again by upholding the ban on contributions of incorporated nonprofit advocacy groups to federal candidates in *Federal Election Committee v. Beaumont*. At the same time, the Supreme Court demonstrated some early concerns with the BCRA provisions and struck down the prohibition on minors under the age of 18 from making political contributions and the requirement that political parties in a general election must choose between making independent or coordinated expenditures on a candidate's behalf (Sherman 2007).

As the Supreme Court's composition changed in 2005 (new Chief Justice John G. Roberts) and 2006 (new Associate Justice Samuel Alito), so too did its interpretation of the BCRA's issue-advocacy advertisement restrictions. This electioneering ad provision (i.e., issue-advocacy advertising) was among the most controversial, as illustrated in *Federal Election Commission v. Wisconsin Right to Life* (2007). More specifically, the Court held that part of the BCRA had been unconstitutionally applied by the FEC to an advertisement that the Wisconsin Right to Life groups sought to air before the 2004 election, and further stated that this advertisement was not an electioneering ad (Utter and Strickland 2008, 204). In this case, the Court's 5–4 ruling under the new Chief Justice, John G. Roberts, left doubts as to whether any part of the electioneering communications provision would survive given the broad exemption. The Court said that ads that truly engaged in a discussion of the issues could not be construed as urging for the support or defeat of a particular candidate. Another 5–4 U.S. Supreme Court decision in 2008, *Davis v. Federal Election Commission*, held that the millionaires' amendment unconstitutionally discriminated against candidates who spent their own money for purposes of getting elected by giving special fund-raising privileges to opponents (Bopp 2008).

Yet another major challenge to BCRA arose over whether Citizens United, a conservative nonprofit organization, could broadcast a documentary that the group produced in 2008 titled *Hillary: The Movie*. The Federal Election Commission enforced the BCRA electioneering provisions prohibiting nonprofits, corporations, and labor unions from expressly advocating for the election or defeat of a candidate for federal office (Welch 2010). In response, Citizens United took the FEC to court. In *Citizens United v. Federal Election Commission* (2010), the Supreme Court struck down a BCRA provision that barred corporations and labor unions from spending general treasury monies to advocate for or against the election of a candidate for federal office. In effect, this decision overturned part of the holding in *McConnell v. Federal Election Commission* (2003), which had upheld the electioneering provision. Many anticipate that the Citizens United ruling will result in a sharp increase in independent expenditures in future federal election campaigns (Jost 2010, 460, 463; Potter 2005, 56). Proponents of the electioneering provisions argue that this decision opens the floodgates and will allow corporations to pour money into campaigns, thus undermining the democratic process, while opponents still maintain that some groups that are able to pool resources, including labor unions and advocacy health care reform advocacy groups, should be able to exercise their free speech rights ("High Court Hears" 2009).

New challenges to the BCRA are being led by David Keating, executive director of the Club for Growth—a political organization that promotes economic growth by advocating for limited government and low taxes. Keating has filed suit in federal court on behalf of SpeechNow.org that calls for the elimination of campaign contribution limits as well as reporting requirements for political action committees that make independent expenditures in federal elections. So far the U.S. Court of Appeals for the District of Columbia has struck down the contribution limits while upholding the reporting requirements. Chief Judge David Sentelle, speaking for the Court of Appeals, said that, given the Supreme Court's ruling in *Citizens United v. Federal Election Commission* (2010), it appears that the government has no interest in limiting the contributions of an independent expenditure group, because this does not create a risk of corrupting federal candidates for office or officeholders (Jost 2010, 460).

State Reform Efforts

In the post-FECA and post-BCRA eras, state governments have also approved campaign finance initiatives. Trying to reduce the role of money in politics, a number of these initiatives sharply limit the amount of campaign contributions, and some states and localities have adopted public financing of campaign measures, which supporters call Clean Elections, Clean Money. Numerous states have launched and won approval of campaign finance reform initiatives.

All states have reporting requirements, with two states mandating reports from political committees only and the rest requiring candidate and committee reports. The majority of states place candidate contribution limits on individuals (37 states), PACs (36 states), candidates themselves (41 states), candidate families (25 states), political parties (29 states), corporations (44 states), and labor unions (42 states). Half of the states completely prohibit anonymous contributions during legislative sessions. Cash contributions in campaigns are unlimited in 19 states, and other states allow varying amounts of cash donations or prohibit them completely.

From 1972 until 1996, 45 referenda and initiatives dealing with campaign and election reform were placed on state ballots, with 75 percent of these efforts occurring since 1985. During this period, the voters supported 36 reforms. These reforms included contribution limits, spending limits, and public financing measures (Hoover Institution 2004). Twelve of the 16 public financing measures were approved. From 1998 until 2006, 30 referenda and initiatives dealing with campaign and election reform were placed on state ballots, with 15 proposals securing passage. These reforms included new measures on public financing and campaign contribution limits. As of 2009, five more states passed "clean election laws" that provide public monies to candidates for political office if candidates accept spending limits, and over 20 states had some type of public financing for select offices (Levinson 2009). In a January 2000 U.S. Supreme Court decision, *Nixon v. Shrink Missouri Government PAC,* the court reaffirmed *Buckley,* stating that state limits to campaign contributions were legal but limits on campaign spending were not. However, the campaign contribution limit could not be so extreme that it prevented the candidate from being able to gain notice or rendered campaign contributions pointless ("Campaign Finance Reform" 2008). The Court further explained this sentiment in *Randall v. Sorrell* (2006), when it struck down a Vermont law that placed strict caps on contributions and expenditures.

In the wake of the U.S. Supreme Court's rejection of campaign expenditure limits in *Buckley v. Valeo* (1976), many states have enacted public financing mechanisms for state elections. Overall, 15 states publicly finance candidates for various offices. The source of public funds for elective office varies, and some states—including Maine, Minnesota, Kentucky, and Rhode Island—rely on more than one source. Fifteen states use a voluntary tax checkoff, similar to the federal government's checkoff system, varying from $1 to $5. Ten states rely on a tax add-on, allowing taxpayers to either reduce their tax refund or increase their tax payment to finance campaigns. Seven states furnish direct legislative appropriations to fund public financing provisions. Eleven states allocate their monies to the taxpayer's designated political party, and three states use a distribution formula to divide the money equitably between the major political parties. The other states allocate money directly to statewide candidates or specify particular types of offices that qualify for public financing (Utter and Strickland 2008, 191–192).

Conclusion

Critics contend that campaign finance reform will never reduce the role of money in politics. They also contend that the BCRA makes it harder to challengers to mount effective campaigns against incumbents, thus dubbing BCRA the "Incumbent Protection Act" (Munger 2006). Public financing provisions enacted at the state level are being challenged in court for placing too many burdens on third-party candidates who try to qualify for public funds (Jost 2010, 464). Supporters of campaign finance reform argue that campaign finance laws are necessary to protect U.S. democracy from corruption (contribution limits), to provide citizens with information that allows them to make informed choices (reporting and disclosure laws), and to give candidates different paths for financing their election campaigns (public financing) (Wertheimer 2010, 473). Now the stage is set for the Supreme Court to decide whether campaign finance deregulation is necessary to protect free speech or to determine whether it should uphold some parts of the BCRA as a means of limiting the influence of wealthy individuals in U.S politics.

Further Reading

Bopp, James Jr., "Millionaires' Amendment Settles Two Key Analytical Issues." June 26, 2008. http://www.jamesmadisoncenter.org/pressreleases/release062608.html

"Campaign Finance Reform." New Rules Project of the Institute for Local Self-Reliance. 2008. http://www.newrules.org/governance/rules/campaign-finance-reform

Ciglar, Allan J., "Issue Advocacy Electioneering: The Role of Money and Organized Interests." In *Law and Politics: The Rules of the Game,* ed. Matthew J. Streb. Boulder, CO, and London: Lynne Rienner, 2005.

Cooper, Mary H., "Campaign Finance Reform." *CQ Researcher* (March 31, 2000): 257–280.

Corrado, Anthony, "Money and Politics: A History of Federal Campaign Finance Law." In *The New Campaign Finance Sourcebook,* ed. Anthony Corrado, Thomas E. Mann, Daniel R. Ortiz, and Trevor Potter. Washington, DC: Brookings Institution Press, 2005.

Farrar-Myers, Victoria A., "Campaign Finance: Reform, Representation, and the First Amendment." In *Law and Politics: The Rules of the Game,* ed. Matthew J. Streb. Boulder, CO, and London: Lynne Rienner, 2005.

Farrar-Myers, Victoria A., and Diana Dwyre, *Limits and Loopholes: The Quest for Money, Free Speech, and Fair Elections.* Washington, DC: CQ Press, 2008.

"High Court Hears 'Hillary: The Movie!' Campaign Finance Case." 2009. http://www.cnn.com/2009/POLITICS/09/09/scouts.campaign.finance

Hoover Institution, "Public Policy Inquiry: Campaign Finance." 2004. http://www.campaignfinancesite.org

Jost, Kenneth, "Campaign Finance Debates." *CQ Researcher* (May 28, 2010): 457–480.

Jost, Kenneth, "Campaign Finance Showdown." *CQ Researcher* (November 22, 2002): 969–992.

Levinson, Jessica A., *State Public Financing Charts.* Los Angeles: Center for Governmental Studies, 2009.

Munger, Michael, "Unintended Consequences 1, Good Intentions 0." Library of Economics and Liberty. January 9, 2006. http://www.econlib.org/library/Columns/y2006/Mungergoodintentions.html

Potter, Trevor, "The Current State of Campaign Finance Law." In *The New Campaign Finance Sourcebook,* ed. Anthony Corrado, Thomas E. Mann, Daniel R. Ortiz, and Trevor Potter. Washington, DC: Brookings Institution Press, 2005.

Sherman, Mark, "Justices' Scales May Be Tipping to the Right." *Houston Chronicle* (June 26, 2007): A1.

Utter, Glenn H., and Ruth Ann Strickland, *Campaign and Election Reform,* 2d ed. Santa Barbara, CA: ABC-CLIO, 2008.

Welch, Matt, "Government Can't Squelch Free Speech." 2010. http://www.cnn.com/2010/OPINION/01/21/Welch.free.expression.campaign/index.html#cnnSTCText

Wertheimer, Fred, "Do Campaign Finance Laws Unduly Restrict Political Speech?" *CQ Researcher* (May 28, 2010): 473.

EXECUTIVE PAY

Carl R. Anderson and Michael Shally-Jensen

The U.S. media have made much out of executive pay recently, which reflects a widespread popular dissatisfaction with the way companies compensate their top officers.

Even as stock prices fell dramatically in the midst of the 2008–2009 financial crisis, for example, some chief executives' compensation remained stable or increased. Is it fair that, in 2009, following massive job cuts at companies such as Ford, Starbucks, Dow Chemical, Whirlpool, and American Express, the CEOs of these organizations received stock options valued at between $17 million (Whirlpool) and $53 million (Ford) (Schwartz 2010)? (Such options, of course, are only part of the standard executive compensation package, which also includes salary, cash bonuses, perks, and other forms of pay.) Is it right that, even as they were being investigated for selling shaky investments to consumers, Wall Street bankers were paying themselves $140 billion in compensation (Grocer and Luccheti 2010)? Can a connection be made between executive pay and company profitability? Or, perhaps more importantly, can a connection be made between executive pay and company stock price? When stock price fell at Home Depot and the CEO's pay increased, the company spokesperson made the argument that the best measure of CEO performance may be company earnings, even though that contradicts the company's proxy statement (Nocera 2006a, 2006b). Many have tried to find explanations for CEO pay but have found little evidence to support very high rates of compensation. This argument got the attention of lawmakers and the public following the government's bailout of various high-profile banks and other firms as part of the Troubled Assets Recovery Plan (TARP) of 2008. Even as some of the funds began to be paid back (with interest) to the government, the incoming Obama administration saw fit to appoint a "pay czar" to ensure that top executives at companies that made use of TARP funds did not receive any untoward cash payments or other unearned rewards.

A Brief Summary of the Basic Issues Involved

There are two distinct sides to this issue. One side asserts that CEOs, other top executives, and the stockholders share a common goal: to increase wealth. If the executives are enriched by enriching the shareholders, then there are no victims. In that regard, no identifiable problem exists, and the system is working well. This side further argues that, if the press makes note of executive pay abuses, those instances are isolated. Market forces, it is believed, will correct abuses. This argument is illustrated in the case of John Thain, former chairman and CEO of Merrill Lynch, who was forced to resign when it was revealed that, despite receiving $84 million in compensation in 2007, he (1) spent over $1 million in company money to make lavish renovations to his office and (2) more seriously, made nearly $4 billion in bonus payments to executives at Merrill Lynch, even while the company was being bailed out through a deal made between the federal government and Bank of America at the height of the financial crisis (*Frontline* 2009). Bad behavior, yes, but the system did what it was supposed to do, it is argued. (Never mind that Thain went on to head CIT Group.)

The other side of the argument is that top corporate executives in the United States are paid far beyond their worth. Their pay is based on factors other than performance,

HIGHEST PAID CEOs

The 10 highest paid CEOs in 2009 were as follows:

Rank	Name	Company	Total Compensation (in Millions of Dollars)	Change from 2008
1	Lawrence J. Ellison	Oracle	$84.5	0%
2	J. Raymond Elliott	Boston Scientific	$33.4	—
3	Ray R. Irani	Occidental Petroleum	$31.4	39%
4	Mark V. Hurd	Hewlett-Packard	$24.2	−29%
5	James T. Hackett	Anadarko Petroleum	$23.5	6%
6	Alan G. Lafley	Procter & Gamble	$23.5	−8%
7	William C. Weldon	Johnson & Johnson	$22.8	8%
8	Miles D. White	Abbott Laboratories	$21.9	−13%
9	Robert A. Iger	Walt Disney	$21.6	−58%
10	Samuel J. Palmisano	IBM	$21.2	1%

Source: "At the Top, Signs of a Slide." *New York Times* (April 10, 2010).

and certainly not on long-term performance. People on this side of the argument assert that boards (typically made up of CEOs from other companies) and the compensation committees of these boards recklessly pay high salaries to chief executives who seem to have more power than they themselves have or in order to influence the market value of CEO pay in general for selfish reasons.

A board of directors has many committees reporting to it. One example is the audit committee. This committee is charged with ensuring that the company's accounting controls are functioning properly and hold up to the scrutiny of an audit. Another example is the compensation committee. The compensation committee is charged with creating a compensation structure for the executives that is fair and beneficial to all parties concerned. Specifically, the compensation committee recommends to the board of directors the pay package for the CEO. This is especially important during the CEO recruitment phase. Furthermore, these committees and boards disguise these high salaries with complicated features and explanations. These complicated features and explanations are created by compensation consultants (often hired by CEOs) who propose handsome pay packages for the chief executive to present to the compensation committee.

Top Executives Are Not Overpaid

This side of the argument is based on the premise that top executives are paid well, but not overpaid. Many people see CEO pay packages but do not look further to see that a

CEO's pay is not the whole story. What are the factors that might support a high executive compensation package?

Only Extreme Cases of Overpay Hit the Press

Proponents of the argument that top executives are not overpaid state that most of the complaints about executive compensation center around extreme cases of overpay, and such cases blind us to the fact that the majority of executives are paid fairly.

One example of this is the case of Lee Raymond, former head of Exxon Mobile. When he retired from the company in 2006, the price of gasoline at the pump was high, $3 per gallon, much to the consternation of consumers. Yet Exxon Mobile rewarded Raymond with a record retirement package—a "golden parachute," as it is known—to the tune of $400 million. The combination of exorbitant CEO pay and painfully high gas prices rubbed most observers the wrong way. A similar situation occurred in the case of Robert Nardelli of Home Depot. When Nardelli retired in 2007 with a pay package worth $210 million, the company he headed had just gone through several straight years of relatively poor performance. People wanted to know why the chief executive received such an exceptional payout.

And yet these are just the extreme cases, say the proponents of substantial executive pay. True, they say, that at the peak of the trend toward higher pay around the turn of the millennium, some CEOs were earning up to 320 times the earnings of the average shop floor worker; however, if the calculation is adjusted by eliminating the extremes and looking at median CEO pay rather than mean pay, the same figure falls by nearly two-thirds, to "only" 120 times. The mean annual CEO pay in 2000–2003, for example, was $8.5 million, while the median was $4.1 million (Carr 2007). In any case, these figures are well below the nine-figure sums that command the attention of the media on occasion. They are also well below the sums made by many top Wall Street traders and hedge fund managers. In 2006, for example, traders could handily bring home bonuses of $40 million to $50 million, while top hedge fund managers could earn in the billions ("The Story of Pay" 2007).

Good CEOs Cost More than Average CEOs

We must now examine a basic theory of economics: you get what you pay for. If a chief executive commands a handsome pay package, then she must have proven to the board of directors that she is worth it.

The board of directors represents the shareholders of the company. The CEO reports to and works for the board of directors. It is through the board that the shareholders can voice their opinions and make their desires known. It is the board's responsibility to act on behalf of the shareholders in carrying out their wishes to management. Management starts with the CEO, who is then responsible for hiring managers to act as agents for the owners (i.e., the shareholders). It is in the best interest of each board member to represent the shareholders to the best of his ability. Board members are elected by the shareholders. If a board member falls out of favor with the shareholders, then he stands the chance of losing his seat on the board. Therefore, if members of the board make a mistake in hiring a chief executive, those members cannot make too many more mistakes, or they will lose their seats on the board.

A basic theory of finance is that the goal of a firm (or company) is to maximize shareholder wealth. Therefore, shareholders look to the board of directors to maximize their wealth. One of the best ways to maximize shareholder wealth is to hire good people, and the most important person to hire is the CEO. Since we expect that good chief executives cost more than average chief executives, the board is certainly working in the shareholders' interest by hiring the most qualified CEO, and that will cost more money. But all interests are served because it is the job of the CEO to see that shareholder wealth is maximized. If you reduce executive compensation, the most talented CEOs will go elsewhere and you risk seeing the value of your shares decline.

CEOs Are Paid to Participate in the Risk with Shareholders

Another tenet of economic theory is that high risk relates to high reward. In a nutshell, this means that to return high rewards to yourself or those to whom you report, you will have to take risks.

As mentioned earlier, CEOs are paid to maximize shareholder wealth. This does not mean simply increasing shareholder wealth during the CEO's time in office. Shareholders' investment in the company is not permanent. Shareholders can sell their shares and invest in another company with relative ease. In fact, it is in the shareholders' interest to invest their money in the best investment they can find. It is not in the company's best interest to have shareholders who want to sell their shares, because that will decrease the share price. A CEO must not only try to increase the company's share price and stock dividends (i.e., maximizing shareholder wealth), but he must do so relative to investments competing for the shareholders' capital.

To maximize shareholder wealth, a CEO must take risks. The CEO is not only putting the shareholders at risk; she is also putting her job and her private fortune at risk. Her private fortune is at risk because she most likely has a large investment in company stock or has the right to buy a large block of company stock (i.e., employee stock options), and she is definitely putting her salary at risk. She is therefore participating in risk with the shareholders, and that is what she is paid to do. If the risks that the CEO takes fail, no one suffers more than the CEO. In conclusion, by acting in her own best interest, she is also acting in the best interest of the shareholders.

Top Executives Are Overpaid

Proponents of this side of the argument assert that executive pay packages not only are excessive but tend to be justified by arguments not related to performance. Proponents on this side also assert that CEOs may be paid well even if a company's performance is declining.

Compensation Committees Keep CEO Pay Artificially High

As mentioned earlier, good CEOs cost more than average CEOs. When the board is considering an offer of employment to a prospective CEO, the board relies on recommendations from the compensation committee. In turn, the compensation committee may hire a compensation consultant to put together a compensation package. This package will be submitted to the board to accompany its offer of employment to the prospective CEO. Additional compensation may also be negotiated with the candidate. The better the candidate, the more negotiating room is available. Compensation consultants are also hired to review existing compensation packages for CEOs.

The process described above can have inherent problems. In the case of making an offer to a CEO candidate, compensation committees often have biases toward a CEO candidate because the board has already expressed its interest in hiring that candidate. Additionally, the board has gone to great expense to find a CEO candidate that it feels is suitable for the job. Good CEO candidates are very difficult to find. As a result, the committee would be at fault if the candidate rejected the offer because the compensation committee's pay package was not satisfactory to the candidate. Sometimes the compensation committee wants to offer an above-average package for the future CEO of its company. This issue tends to increase the committee's pay recommendation. If every CEO is paid above average, then the pay packages are ever increasing. In the case of a compensation consultant reviewing the existing pay package of a CEO, the CEO usually hires the consultant. The CEO then reviews the recommendation. If it is satisfactory to him, he presents it to the board of directors. As a consequence, the CEO will only hire a compensation consultant that will create a very handsome package for him to use as support for an increase in his pay.

The result of this is that CEOs can easily be paid far beyond their worth simply because of the conflicts of interest discussed above. Prior to 2003, in fact, when the rules were changed, chief executives usually sat on the nominating committees that picked potential boards of directors. Clearly, a more favorable board, including a more favorable compensation committee, stood to be elected under those circumstances.

Overpaying a CEO May Indicate Bigger Problems

Many problems in business can be solved with money. But if the money dries up, the problems may reappear twofold. Some have argued that the overcompensation of chief executives is a by-product of bigger problems (Chang 2005). The company can defer the need to address concerns with employees by simply increasing their pay. This is especially true with the highest-ranking employee, the CEO. Overpayment may be indicative of a badly functioning company, a changing product market, lack of resources, or poor corporate governance (Annett 2006).

The issue of paying CEOs and other executives for reasons other than performance has been such a problem that the federal government stepped into the fray with the enactment of the Revenue Reconciliation Act of 1993 (Thomas 2006). This law includes a provision that eliminates the corporate tax deduction for publicly traded companies for senior executive pay in excess of $1 million annually if the pay package is not performance based. The definition of performance in this law is broad and could be achieved even by a poorly performing company and CEO. Although companies must pay attention to compensation packages, if for no other reason than to comply with this law, such a loosely worded regulation is unlikely to create a roadblock to excessive CEO pay.

Similarly, in 2005, as a result of complaints by shareholders, changes in financial disclosure rules were instituted that required companies to count executive stock options as part of a company's operating expenses. Even now, however, such options are often strategically timed or backdated (i.e., listed after the date on which they were issued) by executives in order to maintain personal incomes while avoiding the need to report higher expenses to shareholders ("Executives' Large Pay Packets" 2007). The Securities and Exchange Commission has ruled that backdating is not in itself illegal but that it can be part of fraudulent actions in specific cases and so should be scrutinized.

Tenure, Power, and "Say on Pay"

Many employees have been at their present employer for many years. Those years of experience enable employees to know how things work and who to go to to get things done. This is especially true for high-ranking employees. Longevity at one employer, also known as tenure, is therefore very beneficial to senior executives.

Companies tend to pay top executives with long tenure more than top executives with less tenure. This holds true even if the less-tenured executive has more relevant experience. This also holds true regardless of performance. How can this be explained? Some conclude that pay is driven by power, and power is determined by tenure. Seniority is considered a useful variable when determining pay across levels in most organizations. We tend to believe that those with experience perform better. In some cases, this could be true, but tenure does not necessarily correlate with company performance.

As a check on the effects of tenure, there has developed in recent years a movement of sorts known as "say on pay," in which shareholders expect to have a yes or no vote on the compensation packages offered to top executives. In the beginning, these votes were nonbinding, but more recently they have become binding decisions that boards must act upon. In May 2008, for example, Aflac shareholders approved $75 million in compensation for the company's CEO, Daniel Amos, for delivering exceptional performance ("Shareholders Weigh In" 2008). The opposite occurred two years later in the cases of chief executives from Occidental Petroleum (Ray Irani) and Motorola (Sanjay Jha); shareholders at these companies rejected the proposed CEO pay packages ("Nay on Pay" 2010). Say on pay looks like it could be the wave of the future.

Concentration of Stock Ownership

In large companies, CEOs tend not to be paid above average if there is an individual stockholder with a significant number of shares. This is because stock voting power is concentrated in that one stockholder. That one stockholder can effect change and control situations without having to form a consensus with other shareholders. Forming a consensus is time consuming and replete with compromise, both of which do not lend themselves to swift and targeted corporate governance. Therefore, this inability to control CEO pay through stock concentration gives compensation committees and boards of directors more freedom to approve above-average CEO pay packages.

In small companies, a lack of stock concentration does not lead to the overpayment of CEOs.

Conclusion

In sum, one could find enough information in this controversy to support either view. Many people are trying to understand why top executives are paid so much, and others are trying to understand what all the fuss is about. Much research has been done to find a link between pay and performance, but only a limited connection has been made between compensation packages and performance. One could see how quickly CEO pay could get out of hand, especially in a cash-rich company, if corporate governance is lacking. A well-crafted, balanced executive compensation package would be only one result of good corporate governance. To conclude, then, we ask again: are CEOs overpaid? Many examples of pay for factors other than performance have been explored here. In those cases, one would have to conclude that, yes, many CEOs are overpaid.

See also **Corporate Governance; Corporate Tax Shelters; Financial Regulation; Glass Ceiling**

Further Reading

Annett, Tim, "Great Divide: CEO and Worker Pay." *Wall Street Journal* (May 12, 2006). http://online.wsj.com/public/article/sb114719841354447998-CKSOvdXu2TSMc6ZVSwNaA3zCM tw_20060611.html

"At the Top, Signs of a Slide." *New York Times* (April 10, 2010).

Balsam, Steven, *An Introduction to Executive Compensation.* Burlington, MA: Academic Press, 2002.

Carr, Edward, "In the Money." *Economist* (January 18, 2007).

Chang, Helen K., *CEO Skill and Excessive Pay: A Breakdown in Corporate Governance?* 2005. http://www.gsb.stanford.edu/news/research/compensation_daines_ceopay.shtml

Crystal, Graef S., *In Search of Excess: The Overcompensation of American Executives.* New York: W. W. Norton.

Ellig, Bruce R., *The Complete Guide to Executive Compensation,* 2d ed. New York: McGraw-Hill, 2007.

"Executives' Large Pay Packets Cannot Be Blamed on Poor Governance." *Economist* (January 18, 2007).

Frontline: Breaking the Bank. Documentary. Michael Kirk, dir. Boston: WGBH/Frontline, 2009.

Grocer, Stephen, and Aaron Luccheti, "Traders Beat Wall Street CEOs in Pay." *Wall Street Journal* (April 6, 2010).

Kay, Ira T., and Steven Van Putten, *Myths and Realities of Executive Pay.* New York: Cambridge University Press, 2007.

Kolb, Robert W., ed., *The Ethics of Executive Compensation.* Malden, MA: Blackwell, 2006.

Leonard, Devin, "Bargains in the Boardroom?" *New York Times* (April 4, 2010): B1, B7.

"Nay on Pay." *Economist* (May 15, 2010).

Nocera, Joe, "The Board Wore Chicken Suits." *New York Times* (May 27, 2006). http://select.nytimes.com/2006/05/27/business/27nocera.html

Nocera, Joe, "A Column That Needs No Introduction." *New York Times* (June 3, 2006): C1.

Schwartz, Nelson D., "Striking Gold in Stock Options." *New York Times* (April 4, 2010): B1, B9.

"Shareholders Weigh in on Executive Compensation." *Economist* (May 20, 2008).

"The Story of Pay Is Largely the Story of Share Options." *Economist* (January 18, 2007).

Thomas, Landon, Jr., "The Winding Road to Grasso's Huge Payday." *New York Times* (June 25, 2006). http://www.nytimes.com/2006/06/25/business/yourmoney/25grasso.html

F

FINANCIAL REGULATION

Scott E. Hein

Financial regulations can be viewed as rules or restrictions that subject financial trans-actions or entities to certain guidelines or requirements, generally aimed at maintain-ing the integrity of the financial system, at least in the eyes of those who make these regulations. Financial regulations can be made by either a government or nongovern-ment entity, and the rules and guidelines are monitored by financial regulators. Today, however, the vast majority of financial regulations are put in place by government enti-ties rather than nongovernment or self-regulating entities.

The basic purpose of financial regulation in the United States can be viewed as pro-tecting persons and property, particularly from being taken by force or fraud, and as providing enhanced consumer confidence in financial dealings. There is near universal agreement that there is a role to be played by a "financial constable" to assure that such abuses are prevented.

Financial regulations come with their costs, sometimes explicit and sometimes implicit opportunity costs, imposed on the regulated industry. Another broad concern about the cost of financial regulation relates to the notion of *regulatory capture*, where there exists a cozy, crony relationship between the regulator and the parties being reg-ulated. In this case, the government fails to establish a regulatory state that operates efficiently. But financial regulations also may bring benefits to financial participants. These benefits generally consist of improving participant confidence and convenience as well as circumventing other financial agents' abilities to accumulate and exercise market power to the detriment of others.

Government Financial Regulations and Regulators

Financial regulations in the United States are generally established by lawmakers, and these same lawmakers frequently create financial regulatory agencies to see that the regulations are adhered to through supervision. In the United States, federal lawmakers make laws that are passed by the U.S. Congress and signed into law by the president. In addition, state lawmakers make state laws that are passed by state congressional offices and signed into law by the governor. At both the federal and state levels, regulatory agencies are created to make sure the laws are enforced.

The most heavily regulated area of the U.S. financial system is the banking industry. It has long been recognized in the United States that banks, which accept deposits and make loans, are important in the shaping of financial activities and economic growth. Broadly, government regulations of banks (and other depository institutions) do each of the following: (1) restrict competition, (2) specify what assets a bank can hold, (3) define how bank capital is measured and require banks to hold a minimum level of bank capital, and (4) require that the public be informed about banks' financial conditions.

Since 1863, the United States has had a *dual banking system* with both state-chartered banks and nationally chartered banks. This means that, to even open a bank, one needs to obtain regulatory approval. The National Currency Act of 1863 created the Office of the Comptroller of the Currency to charter, regulate, and supervise all national banks. Coexisting with this federal bank regulator, all states also have their own state departments of banking, which charter, regulate, and supervise state banks, serving as state banking regulators. Thus, today we have both federal and state banking regulators in our financial system.

The Constantly Evolving and Growing Nature of Financial Regulation

While the purpose of financial regulation is simple, the experience in the United States is that financial regulation is both increasing and becoming increasingly complex over time. There are a number of reasons for the growth and increased complexity of financial regulation. First, financial services are becoming increasingly important in the United States. Many individuals have in the past provided their own financial services, such as financial intermediation of lending to family members or self-insuring potential losses, but now find it more advantageous to use a financial agent. Second, there is a general recognition that it is natural for private entities to seek ways around rules that limited profit potential. Edward Kane (1988) has referred to the process as a *regulatory dialectic*. The process starts with new regulation, followed by avoidance of this regulation, as economic agents seek to avoid costly aspects of the regulations, only to be followed by reregulation. Indeed, the term *reregulation* better characterizes most of the evolution of

CREDIT DEFAULT SWAPS

A recent example of a financial innovation is a *credit default swap.* These instruments were not around 20 or 30 years ago, but they became important in the financial crisis of 2008–2009. Credit default swaps can be viewed as insurance products, insuring the holder of the insurance product against default on a particular bond. Suppose you are a large financial institution that owns many General Electric (GE) bonds, for example. If GE were to default on these bonds, then you, as an investor, would lose out financially. To protect yourself against this possibility, you could buy a credit default swap on GE bonds, for which you would pay a premium. If GE never defaults, you, as the credit default swap holder, get nothing in exchange for your premium. On the other hand, if GE defaults, the insurer or underwriter of the insurance product would compensate you for your loss.

The example of a credit default swap is interesting because, although the product was classified as an insurance product above, the insurance regulators did not deem it to be an insurance product. Rather, the insurance regulators saw the instrument to be another example of a *derivative*, an instrument that derives is value from another underlying instrument. Indeed, *swaps,* such as interest rate swaps, are generally thought of as derivatives, not insurance products. But the central point is that credit default swaps, since they were new financial innovations, escaped any real regulatory oversight. Since the insurance firm AIG's financial problems—which came to light during the financial crisis—are generally understood to stem from its underwriting of credit default swaps, it is now felt that someone should have been regulating this financial activity.

financial regulations than the term *deregulation.* Although the term deregulation, meaning the removal of existing regulation, is frequently used, the term deregulation rarely applies, and it would be better to refer to reregulation.

Another reason for the growth in financial regulations stems from *financial innovation.* Financial innovation can be thought of as a new financial product introduced as a result of technological advances or to satisfy some previously unknown demand.

A Broad Chronology of the Evolution of Federal Financial Regulation

In addition to the above reasons for increased financial regulation, each successive financial and economic crisis seems to spawn new financial regulators and regulations put in place by the federal government. For example, it is widely understood that the Federal Reserve System, a banking regulator, was created in 1913 in response to earlier banking panics in the United States. The Federal Reserve Act, among other things, authorized the creation of the country's third central bank, the Federal Reserve, to lend to banks that were solvent but needed liquidity. This lending activity is done through the Federal Reserve's discount window, and the U.S. central bank is referred to as a *lender of last resort.* The Federal Reserve was further authorized to levy *reserve requirements* on member commercial banks, requiring banks to hold a fraction of their deposits in certain liquid forms. The Federal Reserve was further charged with the supervision and examination of banks in the United States.

The McFadden Act was passed by the U.S. Congress in 1927, giving individual states the authority to limit bank branches located in their state. This limitation on branches also applied to national banks located within the state's borders.

Regulations Spawned by the Great Depression

Even with the Federal Reserve in place—or, as many charge (see Friedman and Schwartz 1963), because of the Federal Reserve's poor monetary policies in place—the United States experienced the Great Depression in the early 1930s. As suggested by the thesis that financial and economic crises spawn new financial regulation and regulators, the U.S. Congress imposed a new broad array of financial regulators and regulations not seen before.

Legislation in the Great Depression era, generally referred to as Glass-Steagall after the legislators who proposed the legislation, prevented the commingling of commercial banking (accepting deposits and making loans), investment banking (aiding in the insurance of securities of all types), and insurance (providing either property and causality or life insurance products) from being administered under one single business. Prior to this legislation, financial institutions were much freer in their abilities to offer all such financial services under one corporate structure.

In addition, the Federal Deposit Insurance Corporation (FDIC), another banking regulator, was established by Glass-Steagall. The FDIC was created to offer depositors federal insurance for limited amounts of bank deposits. The legislation also granted the FDIC the ability to supervise and examine banks that offer insured deposits and granted the FDIC the resolution authority to close banks that it deemed as having failed financially.

The Great Depression further led the U.S. Congress to put into law legislation that created the Securities Exchange Commission (SEC). The Securities Act of 1933, together with the Securities Exchange Act of 1934, which created the SEC, was designed to restore investor confidence in capital markets by providing investors and the markets with more reliable information and clear rules of honest dealing. Thinking that abuses in securities markets occurred during the Great Depression that made the economic decline worse, Congress added a new financial constable overseeing securities transactions.

Post–Great Depression Regulation

The economic struggles in the early 1970s led the U.S. Congress to remove limitations on interest rates that banks and other depository institutions could pay on deposits. For years, Regulation Q limited the maximum rate of interest that could be paid on various deposit accounts. These limits were eliminated by Congress in an effort to allow depository institutions to better compete for funds in a rising interest rate environment. The financial and economic difficulties in the United States in the late 1970s and early 1980s, as the nation experienced relatively high inflation, caused Congress to expand this reserve requirement to all commercial banks as well as thrift institutions and credit unions.

The significant numbers of failures for both commercial banks and thrift institutions in the late 1980s and early 1990s led to more regulatory changes. In this case, the term *deregulation* is appropriate. The Interstate Banking and Branching Efficiency Act of 1994 removed many of the limitations placed on depository institutions regarding interstate banking and branching, opening up the United States for the first time to nationwide banking and reversing the McFadden Act.

The late 1990s, while relatively tranquil in terms of economic and financial issues, ushered in another instance of deregulation by reversing the Glass-Steagall Act. In 1999, the Gramm-Leach-Bliley Act allowed financial intermediaries under one corporate structure, the financial holding company, to engage in commercial banking, investment banking, and insurance activities.

Even the terrorist attacks of September 11, 2001, led to banking regulations. In particular, the U.S. Congress amended the Bank Secrecy Act of 1970, with several anti–money laundering provisions and enhanced surveillance procedures under the USA Patriot Act of 2001.

As a response to the financial crisis of 2008–2009, Congress is working on legislation that proposes significant changes in financial regulatory reform. The thinking appears to suggest that, although financial regulations did not prevent the financial crisis, a fine-tuning of these regulations will indeed prevent future crises.

Other Financial Intermediary Regulators

The U.S. financial system includes other financial intermediaries aside from banks. Some of these are other depository institutions like credit unions and thrift institutions. Others provide other financial services like insurance companies and mutual funds.

Regulation of Credit Unions and Thrift Institutions

The United States has other financial institutions that also can be viewed as depository institutions, like *credit unions* and *thrift institutions*. Like banks, these institutions accept "deposit-like" funds and lend these funds out to others. Also like banks, these institutions can be chartered at either the state level or at the federal level. While credit unions and thrifts can be chartered by their individual states, both today generally offer federal deposit insurance. The National Credit Union Administration charters federal credit unions and offers deposit insurance to both state and federal credit unions. The FDIC offers federal deposit insurance to savings and loan associations,

CREDIT RATING AGENCIES

The credit rating agencies such as Fitch Ratings, Moody's Investors Service Inc., and Standard and Poor's Ratings Services, are not generally deemed as regulatory agencies. Although they play an important role in evaluating the default risk of debt securities issued in the United States, they do not have regulations that they monitor. However, credit rating agencies play an important role in the financial system by grading bonds. In many cases, the rating given a particular security will determine whether a regulated investor may buy a given security. Many commentators blame credit rating agencies' lax grading for making the 2008–2009 financial crisis worse (see Kaufman 2010). Because of the critical role of rating agencies in the U.S. financial system, the SEC does serve as the regulator of these agencies, deciding which firms can be nationally recognized rating organizations and which firms cannot be. The U.S. Congress and the SEC are weighing whether it would be wise to change the compensation structure for the credit rating agencies from the current system, in which the issuer of the security pays for the rating, to a system where investors or others should pay for such services.

mutual savings banks, and other thrift institutions. The Office of Thrift Supervision charters and regulates national thrift institutions.

Regulations imposed on credit unions and thrift institutions entail restrictions on the types of loans they can make or the types of investments undertaken. Credit unions generally make loans to consumers and are limited to some extent on the amount of loans they make to businesses. Thrifts, on the other hand, have historically been encouraged to make residential mortgage-related loans. As such, they are generally restricted in the amounts of other types of loans—whether consumer or business—they can make. In addition to having the types of loan activities restricted, credit unions and thrifts are generally restricted in the types of securities they can invest in. Both are not allowed to make investments in common stock of other corporations and are limited in terms of the default risk their bonds can be subject to, generally not being allowed to invest in junk bonds or similarly low-rated debt instruments, as determined by credit rating agencies.

One key aspect of the regulations regarding credit unions in comparison to banks and thrifts relates to their tax treatment. Credit unions are nonprofit financial intermediaries and, as such, pay no income tax. Commercial banks and most thrift institutions (other than mutual savings banks) are for-profit institutions and thus do not get the tax exemption benefits granted to credit unions.

Regulation of Other Financial Intermediaries

In addition to regulating banks and other depository institutions, most states regulate other financial intermediaries such as insurance providers and securities firms. Most insurance activities offered in the United States are regulated at the state level, as state legislators have chosen to create most insurance regulations. Indeed, most states have created either state departments of insurance or state insurance commissions to ensure that the laws passed by the state are enforced and adhered to. Although there is a National Association of Insurance Commissioners, this is simply an organization of state insurance regulators. There is little federal regulation of insurance although the health care insurance legislation signed by President Barack Obama mandating health insurance coverage suggests that this is changing.

Because mutual funds and money market mutual funds generally invest in securities, it is only natural that their activities are regulated by the SEC as well. As an example of such regulation, investors in mutual funds must be provided with a *prospectus* from the mutual fund, detailing the types of investments purchased by the fund, the rules that guide its investment choices, as well as the financial risks to investing in the fund.

Financial Market Regulators

Most states also have passed laws dealing with securities transactions. Today, most states have state securities boards, commissions, or departments to regulate the securities industry in their state and make sure that the state laws are being met. The primary mission of these entities is to protect investors—the buyers of securities—in their states.

In the 19th century, many states also imposed *usury law*, although there was much variation across states. These laws placed a maximum upper limit on interest rates charged in individual states by all lenders. New evidence (see Benmelech and Moskowitz 2010) indicates that these laws came with broad societal costs, such as less credit availability and slower economic growth, but that wealthy political incumbents benefited by a lower cost of capital. Today, only a few states impose usury laws that have any meaningful effect on credit transactions.

The Securities and Exchange Commission

Federal regulations pertaining to the securities industry did not become important in the United States until the establishment of the Securities Exchange Commission in 1934. The SEC is charged with maintaining fair, efficient, and orderly markets by regulating market participants in the securities industry. To the extent that securities transactions are becoming increasingly important in the U.S. financial system, the SEC's role as regulator is also growing over time. The SEC regulates issuers of securities and tells them what types of securities they can issue and the information that must be provided by them to investors—for example, in the form of prospectus and most recently in the Sarbanes-Oxley Act. It also regulates investors and monitors what investors are doing, making sure that investors do not break *insider trading laws* that preclude investors from availing themselves of insider information that is not publicly known and use that to their advantage in trading. To the extent that mutual funds, including money market mutual funds, invest primarily in financial securities, the SEC regulates the mutual fund industry, requiring that mutual funds let investors know the risks and returns investors can anticipate, providing this information in the form of a prospectus. The forms of mutual funds known as hedge funds traditionally have faced less stringent regulation, although under the 2010 Dodd-Frank Wall Street Reform and Consumer Protection Act the reporting (or disclosure) requirements of such funds have increased.

Self-Regulating Organizations

In addition to the numerous governmental entities involved in regulating the U.S. financial system are many *self-regulating organizations*. These include the Financial Industry Regulatory Authority; the Municipal Securities Rulemaking Board; and stock and other financial instrument exchanges and clearinghouses, such as the New York Stock Exchange and the Chicago Mercantile Exchange, to name the largest, most well-known exchanges.

The Commodity Futures Trading Commission (CFTC)

Futures contracts are instruments that allow market participants to buy and sell items, including financial assets, for future delivery but at a price set today. These contracts obligate both parties to fulfill commitments to make or accept delivery. Option contracts, on the other hand, only commit one party, called the writer of the contract, to a particular action, while the buyer of the contract has the option or choice to take a certain action or not. Futures contracts have been traded in the United States for over 150 years, and option contracts have been around for quite some time as well. In 1974, the U.S. Congress passed the Commodity Futures Trading Commission Act, which established the CFTC as the key federal regulator of both futures and options trading activities in the United States. The mission of the CFTC is to protect market participants in futures and options trading from fraud, manipulation, and other such abusive practices and to foster financially sound markets.

Conclusion

Financial regulation in the United States is in a constant state of flux but seems to change the most in response to economic and financial crises. The financial crisis of 2008–2009 does not appear to be an exception to this rule. The U.S. Congress recently passed, and President Obama signed into law, the Dodd-Frank Wall Street Reform and Consumer Protection Act, legislation that will significantly alter the financial regulatory landscape going forward. Indeed, the mind-set in Washington, DC, following the financial crisis is that it was generally a lack of federal financial regulation that led to the crisis. Even with the 2010 act in place, much debate continues to take place as to how the new rules are to be applied by regulators and to what extent they will be shaped by such regulatory actions.

Included in the Dodd-Frank Act is a provision to establish a new Bureau of Consumer Financial Protection that is charged with making sure that consumers are not taken advantage of by "unscrupulous lenders," such as putting home buyers into mortgage loans that are not in the consumer's best interest. While numerous financial regulators were charged with such responsibilities in the past, this new regulator will have this as its chief focus. The Dodd-Frank Act also includes new laws and regulations dealing with the very largest financial institutions in the country that are deemed "too big to fail." The financial crisis has shown evidence of rippling effects throughout the financial system when a large financial institution, like Lehman Brothers, fails. To prevent such rippling effects, many large, systemically important financial institutions were provided federal aid during the crisis to prevent their financial failure. While the new legislation does address many aspects of the too-big-to-fail issue, it does not appear to settle the issue of the optimal method of dealing with large, systemically important institutions that are on the brink of failure. The act also includes some new regulation on derivatives other than futures and option contracts, such as swap agreements.

While the U.S. political leadership today seems to believe that the next financial crisis will be prevented by these new regulatory reforms, a reading of U.S. financial history suggests that future crises are still likely to occur in the not-too-distant future.

See also **Bank Bailouts; Consumer Credit and Household Debt; Corporate Governance; Corporate Tax Shelters; Corporate Crime (vol. 2)**

Further Reading

Benmelech, Efraim, and Tobias Moskowitz, "The Political Economy of Financial Regulation: Evidence from U.S. State Usury Laws in the 19th Century." *Journal of Finance* 65, no. 3 (June 2010): 1029–1073.

Bullard, James, Christopher J. Neely, and David C. Wheelock, "Systemic Risk and the Financial Crisis: A Primer." *Federal Reserve Bank of St. Louis Review* (September/October 2009): 403–417.

Cecchetti, Stephen G., *Money, Banking, and Financial Markets,* 2d ed. Boston: McGraw-Hill Irwin, 2007.

Friedman, Milton, and Anna Jacobson Schwartz, *A Monetary History of the United States, 1867–1960.* Princeton, NJ: Princeton University Press, 1963.

Kane, Edward J., "Interaction of Financial and Regulatory Innovation." *American Economic Review* 78, no. 2 (May 1988): 328–334.

Kaufman, George, "The Financial Turmoil of 2007–09: Sinners and Their Sins." Networks Financial Institute at Indiana State University, March 2010, 2010-PB-01.

NYU Stern Working Group on Financial Reform, "Real-time Recommendations for Financial Reform." December 16, 2009. http://govtpolicyrecs.stern.nyu.edu/home.html

Stigler, George, "The Theory of Economic Regulation." *Bell Journal of Economics* 1 (Spring 1991): 3–21.

FOREIGN DIRECT INVESTMENT

Michael L. Walden

Much has been made about U.S. companies putting jobs and factories in foreign countries. This phenomenon, called outsourcing, has stirred concerns about the United States' competitiveness and the ability of U.S. workers to go head-to-head with foreign workers, many of whom are paid much less.

But perhaps just as important, yet not as thoroughly covered in the popular press, is the opposite flow of money and jobs. This occurs when foreign companies and foreign investors put funds into the U.S. economy. The money is used to build factories and stores or buy financial investments. With the inflow of money usually come jobs and incomes. This process is called foreign direct investment (FDI) and is popularly termed insourcing.

The Size and Origin of Foreign Direct Investment

Foreign direct investment can happen from any country. People and companies from any country can invest in (almost) any other country. For example, there is FDI in China, France, Poland, and Chile. Of course, there is also FDI in the United States, which will be the focus of this entry.

So when we talk about the amount of money foreigners invest in the United States, are we talking about a small or large amount? Figure 1 gives the answer. The dollar amounts in different years in the figure have been adjusted so they have the same purchasing power; therefore, they are directly comparable. As can be seen, FDI in the United States is substantial, at $2.3 trillion in 2008. It has also increased substantially in recent years, rising over 500 percent from 1990 to 2008.

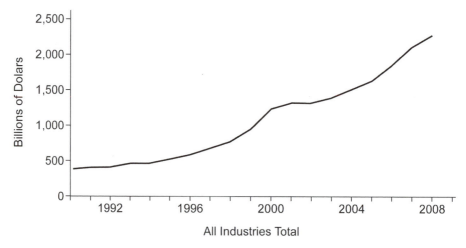

Figure 1. Foreign direct investment in the United States (2008 dollars in billions) (Bureau of Economic Analysis, www.bea.gov)

TABLE 1. Leading Countries of Origin for Foreign Direct Investment in the United States (1990 and 2008)

Country	Share of Total Foreign Direct Investment in 1990 (%)	Share of Total Foreign Direct Investment in 2008 (%)
United Kingdom	25.0	19.9
Japan	21.0	11.4
Netherlands	16.3	11.4
Germany	7.1	9.3
Switzerland	4.5	7.3
France	4.7	7.2
Luxembourg		5.0
Australia	1.7	2.8

Source: Bureau of Economic Analysis. http://www.bea.gov

Who is behind these investments? That information is given in Table 1, which shows FDI in the United States according to the top countries of origin in 1990 and 2008. In both years, the leading investor countries were all in Europe, of European origin (Australia), or Japan. The biggest changes from 1990 to 2008 have been a reduction in the shares of the two leading countries, the United Kingdom (Great Britain) and Japan, and the replacement of Australia in 1990 with Luxembourg in 2008 as a leading investor country.

Why Do Foreigners Invest in the United States?

What motivates foreigners to invest in the United States, and should we be pleased or worried by the interest of foreign investors? These are important questions that help determine how we feel about FDI.

On one level, we should not be surprised that foreigners want to invest in the United States. The United States is the world's largest economy by far, the biggest in aggregate wealth, and has a stable political system that respects the rights of investors. The U.S. economy has more than doubled in size in the past 20 years (1990–2010), and its population is among the fastest growing for developed countries. Against this backdrop, any investor would want part of the action in the United States.

Recently, there has been a demographic reason for FDI in the United States. Compared to Europe, Japan, and soon China, the United States is a relatively young country with a growing population. Europe, Japan, and China are aging rapidly, and their populations may even decline in the decades ahead. Older people tend to be savers and investors so that they can ensure an income in their later years. Younger people, by contrast, are usually borrowers so that they can supplement their income to purchase the homes, cars, appliances, and other assets needed for their lives. Therefore, it makes sense that countries with older populations will lend—which is another way of looking at investing—to countries with a higher proportion of younger people. Indeed, this is exactly the pattern shown in Table 1. The greatest source of FDI in the United States is from the aging countries of Europe plus Japan.

Last, there is a practical reason why foreign citizens invest in the United States. For most of the past 30 years, U.S. businesses and consumers have been purchasing more products and services from foreign countries than foreign businesses and consumers have been buying from the United States. In other words, imports to the United States have exceeded exports from the United States. This means that foreign citizens have been accumulating U.S. dollars. Eventually, these dollars have to make their way back to the United States, and they do so as FDI in the United States. This is one reason to expect China, with which the United States now runs a large trade deficit, to soon become a major source of FDI. The Chinese computer giant Lenovo's purchase of IBM's personal computer unit in 2004 and the Chinese auto company Geely's purchase of Volvo from Ford in 2009 are examples of what is likely ahead.

Impact of FDI on Employment

Like any investment, FDI in the United States creates jobs. But how many jobs, and where are they and what do they pay?

Table 2 shows the latest data on the distribution of jobs by industry created by foreign investments in the United States. More than 5.3 million jobs in the United States are

TABLE 2. Employment Associated with Foreign Direct Investment in the United States (2008)

Sector	Number of Jobs	Percent of Total
All industries	5,334,200	100.0
Manufacturing	2,063,900	39.0
Wholesale trade	614,700	11.5
Retail trade	563,800	10.6
Hotels and food service	358,100	6.7
Transportation and warehousing	233,100	4.4
Information	225,700	4.2
Finance	215,300	4.0
Professional, scientific, and technical	202,100	3.8
Agriculture and mining	82,900	1.6
Construction	74,500	1.3
Real estate	44,000	0.8
Utilities	28,000	0.5
Other	628,000	11.8

Source: Bureau of Economic Analysis. http://www.bea.gov

RISE OF FOREIGN-OWNED AUTO FACTORIES IN THE UNITED STATES

Manufacturing is the leading sector attracting foreign direct investment to the United States, and, within manufacturing, vehicle production has become a popular venture for foreign investors. There are now 10 foreign auto companies with factories operating in the United States, and more are planned for the future. Additionally, there are foreign-owned factories producing vehicle parts that then supply their output to the vehicle assembly plants.

Employment in foreign-owned auto factories in the United States steadily increased from the mid-1990s, rising 52 percent between 1995 and 2005. In contrast, domestic U.S. vehicle assembly and parts factories cut 350,000 jobs between 2000 and 2005, with more reductions in the wake of the 2008–2009 financial crisis. Thus, the gains in foreign-owned vehicle factories have not matched the cuts from domestic plants, so total employment in vehicle production in the United States has continued to fall.

The rise of foreign vehicle production in the United States and the decline of production from domestically owned companies have paralleled their sales trends. U.S. auto companies first trailed their foreign competitors in developing smaller, fuel-efficient vehicles in the 1970s and 1980s. Then they lagged in quality and customer satisfaction in the 1990s and 2000s. U.S. auto companies were not able to close these gaps, and they suffered severely during the financial crisis. (General Motors and Chrysler were bailed out by the government, and Ford sales dropped before evening out at a much lower volume than before.) Currently, the Big Three are in the process of becoming smaller in scale even while foreign producers have plans to grow.

U.S. and foreign vehicle companies have also differed in terms of their locations within the United States. Traditionally, U.S. vehicle companies located their production facilities in the Midwest, in states like Michigan, Ohio, and Indiana. Foreign vehicle companies have sited most of their factories in the South, including Alabama, Texas, and South Carolina. Lower labor costs and access to centers of growing population have been the main reasons pulling foreign factories to southern locations.

Although many Americans may be suspicious of foreign ownership, they have voted with their purchases and dollars in favor of foreign auto companies. The pay and prestige that a foreign vehicle production plant brings to a locality has set off intense competition between states for landing these so-called trophy firms.

directly associated with FDI, accounting for approximately 4 percent of all jobs in the country. Perhaps the most striking feature is the concentration of jobs in the manufacturing sector. Of the 5.3 million jobs, over 2 million of them are in manufacturing. This is 39 percent of the total FDI jobs. In comparison, in 2004, only 10 percent of all U.S. jobs were in manufacturing. An interesting feature of FDI is the growth of production and jobs in foreign-owned vehicle manufacturing factories placed in the United States.

FDI employment in the United States also pays well. In 2004, for example, FDI jobs paid an average of $62,959 in salaries and benefits, compared to $48,051 for all

U.S. jobs. Hence, the average FDI job paid over 30 percent more than the average U.S. job in the country. So foreign investors are not creating low-paying positions in the United States; they are creating just the opposite—jobs that pay at the upper end of the wage scale.

Comparing Insourcing and Outsourcing

How does FDI in the United States (insourcing) compare to U.S. direct investment in foreign countries (outsourcing)? Although FDI in the United States has been growing substantially, U.S. investment in foreign countries is larger still. The total value of U.S. investments in foreign countries is almost one-third larger than the corresponding foreign investment in the United States. Also, there are about two jobs in U.S. foreign factories and offices for every one job in the United States in a foreign-controlled company. So, by these standards, it can be said that outsourcing is larger than insourcing.

But before the conclusion is reached that this is bad, consider two counterpoints. First, since the U.S. economy is the largest in the world, it makes sense that U.S. companies will have more operations in foreign countries than foreign countries have in the United States. Second, foreign investments by U.S. companies can be complementary to domestic operations, making the domestic operations more efficient and profitable. Stated another way, putting some jobs in foreign countries, where costs may be lower or where access to important inputs is easier, can actually save jobs at home by making the operating company stronger and healthier.

Are Foreigners Buying Up the United States?

Although many positive aspects can be stated for FDI, there are a couple of nagging questions that frequently bothers people: Will foreign investments give the foreign owners control over the U.S. economy? Would these owners then pursue policies that are contrary to the national interests of the United States and its citizens?

From an economic perspective, these concerns are unlikely to be realized. This is because any investor, domestic or foreign, has two main objectives: preserving its investment and earning income on that investment. Pursuing destructive policies that damage the investment or its income-earning ability are simply not consistent with basic investment philosophy.

Another way of answering the questions is to calculate the proportion of the U.S. economy that foreigners own. This is found by taking foreign-owned assets as a percentage of all assets in the United States. In 2008, this percentage came to a little over 12 percent ($23.4 trillion of $188 trillion). Although this is double the percentage in the late 1990s, foreign gains have not come at the expense of domestic ownership. Between 1997 and 2008, foreign-owned assets in the United States increased by more than $5 trillion, but U.S. domestically owned assets rose by about $30 trillion.

The World Is Our Economy

It is likely that FDI, both in the United States by foreign citizens as well as in foreign countries by U.S. citizens, will increase in coming years. The reason is simple: globalization. With trade barriers lower and technology making travel and communication among countries in the world easier, we should expect money flows between nations and regions to likewise surge. Just as a century ago local financial markets in the United States expanded to become nationwide financial markets, world markets are now supplanting national markets. Our perspective of what is normal and common will have to adjust.

See also **Free Trade; Globalization; Outsourcing and Offshoring; Trade Deficits (and Surpluses)**

Further Reading

Crystal, Jonathan, *Unwanted Company: Foreign Investment in American Industries.* Ithaca, NY: Cornell University Press, 2003.

Gálvez-Muñoz, Lina, and Geoffrey G. Jones, eds., *Foreign Multinationals in the United States: Management and Performance.* New York: Routledge, 2001.

Maunula, Marko, *Guten Tag, Y'all: Globalization and the South Carolina Piedmont, 1950–2000.* Athens: University of Georgia Press, 2009.

Maynard, Micheline, *The End of Detroit: How the Big Three Lost Their Grip on the American Car Market.* New York: Broadway Books, 2004.

Maynard, Micheline, *The Selling of the American Economy: How Foreign-Owned Companies Are Remaking the American Dream.* New York: Broadway Books, 2009.

Wilkins, Mira, *A History of Foreign Investment in the United States, 1914–1945.* Cambridge, MA: Harvard University Press, 2004.

FREE TRADE

Diane H. Parente

Free trade is one of those concepts espoused by economists that makes perfect sense in the abstract. When one looks a bit closer, however, questions can be raised about whether we as citizens and consumers should support the implementation of free trade principles and policies. Ultimately, it depends on one's point of view.

What Is Free Trade?

Simply put, free trade is the exchange or sale of goods or services without the addition of any tariff or tax. It is common for import taxes to be levied when goods are brought into a country. Often, products that are produced outside a country are taxed, sometimes heavily, when foreign manufacturers bring these products into the home country for sale.

The notion of free trade says, for example, that there should be no additional taxes on foreign imports of cars vis-à-vis domestically produced automobiles.

What Is Nonfree Trade?

Another label for nonfree trade is protectionism. In this case, tariffs or taxes, trade restrictions, or quotas may be placed on the import of goods and services into a country. This is done to protect businesses in the home country from competitors. Opponents of free trade sometimes call this practice fair trade.

On the surface, for a resident of the home country, higher prices for imported goods means that the home country's goods will be purchased equally if not more robustly than a foreign competitor's products and moreover that those purchases will sustain businesses and save jobs in the home country. The truth, however, is more complicated. Adding tariffs in order to level the playing field between foreign and domestic competition actually ends up taxing consumers and causing them to pay higher prices.

Back to Basics

The fundamental laws of trade were first hypothesized in 1776 by Adam Smith in his treatise *The Wealth of Nations*. In this document, Smith had a simple make-buy argument: do not make at home what you can buy cheaper elsewhere. This applies to countries as well as to individuals. Thus, if one country (say, China) can make shoes cheaper than another (say, the United States), then it would make sense for Americans to buy shoes that are made in China. Smith's argument is logical in that we can do the things that we do well and buy goods and services from other countries that do those things well. This argument makes very good sense in the abstract.

As we can see in Figure 1, country 1 has a lower cost (C1) than the cost for the product produced in country 2 (C2) for the product being made. If we presume the same profit, X, then the price (P1) of the product produced in country 1 will be lower than the price (P2) of the product produced in country 2. This should be fundamentally good for consumers. However, if a tax (T) is added to the price for the good produced in country 1, as shown in Figure 3, then consumers will pay the same amount for the product and not realize any potential savings for efficiencies, as seen in Figure 2.

The example begs the question of what would happen if the tax were not imposed and free trade were enabled. Figure 3 illustrates the value to the consumer of free trade. In the example, both countries produce wine and wheat. However, country 1 produces wheat at a lower cost than country 2. Likewise, country 2 produces wine at a lower cost than country 1. If a consumer was able to buy wine from country 2 and wheat from country 1 (without any interference from tariffs), she would expend less money for both products.

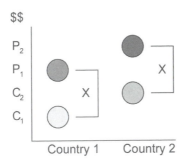

Figure 1. Costs and Corresponding Prices

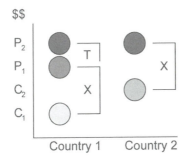

Figure 2. Prices under Nonfree Trade

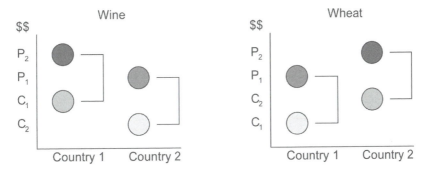

Figure 3. Tariff-Free Spending

What Are the Issues that Prompt Free Trade among Nations?

There are two fundamental factors that prompt nations to engage in free trade. One is buying power (or selling power), and the other is cost.

Consider the trading power of a nation. In our prior example, the more products a trading unit (i.e., a nation) has that it can produce at a low cost, the more opportunities it will have to trade. If each state in the United States were acting independently, it would have to be very efficient at organizing trades that would take a small number of products and obtain all of the products that the individual state would need. However, with all 50 states operating without trade barriers, the movement of goods and services is free flowing. Consumers do not have artificial pricing increased by taxes. Trading power is enhanced in a free trade environment.

Cost is the second issue prompting free trade. Think about the possibility that a truckload of product would need to stop at the border of each state to continue. In addition to the time lost in the stops, a tax would be charged at each checkpoint. The total cost of the product in such a scenario would be increased dramatically. In fact, at one time, the truck transportation cost was estimated to be twice as much in Europe as it was in the United States due to border checkpoints where inspections would be made and taxes levied. Therefore, we can presume that total cost in a nonfree trade environment would be higher.

Where Is Free Trade?

One of the classic examples of an implementation of free trade policies is the formation of the European Union (EU). The countries in Europe maintained separate governments, currencies, and standards over centuries. The EU was formed to enhance political, social, and economic cooperation. As an example, prior to the formation of the EU, there was no free movement of people from country to country. Licensing standards for medical and professional personnel were neither consistent nor even recognized from one country to the next. In fact, these standards were so different and so ingrained in the laws of each country that it took 17 years to reach agreement on the qualifications for an architect. Architects, like other professionals, could not move freely from one country to another. Once the EU was established, architects could move from one country to another because they would be licensed in all of the countries in the EU. Licensing standards for doctors and other medical personnel were among those that would be harmonized, or standardized.

Uniting Europe was done for two stated reasons: preventing another world war and creating an economic unit as strong as the United States. The issues in the EU were many, and the task was very daunting in the beginning. Issues included a difference in tax rates (i.e., high in the United Kingdom and low in southern European countries), government (i.e., monarchy vs. democracy), currencies (each country with its own currency), and wages (i.e., high in the heavily industrialized countries and low in other countries). The common currency, the euro, came into use officially in 1999, and many of the other issues are either unresolved or have been recently resolved. So we might say that the jury is still out on the EU's success. (The global economic crisis of 2008–2009 caused some frayed relations but left the system intact; and even the collapse of the Greek economy in 2010 was being dealt with by means of EU policies and procedures.)

The North American Free Trade Agreement (NAFTA) was launched in 1994. Canada, Mexico, and the United States formed the world's largest free trade area. Unlike the EU, there is no supraorganization over the independent participants. The agreement called for the elimination of duties on half of all U.S. goods shipped to Mexico and Canada immediately and for the phasing out of other tariffs over a period of 14 years. The treaty protected intellectual property and also addressed the investment restrictions between the three countries.

Several reports have been published that address the progress of the NAFTA agreement 10 years later. The *Yale Economic Review* reports that, during the five years before NAFTA, Mexican gross domestic product grew at 3 percent (U.S. Department of Commerce 2004). After the agreement, however, this rate increased to a high of 7 percent (prior to the global economic crisis). During the 10 years post-NAFTA, exports from the United States to Canada increased by 62 percent, and exports to Mexico increased by 106 percent. Canada's success with NAFTA is also well established.

What Are the Issues?

There are a number of issues and questions regarding free trade. The issues concern the economy, the political situation, and social matters.

One question has to do with workers' rights. Stories abound of child labor in foreign countries and poor wages, such as 50 cents per hour. The presumption is that these wages are slave labor rates in comparison to those of the United States. However, wherever globalization has taken hold, workers most often have seen dramatic improvements in their working conditions. Since foreign-owned companies are likely to provide similar conditions to their overseas versus domestic workers, local firms are forced to compete. Foreign-owned companies typically pay more than local businesses and provide a better environment to attract the best possible workers.

Another question relates to the environment. One view is that companies will set up shop at locations where they might avoid environmental constraints. However, this is usually a minor issue in the siting of a facility. Higher on the list of requirements are tax laws, legal systems, and an educated workforce. Infrastructure, such as transportation and packaging facilities, are also high on the list. Empirical evidence shows that the environmental standards of countries with free trade actually improve and do not deteriorate.

How does free trade affect manufacturing? Free trade, in the view of most, if not all, economists, is actually an advantage to U.S. manufacturing. Increasing productivity and decreasing costs force innovation and an increase in profitability. In fact, during the period 1992 to 1999, when the U.S. economy increased by 29 percent overall, manufacturing output increased by considerably more: 42 percent.

So we need to ask whether free trade enables movement of people across borders. Is immigration bad for the United States? The answer actually is no. Immigrants tend to fill gaps in worker shortages and often bring technical skills with them. Furthermore, a study by the National Research Council found that immigrants and their children actually pay more in taxes than they consume in services (Simon 1995).

LOSS OF JOBS AS A PERSONAL ISSUE

The steel business was a major industry in Buffalo, New York, employing nearly 60,000 people at its peak. The purchase of Lackawanna Steel by Bethlehem Steel was critical for location and access to the Buffalo and Detroit auto plants. Power was inexpensive due to the proximity to the Niagara Power Project, although a strong union position served to increase costs. As the industry gradually left the United States for offshore locations, initially to Southeast Asia, a cry concerning the impact of free trade and the loss of jobs as a result was heard throughout the area. Although that claim can be empirically disproved, it is a tough sell to a family whose father or mother is now one of those unemployed, with little prospect for obtaining work in another steel plant and few alternatives.

What about the phenomenon called brain drain? This is when nations or regions lose skilled or educated workers owing to the availability of better-paying jobs elsewhere. Poor countries often educate their population in specific jobs in medical areas and other professions in the hope that they will stay, only to find that some rich countries try to attract them away. The BBC reports that one-third of doctors in the United Kingdom are from overseas (Shah 2006). The report goes on to state that African, Asian, and Latin American nations are plagued by the brain drain issue.

Finally, free trade always spurs a discussion on jobs. While imported goods may take some jobs away from a country, such jobs generally are in industries that are less competitive. More often than not, technological changes, shifts in monetary policy, and other nontrade factors lie behind the loss of jobs. Increasing imports, it is generally considered among economists, actually increases jobs and serves to make workers more productive. (Remember, however, that this effect is in the aggregate, not in specific industries.)

What Are the Various Perspectives?

The benefits to the individual consumer are well documented. As seen in Figure 3, the individual will pay less overall for goods and services under a free trade economy. Furthermore, he will be able to buy higher-quality goods at lower prices than without free trade. The downside, of course, is that, while the long-term benefit is clear, the short term presents problems, especially if one's job is impacted by the movement abroad.

Countries that engage in free trade, or at least lower trade barriers, enjoy higher standards of living overall. As noted by Griswold (1999), trade moves to those industries where productivity and returns are higher. Thus, workers will have more job opportunities at higher wages.

There are also national implications from the value of the U.S. dollar (or the home currency). If trade barriers are imposed, imports are restricted. Americans then spend less on foreign goods, which makes its currency higher with respect to other currencies. Thus, any industry that is not protected by tariffs becomes less competitive in world markets, and the United States is less able to export. It is a vicious cycle: restricting imports creates higher currency value, which then inhibits exports.

From the corporate perspective, with free trade, raw materials may be purchased more cost-effectively, manufacturing becomes more streamlined, and lower costs make products more profitable. When we consider the changes in industries that will make one industry more profitable, we should also examine whether a change in one industry places even more pressure on another. In our steel example (see sidebar "Loss of Jobs as a Personal Issue"), if quotas are imposed once steel moves off shore, then automobiles become less competitive domestically.

Continuing with the steel example, some of the "buy American" slogans may be misleading when we examine them further. According to Blinder (2002), the estimated cost

AN EXAMPLE OF THE CURRENCY ISSUE

Assume that a component—say, a circuit board—can be made in both the United States and Thailand. The cost (in U.S. dollars) is represented in the following table, both with and without tariffs.

	U.S. Product	Thai Product without Tariff	Thai Product with Tariff
Cost	$100	$60	$60
Tariff			$50
Final price	$100	$60	$110

If, as is usually the case, the circuit board is used as a component part in a larger manufactured good, the final good will be least expensive if the Thai component is used without a tariff. The idea here is that if there are no tariffs, then the corporation would tend to use the lowest-cost raw material. Thus, we could assume that, under the condition of no tariffs, the final price of the finished good might be as much as $40 less than if the U.S. circuit board were used.

If the U.S. circuit board were used (or the Thai product with the tariff applied), then the final product would cost more. A consumer would have less disposable income and would not be able to buy as many other goods as a result, reducing trade overall.

Since there would be fewer imports, there would be fewer U.S. dollars on the international market, raising the dollar's value. The result is that we would be selling less on the export market and actually decreasing trade.

If, on the other hand, we were to use the Thai product without tariffs, the cost of the final product would be less, and we would be able to spend more and buy more imports. This would cause the currency to be lower in value with respect to other countries and encourage export sales. The overall result is an increase in trade.

of saving jobs by implementing protectionism is staggering. He cites costs of restricting imports in the automobile industry "at $105,000 per job per year, one job in TV manufacturing at $420,000, and one job in steel at $750,000/year." No wonder the steel industry was one of the earliest to leave U.S. shores.

What Are the Options?

One option for free trade is balanced trade. In this model, countries must provide a balance from each country. Neither country is allowed to run deficits at the risk of penalties. Some critics of this approach think that innovation may be stifled.

Another option is called fair trade. In this scenario, standards are promoted for the production of goods and services, specifically for exports from lesser-developed countries to well-developed (First World) countries.

Another alternative is an international or bilateral barter program, which would force the matching of imports and exports. Finally, establishing increased credit risk for international loans, especially those brought on by trade imbalance, would lower the volume of uneven trade and look to the economic market for discipline.

Conclusion

Free trade is the movement of goods, services, capital, and labor across boundaries without tariffs or other nontariff trade barriers. Arguments against it and for the use of tariffs are intended to save jobs, but actually the application of tariffs costs consumers more for final goods and services and restricts competition in a number of fundamental ways. Free trade is not a main factor in the loss of jobs. Rather, free trade helps to improve productivity and, ultimately, raise the standard of living overall.

See also **Foreign Direct Investment; Outsourcing and Offshoring; Trade Deficits (and Surpluses)**

Further Reading

Bhagwati, Jagdish, *Free Trade Today.* Princeton, NJ: Princeton University Press, 2002.

Blinder, Alan S., "Free Trade." *The Concise Encyclopedia of Economics,* 2d ed. 2002. www.econlib.org/library/enc/freetrade.html

Griswold, Daniel, "Trade, Jobs, and Manufacturing: Why (Almost All) U.S. Workers Should Welcome Imports." Trade Briefing Paper, September 30, 1999. http://www.cato.org/pub_display.php?pub_id = 6812

Irwin, Douglas A., *Free Trade under Fire,* 3d ed. Princeton, NJ: Princeton University Press, 2009.

Roberts, Russell D., *The Choice: A Fable of Free Trade and Protectionism.* Upper Saddle River, NJ: Pearson Prentice Hall, 2007.

Shah, Anup, "Criticisms of Current Forms of Free Trade." *Global Issues* (March 31, 2006). http://www.globalissues.org/article/40/criticisms-of-current-forms-of-free-trade

Simon, Julian L., *Immigration: The Demographic and Economic Facts.* Cato Institute, December 11, 1995. http://www.cato.org/pubs/policy_report/pr-immig.html

U.S. Department of Commerce, International Trade Administration, Office of Industry Trade Policy, "NAFTA 10 Years Later." 2004. http://www.trade.gov/td/industry/otea/nafta/nafta-index.html

G

GLASS CEILING

William M. Sturkey

What Is the Glass Ceiling?

Glass ceiling is a term used to refer to the alleged limits of advancement that minorities, including women, experience in the U.S. workplace. It has been observed that the highest-ranking positions in organizations are dominated by heterosexual white men. This observation has led to the theory that minorities within organizations have a limited level to which they can advance. That ceiling for advancement is said to be transparent, or obviously biased, unlike other ceilings, which require various degrees of experience or education. Hence the term glass ceiling has been used to describe this phenomenon.

Does the Glass Ceiling Exist?

The term *glass ceiling* was first used by Carol Hymowitz and Timothy Schellhardt in the March 24, 1986, edition of the *Wall Street Journal* to describe the limits of advancement that women face in the workplace (Hymowitz and Schellhardt 1986). When originally used, the term drew widespread criticism because it claimed that women did not achieve high levels of advancement in the workforce because they were consumed by family life or did not obtain the required levels of education and/or experience. Since then, the term and the arguments surrounding it have developed to encompass all minorities in the workplace.

According to a great deal of research, the glass ceiling is a very real characteristic of the U.S. corporate atmosphere. A 1995 study by the Federal Glass Ceiling Commission found that 97 percent of the senior managers of the Fortune 1000 Industrial and Fortune 500 were white, and 95–97 percent were men. This is not demographically representative, considering that 57 percent of the workforce consists of ethnic minorities, women, or both. In 1990, Jaclyn Fierman (1990) found that less than 0.5 percent of the 4,012 highest-paid managers in top companies in the United States were women, while fewer than 5 percent of senior management in the Fortune 500 corporations were minorities. More recent figures show that gains have been made in some areas—for example, among Fortune 500 company boards of directors, women now make up 15 percent of the total (Catalyst 2008)—but clearly there is room for improvement. The conclusion reached from studies such as these is that there are invisible barriers that exclude women and ethnic minorities from upper management positions.

Despite evidence to the contrary, many argue that the glass ceiling concept does not exist. Those who argue that the glass ceiling does not exist focus mainly on the status of women and argue that the glass ceiling ignores pertinent evidence that disproves the theory and that it is an unrealistic conspiracy theory that simply reflects women's chosen positions in U.S. society.

One of the forms of evidence that glass ceiling detractors claim is ignored is the education of high-ranking executives. They argue that these executives are more qualified because they have achieved a higher level of education than most women. They argue that women are not well represented in upper-level management because of a lack of women receiving master of business administration (MBA) degrees.

Those who argue against the existence of the glass ceiling also argue that women are not represented in upper-level management because women do not aspire to such positions, partially because of the characteristics of U.S. society. It is argued that men work better in teams and under a chain of command than women, who take less dangerous jobs, are not willing to work long hours like men, and wish to have more maternal positions, such as nurse, child care provider, or secretary. Of course, the issue of childbirth and maternal instincts are also factors that many claim prevent women from holding high-level positions. Glass ceiling detractors often take as fact that women cannot be highly successful and raise children. Surprisingly, a great number of these types of arguments are being made by women with experience in the business world who do not see themselves as victims. Instead, they deny their advancement potential by claiming that they have decided to make another choice.

Those who argue against the glass ceiling in terms of how it affects ethnic minorities use similar arguments and often expand them to include stereotypes, the most common being that African Americans and Latinos are not self-directed or would rather perform labor-centered tasks. Other reasons used include a lack of education, inability to understand the English language or Western society, and a desire to hold certain types of positions (e.g., linking Asian Americans to computer and science jobs).

The argument against the existence of the glass ceiling is compelling; however, the enormous disparities between the minority and majority when it comes to senior management positions make the analysis of this issue necessary, whether the concept is seen as bona fide or not.

Groups Affected by the Glass Ceiling

Women

For most of the 20th century, the levels of education achieved by men and women were disproportionate. However, recent decades have seen the end of unequal access to education in terms of gender. In 2008, 49 percent of the Yale undergraduate class was female, the entering class of the University of California, Berkeley's law school was 55 percent female, and Columbia University's law school (in toto) was 48 percent female. Over 50 percent of medical school applicants are now women, as are half of undergraduate business majors. So how has the discrepancy between men and women in high-ranking positions evolved?

One major and incontrovertible difference between men and women is that women give birth and men do not. This leads to one of the most common reasons given for the existence of a glass ceiling. Many argue that women simply choose other paths than their careers. One example comes from business. A Harvard Business School survey found that only 38 percent of women from the MBA classes of 1981, 1985, and 1991 were working full-time. Of white men with MBAs, 95 percent are working full-time, while only 67 percent of white women with MBAs have full-time positions (McNutt 2002).

Many women are discriminated against in the workplace. Often, when a woman is hired, she is hired under the assumption that she will leave her job or not work as hard when she gets married or has children. This type of attitude places women in the types of jobs that can be seen as temporary. Women may be working on small projects instead of being heavily involved with the infrastructure of a corporation. This type of job discrimination may go so far as to place women with college degrees as administrative assistants or secretaries. It is with this type of discrimination that many women's careers begin. Perhaps one of the reasons that women opt out of the workplace to raise children is because of the pressure and stress that come along with being a woman in the business world.

In addition, many of the same factors that affect ethnic and racial minorities also affect women. The next section addresses these issues specifically.

Ethnic and Racial Minorities

The barriers that ethnic and racial minority managers encounter are common to the experience of other minorities. These barriers operate at the individual and organizational levels. They range from overt racial harassment experienced in the workplace to specific segregation practices. These barriers are believed to be responsible for the lack of ethnic minority senior executives in large organizations.

Bell and Nkomo (2003) have identified three major individual barriers that ethnic minorities experience: (1) subtle racism and prejudice, (2) managing duality and bicultural stress, and (3) tokenism and presumed incompetence.

This subtle form of racism and prejudice does not resemble the outright hostility that U.S. culture has rejected since the civil rights movement of the 1950s and 1960s but instead takes the form of what Essed (1991) has termed everyday racism. This includes acts of marginalization, which refers to the exclusion of African American managers from mainstream organizational life, thus maintaining their outsider status, and problematization, which includes the use of stereotypes to justify the exclusion of African American managers without seeming to be prejudiced or racist.

Another important form of an individual barrier includes racial harassment. Racial harassment occurs when an individual or group of employees is continually subjected to racial slurs, jokes, pranks, insults, and verbal or even physical abuse because of their race. Obviously, threats of violence and abuse are detrimental to any working environment, but racial harassment takes many forms and is often precipitated by fellow employees who are unaware of the harassment they inflict. Racial jokes are a good example of unconscious racial harassment. Another example would include a negative reaction to

EXAMPLES OF EVERYDAY RACIAL HARASSMENT

- Any type of racialized joke.
- Racial comments about public figures such as politicians, entertainers, athletes, or even criminals—for example, pointing out that the city councilman accused of fraud is "the black one."
- Asking individuals questions pertaining to their entire race—for example, Why do black people like chicken so much? or Why are Asians so good with computers?
- Using phrases that encompass derogatory terms—for example, nigger-lip, Asian eyes, black booty, or black music.
- Any comments or questions pertaining to a physical difference between the ethnic minority and white employees, including skin color, hair, or any other prominent features.
- Displaying symbols that could be racially offensive—for example, a swastika, Confederate flag, or any symbol resembling a racist organization. The display of a logo of a popular sports team may also be offensive. The most objectionable are those that portray Native Americans in a negative light. The display of this type of symbol may be considered racial harassment.
- Discussing or using quotes from racist films or music.

a news event involving a minority that reflects negatively on that minority's race or ethnicity.

The second level of individual barriers is referred to as bicultural stress. As Bell and Nkomo (2003) noted, in the organizational world, there is little tolerance or appreciation for cultural diversity in terms of behavioral styles, dress, or alternative aesthetics. Bell and Nkomo pointed out that most business environments rely on norms from mostly white Western society that may conflict with other dimensions of these minority managers' normal lives or backgrounds. If the manager is from a non-Western country, this conflict can only increase. The challenge of balancing these contrasting aspects of life often creates stress and tension between the workplace and one's private life. This tension becomes a barrier when ethnic minorities feel compelled to suppress one part of their identity to succeed in one or both of the cultural dimensions in which they exist.

The third level of individual barriers is tokenism. Tokenism is the process of hiring a token number of individuals from an underrepresented minority group to comply with government or organizational affirmative action policies. The people who are token hires are often viewed as representative of their entire race rather than as individuals. Their performance on the job and their personal lives are carefully examined and taken out of context. Because of these stereotypes and general animosity toward affirmative action policies, many other employees believe that these tokens received their jobs not because of individual merit but because of their minority status.

The psychological effects of being treated as a token negatively affect job performance. To overcome the stereotypes associated with each ethnic or racial group, the minority employees often feel that they have to perform at a higher level than other employees just to maintain equal status. They also have to spend a disproportionate amount of time validating their existence in the workplace. They are often aware that because they are perceived to represent their entire race, performing poorly will negatively contribute to the negative stereotypes attributed to their ethnic minority.

Entering a work environment is different for ethnic minorities than it is for white men and women. There are often a multitude of factors that must be juggled just to achieve equal status to that of white employees. The disadvantages that ethnic minorities experience in the workplace are prevalent from the first day on the job, and maybe even before.

Organizational-Level Barriers

Bell and Nkomo (2003) pointed out various organizational-level barriers that exist for ethnic minorities in the workplace. These include (1) lack of mentorship, (2) unfair promotion and evaluation processes, and (3) segregation into staff-type jobs.

Mentors are important in any large business environment. A mentor helps to increase self-confidence, motivation, career skills, career enhancement, career planning, networking opportunities, and, perhaps most importantly, mentors reduce isolation. Mentors are most likely to have mentees who have similar backgrounds. This is perfectly understandable because people tend to sympathize with and coach those in similar situations or from similar backgrounds as themselves. A problem is that mentors may pass over a potential protégé who belongs to an ethnic minority group because of racial stereotypes that may make the mentor see the minority as a risky protégé.

Many employees from ethnic minority groups find it difficult to find mentorship. Friedman and Carter (1993) found that 53 percent of National Black MBA Association members felt that they did not have the support of a mentor. Without equal access to mentors, ethnic minorities are without one of the most important aspects of successful career advancement. It limits their networking opportunities, exposure within the company, and potential supporters. It also denies them the important basic advantages that a mentor provides as far as career planning and the transition into a new organization.

Over the past 20 years, numerous studies have been done that show that white supervisors rank managers from ethnic minority groups below white managers in their evaluations (Bell and Nkomo 2003). They rank them lower in terms of job performance and how they interact with other employees. Part of this is because of racial stereotypes. If supervisors consider ethnic minority managers to be doing a fine job, then their performance is attributed to the support structure they have around them that makes their job easier. For whites, top performance is attributed to effort and competence. As negative feedback builds, it has a snowball effect on African American managers as they lose their confidence and begin to question their own abilities. Low performance ratings have negative effects on an individual's long-term career prospects and self-prescribed potential for advancement within the organization.

There are clear trends in the career paths of the vast majority of CEOs of large organizations. The critical career paths have historically been through marketing, finance, and operations. The people who head companies are often funneled through these departments. Collins (1989) has pointed out that African Americans have been relegated to racialized jobs outside of those departments that produce the most upper-level managers. She suggested that African Americans are often placed in jobs dealing with public relations, community relations, affirmative action, and equal employment opportunity. Among 76 of the highest-ranking African American managers, she found that 66 percent held jobs that dealt with affirmative action or consumer issues. Because of the types of jobs that African American employees are often relegated to, it becomes more difficult for them to advance up the corporate ladder because they do not get experience in the most important functions.

Conclusion

The glass ceiling concept for women and ethnic and racial minorities is hotly contested. Those who argue that it does not exist for women claim that women are not represented in upper management well because they put their families before their careers. The argument against the glass ceiling concept as it concerns ethnic and racial minorities basically hinges on racial stereotypes. Opponents claim that groups like African Americans and Latinos are lazy and that they are not willing to do what it takes to get to the top.

The argument backing the glass ceiling concept for women accepts that many women do choose to leave the workplace to make a family but that those who do not have suffered because of the common misconception and stereotypes surrounding all women. Arguments backing the glass ceiling concept for ethnic and racial minorities claim that basic racist ideas as well as cultural conflicts hinder the ability of people of color to reach upper levels of management. Arguments that the glass ceiling does exist are the most convincing because they are all backed by facts that do indicate, for one reason or another, that minorities are not represented demographically in upper levels of management.

See also **Affirmative Action; Class Justice (vol. 2); Employed Mothers (vol. 3)**

Further Reading

Barreto, Manuela, et al., eds., *The Glass Ceiling in the 21st Century: Understanding Barriers to Gender Equality.* Washington, DC: American Psychological Association, 2009.

Bell, Ella L. J., and Stella M. Nkomo, *Our Separate Ways: Black and White Women and the Struggle for Professional Identity.* Cambridge, MA: Harvard Business School Press, 2003.

Catalyst, *2008 Catalyst Census of Women Corporate Officers and Top Earners of the Fortune 500.* December 2008. http://www.catalyst.org/publication/282/2008-catalyst-census-of-women-board-directors-of-the-fortune-500

Collins, S., "The Marginalization of Black Executives." *Social Problems* 36 (1989): 317–331.

Essed, Philomena, *Understanding Everyday Racism: An Interdisciplinary Theory.* Newbury Park, CA: Sage, 1991.

Federal Glass Ceiling Commission, *Good for Business: Making Full Use of the Nation's Human Capital.* Washington, DC: 1995.

Fierman, Jaclyn, "Why Women Still Don't Hit the Top." *Fortune* 122 (1990): 40.

Friedman, R. A., and D. Carter, "African American Network Groups: Their Impact and Effectiveness." Working Paper 93–069. Cambridge, MA: Harvard Business School, 1993.

Hymowitz, Carol, and Timothy Schellhardt, "The Glass Ceiling." *Wall Street Journal* (March 24, 1986).

Karsten, Margaret Foegen, *Gender, Race, and Ethnicity in the Workplace: Issues and Challenges for Today's Organizations.* Westport, CT: Praeger, 2006.

McNutt, L., *The Glass Ceiling: It Can't Be Shattered If It Doesn't Exist.* 2002. http://www.ifeminists.net/introduction/editorials/2002/1217c.html

GLOBALIZATION

Peter H. Denton

One big planet, a global community, the vision of everyone and everything together from pictures of the Earth from space first sent back by *Apollo 8*—globalization can be romantically portrayed as any of these. From the dark side, it can also be seen as something that shatters local communities, takes away individual autonomy, destroys local cultures, and renders everyone helpless in the face of overwhelming power from somewhere else.

That globalization can be seen as both the happy inevitability of a bright future and the dismal gray of a grinding disaster reflects the reality of a significant conflict between opposing perspectives. Globalization can be represented in economic, cultural, socio-political, and environmental terms, each of which has its own means of measuring the difference between heaven and hell.

Patterns from the Past

To some extent, globalization has always been with us. Looking to identify the means by which people or cultures have sought to spread around the planet and why, one can argue that the primary means has been military, conquering the world through the use of force. For historical examples, we can look to Alexander the Great, the emperors of Rome, Genghis Khan, and so on. In such instances, the means becomes the object; there is no particular value to be gained by conquest, yet the conquest continues because the military machine, so unleashed, has no particular boundary or end to its use. Like a for-est fire, globalization by such means continues until it reaches some natural boundary—like a river or an ocean—or it runs out of "fuel" to sustain it.

On the heels of military globalization, the means by which the gains of conquest are maintained and the benefits accrue to the state or group that initiated the conquest are primarily political. One of the reasons for the failure of Alexander's empire was the fact he absorbed the local political structures, virtually unchanged, into his own; when he died, of course, that was the end of the empire. The Roman Empire, by contrast, brought with it Roman forms of government and social organization, structures that tended to be imposed on the local populations that were controlled and directed by Roman law and institutions. Caesars and other leaders came and went, but the empire continued until the center fell apart, and the institutions—though not the roads—also fell apart. Political organization may be combined with religious organization, however, and, although certain Roman institutions lost their sway in the outlying areas, the re-ligion that was propagated through the military and political structures continued and spread.

With military and political impulses to globalization come economic considerations. In the first instance, to the victor the spoils, for the fruits of conquest are inevitably monetary—someone, after all, has to pay the costs of the operation and make it pos-sible for further conquest. In the second instance, the establishment of political institu-tions makes an economic return on conquest more than the immediate spoils of war; a steady flow of money back to the state at the center of the empire enables the main-tenance of a structure from whose stability everyone benefits, at least to some extent.

Trade flourishes in the context of political stability, and military power protects such trade from the natural depredations of those who want to profit through force and not commerce.

Naturally, to maintain this kind of structure in the longer term requires both common currency and common language; in the wake of military and political conquest inevitably comes the standardization of currency (the coin of the empire) and some common language for the exercise of political and economic power. Latin—and particularly Latin script—became the language of the Roman Empire to its farthest reaches, providing a linguistic uniformity and continuity that outlasted the empire itself by a thousand years. With linguistic uniformity comes intellectual constraints; whether it was previously possible to articulate dissent or rebellion in the language of the peoples, over time their linguistic armory is depleted by the acceptance and use of the language—and the philosophy it reflects—of the conquering culture. The longer an empire has control over the political, social, and religious institutions of the areas it has conquered, the less able the conquered people are able to sustain an intellectual culture distinct from that of their conquerors—thus increasing the likelihood that such an empire will continue, because no one can conceive of another way of making things work.

Colonialism—a practice that existed long before the European powers made it an art in the 19th century—was the means by which the empire was not only propagated but also sustained, through the use of military, political, economic, religious, and intellectual tools.

This is a coercive model of globalization, but it tends to be the one first thought of when discussing how to overcome the various geographical, social, and cultural barriers that divide various groups. It is also the model that is reflected most obviously in history, which tends to be a record of the various conquests of one people or nation by another.

Is it possible, however, for there to be an impulse to "one planet" that is not inherently coercive? Is it possible for these kinds of boundaries to be overcome through mutual goodwill or a collective self-interest, in which all parties cooperate because it is to the advantage of all players that they do so? This is the million-dollar question, because, in the absence of some way in which such cooperation might take place, all that remains is a coercive model, however well the coercion is disguised.

Money and Merchandise

Of the current models for breaking down regional boundaries, most of them are economic and arguably coercive in nature. There is the International Monetary Fund (IMF) coupled with the World Bank, both operating within the framework approved (if not designed) by the countries of the G8 (and now G9, if one includes China). Within that framework, although countries identified as "developing" are offered financial assistance, the assistance is tied to certain monetary and trade policies in such a way that they are, in effect, coerced into compliance. Where countries—including members of the G9—try to go their own way, it is still within the framework of international trade agreements (such as the General Agreement on Tariffs and Trade [GATT]) and under the watchful eyes of global currency markets whose volatility is legendary. In the absence of a global gold standard, certain economies set a global economic standard through their national currency; for example, the value of other currencies used to be measured primarily against the U.S. dollar, though increasingly it is measured as well by the Japanese yen and by the euro from the European Union.

It would be one thing if this approach to globalization was successful, but for too many people, it is not; and the number of critics from all perspectives grows. Oswaldo de Rivero (2001), the head of the Peruvian delegation to a round of the GATT talks, lays out very clearly in *The Myth of Development* why the current structure not only favors the wealthy but also entails the failure of the economies of developing countries in the South. Similarly, Joseph Stiglitz (2003), 2001 Nobel Prize winner in economics, reached the same conclusions about the unequivocal failures of the IMF and the World Bank from the perspective of an insider in *Globalization and Its Discontents.* For those who wonder why and how such a situation came about, in *The Wealth and Poverty of Nations: Why Some Are So Rich and Some So Poor,* historian of technology David Landes (1999) set out the historical development of industrial economies through to the present and makes it clear why there are winners and losers.

There is a difference, however, between the macroeconomic globalization that organizations such as the IMF and the World Bank promote and what can be termed commercial globalization. Commercial globalization, through the merchandising of certain products worldwide, promotes an economic model of consumption that is not restricted by national boundaries. Because the objects sold through such global channels are always value laden, this reflects a globalization, if not of the commercial culture itself that produced the items, at least of some of its values and mores. For example, it is not possible for McDonald's restaurants to be found worldwide without there also being an element of the American burger culture that is found wherever there are golden arches, regardless of what food is actually served (even the McLobsters that seasonally grace the menu in Prince Edward Island). Given the worldwide availability—albeit at a higher price—of virtually any item to be found on the shelves of a North American supermarket or department store, and the capacity of advertising to be beamed simultaneously to multiple audiences watching television from the four corners of the globe, it becomes understandable how and why commercial globalization has become a potent economic, political, social, and cultural force in the 21st century.

Thus, the material aspirations of a 21-year-old in Beijing may well be parallel to someone of the same age in Kuala Lumpur, or Mumbai or Dallas or Moose Jaw. Exposed to the same images and advertising, their material desires in response are likely to be the same; regardless of their culture of origin, their culture of aspiration is likely to include cars, computers, iPods and fast food.

One might say the primary implication of commercial globalization is the globalization of consumer culture, specifically Western consumer culture. Whether such a culture is good or bad in and of itself, its implications are arguably negative in terms of what it does to the local culture through supplanting local values and replacing them with (usually) more alluring and exciting values from far away.

In addition, the diversity of local cultural values—reflected in everything from forms of government to traditions around medicine and healing to cultural practices related to agriculture, cooking, and eating to religious belief systems and habits of dress—is endangered by the monoculture of mass consumerism as it is represented in the venues of mass media.

The Global Village?

There is a difference, however, between globalization and standardization. It is important to distinguish the two, especially in light of the social and cultural requirements of industrial (and postindustrial) society. A very strong case can be made that the impulse to globalize is an effort to regularize and systematize the messy world of human relations into something that fits a mass-production, mass-consumption model. From the introduction of the factory system (1750) onward, industrial processes have become more and more efficient, systematizing and standardizing the elements of production, including the human ones. Ursula Franklin (1999) refers to the emergence of "a culture of compliance" in which the activities of humans outside the manufacturing process become subject to the same terms and conditions as are required in the process of mass production. This culture of compliance requires individuals to submit to systems; it requires them to behave in socially expected as well as socially accepted ways, thus removing the uncertainties and vagaries of human behavior from the operations of society. Although in the mechanical sphere of production, such habits of compliance are essential for the smooth operation of the system, taken outside into the social and cultural spheres in which people live, the antihuman effects of such standardization—treating people in effect like machines to be controlled and regulated—are unpleasant, if not soul-destroying.

Thus, in any discussion of globalization, it needs to be established from the outset what the benefit is, both to individuals and to societies, of some kind of uniformity or standardization in the social or cultural spheres. What is lost and what is gained by such changes, and by whom? Much has been made of the comment by Marshall McLuhan that humans now live in a "global village," thanks to the advent of mass communication devices such as the radio, the television, the telephone, and now the Internet. Yet studies were done of what television programs were being watched by the most people around the world and therefore had the greatest influence on the development of this new "global" culture that was replacing local and traditional cultures. Imagine the consternation when it was discovered that the two most watched programs were reruns of

Wagon Train and *I Love Lucy!* Globalization and the cultural standardization that mass-production, mass-consumption society assumes to be necessary may mean that the sun never sets on the fast food empires of McDonald's or Pizza Hut, just as 150 years ago it was said to never set on the British Empire. Yet if the dietary habits of local cultures, in terms of both the food that is grown or produced and the ways in which the food is eaten, are merely replaced by standardized pizzas or burgers (or McLobsters, instead of the homemade variety), one cannot help but think something has been lost.

In the same way as colonies were encouraged to supply raw materials to the homeland and be captive consumers of the manufactured goods it produced (along with the culture and mores that the homeland dictated), so too the commercial colonization of mass-production/mass-consumption society requires the same of its cultural colonies. The irony, of course, is that the homeland is much less identifiable now than it was in the days of political empires; although corporate America is often vilified as the source of the evils of globalization, the reality is that corporate enterprises are much less centralized and less entrenched than any nation state. Certainly the burgeoning economic growth of the European Union (with its large corporate entities that not only survived two world wars and a Cold War but even thrived on them), along with Japan, and the emergence of China and India as economic superpowers indicates that the capital of empire today is entirely portable. The reality that some corporations have larger budgets and net worth than many of the smaller nations in the world also indicates that borders are neither the boundaries nor the advantages that they used to be.

Broader Impacts

Although the economic examples of globalization today are arguably coercive (despite the inevitable objections that no one is forcing us to buy things), it is possible at least to conceive of other ways in which globalization might be noncoercive, incorporating mutually beneficial models instead. In a subsequent book, *Making Globalization Work,* Joseph Stiglitz (2007) works through the ways in which the current problems he and others identify with economic globalization could be overcome; while he proposes solutions to the major problems, he does not effectively address the motivational change that would be required for decision makers to make choices reflecting social responsibility on a global scale.

Politics and Resistance

In the political realm, the United Nations (UN) has, in theory, the potential to be a body that—while respecting the national boundaries of its member states—works to find constructive ways of collectively responding to regional and global issues. Whether its first 60 years reflects such an ideal or whether instead the UN has been a facade behind which coercion has been wielded by one group against another is a subject for debate; in the absence of a clear global mandate for intervention or the effective economic and military means to intervene, moreover, even within a coercive framework, it is hard to see the UN as a model for good global government.

(In terms of any other models of globalization, one might point to the Olympic movement, but, because it has always been a stage for personal and national self-aggrandizement, it is hard to see how it could become a step to some positive global culture.)

In the larger scope history provides, there are positive signs for political organizations that transcend the boundaries of the nation-state and in which participation is voluntary, benefits accrue to all, and the elements of coercion become less significant over time. No one who witnessed the aftermath of the Napoleonic era, the revolutions of 1848, the Franco-Prussian War, the Great War, World War II, and the Iron Curtain ever would have expected either the peaceful reunification of Germany or the formation (and success) of the European Union. Begun first as an economic union, it has continued to grow and mature into a union that has lowered many of the barriers to social, cultural, and political interaction that hundreds of years of nationalism had created.

Whether the EU model is exportable to other parts of the world raises some serious questions about how political globalization might succeed. The EU is regional, involving countries with a long and similar history, even if it was one in which they were frequently at war. The export of its rationale to other areas and cultures, with a different range of historical relations, is unlikely to meet with the same success. There should be some considerable doubt that democracy—as a Western cultural institution—will be valued in the same way in countries that do not have a similar cultural heritage or as desirable to the people who are expected to exercise their franchise. William Easterly (2006), in *The White Man's Burden,* is quite scathing in his account of why such cultural colonialism has done so little good, however well-meaning the actors or how noble their intentions.

Certainly the effects of globalization are far from being only positive in nature; globalization in the absence of political and economic justice that is prosecuted through military and economic coercion creates not only more problems than it solves but also arguably bigger, even global, ones. Whatever the potential benefits of a global perspective, they are undercut by what globalization has come to mean in practical terms for many people—as the articles in *Implicating Empire: Globalization and Resistance in the 21st Century World Order* (Aronowitz and Gautney 2003) so clearly represent. After the events of September 11, 2001, one might easily argue against globalization of any sort given that previously localized violence has been extended worldwide as a consequence of what is now the "global war on terror."

All of these issues combine to ensure what John Ralston Saul (2005) describes as "the collapse of globalism." He sees recent events as sounding the death knell for the free-market idealisms of the post–World War II period, noting that the promised lands of milk and honey that were to emerge from the spread of global markets and the demise of the nation-state have simply failed to materialize. In fact, the current reality is so far from the economic mythology that, in retrospect, it perhaps would not be unfair to regard the architects of this plan as delusional and their disciples as blind.

Saul does add a subtitle to his book, however, in which the collapse of globalism is succeeded by "the reinvention of the world." Out of the ashes of this kind of economic globalism, in other words, and the unmitigated disaster it has spawned, it might be possible to reinvent a shared perspective on global problems that seeks to find a way other than those that have failed. Although Saul is rather bleak in his outlook and much more effective in describing the collapse of globalism than in setting out the character of such a reinvention, he makes a useful point. The failures of economic globalism are so painfully obvious that there can be no reasonable doubt that some other means of working together must be found.

Environmental Issues

If there is a perspective that has potential to be a positive rationale for globalization, it might be an environmental or ecological one. One of the most significant issues pushing some cooperative means of globalization is the environment, as we consider the ecological effects of human activities on a planetary scale. Global warming, ozone depletion, and the myriad means of industrial pollution whose effects are felt worldwide make it clear that, in the absence of a global response, we will all individually suffer serious consequences.

As much as we like to divide up the planet in human terms, laying out the grid lines of political boundaries and economic relationships, the fundamental limitations of the planet itself establish inescapable conditions for what the future holds. Although this may seem just as counterintuitive as Saul's analysis of the failure of global economic systems reinventing the world, the global spread of pollution combined with catastrophic climate change may catalyze changes that overcome local self-interest in favor of something bigger than ourselves. The artificial boundaries that humans create—everything from the notion that one can possess the land to the idea that one can control a part of the planet—are seen through even a crude ecological lens to be nonsensical and even dangerous. If the idea that people have the right to do what they please with the land, water, or air that they "own" is replaced by some more ecologically responsible understanding, then there may be a common ground for cooperation on a planetary scale that does not yet exist. Whether such global cooperation will be in response to some global disaster or whether it will be the result of some new and more positive understanding remains to be seen.

It may seem like pie in the sky, but there are noncoercive ways of conceiving of a global community in which globalization consists of the universal acceptance of ideals and values. If justice, human rights, and respect were tied to the provision of the necessities of life to people in all areas of the planet, and peaceful means were used to settle whatever disputes might arise, then a global culture that reflected these things would be good for everyone.

This is not a new idea, but it is one that Albert Schweitzer (1949) elaborated on in his book *The Philosophy of Civilization*. The first two sections were written "in the primeval forest of Equatorial Africa" between 1914 and 1917. The first section of the book, "The Decay and Restoration of Civilization," locates the global problem not in economic forces but in a philosophical worldview that has undermined civilization itself; for Schweitzer, the Great War was a symptom of the spiritual collapse of civilization, not its cause. He asserts that society has lost sight of the character of civilization and, having lost sight of it, has degenerated as a result. That degeneration is primarily ethical; civilization is founded on ethics, but we are no longer aware of a consistent ethical foundation on which we can build a life together. The second section, not surprisingly, is titled "Civilization and Ethics"; in it, Schweitzer explores this ethical (and spiritual) problem. Schweitzer's answer, reached in the third section, published after the war, was to found ethical action on a principle Schweitzer called "the reverence for life." By doing this, he said, it would be possible to make decisions that were more fair, just, and life-giving than society at the present time was making. He noted that the principle was a general one, for it was not only human life, but all living things, for which people were to have reverence.

The idea of "reverence for life" entailed not only an ecological view of life but also one in which a spiritual dimension in all living things was acknowledged and respected. Moreover, it was not merely a Christian spirituality that Schweitzer said must underpin ethics in civilization, but it was a spirituality in general terms that—across religious boundaries as well as cultural and political ones—had not just a respect for life, but a reverence for it.

Conclusion

In the search for some noncoercive means of uniting people across social, political, cultural, and economic as well as geographic boundaries, working out some vague consequentialist environmentalism to guide the activities and choices of individuals in the global community is not likely going to be enough. There does, however, need to be some ethical framework within which to consider options that, in some form and in the service of some greater, global good, will not have negative effects on people, places, and human institutions. Such a framework will be difficult to find, to articulate, and to accept. Perhaps Schweitzer's idea of reverence for life might turn out to be as useful an ethical touchstone for global decision making today as he thought it would be nearly a century ago.

See also Free Trade; Outsourcing and Offshoring; Social Justice (vol. 2); Environmental Justice (vol. 4)

Further Reading

Aronowitz, Stanley, and Heather Gautney, eds., *Implicating Empire: Globalization and Resistance in the 21st Century World Order*. New York: Basic Books, 2003.

De Rivero, Oswaldo, *The Myth of Development: The Non-Viable Economies of the 21st Century*. New York: Zed Books, 2001.

Easterly, William, *The White Man's Burden: Why the West's Efforts To Aid the Rest Have Done So Much Ill and So Little Good*. New York: Penguin, 2006.

Faber, Daniel, *Capitalizing on Environmental Injustice: The Polluter-Industrial Complex in the Age of Globalization*. Lanham, MD: Rowman & Littlefield, 2008.

Franklin, Ursula, *The Real World of Technology*, 2d ed. Toronto: Anansi, 1999.

Hilton, Matthew, *Prosperity for All: Consumer Activism in an Era of Globalization*. Ithaca, NY: Cornell University Press, 2009.

Landes, David S., *The Wealth and Poverty of Nations: Why Some Are So Rich and Some So Poor*. New York: W. W. Norton, 1999.

Saul, John Ralston, *The Collapse of Globalism and the Reinvention of the World*. Toronto: Viking, 2005.

Schweitzer, Albert, *The Philosophy of Civilization*. Translated by C. T. Campion. New York: Macmillan, 1949.

Stiglitz, Joseph, *Globalization and Its Discontents*. New York: W. W. Norton, 2003.

Stiglitz, Joseph, *Making Globalization Work*. New York: W. W. Norton, 2007.

GOVERNMENT SUBSIDIES

E. C. Pasour Jr.

A subsidy refers to an economic benefit from government to individuals or business firms. A subsidy may lower the price of a product or service to individuals or raise the price received by those who produce it. It may also benefit producers by lowering the cost of production. Governments—federal, state, and local—subsidize a wide range of economic activities in the United States. Well-known subsidies include government assistance to farmers, food stamps, college student loans, and economic incentives (such as tax breaks) by state and local governments to attract sports teams and manufacturing or research facilities.

Subsidies began in Great Britain in the 1500s with a grant of money by the British Parliament to the king to finance military expenditures. The money was raised by a special tax. The subsidy concept has long since been generalized and now refers to any economic favor by government to benefit producers or consumers. Though some subsidies may benefit the public at large, many subsidies today do not and frequently, quite appropriately, are referred to as political pork or corporate welfare.

What are the main kinds of subsidies in the United States? How do some of the familiar and not-so-familiar subsidy programs work? Why do subsidies typically lead to too much of the subsidized activity being produced and used? Subsidies generally benefit a

POLITICAL PORK AND CORPORATE WELFARE

In the literal sense, a pork barrel is a barrel in which pork is kept. The term is thought to have originated on southern plantations, where slaves were given a barrel with the remainder of slaughtered hogs—the pork barrel. In the political arena, pork barrel legislation is a derogatory term referring to government spending meant to shore up constituent support in a politician's home state. Pork barrel legislation provides rich patronage benefits to incumbent politicians. Public work projects and agricultural subsidies are commonly cited examples of pork. Increased pork might be ladled out for existing government programs that benefit particular groups such as corn producers, sugar producers, textile manufacturers, or workers in auto factories. It also might go for government spending on a new project, such as a new post office building, where economic benefits are concentrated in a specific congressional district.

Pork barrel projects providing subsidies to favored groups are added to the federal budget by members of the appropriation committees of Congress. The congressional process often provides spending on federally funded projects in the congressional districts of members of the appropriation committee. Pork barrel projects frequently benefit major campaign contributors. Politicians often are judged by their ability to deliver pork to their constituents, and candidates for political office sometimes campaign with the promise that, if elected, he or she will secure more federal spending for that state or congressional district.

Pork barrel legislation may also give rise to so-called corporate welfare, which describes a wasteful government subsidy to a large company. The government subsidy may be in the form of grants of money, tax breaks, or some other form of special treatment. Corporate welfare, which benefits particular business corporations, generally comes at the expense of other corporations and the public at large.

Political pork and corporate welfare, like beauty, may be in the eye of the beholder. For example, the prospect of large numbers of unhappy voters may cause the federal government to bail out a large corporation when it faces bankruptcy—as happened, for this and other reasons, in the case of General Motors and Chrysler in 2008–2009. The justification given may be that the loss of jobs and economic activity accompanying bankruptcy is so large that a bailout by the government to avoid bankruptcy would benefit the public at large. In the airline industry, for example, some firms may not be able to survive ongoing losses without government subsidies. Such bailouts, however, may not be beneficial. Bankruptcy of less efficient firms is an inevitable feature of a competitive market process, and profit and loss signals lose their ability to channel resources efficiently if business firms are not allowed to fail. Moreover, business firms seeking government aid often succeed when the benefits are highly concentrated on a relatively small group and the costs are borne by taxpayers generally, as in the case of the Wall Street bank bailouts of 2008–2009. Are such bailouts helpful or harmful to the public at large? Are they best thought of as corporate welfare or as a means of keeping the economy running when the stakes are high? In this and other such cases, opinion is sharply divided and perhaps only time will tell.

small group at the expense of the general population, and many are harmful to the general public. How, then, do harmful subsidy programs get enacted into law in a democratic society that makes decisions on the basis of majority vote? The following sections consider these questions and clear up some of the confusion about subsidies.

Types of Subsidies

Subsidies take many different forms and can be classified in different ways.

Money versus In-Kind Subsidies

A subsidy or so-called transfer from the government to an individual or business firm may be in the form of money or in-kind benefit. Well-known money transfers include agricultural subsidies, veterans' benefits, and Medicaid. Common in-kind benefits include food stamps, school lunches, rent subsidies, medical assistance, and other programs that do not involve the exchange of money. In some cases, an in-kind subsidy program may require the recipient to pay some of the cost. For example, the school lunch program is said to be means tested: depending on the parents' income, some students receive free meals, while students from families having higher incomes must pay, but the price paid is below the cost of the meal.

Business Subsidies versus Subsidies to Individuals

Business Subsidies

Federal, state, and local governments subsidize a wide range of producer activities. Farmers, for example, may receive financial assistance when crop prices are low or crop yields are lowered due to drought, hail, or other unfavorable weather conditions. Governments sometimes subsidize large corporations such as auto or steel companies. Assistance may be direct, as in the case of a financial bailout, or it may be indirect, including tariffs and import quotas that limit domestic sales of competing goods from foreign countries.

Quite often, a government subsidy is targeted to a specific business firm. State and local governments may attempt to lure a corporation to locate a manufacturing facility within its borders by providing property tax holidays or other financial incentives. For example, South Carolina, Alabama, and other states have used tax breaks to induce foreign auto companies, including Toyota and Mercedes, to locate manufacturing facilities within their states. Similarly, local governments often subsidize the construction of sports facilities to lure sports teams.

Similarly, large industries may induce the federal government to restrict competition from foreign firms producing similar products. Subsidies of this type include import tariffs on autos, steel, textile products, and agricultural products. An import tariff on autos, for example, means that Ford, General Motors, and other domestic auto producers can charge somewhat higher prices for their products in the United States (even though, under current conditions, they must also offer economical models and provide low financing).

The federal government also subsidizes the export of products from the United States to other countries. For example, the export of agricultural products has been subsidized for more than 50 years. The best known program, known as Public Law 480, was first enacted in 1954. The program was begun to reduce stocks of food that the government acquired through its farm subsidy programs. The program reduces the cost of U.S. food in foreign countries. Some of the food is sold to foreign buyers with long repayment periods at low interest rates, which is a monetary subsidy. Some of the food subsidies are in-kind: the U.S. government donates food products to people in foreign countries in response to devastation caused by floods, earthquakes, famine, and so on. Still other agricultural export subsidies go to private companies and to state and regional trade groups to promote sales of U.S. farm products in foreign countries.

With the exception of subsidies for disaster aid, all export subsidies are inconsistent with free trade between countries. Programs that subsidize exports of U.S. agricultural products help to insulate U.S. farmers from world market prices and often work against the interests of low-income farmers in less developed countries. Moreover, U.S. export subsidies tend to cause recipient countries to retaliate by creating their own export subsidies and thereby foster increased protectionism by producer interests in those countries.

Subsidies to Individuals

Federal, state, or local governments may subsidize a product to increase the use of the product subsidized; such subsidies generally target lower-income consumers and are no less common than producer subsidies. Some consumer subsidies targeting low-income individuals, including food stamps and the school lunch program, have been operating for decades.

Other consumer subsidies of more recent origin are much less dependent on the individuals' incomes. For example, a recently enacted federal program provides an income tax credit for the purchase of hybrid cars—cars with both electric motors as well as internal combustion engines—which is available to all taxpayers. In this case, purchasers of hybrid cars may reduce their federal income taxes by a specified amount in the year that the car is purchased. For example, some buyers of hybrid cars, if purchased during 2006, were able to reduce their 2006 federal income taxes by as much as $3,150.

The hybrid car subsidy ostensibly was begun to reduce U.S. dependence on imports of petroleum. The long-term prospect for hybrid cars remains in doubt, and the huge tax credit required to make hybrids competitive with conventional gasoline-powered cars suggests that the subsidy may not be socially beneficial. It also raises a question as to whether future increases in technology will make hybrid cars competitive with conventionally powered autos. The crucial public policy problem is that temporary subsidies to enable a new technology to become established often become permanent subsidies, even when the new technology does not pan out.

Effects of Subsidies

Why Do Subsidies Lead to Overproduction and Overuse?

When production of an activity is subsidized, producers increase output. When a business enterprise is operating under competitive conditions—in which it has little ability to influence the market price—it will continue to produce an additional unit of the product as long as the expected return is greater than the cost of producing the unit. For example, if the cost of producing another widget is $10, but the widget can be sold for more than $10, it is profitable to produce the widget. But if it costs more—say, $12—than it can be sold for—say, $10—it is neither profitable nor socially beneficial to produce it. The profit and loss system in this way provides a check on wasteful production.

However, if the government subsidizes production, a business firm may find it profitable to produce and sell too much. In the above example, a subsidy of $3 per widget makes it profitable to produce and sell another unit for $10, even if it costs $12 to produce: $10 from the buyer plus $3 from the government is more than the cost of production. In this case, the government subsidy overrides the loss signal—the resources used in production are worth more than the value of the product! Agricultural subsidies are a good example. Government subsidies to farmers lead to overproduction. This also may be the case for ethanol, a substitute fuel for gasoline. The ethanol subsidy also illustrates how government subsidies generally are supported by vested interests. It is shown in the following section how small groups are able to maintain their transfer programs, regardless of whether they are beneficial to the public at large.

The Ethanol Subsidy

The far-reaching energy legislation enacted by the U.S. Congress in 2005 illustrates a number of issues related to producer subsidies. With higher petroleum prices and increased uncertainty about oil production in the Middle East, there was increased interest in biomass-derived fuels. Biomass refers to all bulk plant material. One of the first provisions of the 2005 legislation to take effect mandated an increase in the production and use of ethanol, currently made from corn or sugar. Gasohol, a mixture of gasoline and ethanol, is the primary fuel of this type.

Ethanol production recently has become a much more important public policy issue in the United States. However, interest in ethanol as an auto fuel is not new. Congress enacted legislation providing for subsidies for ethanol and other biomass-derived fuels more than 30 years ago, following the Arab oil embargo of 1973. The subsidy was in the form of exemptions from federal excise taxes, which have been in the range of 50 to 60 cents per gallon of ethanol. The subsidy amounted to more than $10 billion between 1979 and 2000. In 2005, more than 4 billion gallons of ethanol were used in gasohol in the United States out of a total gasoline pool of 1.22 trillion gallons. Corn farmers became staunch supporters of the ethanol program—no surprise because it increases the use and market price of corn.

Most energy experts believe that using corn to make ethanol is not an economically feasible substitute for gasoline. Although ethanol is sold to the public as a way to reduce dependence on oil, the net amount of oil saved by gasohol use, if any, is small. Indeed, widely cited research suggests that it may take more than a gallon of fossil fuel to make one gallon of ethanol. The growing, fertilization, and harvesting of corn and the fermentation and distillation processes that convert corn to ethanol require enormous amounts of fossil fuel energy. Although there is no consensus among energy experts as to whether ethanol production reduces dependence on fossil fuel, there is little doubt that ethanol subsidies are driven far more by congressional lobbying and farm-state politics rather than by the fact that it is a practical, long-term alternative to petroleum.

Why Are Subsidies Often Harmful?

Government subsidies were originally viewed as a grant of money or special privilege advantageous to the public. More often, however, as in the case of farm programs, subsidies work against the interests of the public at large because they lead to too much production; that is, the cost of production exceeds the value of the product produced. Moreover, the very process through which special interest groups gain an economic advantage through government legislation creates additional waste. Typically, as in ethanol production, a subsidy can be traced to so-called privilege-seeking behavior by those who stand to gain. Privilege seeking occurs when individuals or groups, such as corn farmers or sugar producers, attempt to influence the political process for their own financial benefit.

Why is privilege-seeking behavior harmful from the standpoint of the public at large? It is neither easy nor cheap to influence the political process—to obtain a government favor. Individuals and groups spend large amounts of time and money on campaign contributions, lobbying, and so on to obtain government subsidies. The time and money to influence the political process to obtain legislation that restricts competition is wasted, at least from the standpoint of consumers and taxpayers generally. The valuable resources used to obtain the subsidy could have been used to produce additional goods and services that would have benefited the public at large.

The sugar program is a prime example of how privilege-seeking behavior can lead to bad public policy. The sugar price support program raises sugar prices to U.S. producers of sugar cane and sugar beets by restricting imports of sugar from Brazil and other countries that can produce sugar more cheaply than the United States can. U.S. import quotas limit the amount of sugar coming into the United States from other countries and keep the domestic price of sugar in the United States higher than the world price of sugar—it has sometimes been twice as high. The cost of the sugar subsidy is borne largely by U.S. consumers and manufacturers of sugar products, who must pay much higher sugar prices than they would have to pay if there were no sugar program. This sugar tax, in the form of higher retail sugar prices, according to the General Accounting Office, costs U.S. consumers some $2 billion per year.

Who benefits from the sugar subsidy? It benefits relatively few U.S. farmers—growers of sugar beets, sugar cane, and corn—and domestic manufacturers of sugar substitutes. It should not be surprising that sugar interests donate large amounts of money to political candidates. The Florida cane-growing company Flo-Sun contributed $573,000 to candidates in recent elections. American Crystal, a sugar beet cooperative in the Red River Valley of North Dakota and Minnesota, donated $851,000 in the 2004 elections.

The sugar subsidy benefits corn farmers as well as sugar producers. How do corn farmers benefit from the sugar subsidy? The sugar price support program not only raises the price of sugar, it also spurs the development and production of sugar substitutes because it makes them more competitive with sugar. For example, U.S. consumption of corn-based sweeteners now is larger than that of refined sugar. The sugar subsidy is defended by lobbyists representing both corn farmers and producers of corn-based sweeteners. The added support for the sugar subsidy helps to maintain what almost all objective analysts agree is a bad public policy.

Why Not Just Abolish Bad Subsidies?

Why is it that getting rid of a harmful subsidy is easier said than done? A subsidy program may be proposed for a variety of reasons that are generally misleading and often erroneous. These arguments made by subsidy proponents quite often divert attention from the actual reason. For example, the sugar subsidy, which virtually all objective analysts agree raises the sugar price, is sold to the public as a way to stabilize the sugar market or prevent swings in sugar prices.

Consumers, of course, benefit when prices are low some of the time instead of being high all of the time, as they are under the sugar price support program. In reality, the sugar subsidy can be chalked up to favor seeking by producers of sugar and sugar substitutes.

The sugar program is a classic example of how a government program may last a long time, even though the number of consumers and taxpayers harmed is far, far larger than the number of individuals and business firms benefiting from the subsidy. The direct beneficiaries of the U.S. sugar subsidy, for example, are highly concentrated on the approximately 10,000 domestic producers of sugar and sugar substitutes. Each sugar cane and sugar beet farmer may benefit by thousands of dollars from the sugar subsidy. For example, a U.S. Department of Agriculture study reported that each one-cent increase in the sugar price was estimated to average $39,000 per sugarcane farm and $5,600 per sugar beet farm (Lord 1995).

The sugar subsidy program also is highly beneficial to the industry producing high fructose corn syrup, the sweetener used in many soft drinks. It should not be surprising that Washington lobbyists for corn refiners are highly effective advocates for the sugar subsidy. Archer Daniels Midland Corporation (ADM), a large agribusiness firm, for example, is a driving force behind the sugar lobby in the periodic congressional battles over sugar legislation. Although ADM does not directly produce sugar, it does produce high fructose corn syrup. As the sugar price increases, so does the demand for and price of high fructose corn syrup and other sugar substitutes.

The sugar subsidy creates a price umbrella under which ADM can profitably operate to produce the corn sweetener substitute. If there was no price support program for sugar, sugar prices in the United States would be much lower, and ADM probably would not be able to produce high fructose sweetener at a price low enough to compete with sugar. Since the benefits of the sugar subsidy are highly concentrated on a relatively small number of sugar farms and agribusiness firms, such as ADM, it is in their financial interest to make sure that well-paid lobbyists exert a lot of pressure in Congress to maintain the sugar subsidy.

While the benefits of the sugar subsidy are highly concentrated on a small number of producers of sugar and sugar substitutes, the cost of the sugar subsidy is divided among 300 million users of sugar in the United States. The average consumer uses about 100 pounds of sugar per year. Even if the sugar producer subsidy doubles the retail sugar price, the cost to the individual consumer is quite small (almost certainly less than $100 annually). What is the implication? Individuals supporting the sugar subsidy can afford to spend huge amounts of money lobbying Congress to maintain the sugar program, but individual consumers cannot afford to spend much time or money fighting the sugar program because the amount of money each spends on sugar is just too small. This is the main reason the United States sugar subsidy has lasted for decades, even though it is harmful not only to consumers buying sugar but to manufacturers using sweeteners in candy, cookies, and other food products as well.

Conclusion

The term *government subsidy* originally referred to a grant of money from the British Parliament to the king to finance military expenditures. Subsidy now refers to a wide range of government favors to business firms or individuals. Current subsidies often face widespread criticism, especially corporate welfare, a derisive term for subsidies made to large business corporations.

A subsidy program may be enacted to benefit individuals or business enterprises. Common subsidy programs to individuals include federal and state education subsidies, food stamps, rent subsidies, medical subsidies, school lunch subsidies, and subsidies to reduce energy use in autos and home heating and cooling systems. Business subsidy programs include subsidies to farmers, agribusiness firms, steel producers, auto producers, textile producers, sports teams, and so on.

While a subsidy may sometimes be warranted—that is, it is advantageous to the public at large—typically, this is not the case. Quite often, the cost of the output exceeds its value—too much is produced from the public's point of view. What explains the prevalence of harmful government subsidies? Most public subsidies can best be explained by favor seeking by narrowly focused producer and consumer groups who successfully further their own interests through the legislative process at the expense of the public at large. In other words, programs presumably enacted to further the public interest frequently transfer wealth from individual consumers and taxpayers to special interest groups—including the auto industry, airline industry, steel producers, textile producers, farmers, and ship builders—even when they are harmful to the public. Ethanol and sugar subsidy programs are prime examples.

In a democratic society operating on a one person–one vote basis, how can a small group of individuals or business firms obtain legislation that benefits them at the expense of the public at large? Economists, using public choice theory, a new subfield of economics, only recently have begun to understand this phenomenon. If the benefits of a subsidy are highly concentrated on a small group and the costs are widely dispersed over the entire population, as is often the case, the subsidy may be enacted and last for a long time. Consequently, the burden of proof for any subsidy should be on those who defend it. Citizens in a democratic society should question current and proposed government programs that confer benefits on particular business firms or individuals at the expense of the rest of society.

See also **Bank Bailouts; Corporate Tax Shelters; Election Campaign Finance; Interest Groups and Lobbying**

Further Reading

Hyman, David N., *Public Finance: A Contemporary Application of Theory to Policy,* 6th ed. Orlando, FL: Dryden Press, 1999.

Johnston, Mark C., *Free Lunch: How the Wealthiest Americans Enrich Themselves at Government Expense.* New York: Portfolio, 2007.

Lord, Ron, *Sugar: Background for 1995 Legislation.* Washington, DC: U.S. Department of Agriculture Economic Research Service, 1995.

Pasour, E. C., Jr., and Randal R. Rucker, *Plowshares and Pork Barrels: The Political Economy of Agriculture.* Oakland, CA: Independent Institute, 2005.

Peterson, E. Wesley F., *A Billion Dollars a Day: The Economics and Politics of Agricultural Subsidies.* Malden, MA: Wiley-Blackwell, 2009.

Sorkin, Andrew Ross, *Too Big to Fail: The Inside Story of How Wall Street and Washington Fought to Save the Financial System from Crisis—and Lost.* New York: Viking, 2009.

H

HEALTH CARE

Jennie Jacobs Kronenfeld

Health care is a complex issue. Many aspects of the health care system in the United States are in the process of change, partially because of the enactment of new legislation that modifies aspects of health care insurance in the United States. This new legislation has a goal of increasing access to health care through providing greater access to health care insurance among Americans and will be discussed in more detail at the end of this entry.

History and Background of the U.S. Health Care System

At one point in time, the U.S. health care system was dominated by physicians who worked in private practice as independent practitioners and was even described as a cottage industry since many physicians had their offices in their homes (Starr 1982). During that time period (up to 1900 at least and probably later), most people who had other options tried to avoid hospitals, because hospitals were viewed as a place to go to die for people with no other option and for people who were too poor to be able to remain in their homes. In addition, during the same time frame, there was not much care that could be provided for a person in the hospital that could not occur in the homes of people of economic means. This worked as the system for some period of time. Most people paid doctors as they received their care, and health insurance was not important for most people to obtain care. By 1900, there began to be some types of health insurance policies that people could purchase, often as a mix of coverage for actual health care costs and coverage for being out of work. Gradually, sick leave policies and disability policies replaced those aspects of health insurance, and health insurance became coverage for the major health care costs. Discussions grew about the need for people to have coverage. This related to improvements in medicine and surgery, so that surgery became safer and less scary through the use of anesthesia and an understanding of the need to control infection to facilitate safe recovery from surgery. New technologies such as X-ray machines also made the use of hospital services desirable, and people then wanted a way to pay the higher medical bills. During the presidency of Theodore Roosevelt, the first major attempt to pass some type of heath reform and health care coverage for many Americans occurred. During the same period, the efforts of the labor movement in the United States and such groups as the American Association for Labor also began, with these groups pushing health insurance programs mostly through state government efforts prior to World War I.

Push for Health Insurance from the 1920s to 1965

In 1921, a partial effort to provide health insurance coverage to mothers and children was passed: the Maternity and Infancy Act (also known as the Sheppard-Towner Act). This was a grant to states in the area of health and was an early successful effort to expand the role of the federal government into the provision of health care assistance to specialized groups of citizens. Although the goals of this program may seem simple and not controversial today, the program was very controversial in the 1920s and generated great criticism from conservative political groups and from the American Medical Association. The criticism was loud, and the commitment to the program by the political powers of the time was fairly limited, so the act was not renewed in 1929 and the program ceased to exist.

The idea of a Medicare program, or provision of health care insurance for the elderly, was rejected as part of the Social Security legislation in the 1930s because of opposition from the American Medical Association. Franklin Roosevelt wanted to be sure that the essential Social Security legislation creating an old-age pension system was enacted and quickly backed off from a Medicare-type provision when it became clear that it would be more controversial than the rest of the program and could potentially threaten the passage of the overall Social Security legislation. Although Medicare-type legislation continued to be introduced into most sessions of Congress once World War II ended, these pieces of legislation had little chance of success in the late 1940s and 1950s. Medicare did eventually pass, of course, in 1965 as part of the Great Society legislative efforts of President Lyndon Johnson. This program was created as a federally administered program, with the same benefits for all Social Security recipients regardless of which state they resided in. The program was designed to be similar to the health insurance that most working Americans had through their jobs at that time (although the latter was privately contracted between employers and insurers). At the same time, the Medicaid program that provided health coverage to selected groups of the poor was also passed, though as a federal-state joint program rather than as a national program. Over the past 40-plus years, both of these programs have become the major efforts of the government in the provision of health care insurance and health care services to parts of the U.S. population. They have also grown to be very complex programs, with many detailed and specific provisions and many important limitations that have been the subject of much critique and many policy debates. Both programs have changed and evolved a great deal.

Medicare, Medicaid, and Health Insurance for the Rest of the Population

Once Medicare was passed, the elderly had access to a health insurance plan that resembled what many working-age Americans had through their jobs, because a central goal of Medicare was to bring the elderly into the mainstream of U.S. medicine. Another basic assumption was that Medicare would provide all elderly with the same health insurance coverage, whatever a person's income level before retirement or after retirement. A third assumption of the architects of the basic Medicare legislation was that Medicare was the beginning of a government role in health insurance, perhaps a first step toward a more universal health insurance system. This did not really happen, with a few small exceptions such as adding coverage for people with kidney disease and then the extension of coverage to more children under the State Child Health Insurance Program (SCHIP) in the 1990s.

The basic coverage of Medicare was hospital coverage, known as Part A of Medicare, In addition, most people 65 and older also purchased Part B coverage for physician's fees. Social Security recipients pay for the Part B coverage, although the amount is deducted from their Social Security checks before they are issued so that some elderly do not know how much they pay for this coverage each month. The general premium in 2009 was $96.40 per month for most people, although the premium can be higher if the income of the person or couple is high enough. The costs of Medicare were higher than early estimates, and they continued to increase as the costs and complexities of health care increased and as the absolute numbers of people aged 65 and over increased. By the end of the first year of the operation of Medicare, 93 percent of the elderly (about 19 million people at that time in the United States) had enrolled in Part B. Beyond enrollment, usage of the program grew rapidly. By the end of the first year of operation, one in five of the elderly had entered a hospital using their Medicare benefits, and 12 million of the elderly had used Part B services. On average, about 80 percent of the hospital expenses of the group using hospital services were paid that year by Medicare.

There were some early implementation problems such as delays in payment to providers, especially during the first summer of operation. Fears about overcrowding of hospitals did not occur. Despite physician opposition to the program before it was passed, Medicare benefited physicians after its passage. Physicians initially received substantial income supplements from the Medicare program, and most physicians ended up being reimbursed for services they previously provided for free or at a reduced cost to the elderly before Medicare. In a variety of ways, costs ended up being higher than expected. In its early years, Medicare costs exceeded the actuarial projections that were made at the time of its passage. One explanation is that both hospital and doctor fees rose, partially because the arrangements for paying physicians were quite generous. There are estimates that physician fees initially rose 5 to 8 percent, and physician incomes went up 11 percent (Marmor 2000). Similar problems, perhaps even more serious, existed in the area of hospital prices. The Labor Department's consumer price survey showed that the average daily service charge in U.S. hospitals increased 21.9 percent in the first year of operation of Medicare. In 1968 and 1969, Medicare costs rose around 40 percent each year, leading to Medicare acquiring a reputation, both in Congress and in the administrative branch, as a program with a potential to be an uncontrollable burden on the federal budget.

One clear result of the first two years of experience was that the rise in medical costs did initially lead to increased interest in national health insurance. For example, in 1968, an organized labor–supported Committee for National Health Insurance was created, and the American Hospital Association announced that it planned to study the feasibility of a national health insurance plan. From 1965 to the present, the U.S. health care system has had a number of important changes, but one thing that has not changed greatly is that, except for people whose health insurance is provided through a government program such as Medicare or Medicaid, most people obtain their health insurance through their jobs.

Having good health insurance coverage has been one of the most basic indicators of access to health care in the United States since the end of World War II. Although estimates vary regarding the numbers of people uninsured and underinsured in the United States from the early 1980s to the present, most sources agree that there was an increase in the numbers of uninsured from the late 1970s to the early 1990s. In the late 1970s, the best estimates were that 25 million to 26 million people in the United States were without health care insurance, or about 13 percent of the population under 65. The numbers of uninsured grew in the 1980s. Estimates ranged from a low of 22 million to a high of 37 million by the late 1980s. In a review of statistics from 1980 to 1993, one source estimated that the uninsured population increased from 13 percent to 17 percent in that time period (Andersen and Davidson 1996). Medicaid coverage increased (from 6 percent to 10 percent) as part of some of the expansions already discussed, but coverage by private health insurance decreased (from 79 percent to 71 percent). The proportion covered by private health insurance decreased for every age group, and the decline was especially noticeable for children under 15.

Critical to understanding how some groups of people have no health insurance in U.S. society is the realization that most private health insurance in the United States is purchased through employer-based group insurance policies, representing 75 percent to 85 percent of all private coverage. One major factor in the increase in the number of uninsured during the 1980s and early 1990s was the growth in unemployment in the early 1980s and again in the early 1990s, as well as in the last few years. Those with a history of serious medical problems comprise another group of people with no insurance. Many people with serious health problems do maintain health insurance coverage as long as they keep their jobs. If they lose their jobs due to the general economy or their health but can still work, they may experience problems in finding employment due to their health. People who are medically uninsurable are a small part of those without health insurance, but they are important because they are very high utilizers of health services.

These kinds of issues have led at different points to calls for national health insurance reform. As various political issues shifted in the 1970s, no major national health insurance reform was passed. From the 1970s on, there have been a number of times when health care reform was a major topic of discussion and when expectations for the passage of some type of program were high, but the efforts did not succeed. In the Nixon administration, there was a major attempt to pass health insurance legislation, and many expected it to succeed, but Watergate and the political fallout from that scandal blew apart the attempt to create a Republican-Democratic consensus on reform legislation. When Jimmy Carter was elected president, there were planks in the Democratic party platform that called for major health care reform, but economic issues took center stage, and no program that had any realistic chance to pass was ever introduced into Congress at that time. The last major push for major health care reform before the Obama administration's current effort was the failed attempt by the Clinton administration to pass health care reform at the beginning of Bill Clinton's first term as president in 1993. After this, the Clinton administration focused on expanding coverage for children, which resulted in the passage of the SCHIP program. The only major health care coverage expansion during the George W. Bush administration was the expansion of Medicare to include drug coverage.

Recent Expansions of Publicly Funded Insurance: SCHIP and Changes in Medicare

Some important expansions have been passed in the last decade, especially the State Child Health Insurance Program, which has expanded the provision of government-provided health care insurance to the children of the working poor, and the drug coverage provision of the Medicare program, which has dealt with one major criticism and weakness of the Medicare program, the lack of inclusion of coverage for drugs.

In fall 1997, Congress passed the joint federal-state SCHIP as part of the Balanced Budget Act of 1997, which began in fiscal year 1999. As an expansion, this program focused on providing coverage to children, a group that previous surveys found was viewed

HEALTH CARE COSTS

A half century ago (1960), an average of $148 was spent by every person in the country on health care, and health care spending accounted for 5 percent of all spending in the economy. In 1980, these amounts had increased to $1,100 and 9 percent, and in 2008, they had jumped to $7,680 and 16 percent. The current amounts for the United States are higher than comparable measures in virtually all other countries.

While spending amounts will rise over time because of general inflation, the spending amounts above have been adjusted for general inflation, so we cannot blame the increase in health care spending on the general rise in prices.

Many citizens and policymakers look at the steady climb in health care expenditures and health care's share of the economy with alarm. Is it a result of waste in the health care system, meaning that all we need to do is eliminate the waste and health care costs will fall? Or are other factors at work that make the rise in health care expenditures more complicated and less ominous?

We Are Aging

One simple reason why health care spending is rising is that we are an aging population. In 1960, 9 percent of the population were aged 65 years or older, whereas in 2008, just over 12 percent were. It is a simple fact that older persons use more health care. People in their seventies spend more than 6 times more on health care than people in their twenties, thirties, and forties, and folks in their eighties spend 15 times more. Our aging population can account for as much as 25 percent of the increase in health care expenditures per person between 1960 and 2008.

However, this still leaves the majority of the rise in health care spending in recent decades owing to factors other than aging. What are they, and what do they imply for efforts to tame the health care money-eater?

Are We Getting More for Our Money?

An economic fact of life is that spending on any product or service equals the price charged per unit of the product or service multiplied by the number of units purchased. So, for example, if one hamburger has a price of $1, and you purchase 10 hamburgers, then your spending on hamburgers is $1 (per unit) times 10 (units), or $10.

Therefore, when we notice that total spending on health care is rising, the increase can occur because (1) the price per unit of health has risen, (2) the number of units of health care purchased has increased, or (3) a combination of both has occurred.

We already know that the number of units of health care purchased has been increasing due to the country's aging population. But the quality and scope of health care provided to the entire population also has been increasing. Modern health care, with its high-tech equipment and ever-increasing knowledge, can perform more operations, successfully treat more diseases, and extend healthy life spans to a much greater degree than ever

(*continued*)

(*continued*)

before. Stated another way, modern health care spending can do much more than health care spending in the past. The costs are greater, but so, too, are the benefits.

Some economists therefore argue that because modern health care is accomplishing so much more, its price per unit has actually fallen, and all of the increase in spending is because of the increased consumption of units of health care. Admittedly, while this is a difficult as well as controversial conclusion to reach, it does direct attention away from total spending to its components—price and both quantity and quality consumed.

Who Pays Matters

In the typical buying situation, a person evaluates the benefits of a product or service and then judges whether those benefits are greater than the price the person must pay to obtain the product or service. So if hamburgers cost $1 each, you will buy hamburgers up to the point where the last one bought gives you a benefit (satisfying your hunger or the enjoyment of eating) of $1. Since you are paying for the hamburgers, you have a big motivation to compare the costs and benefits of buying them. Usually, the initial units of a product or service give higher benefits than the later ones. So when the price of hamburgers is lower, you will buy more burgers.

What if someone else pays, or partially pays, for the burgers? Say the government subsidizes the cost of hamburgers at the rate of 50 cents per burger. This means that, for every burger with a price of $1, the government pays 50 cents and you pay 50 cents.

What will this do to the number of hamburgers you buy? It will certainly increase it. Now you will purchase burgers up to the point where the last one bought provides a benefit of only 50 cents. Maybe you will not eat all of them at once but take some home and save them for later. But the two important points to realize are that (1) you will buy more burgers and (2) the benefit of the burgers to you does not have to be as great as when you paid the entire bill.

What does this have to do with health care costs? Plenty. Health care costs faced by consumers are heavily subsidized in two ways. First, the government—primarily through Medicare and Medicaid—pays for almost half (45 percent) of all health care expenditures. Second, private insurance pays a little more than one-third (36 percent). This means that the consumer of health care only pays directly less than 15 cents on the dollar (14 percent) of its cost.

Of course, consumers pay for the government subsidy through taxes and for the insurance subsidy via insurance premiums. But there is no direct relationship between the amount of health care a person uses and the taxes he pays. Also, insurance premiums are first paid, and then health care is used later. So if there is any correspondence between the use of health care and insurance premiums, it certainly is not one to one.

What this means is that the heavy subsidization of health care has motivated people to use more health care. In fact, that is likely the purpose of the subsidization. Indeed, as the subsidization of health care has increased, so has spending on health care. Back in 1960, consumers directly paid for 60 percent of health care expenditures, and in 1980, their share was 30 percent. As the consumer's direct share has dropped, spending on health care has climbed—just as economists would predict.

Yet is it not a good thing that these subsidies encourage people to use more health care than they would have if they directly paid all the costs? Most people would answer yes, yet economists point out that there is an issue. When a person pays for all the health care she uses, this guarantees that every dollar spent on health care is perceived as at least being worth a dollar of benefits to her. When health care spending is subsidized, this is not the case—every dollar spent on health care is not necessarily worth a dollar of benefits to the person receiving the care.

This implies that health care may be overutilized. Tests, procedures, and medicines are being used that are valued at less than their cost to the consumer.

Consumers and society might be better off if some of that spending was redirected to other things, including preventive care, proper diet, exercise, and sleep.

—Michael L. Walden

Sources: Centers for Medicare and Medicaid Services, Department of Health and Human Services, *NationalHealthExpendData*. Table. http://www.cms.gov; Administration on Aging, Department of Health and Human Services, http://www.aoa.gov/; Centers for Disease Control, "Health, United States, 2009," http://www.cdc.gov/nchs/data/hus/hus09.pdf

by most of the public as an important group to have coverage for health care. When SCHIP was passed, around 10 million children under the age of 18 were estimated to be without health insurance coverage in the United States, or about 12 percent of children under the age of 18. Children in some parts of the country and some population groups were more likely to be without health insurance. This included children living in the South and the West, children living outside metropolitan areas, and Native American and Hispanic children, as well as the main target group of the legislation, children in lower income brackets. SCHIP represented the largest expansion of health coverage since the passage of the Medicare and Medicaid Program.

SCHIP has had some success in improving the insurance levels of children. By 1999, 23 percent of children were covered by public programs such as Medicaid and SCHIP, compared to only 11 percent in 1987, before SCHIP and some of the Medicaid expansions (Federal Interagency Forum on Child and Family Statistics 2001). SCHIP grew to be a major program, with the expenditures for the program totaling $2.1 billion in fiscal year 2000, or 0.8 percent of total state health care spending and 0.2 percent of all state spending. The program has continued growing. Estimates are that, since SCHIP was created in 1997, the number of uninsured low-income children in the United States has decreased by one-third. In 2006, 91 percent of children who were covered by SCHIP had incomes at or below 200 percent of the federal poverty level ($20,650 for a family of four in 2007). Combined with the Medicaid program that covers children in families with the lowest incomes, SCHIP and Medicaid provide health insurance coverage to one-quarter of all children in the United States and almost half of all low-income children.

There are important differences between SCHIP and Medicaid. Medicaid is a joint federal-state entitlement program in which federal funding increases automatically as health care costs and caseloads increase. In contrast, SCHIP is a block grant with a fixed annual funding level. The initial program was authorized for 10 years, and, to continue, the program needed reauthorization. There was a debate over this, and eventually only a continuing resolution let the program remain in place by the end of the Bush administration in 2008. Once Barack Obama became president, the reauthorization of the SCHIP program was the first piece of health legislation passed, signed on February 4, 2009. The signed bill reauthorized and expanded SCHIP to an additional 4 million children. In the new legislation, children in families with incomes of up to three times the federal poverty level will qualify for the program. The legislation also requires states to offer dental care through SCHIP and to provide equal coverage of mental and physical illnesses.

As mentioned, one major change in Medicare occurred during the Bush administration. There was growing concern about the rising costs of health insurance, but the major health-related effort in the second half of 2003 was a push for a Medicare reform bill. This passed at the end of November 2003 as, in some ways, a political compromise between Democrats and Republicans so that both sides could claim some success in improving Medicare as they ran for reelection. The law provided a new outpatient prescription drug benefit under Medicare beginning in 2006. In the interim, it created a temporary prescription drug discount card and transitional assistance program. The Part D drug option was a major addition to the Medicare program and partially dealt with what had been a major criticism of Medicare, the lack of drug coverage. Prior to the enactment of the Part D drug benefit, around one-third of seniors had no drug coverage. People without drug coverage generally had higher out-of-pocket costs and were less likely to fill prescriptions.

Medicare Part D is a prescription drug insurance plan that provides beneficiaries with prescription drug benefits. To receive these benefits, people must pay a monthly premium as part of enrolling in the plan and continue to pay it each year, or else they will have an interruption of coverage. People must choose among available plans in their state. The costs for the plans vary, as do the specific drugs that are covered. This potentially makes the choice confusing to consumers, and this was an initial concern. Because not every plan will cover the same drugs, people must search current medications for coverage under the Medicare Part D plans available to them. Although consumers were confused initially, most are now choosing to enroll in a plan (unless they have supplemental coverage through a retirement work-based plan or other supplemental plan that provides drug coverage that is as good as the typical Part D plan).

One concern about the plan is that there is a coverage gap; during this portion of spending, plans are not required to provide any coverage to beneficiaries. The gap, or doughnut hole, was created as a way to provide a large amount of coverage (75 percent) to most Medicare beneficiaries after the modest deductible but to hold down the cost of maintaining it throughout the year. For those with extremely high drug costs, catastrophic coverage resumes (once a person has spent over $4,550 on drug costs as of 2010) and covers the rest of one's drug expenditures in that year. The doughnut hole became one of the most controversial aspects of the Part D plan. One study found that, for the 12 percent of people who reached the Part D coverage gap, there was a decrease in essential medication usage. Zhang and colleagues (2009) found that those lacking coverage for drugs in the doughnut hole period reduced their drug use by 14 percent. The proportion of beneficiaries reaching the doughnut hole increased as the number of chronic conditions that a person has increased.

Both of these new programs or extensions to existing programs have been successful efforts at expansion of the role of the federal government in the provision of health insurance coverage to Americans. But both also have created new complexities in the case of drug coverage for those on Medicare and new variation in coverage across states in the case of SCHIP, since the program, as with the Medicaid program, is jointly administered at the federal and state levels and has some differences in eligibility and some differences in coverage across states.

The Need for Health Insurance Coverage and Obama Reforms

The lack of health insurance among a substantial group of Americans is not a new issue, but as the recession hit and more people lost jobs and younger people had trouble finding jobs initially, the issue of the link between employment and health care became clearer and problematic. Also, there were concerns for older people who either planned an early retirement before the age of 65 or who lost a job in their fifties and discovered how difficult it was, in a time of recession, to find new jobs with health insurance or to be able to purchase a private health insurance policy. For people who already had health problems, many insurance companies would not provide coverage for preexisting conditions.

There were also discussions about how programs such as Medicaid did not cover all of the poor and about the groups of people with low incomes who nevertheless earned too much or had too many assets to qualify for Medicaid in many states. The percentage of people in poverty has been increasing and was 13.2 percent in 2008, up from 12.5 percent in 2007. The number of people without health care insurance has been increasing over the past decade. About 39.8 million people had no insurance in 2000, and this increased to more than 45 million people with no coverage in 2005, a 13 percent increase from 2000. The number of people without health insurance coverage continued to rise, though not as rapidly, from 45.7 million in 2007 to 46.3 million in 2008, while the percentage of uninsured remained unchanged at 15.4 percent (DeNavas-Walt, Proctor, and Smith 2008). In addition, during this period, there was a decrease in employer-provided health care coverage, from 69 percent of employers providing coverage in 2000 to 60 percent in 2005. The number of people covered by all types of private health insurance continued to decrease from 2007 to 2008, with absolute numbers decreasing from 202 million to 201 million. The number covered by employment-based health insurance declined from 177.4 million to 176.3 million. Numbers of uninsured overall did not increase more, because the number covered by government health insurance climbed from 83 million to 87.4 million. These figures and concerns are the backdrop for some of the renewed push for health care reform after the election of Obama.

Shortly after the election, discussion began about health care reform. One initial approach of the Obama administration was to try and have Congress work through and develop the legislation. Partially, this was a reaction to the failure of the Clinton plan and the consensus that the administration in that case had become too involved in the details and Congress did not feel invested in the plan being developed. During 2009, some criticism of this approach arose, with people arguing that, to pass controversial, major legislation, the president had to become more involved. At one point, there was a feeling that Obama and the Democratic party would have the votes available to pass major legislation, especially given the conversion of the formerly Republican senator from Pennsylvania, Arlen Specter, to the Democratic party, which gave the Democrats a veto-proof majority in the Senate. Things moved slowly, however, and no legislation had been passed by the time of the elections in November 2009, when the Democratic Senate seat held for decades by Ted Kennedy in Massachusetts was open due to Kennedy's death. A shock occurred in that election, with a Republican capturing the seat. This meant that passage of the bill might not be possible without use of the so-called reconciliation approach, which required only a majority of votes (the Democrats still had 59 seats in the Senate). The initial Senate version of the bill was passed in late 2009. The U.S. House of Representatives passed the bill to reform health care in March 2010 by a vote of 220 to 211. The House also passed a bill, which then was sent back to the Senate to modify some versions of the Senate bill. That bill was also passed in March 2010. The bill was signed by President Obama on March 23, 2010.

When fully phased in, the legislation will cover around 32 million Americans who are currently uninsured. Major coverage expansion begins in 2014, with exchanges being created and the requirement that most people have health insurance. Beginning in 2010, insurers must remove lifetime dollar limits on policies, and some subsidies to small businesses to provide coverage to employees will become available. Insurance companies will be barred from denying coverage to children with preexisting conditions. Children will be allowed to stay on their parents' insurance policies until their 26th birthday.

Gradually, a number of other changes will be put into place. Medicaid will be expanded, the doughnut hole in the Medicare drug plan will gradually disappear, and certain preventive services in Medicare will be available without a copayment. There will be reductions in Medicare advantage plan payments that will help to extend the life of the Medicare trust fund. An independent advisory board will be created to make recommendations for other cost savings. The legislation will establish the Community First Choice Option, which will create a state plan option under section 1915 of the Social Security Act to provide community-based attendant supports and services to individuals with disabilities who are Medicaid eligible and who require an institutional level of care, to try and begin to deal with some of the needs of the elderly and disabled for less intensive community-based services. There will be the creation of some demonstration programs for certain types of home care and modifications to some of the rules for nursing homes that receive Medicare payments. A number of new taxes and fees—some on people through Medicare taxes and others on drug makers and employers—will begin in various years, such as 2011 for drug makers and fines on employers mostly beginning in 2014. Taxes on high-cost health plans will not begin until 2017.

Continuing Concerns and Unresolved Issues

Although there are high hopes that the new reforms in health insurance—a more accurate description of the Obama changes than "health care reform"—will lower the rates of the uninsured, many problems were not dealt with. In much of the discussion, there was talk of a public option, a way to be sure that there was an affordable option for everyone. This did not end up in the legislation, and, while insurance companies will have to offer coverage to a person and there will be health care exchanges, there is not a limit on what can be charged, so costs of health insurance may not be well controlled. In addition, the bill has few mechanisms in place to control rising costs of health care and of drugs, so that some experts fear that, as happened with the passage of Medicare and Medicaid in the 1960s, costs will increase and there will be need for additional reforms to deal with costs. Some issues in Medicare were dealt with (the doughnut hole in the drug plan and some beginnings of experimentation with aspects of long-term care), but the major issue of long-term care for the elderly, a growing program as the large baby boom group in the population begins to age, is not really covered. How the new taxes will actually work and how fines and mechanisms to ensure that all people purchase coverage remain to be seen as the different provisions of the Obama plan come into effect in future years.

See also **Interest Groups and Lobbying; Prescription Drug Costs; Social Security**

Further Reading

Andersen, Ronald M., and Pamela L. Davidson, "Measuring Access and Trends." In *Changing the U.S. Health Care Delivery System*, ed. by Ronald M. Andersen, Thomas H. Rice, and Gerald F. Kominski. San Francisco: Jossey-Bass, 1996.

DeNavas-Walt, Carmen, Bernadette D. Proctor, and Jessica C. Smith, *Income, Poverty, and Health Insurance Coverage in the United States: 2007.* U.S. Census Bureau, Current Population Reports, P60–235, Washington, DC: U.S. Government Printing Office, 2008.

Federal Interagency Forum on Child and Family Statistics, *America's Children: Key National Indicators of Well-Being, 2001.* www.ncjrs.gov/pdffiles1/ojjdp/188155.pdf

Greenwald, Howard P., *Health Care in the United States: Organization, Management, Policy.* San Francisco: Jossey-Bass, 2010.

Kronenfeld, Jennie Jacobs, *Expansion of Publicly Funded Health Insurance in the United States: The Children's Health Insurance Program and Its Implications.* Lanham, MD: Lexington Books, 2006.

Kronenfeld, Jennie Jacobs, and Michael Kronenfeld, *Health Care Reform in America.* Santa Barbara, CA: ABC-CLIO, 2004.

Marmor, Theodore H., *The Politics of Medicare,* 2d ed. New York: Aldine De Gruyer, 2000.

Quadagno, Jill, *One Nation Uninsured: Why The U.S. Has No National Health Insurance.* New York: Oxford University Press, 2005.

Skocpol, Theda, *Protecting Soldiers and Mothers: The Political Origins of Social Policy in the United States.* Cambridge, MA: Harvard University Press, 1992.

Starr, Paul, *The Social Transformation of American Medicine: The Rise of a Sovereign Profession and the Making of a Vast Industry.* New York: Basic Books, 1982.

Zhang, Yuting, Julie Marie Donohue, Joseph P. Newhouse, and Judith R. Lave, "The Effects of the Coverage Gap on Drug Spending: A Closer Look at Medicare Part D." *Health Affairs* 28, no. 2 (2009): w317–w325.

I

IMMIGRANT WORKERS

Kenneth Louie

Immigration policy in the United States has become a highly contentious issue, one that is likely to play an increasingly important role in affecting electoral outcomes at the local, state, and national levels. Currently, members of the U.S. Congress as well as elected public officials in locales across the country are embroiled in an emotionally charged debate over the immigration issue. The country will eventually have to grapple with a host of concerns, but some of the key policy areas of contention include how to control unauthorized (illegal) immigration into the United States, how to resolve the status of the illegal aliens who are already working in the United States, whether we should establish a so-called guest worker program that will allow foreigners to work in the United States temporarily, and whether, on balance, immigrant workers have a positive or negative economic effect on native U.S. workers.

Many Americans believe that, as a nation, we should continue to uphold the principle of openness so eloquently captured by the words at the Statue of Liberty: "Give me your tired, your poor, your huddled masses, yearning to breathe free." These individuals also contend that immigrants contribute positively to the economic, political, and social vitality of the country. Many other Americans, on the other hand, believe that uncontrolled immigration, especially of the illegal kind, will create significant adverse economic consequences for the nation that may spill over into the political and social arenas.

It is interesting to note that some of the elements in the current debate are not new. In the 1980s, for example, U.S. officials faced increasing political pressure to do something about the growing number of unauthorized workers from Mexico and to counteract the widespread perception that U.S. employers who hired illegal aliens were seldom prosecuted. In response, Congress passed the Immigration Reform and Control Act (IRCA) of 1986. Although the IRCA was intended to strengthen enforcement by imposing penalties on U.S. employers who knowingly hired undocumented workers, it did not succeed in significantly reducing illegal immigration, partly due to underfunding of the enforcement efforts and the widespread use of fraudulent documents by unauthorized workers (Martin and Midgley 2003). IRCA also addressed the question of how to treat illegal immigrants who were already in the country, another issue that is looming large in the current debate, essentially by granting legal status to 2.7 million unauthorized foreigners in the United States. Another revision of the immigration system was tried in 2005–2006 but failed to pass. While many facets of the current immigration debate have historical antecedents, it remains to be seen how the United States will address this important issue as the second decade of the 21st century progresses.

Arguments for and against Immigration

Advocates on both sides of the immigration issue have at one time or another put forth arguments based on history, philosophy, politics, culture, or religion in support of their cause. For example, one of the common arguments put forth by advocates of an open immigration policy is that, since its founding, the United States has always been a nation of immigrants, and the country should therefore maintain its immigrant heritage by continuing to welcome foreigners to its shores. Other advocates of unrestricted immigration maintain that, by introducing greater diversity, immigration strengthens and enriches the United States' political, social, and cultural institutions. Religious organizations, such as the Roman Catholic Church, are generally in favor of unrestricted immigration because of humanitarian reasons and sometimes issue official pronouncements opposing barriers to human migration.

Those in favor of restricting immigration have argued that the changing ethnic composition of the U.S. immigrant population (which, as will be documented subsequently, is becoming increasingly Hispanic and Asian) will pose difficult political challenges, such as deciding whether to offer bilingual education in public schools. A related argument is that, unless assimilation into the society on the part of immigrants occurs quickly and smoothly, the increased ethnic diversity associated with a rapidly changing immigrant population may weaken the social and cultural fabric that unites the country. It is interesting to note that even Benjamin Franklin expressed concern about the rate of assimilation by German immigrants into U.S. society in the late 18th century by asking, "Why should Pennsylvania, founded by the English, become a colony of aliens, who will shortly become so numerous as to Germanize us, instead of our Anglifying them?" (Degler 1970, 50). Proponents of immigration restrictions also point to the additional political challenge of having to deal with increasingly severe strains placed on the health care and law enforcement systems as a result of high levels of immigration. Of course, superimposed on all these arguments for restricting immigration are the concerns for national security that arose after the terrorist attacks on the United States on September 11, 2001.

But perhaps the most controversial, and hence most scrutinized, arguments put forth by advocates on both sides of the debate are the ones concerning the economic impact of immigration. Those who advocate open borders argue that immigration is economically beneficial both to the immigrants and to the native U.S. population. For example, when immigrants come to the United States from other comparably developed countries, mutual benefits come in the form of new ideas generated from human interaction that ultimately lead to economic growth and higher standards of living for all. According to the proponents of unrestricted immigration, even immigrants who come to the United States from poorer countries benefit from the higher U.S. standard of living at the same time that they contribute to the output, or gross domestic product (GDP), of the U.S. economy.

In contrast, those who argue for restrictions on immigration contend that immigrant workers create significant negative effects for the U.S. economy. For example, in labor markets where immigrants compete for the same jobs with native-born workers, the earnings and employment opportunities of native-born workers will both be reduced. Additionally, immigrants may create net fiscal burdens for governments at the national, state, and local levels if they contribute less in tax revenues compared to their drain on government resources.

Evidence on the Economic Effects of Immigration

Because such a big part of the debate centers on the economic impact of immigration, it is not surprising that economists have conducted extensive research into this very question (see, e.g., Borjas 1994). So what does the empirical evidence tell us?

Studies in the late 1970s seemed to suggest an optimistic outcome for immigrant workers in the United States. Specifically, researchers reported that immigrants were able to achieve earnings comparable to those of native-born workers with similar socioeconomic characteristics within a relatively short time. Indeed, the rapid rise of their earnings implied that many immigrant workers appeared to earn more than comparable native-born U.S. workers within one or two decades after entering the United States. Furthermore, these earlier studies did not provide any strong evidence that immigrant workers reduced the employment opportunities of native-born workers. Consequently, the empirical findings up until the mid-1980s were consistent with the view that immigration was mutually beneficial to immigrant workers (because of their very steep earnings profiles) as well as to the U.S. economy (because of the additional output and income generated).

Starting in the mid-1980s, however, a somewhat different picture emerged as economists conducted new research studies as well as reassessed earlier ones. Partly as a result of discovering methodological weaknesses in some of the earlier studies and applying more elaborate statistical techniques to new data sets, economists began to revise their views on the economic impact of immigration.

For example, especially in light of the fact that the skill levels of immigrants into the United States were shown to have been declining during the postwar years, the new view was that recent immigrants were unlikely to achieve the same earnings levels as native-born workers, even over the entire course of their working years. Moreover, many of the new research studies concluded that immigration may in fact have lowered the earnings of unskilled native-born U.S. workers during the 1980s, although the magnitude of the effect appears to be small. The consensus at present seems to be that immigration has reduced the wages of low-skilled U.S. workers, especially those without a high school degree, by about 1–3 percent (Orrenius 2006).

In addition to these labor market effects, immigration may also create fiscal impacts on government budgets. For instance, highly skilled immigrants in the technology, science, and health fields have a significant positive effect on the U.S. economy not only through their contributions to the nation's GDP but also through their contributions to tax revenues. Because so much attention is focused on illegal or low-skilled immigrant workers, it may be surprising to many that about 40 percent of the doctoral scientists and engineers in the United States are foreign-born immigrants (Orrenius 2006). These foreign-born workers are likely to create a net fiscal benefit for the U.S. economy.

The net fiscal impact of low-skilled immigrant workers is less certain, however. While these immigrants still contribute to the nation's output, they may have a negative fiscal impact if they draw on more public services, such as education and health care, compared to their tax contributions. Furthermore, the distribution of the fiscal burden of these immigrants may become an important policy issue, since most of the fiscal benefits (in the form of employment taxes) go to the federal government, while much of the cost (such as health care and educational expenses) must be borne by state and local governments. Recent studies suggest that, overall, legal immigrants and their descendants actually end up paying more in taxes compared to what they receive in government benefits, with the difference (measured over the course of the immigrants' lifetimes) estimated at about $80,000 per immigrant (Smith and Edmonston 1997; Lee and Miller 2000).

What about the economic effects of *illegal* immigration? In the current debate, there is much concern that illegal immigration has unambiguous negative fiscal effects in the U.S. economy. But there are several reasons why this may not be the case. For example, illegal immigrants may contribute less to government tax revenues (although they may still have to pay payroll and sales taxes, which are hard to avoid). But illegal immigrants are also ineligible for many government programs such as Social Security and unemployment insurance. Therefore, illegal immigrants do not necessarily create a net fiscal burden. Indeed, since illegal immigrants enter the United States primarily to work, lured

BRIEF HISTORY OF U.S. IMMIGRATION POLICY

1776–1880s: Period of Openness

For almost 100 years after achieving independence, the United States adhered to a policy of virtually unrestricted immigration. As a result, immigration increased steadily, especially after 1840, due to industrial and political transformations that started to occur in the United States and Europe.

1880s–1920s: Period of Restrictiveness

Beginning in 1880s, the United States began to restrict immigration by certain types of foreigners. These early restrictions reduced the flow of immigrants briefly, but immigration picked up again and reached a peak in the first decade of the 20th century. In 1921, Congress passed the Quota Law, which set annual quotas for immigration on the basis of national origin. Partly driven by fears that the influx of unskilled immigrants from Eastern and Southern Europe would negatively affect native-born U.S. workers, the quota system favored immigrants from Northern and Western Europe instead.

1960s–1990s: Period of Reform

In 1965, Congress passed the McCarran-Walter Immigration and Nationality Act (INA), which eliminated the quota system based on national origin. Instead, the INA, which was amended in 1990, set immigration quotas based on the following purposes: (1) family reunification, (2) the need for professional and high-skilled workers from abroad, and (3) increasing so-called diversity immigrants from historically underrepresented countries. No limits were placed on political refugees who faced the risk of persecution in their home countries.

In 1986, Congress passed the Immigration Reform and Control Act (IRCA), which granted legal status to 2.7 million illegal immigrants who were already working in the country. IRCA was also intended to discourage future illegal immigration by imposing sanctions on employers who knowingly hired illegal aliens.

The rapid growth of technology led Congress to pass the Immigration Act of 1990, which authorized the Immigration and Naturalization Service to issue 60,000 H-1B visas each year to applicants with higher education in an effort to attract high-skilled workers to the United States. The number of H-1B visas was increased to 115,000 for 2000.

1996 to Present: Period of Safeguarding National Security

In 1996, Congress passed three laws relating to immigration: the Antiterrorism and Effective Death Penalty Act, the Personal Responsibility and Work Opportunity Reconciliation Act, and the Illegal Immigration Reform and Immigrant Responsibility Act. These laws were intended to prevent terrorist acts as well as to address the issue of welfare eligibility for legal immigrants.

In 2001, in response to the September 11 terrorist attacks, Congress passed the Uniting and Strengthening America by Providing Appropriate Tools Required to Intercept and Obstruct Terrorism (USA PATRIOT) Act, which provided funds for additional border

(continued)

(*continued*)
security and gave the U.S. attorney general the authority to detain foreigners who were deemed to pose potential risks to national security.

In 2005–2006 and again in 2010, lawmakers struggled to reform the immigration system by balancing social and economic arguments in favor of increased immigration against security issues and other arguments against immigration. The first effort (2005–2006) failed, but the second (in 2010) gained traction—in both directions—after the state of Arizona passed a restrictive law permitting police officers to stop and question anyone suspected of being in the country illegally.

by the prospects of a higher standard of living, they contribute to the output and economic growth of the country. All these considerations lead some analysts to argue that illegal immigrants may very well make a net positive contribution to the U.S. economy (Ehrenberg and Smith 2006).

Some Key Immigration Policy Issues

Although immigration reform is currently (mid-2010) in a state of flux, President Barack Obama has stated that he is in favor of making changes to the system. He has called for continued enforcement of existing immigration laws at the borders and at the same time has urged lawmakers to explore a guest worker program or something similar to it in order to address the issue of unauthorized foreigners who are already working here. Under the proposed guest worker program from 2005 to 2006, for example, unauthorized foreign-born individuals in the United States with jobs would have had the opportunity to apply for legal immigrant status after working in the country for 6 years and to apply for U.S. citizenship after 11 years. As the new administration takes up this issue, any such specifics could, of course, change.

Another key issue is employer verification of their immigrant workers' legal status. In 2005, for example, a bill passed by the U.S. House of Representatives (but never signed into law) required that all employers submit the Social Security and immigration numbers of their new workers to the relevant government agencies within three days of hiring them. Employers who did not follow these procedures or who otherwise violated immigration laws would, under the bill, be subject to substantial fines up to $25,000. Unauthorized presence in the United States would become a felony, jeopardizing the chances of those who are currently illegal immigrants in the United States to become guest workers or legal residents in the future. One provision of the bill also stipulated penalties of up to five years in prison for those who shield illegal immigrants from apprehension or prosecution by authorities.

In addition to the House bill, the U.S. Senate passed legislation in May 2006 (but again never signed into law) that would have allowed illegal immigrants then living in the United States for five years or more (about 7 million people) an opportunity to apply for citizenship if they continued to maintain a job, adequately passed background checks, paid up all past fines and back taxes, and enrolled in English classes. Illegal immigrants who lived in the country for two to five years (about 3 million people) would have been required to leave the country briefly and apply for a temporary work visa before returning to the United States as a guest worker. They would eventually be given the opportunity to apply for permanent residency and then U.S. citizenship. Illegal immigrants who lived in the country for less than two years (about 1 million people) would have been required to leave the United States completely but were eligible to apply for the proposed guest worker program (Swarns 2006).

Clearly, the issues of establishing a guest worker program, creating a "path to citizenship" for those who are now in the country unlawfully, expecting employers to share in the responsibility of verifying the status of their employees, and maintaining effective law enforcement with respect to illegal immigration will all form a part of any ensuing House and Senate debates as the matter of reforming immigration is considered anew under the Obama administration.

Some Basic Statistics on the U.S. Immigrant Population

As noted previously, a big part of the immigration debate centers around the impact of immigration on native U.S. workers as well as on how to stem the tide of illegal immigration. So just what are the facts concerning the extent of immigration, both legal and illegal?

The total number of foreign-born residents in the United States in 2005 was estimated to be in the range of 36 to 37 million, making up approximately 12 percent of the country's overall population. This total figure includes 11.5 million individuals who were naturalized U.S. citizens, 10.5 million who were legal immigrants, and between 11 and 12 million who were unauthorized immigrants (Martin 2006). Of course, the current number of foreign-born residents in the United States is the result of annual immigrant flows that have entered the country over the course of many years. Table 1 shows the number of immigrants that have legally entered the United States in each decade since 1821. As Table 1 indicates, immigrant flows into the United States rose steadily throughout the 19th and early 20th centuries, reflecting the nation's essentially open-door immigration policy during its first 100 years of independence. (During this period, the only groups who were subject to significant immigration restrictions were convicted criminals and individuals from Asia; see Ehrenberg and Smith 2006.) While the absolute number of immigrants grew, especially after 1840, the annual rate of immigrant entry for any decade never exceeded 10 per 1,000 U.S. population until the beginning of the 20th century. The U.S. immigration rate reached a peak of 10.4 per 1,000 U.S. population (an annual rate of more than 1 percent of the population) during the first decade of the 20th century, after which it has been declining. Thus, although many who are involved

TABLE 1. Immigration to the United States, 1821–2009

Time Period	Number of Immigrants	Annual Rate (per 1,000 U.S. Population)
1821–1830	143,439	1.2
1831–1840	599,125	3.9
1841–1850	1,713,251	8.4
1851–1860	2,598,214	9.3
1861–1870	2,314,824	6.4
1871–1880	2,812,191	6.2
1881–1890	5,246,613	9.2
1891–1900	3,687,564	5.3
1901–1910	8,795,386	10.4
1911–1920	5,735,811	5.7
1921–1930	4,107,209	3.5
1931–1940	528,431	0.4
1941–1950	1,035,039	0.7
1951–1960	2,515,479	1.5
1961–1970	3,321,677	1.7
1971–1980	4,493,314	2.0
1981–1990	7,338,062	3.1
1991–2000	9,095,417	3.4
2001–2009	9,488,544	3.0

Source: U.S. Department of Homeland Security, Yearbook of Immigration Statistics, 2009. Table 1. April 2010. http://www.dhs.gov/files/statistics/publications/LPR09.shtm

in the current debate often refer to the so-called unprecedented surge in immigration, it is important to remember that the percentage of the U.S. population that is foreign born was actually higher in 1910 (at 15 percent) than it is today (at 12 percent) (Martin and Midgley 2003).

One important feature of immigration into the United States is the gradual change over time in the countries of origin of the immigrants. Between the 1960s and the 1990s, the percentage of legal immigrants who were from Europe fell to 13 percent from 40 percent. During the same period, the percentage of immigrants from Latin America increased to 51 percent from 38 percent, while the percentage from Asia increased to 30 percent from 11 percent.

Because a large part of the current debate on immigration centers on the economic impact of immigrants, it is instructive to look at some statistics from the U.S. government's Current Population Survey that reveal some interesting demographic and economic characteristics of the foreign-born population in the United States.

The average age of foreign-born residents in the United States who worked full-time for at least part of the year in 2001 was 39 years, compared to an average age of 41 years for U.S.-born workers. As a group, foreign-born residents accounted for almost 15 percent of all U.S. workers who were employed full-time for at least part of the year in 2001; however, median annual earnings were $24,000 for foreign-born workers, compared to $31,200 for U.S.-born workers. In addition to the changes in the countries of origin, there have been changes in the demographic and economic profiles of recent U.S. immigrants. The foreign-born residents who came to the United States after 1990 tend, on average, to be younger (average age of 32 years), less educated (34 percent do not have a high school diploma compared to 16 percent of U.S.-born residents), and have lower median earnings ($20,000). In 2002, about 16 percent of the foreign-born population earned incomes that were below the official poverty line compared to 11 percent of U.S.-born residents. Almost a quarter (24 percent) of U.S. households that were headed by foreign-born residents received a means-tested federal benefit (i.e., one that uses income level to determine eligibility, such as Medicaid) in 2001 compared to 16 percent of households that were headed by U.S.-born residents (Schmidley 2003; Camarota 2002).

The Extent of Illegal Immigration

For purposes of immigration policy, the U.S. government considers foreigners who are in the country without a valid visa and who are therefore violating U.S. immigration laws to be unauthorized immigrants (also called undocumented or illegal immigrants). It is estimated that 850,000 foreigners entered the United States without authorization in 2005, while other illegal immigrants left the country, became legalized residents, or passed away, so that, on balance, the number of unauthorized foreigners in the United States increased by 400,000 during the year (Passel 2006). It is estimated that anywhere between 350,000 and 500,000 illegal immigrants enter and reside in the United States each year, while many others enter to stay temporarily and then leave within the same year. The U.S. Immigration and Naturalization Service reported 1.4 million apprehensions of illegal aliens in 2001 (an individual may be apprehended more than once during the year for trying to enter illegally, and each incident is reported as a separate apprehension) (Martin and Midgley 2003). And in 2005, 1.2 million individuals were apprehended just along the U.S.-Mexico border (Bailey 2006).

A big reason why illegal immigration into the United States has generated so much concern and controversy is that it has grown dramatically in recent years. In fact, it is estimated that most of the illegal immigrants came to the United States during the last decade: two-thirds have been in the United States for less than 10 years, and 40 percent have been here for less than 5 years. Most of these unauthorized foreigners come from three major regions of the world: over half (56 percent) come from Mexico, 22 percent come from Latin America, and 13 percent come from Asia. Six percent of illegal immigrants in the United States come from Europe, and 3 percent come from Africa and elsewhere in the world (Passel 2006; Bailey 2006).

Table 2 shows the estimated size of the unauthorized resident population in the United States as well as the 10 states with the largest number of unauthorized foreigners in 1990 and 2000. As Table 2 indicates, the total number of unauthorized foreigners in the United States doubled in the decade from 1990 to 2000, from 3.5 million to an estimated 7 million individuals. Since it is estimated that 11–12 million unauthorized immigrants were residing in the United States in 2005, this means that the number of illegal immigrants increased by another 55–70 percent in the five-year period from 2000 to 2005 alone.

Unauthorized foreigners are not distributed evenly across the country, however. For instance, the top 10 states with the largest number of unauthorized residents accounted for almost 80 percent of the total unauthorized population in the United States in 2000 (Table 2). While California and Texas experienced the largest increase in the absolute

TABLE 2. Estimated Unauthorized Resident Population, Top 10 States, 1990 and 2000

State of Residence	Estimated Unauthorized Resident Population (thousands)*			Percent of Total Unauthorized Population		U.S. Population, 2000 Census	
	1990	2000	Percent Change, 1990–2000	1990	2000	Total Population in 2000 (thousands)*	Percent Unauthorized
All States	3,500	7,000	100.0	100.0	100.0	281,422	2.5
California	1,476	2,209	49.7	42.2	31.6	33,872	6.5
Texas	438	1,041	137.7	12.5	14.9	20,852	5.0
New York	357	489	37.0	10.2	7.0	18,976	2.6
Illinois	194	432	122.7	5.5	6.2	12,419	3.5
Florida	239	337	41.0	6.8	4.8	15,982	2.1
Arizona	88	283	221.6	2.5	4.0	5,131	5.5
Georgia	34	228	570.6	1.0	3.3	8,186	2.8
New Jersey	95	221	132.6	2.7	3.2	8,414	2.6
North Carolina	26	206	692.3	0.7	2.9	8,049	2.6
Colorado	31	144	364.5	0.9	2.1	4,301	3.3
Total, top 10 states	2,978	5,590	87.7	85.1	79.9	136,182	4.1
All other states	522	1,410	170.1	14.9	20.1	145,240	1.0

*The population figures shown must be multiplied by 1,000. Thus, for example, 3,500 becomes 3.5 million.

number of unauthorized foreigners, the states that showed the largest percentage increase over the last decade were North Carolina, Georgia, and Colorado.

Of the 11–12 million unauthorized immigrants in the United States in 2005, it is estimated that about 7.2 million were in the labor force, accounting for almost 5 percent of all U.S. workers. Unauthorized foreign-born workers make up at least one-fifth of the total work force in each of the following labor categories: agricultural workers (29 percent), grounds maintenance (25 percent), construction laborers (25 percent), maids (22 percent), painters (22 percent), cooks (20 percent), and hand packers (20 percent) (Passel 2006). Additionally, and perhaps somewhat contrary to popular perception, it is estimated that 20 percent of computer hardware engineers in the United States are illegal immigrants (Bailey 2006).

Conclusion

Immigration is an important national issue worthy of serious and objective discussion. Given the many controversial aspects surrounding the nation's immigration policy, it is inevitable that there will be disagreement and highly unlikely that any single comprehensive reform measure will satisfy the preferences of all who are engaged in the debate. Indeed, the debate over immigration policy has gone on for a long time and will likely continue with every change in domestic or international circumstances. The important thing to keep in mind is that any immigration policy should carefully balance the interests of all those who will be affected by the policy since the livelihood and standard of living of millions of individuals, both native and foreign-born, will be affected.

See also **Immigration and Employment Law Enforcement (vol. 2); Immigration Reform (vol. 3)**

Further Reading

Bacon, David, *Illegal People: How Globalization Creates Migration and Criminalizes Immigrants.* Boston: Beacon Press, 2008.

Bailey, Holly, "A Border War." *Newsweek* (April 3, 2006): 22–25.

Borjas, George J., "The Economics of Immigration." *Journal of Economic Literature* 32 (1994): 1667–1717.

Borjas, George J., *Heaven's Door: Immigration Policy and the American Economy.* Princeton, NJ: Princeton University Press, 2001.

Camarota, Steven A., "Immigrants in the United States—2002." *Backgrounder* (November 2002). http://www.cis.org

Degler, Carl N., *Out of Our Past: The Forces that Shaped Modern America,* 2d ed. New York: Harper & Row, 1970.

Ehrenberg, Ronald G., and Robert S. Smith, *Modern Labor Economics: Theory and Public Policy.* Boston: Pearson Addison-Wesley, 2006.

Lee, Ronald, and Timothy Miller, "Immigration, Social Security, and Broader Fiscal Impacts." *American Economic Review* 90 (2000): 350–354.

Martin, Philip, *The Battle over Unauthorized Immigration to the United States*. 2006. http://www. prb.org/Articles/2006/TheBattleOverUnauthorizedImmigrationtotheUnitedStates.aspx

Martin, Philip, and Elizabeth Midgley, "Immigration: Shaping and Reshaping America." *Population Bulletin* 58 (2003): 30–31.

Orrenius, Pia, "On the Record: The Economics of Immigration." *Southwest Economy* (March/April, 2006).

Passel, Jeffrey, *The Size and Characteristics of the Unauthorized Migrant Population in the United States*. Research Report 61. Washington, DC: Pew Hispanic Center, 2006.

Schmidley, Dianne, "The Foreign-Born Population in the United States: March 2003." *Current Population Reports* 20 (2003).

Smith, James P., and Barry Edmonston, eds., *The New Americans: Economic, Demographic, and Fiscal Effects of Immigration*. Washington, DC: National Academy Press, 1997.

Stout, Robert Joe, *Why Immigrants Come to America: Braceros, Indocumentados, and the Migra*. Westport, CT: Praeger, 2008.

Swarns, Rachel L., "Senate, in Bipartisan Act, Passes an Immigration Bill." *New York Times* (May 26, 2006). http://www.nytimes.com

INCOME TAX, PERSONAL

David N. Hyman

All working Americans are familiar with the April 15 deadline for filing personal income tax returns. Taxes on personal income accounted for 44 percent of total revenue raised by the federal government in the United States in 2009. All but seven state governments also tax personal income, which now accounts for 30 percent of state revenue. Many view income as a good measure of ability to pay taxes, and the income tax enjoys broad political support in the United States. However, it is also reviled as having become incredibly complex, and there are continual calls to reform the income tax to make it fairer and simpler and to reduce the distortions it causes in economic decision making.

To understand the impact of the income tax on our decisions and the way its burden is distributed among taxpayers, it is first necessary to define the concept of income.

What Is Income?

Income is a flow of purchasing power from earnings of labor, capital, land, and other sources that a person receives over a period of one year. The most comprehensive definition of income views it as an annual acquisition of rights to command resources. Income can be used to consume goods and services during the year it is received, or it can be stored up for future use in subsequent years. Income stored up for future use is saving, which increases a person's net worth (a measure of the value of assets less debts). The most comprehensive measure of income views it as the sum of annual consumption plus savings, where savings is any increase in net worth that can result from not spending

TAX EXPENDITURES

Every adjustment, exemption, exclusion, and deduction from the gross income of taxpayers reduces the amount of income that is actually taxed. The many special provisions of the personal income tax code that make taxable income less than actual income therefore reduce the revenue collected by the U.S. Treasury. Indirectly, the reduction in revenue ends up increasing the after-tax income of taxpayers who engage in those transactions for which the tax code affords preferential treatment. This loss in income tax collected can be thought of as subsidizing the activities that people engage in to reduce their income tax burdens.

The federal government is required by law to estimate this loss in income tax revenue and report the losses as tax expenditures, which are indirect subsidies provided through the income tax. In effect, tax expenditures are a form of federal government spending financed by loss in tax revenue. The table below shows selected tax expenditures resulting from provisions of the federal income tax code reported by the Office of Management and Budget (OMB):

Selected Tax Expenditure Resulting from Preferential Treatment of Income (Fiscal Year 2007)

Provision	Revenue Loss (in Billions of Dollars)
Exclusion of employer contributions for medical insurance premiums	146.8
Capital gains exclusion on home sales	43.9
Deductibility of mortgage interest on owner-occupied homes	79.9
Deductibility of property taxes on owner-occupied homes	12.8
Exclusion of interest on public purpose state and local bonds	29.6
Deductibility of nonbusiness state and local taxes (other than taxes on owner-occupied homes)	27.2

Source: Office of Management and Budget, *Budget of the United States, Fiscal Year 2007.* http://www.whitehouse.gov/omb/budget/fy2007

This is just a small selection of the more than $800 billion of tax expenditures from special provisions of the federal income tax reported each year by OMB. The exclusion of employer-provided medical insurance from the taxable income of employees subsidizes health expenditures. The exclusion of capital gains on home sales subsidizes home ownership in the United States, as does the deductibility of mortgage interest and property taxes. These three tax expenditures together subsidized homeowners in the United States by nearly $140 billion in 2007. Indirectly, the deductibility of property taxes also subsidizes local government by making it easier to get tax increases approved because

(continued)

(continued)

those taxes mean that part of their burden is shifted to the federal government through reduced federal tax collection.

Similarly, OMB views deductibility of all other nonbusiness state and local taxes as indirect aid to state and local government. Exclusion of interest on state and local debt from federal taxable income makes it possible for these governments to borrow at lower rates than otherwise would be the case. The nearly $30 billion in revenue that the federal government did not collect because of this special provision is also aid to state and local governments.

Tax expenditures make it clear that the personal income tax is used as a mechanism to promote social outcomes, such as home ownership, subsidized health care, and aid to state and local governments, to name a few, in addition to raising revenue to finance federal expenditures. The use of the personal income tax in this way is, in part, responsible for its complexity. As proposals to reform the tax code are considered, those who benefit from these tax expenditures often resist their abolition.

earnings and other forms of income or from increases in the market value of such assets as stocks, bonds, or housing that a person might own. The annual increase in the value of a person's existing assets are capital gains, which can either be realized (converted to cash) by selling an asset or unrealized (not turned into cash in the current year).

A comprehensive income tax would be levied on the sum of a person's annual consumption plus savings. Consumption plus savings in a given year would represent the uses of the taxpayer's earnings and other sources of income.

A Flat Rate Income Tax

The simplest form of an income tax would be a flat rate tax. Individuals would report their income based on the comprehensive definition discussed previously, and a flat rate would be levied to collect the tax. For example, if, through the political process, it was decided to raise all revenue from the income tax and that a 15 percent rate on income would raise enough revenue, then every citizen earning income would have to pay 15 percent tax on that income to the government to finance public services. All income, irrespective of its source or use, would be subject to the tax. Tax forms would be very simple, with only three lines: one to report income, one to indicate the tax rate, and the other to show the product of the tax rate when multiplied with income. If your income was $30,000 this year, you would multiply that income by 0.15 if the tax rate was 15 percent, and your tax bill would be $4,500.

Under a flat rate comprehensive income tax, those with higher income would pay proportionately higher taxes. For example, a person with $10,000 annual income would have a tax bill of $1,500. A person with an annual income of $100,000 would pay

$15,000 in taxes, while a person with $1 million in income would pay $150,000 in taxes. So under a flat rate income tax, the rich would pay more than the poor, even though the tax rate is the same for all taxpayers.

Under a comprehensive income tax, there would be no need for a separate tax on corporation income. Corporations are owned by their stockholders. A corporation's net income would simply be allocated to shareholders in proportion to their share of ownership. For example, suppose the XYZ Corporation has 100,000 shares of its corporate stock outstanding and earned $1 million in profit this year. If you own 10,000 shares of the outstanding stock, amounting to a 10 percent share in the ownership of the corporation, then 10 percent of the $1 million profit, or $100,000, would be allocated to you, and you would have to include this amount in your personal income. Under a 15 percent flat rate tax, your tax liability on your share of the corporation's profit would be $15,000 this year.

The flat rate income tax would be easy to administer. Time spent figuring taxes and keeping records would be minimal, and there would be no need for an army of tax accountants and lawyers to help people wade through complex tax laws.

However, even a flat rate income tax can cause distortions in behavior that could impair the efficiency of operation of the economy. The tax would reduce the net return to work and to saving and investment. This is easiest to see if taxes are withheld from earnings as those earnings are received during the year. If you earn $3,000 per month from your job, and the 15 percent income tax is withheld from your paycheck, then your net earnings from work after tax would be $3,000 minus $450, to give you net pay of $2,550. When deciding how many hours to work, you will base your choice on your net pay rather than the gross amount actually paid by your employer. The reduction in the net wage or salary due to the income tax could impair incentives to work.

The flat rate tax would also reduce the net return to saving and investment. All interest earned on savings, all corporate profits, capital gains, and any other income from use of capital would be taxable. The net return to saving and investment would fall below the actual gross return earned. Because saving and investment decisions are made on the basis of the net, after tax, return, there is the potential for a decline in saving and investment below the amounts that would prevail without taxation.

For example, if you have a savings account in a bank and earn 5 percent interest, then you will have to pay tax on the interest you earn during the year. With a 15 percent flat rate tax, your net interest would amount to 4.25 percent, calculated by subtracting 15 percent of the 5 percent from the gross interest earned:

$$\text{net interest} = \text{gross interest} \, (1 - \text{tax rate}).$$

In this case, your net interest earned is 85 percent of the 5 percent interest rate.

If the lower net interest rate decreases the incentive to save, then total saving in the nation will decline. As saving declines, funds financing for investment will become

HOW IS THE BURDEN OF PAYING THE FEDERAL PERSONAL INCOME TAX DISTRIBUTED?

The federal personal income tax has a progressive tax rate structure but is also riddled with special provisions that allow taxpayers to avoid paying taxes by taking advantage of the various adjustments, exclusions, exemptions, and deductions as well as tax credits. Do the effects of special provisions cancel out the impact of the progressive tax rates on the distribution of the payments of taxes? In other words, does the progressive income tax really result in the rich paying higher tax rates than the poor?

To find out, the Congressional Budget Office (CBO) conducted an analysis of the distribution of the tax burden of the federal personal income tax for 2003, a year when major tax rate cuts and other changes in the tax code became effective. The study began with a comprehensive measure of income and ranked taxpayers according to the amount of income they earned. Taxpayers were grouped into quintiles, starting with the fifth with the lowest income. The CBO then estimated effective (actual) income taxes paid under the provisions of the income tax code and divided total taxes paid in each quintile of households (adjusted for size) ranked according to their incomes by total income earned in that quintile. A household consists of people who share housing, regardless of their relationship (see Congressional Budget Office 2005 for details of adjustments and comprehensive measurement of income).

The following table shows the results of the CBO study.

Effective Federal Personal Income Tax Rates, 2003

Income Category	Effective Tax Rate (%)
Lowest quintile	−5.9
Second quintile	−1.1
Middle quintile	2.7
Fourth quintile	5.9
Highest quintile	13.9

Source: Congressional Budget Office, U.S. Congress, *Historical Effective Federal Tax Rates: 1979 to 2003.* December 2005. http://www.cbo.gov/ftpdocs/70xx/doc7000/12–29-FedTax Rates.pdf

Notice that the two lowest quintiles actually have negative effective tax rates because the earned income tax credit for low-income taxpayers results in net payments to these households from the U.S. Treasury instead of collection of income taxes.

The results of the study show that the distribution of the burden of paying federal personal income taxes is such that upper-income groups do indeed pay higher average tax rates than lower-income groups in the United States. The estimated average effective rate for all households in 2003 was 8.5 percent. The top 1 percent of households ranked according to income were estimated to pay an average effective tax rate of 20.6 percent in 2003. Effective tax rates are progressive.

scarcer, and market interest rates could rise, discouraging investment. Investment could also directly decline because the tax will be levied on all capital income, including corporate profits, rents, and capital gains, decreasing the net return to investment after taxes. A decline in investment could slow the rate of growth of the economy and decrease future living standards by contributing to a decline in the rate of growth of wages and salaries as worker productivity growth slows because of the slowdown in the supply of new capital equipment and technology that investment makes possible.

In short, a flat rate income tax could reduce the size of the economy by contributing to a decrease in work effort. Over the longer term, the tax could also slow economic growth if it adversely affects saving and investment.

The Personal Income Tax in Practice

The personal income tax in the United States does not comprehensively tax all income. Instead, because tax law allows a host of adjustments, exemptions, deductions, and exclusions from income, taxable income falls far short of total income. For tax purposes, gross income includes wages and salaries, taxable interest, dividends, realized capital gains (although long-term gains on many assets are taxed at preferentially low rates), rents, royalties, most pension income, and business income from proprietorships and partnerships. Taxpayers can, to some extent, control their income tax bills by adjusting the sources and uses of their income. This leads to distortions in behavior as people make decisions based, in part, on the tax advantages of engaging in particular economic transactions, such as buying homes; providing employees with compensation in the form of nontaxable fringe benefits instead of cash; or buying municipal bonds, for which interest payments are exempt from federal taxation.

The federal personal income tax uses a progressive tax rate structure. Instead of one flat rate, there are several rates. The tax rate applied to additional income after a certain amount is received is called the taxpayer's marginal tax rate. Low marginal tax rates apply to lower ranges of income. Each range of income is called a tax bracket, and, as income increases, the amounts falling into higher tax brackets are taxed at higher marginal tax rates. Many citizens believe that a progressive tax rate structure is fairer than a flat rate tax because it subjects those with higher incomes to higher tax rates.

As of 2010, the federal income tax had six tax brackets subject to positive tax rates, with income in the highest bracket subject to a 35 percent tax rate. The lowest positive tax rate was 10 percent. Intermediate brackets were 15, 25, 28, and 33 percent. These tax rates are levied on taxable income. Under a progressive income tax system, marginal tax rates exceed average tax rates. Average tax rates can be calculated by simply dividing taxes due by taxable income. For example, a single taxpayer with a taxable income of $74,200 in 2006 would pay $15,107.50 in federal income tax. This taxpayer's average tax rate would be $15,107.50/$74,200 = .2036 = 20.36 percent. However, the taxpayer would be at the beginning of the 28 percent tax bracket with that amount of income, and each extra dollar of taxable income would be subject to a 28 percent marginal tax rate. Marginal tax rates are important for determining the impact of taxes on economic decisions, because they influence the net return to going to the effort of earning additional income.

Most taxpayers are entitled to personal exemptions and a standard deduction or can itemize deductions. Tax credits for such expenses as child care can be directly subtracted from tax bills. The standard deduction varies with filing status (single, married filing jointly or separately, or head of household). Adjustments for contributions to retirement accounts and other expenses can also reduce the portion of gross income that is subject to tax.

The personal exemption, the standard deduction, and the beginning points for each tax bracket are adjusted for inflation each year. In 2010, a taxpayer could claim a personal exemption of $3,650 if not claimed as a dependent on some other tax return. Taxpayers can also claim personal exemptions for dependents. A single taxpayer could claim a standard deduction of $5,700 in 2010 or itemize deductions for such expenses as state and local income taxes, property taxes, charitable contributions, interest paid on mortgages, and a host of other expenses eligible to be itemized under the income tax code. If the single taxpayer chooses to take the standard deduction and is eligible for a personal exemption, then $9,350 of gross income would not be taxable. (Under the tax law prevailing in 2010, taxpayers with relatively high incomes have their personal exemptions and itemized deductions reduced, and eventually eliminated, as income increases.)

Finally, there are provisions of the U.S. tax code that result in some low-income taxpayers, particularly those with dependent children, paying negative tax rates. The provision is called the earned income tax credit (EITC) and allowed as much as $5,666 per year to be paid to a low-income taxpayer with dependent children by the U.S. Treasury in 2010. The EITC is a way of using the tax system to increase the incomes and living standards of low-income workers through a tax credit that is payable to the worker by the U.S. Treasury.

The actual personal income tax in the United States can affect incentives to work, save, and invest, just like the flat rate income tax. However, because of complex provisions allowing taxpayers to influence their taxable income tax bills by adjusting the sources and uses of their income, the income tax in the United States effectively subsidizes some activities over others. Provisions in the tax code allowing homeowners to deduct interest on mortgages and property taxes on homes as well as those exempting up to $500,000 in capital gains from the sale of a principal residence from taxation encourage investments in housing. Reduced taxation of long-term capital gains benefits upper-income taxpayers with assets and could encourage them to invest. Exemption of some fringe benefits, such as employer-provided health insurance, encourages compensation of workers in that form instead of in taxable wages. In addition, the complexity of the tax code imposes a burden on taxpayers to keep up with the tax law, keep records, and pay professional tax consultants to help them in filing their tax returns.

Issues and Problems in Income Taxation and Prospects for Reform of the Tax Code

The federal personal income tax has been reformed many times. Each time, it seems to get more complex. Reforming the income tax code is very difficult because there will be both gainers and losers in the process, and the losers use political action to prevent changes that will make them worse off. The most extreme reform would be to move to a flat rate income tax. If this were done, all exemptions and deductions from income would be eliminated, and the average tax rate could be reduced because a much larger portion of actual income received would be subject to taxation. Under a flat rate tax, the average tax rate is equal to the marginal tax rate. A single lower marginal tax rate could reduce the distortions in decision making that result from the impact of taxes on net returns to work and saving. However, many object to a shift to a flat rate tax, because it would lower the tax rate for upper-income individuals while raising the tax rate for many lower-income taxpayers.

A less extreme approach to tax reform would eliminate some exemptions, deductions, and exclusions from taxable income to allow lower marginal and tax rates while retaining a progressive tax rate structure. For example, the report of the President's Advisory Panel on Federal Tax Reform in 2005 recommended limiting deductions for interest on home mortgages and eliminating deductions for state and local income and property taxes. Elimination of deductions generates tax revenue and allows tax rates across the board to decrease without tax revenue collected falling. However, such changes could have adverse effects on homeowners. As the tax advantages to homeownership are reduced, the demand for homes could decline, and this would decrease home prices, reducing the net worth of many households. The President's Advisory Panel on Federal Tax Reform recommended that the mortgage interest deduction be replaced with a tax credit for such interest that would be available to all taxpayers regardless of whether they itemize deductions. The panel also recommended a cap on the amount of interest that could be claimed as a credit so that the benefit to upper-income households with expensive homes and mortgages in excess of $300,000 would be reduced. This could sharply reduce demand for luxury homes but could increase demand and prices for modest homes.

Similarly, the current deduction for state and local taxes cushions those tax bills for those who itemize deductions by, in effect, allowing them to pay some of those bills through a reduction in federal tax liability. If the deduction were eliminated, it would be more difficult for state and local governments, particularly those whose tax rates are already high, to raise tax rates in the future and could result in political action to decrease tax rates.

The personal income tax system has been used as a means of encouraging individuals to favor one activity over another through its extensive use of adjustments, exemptions, deductions, and credits. This, too, has contributed to the complexity of the code. Congress often enacts tax deductions or credits for such activities as child care or education but limits availability to upper-income households. As a result, the amount of the benefits are often reduced as a taxpayer's adjusted gross income increases, and the tax forms necessary to calculate the reduction in credits or deductions are often quite complex.

Another reform often suggested is to change the tax system to encourage saving and investment. Because of concern about the impact of the current system of income taxation on incentives to save and invest, some economists advocate allowing taxpayers to deduct all of their savings from taxable income and exempting interest from taxation unless it is withdrawn. In effect, such a scheme would tax only consumption, because income less saving is equal to consumption.

Conclusion

The tax reform process is inevitably tied to politics, because it always results in some people gaining while others lose. The prospects for a radical reform of the tax code, such as a shift to a flat rate tax, are remote. Instead, small, incremental changes in tax deductions and credits, and simplification of complex provisions of the tax code are more likely. Elimination of these special provisions that reduce revenue can allow across-the-board decreases in average and marginal tax rates and reductions in the distortions in decision making from the income tax.

See also **Consumer Credit and Household Debt; Corporate Tax Shelters; Debt, Deficits, and the Economy; Government Subsidies**

Further Reading

Boortz, Neal, and John Linder, *FairTax, the Truth: Answering the Critics.* New York: Harper, 2008.

Cordes, Joseph, Robert D. Ebel, and Jane G. Gravelle, eds., *The Encyclopedia of Taxation and Tax Policy,* 2d ed. Washington, DC: Urban Institute Press, 2005.

Diamond, John W., and George R. Zodrow, *Fundamental Tax Reform: Issues, Choices, and Implications.* Cambridge, MA: MIT Press, 2008.

Hyman, David N., *Public Finance: A Contemporary Application of Theory to Policy,* 10th ed. Mason, OH: South-Western College Publishing, 2010.

Slemrod, Joel, and Jon Bakija, *Taxing Ourselves: A Citizen's Guide to the Debate over Taxes.* Cambridge, MA: MIT Press, 2008.

Steuerle, C. Eugene, *Contemporary U.S. Tax Policy,* 2d ed. Washington, DC: Urban Institute, 2008.

INTELLECTUAL PROPERTY RIGHTS

Jason A. Checque and Michael Shally-Jensen

Historically, ideas have changed the world. They impact cultures, governments, and religions. Ideas also shape businesses on many different levels, influencing marketing, management, and operations decisions on a daily basis. Today, businesses operate in an ever-changing global market, requiring access to information via high-speed communications. The explosion of technological innovation has increased competition and forced businesses to find alternate means to generate profits.

For example, in 1999, Research in Motion Ltd. (RIM), an Ontario-based firm that designs and manufactures wireless mobile devices, introduced the BlackBerry wireless platform (commonly called a BlackBerry). The BlackBerry is a handheld palm computer that uses a radio frequency technology to allow millions of users to instantly access their e-mail, phone messages, Internet, and business data. The introduction of the BlackBerry revolutionized communication capabilities for corporate executives, small businesses, elected officials, and law enforcement agencies. In 2001, NTP Inc., a small patent holding company, filed a patent infringement lawsuit against RIM. NTP claimed that it held the patents to the radio frequency technology used for the BlackBerry and feared that RIM misappropriated the patents without paying royalties. In 2002, a federal jury agreed that RIM had infringed on NTP's patents. In 2003, the court entered a final judgment in favor of NTP and imposed a permanent injunction against RIM for the further manufacture or sale of BlackBerry products. The injunction was stayed pending RIM's appeal. In January 2006, the U.S. Supreme Court declined to hear RIM's appeal (Locy 2006; Spencer and Vascellaro 2006).

In March 2006, with an impending shutdown of all BlackBerry products, NTP and RIM settled out of court for $612 million before the trial judge issued a final opinion regarding the form of injunctive relief. The settlement saved approximately 4 million users from life without their so-called CrackBerries. In May 2006, Visto Inc. filed a patent infringement lawsuit against RIM, alleging that it held the patents to the e-mail technology used in BlackBerry products (Wong 2006; "BlackBerry Maker" 2006). The case was settled in July 2009. However, in January 2010, Motorola filed a request with the International Trade Commission to ban BlackBerry imports, alleging that the device's early-stage innovations drew on Motorola patents. Meanwhile, BlackBerry continues to dominate the business smart phone market, capturing a 61 percent share (Rysavy 2009).

The lawsuits against BlackBerry manufacturer RIM provide insight on two important concepts: (1) the importance of innovation in technology, usually in the form of intellectual property, and (2) the importance of protecting those innovations from piracy.

The Importance of Intellectual Property

The idea of protecting intellectual property dates back to ancient times. In Greek mythology, Prometheus arguably committed an infringement when he stole fire from the Olympian gods to give to mankind. Zeus punished Prometheus by chaining him to a mountainside, where an eagle devoured his rejuvenated liver each day. As a consequence of Prometheus's actions, mankind still has fire to the present day.

During the Middle Ages, protection for intellectual property was granted from the crown or a sovereign. Publishing patents were granted to printers of books like the Bible or legal treatises (factors include relative expense and /or politics). Additionally, the Stationers' Company in England maintained a monopoly of registered books, where the government allowed a printer or bookseller, but not the author, copyright protection on a written work. Publishers paid large sums of money to authors not to sell their works (e.g., John Milton's contract for the sale of *Paradise Lost* in 1667) (Posner 2009).

Modern protections of intellectual property formed with the spread of the Industrial Revolution. In 1710, England instituted the first modern copyright law (Posner 2009). At the Constitutional Convention in 1788, the Founding Fathers recognized the importance of intellectual property when they granted Congress the power to "promote the Progress of Science and useful Arts, by securing for limited times to Authors and Inventors, the exclusive Right to their respective Writings and Discoveries" (Friedman 2004, 426). In comparison with imperial China, "Chinese culture placed continuity with the past, and its suspicion of novelty, both of which encouraged copying" (Posner 2009, 393).

Congress established the Patent and Trademark Office under the auspices of the Department of Commerce. One of the deputy undersecretaries of commerce is the deputy undersecretary of commerce for intellectual property. The Patent and Trademark Office "examines patent and trademark applications, issues patents, registers trademarks, and furnishes patent and trademark information and services to the public" (Garner 1999, 1149). In 1879, Eaton S. Drone published *A Treatise on the Law of Property in Intellectual Productions,* one of the earliest hornbooks on intellectual property law.

Intellectual property is divided into four categories: (1) patents (ideas), (2) copyrights (expressions), (3) trademarks (source indicators), and (4) trade secrets (business processes).

TOP 10 COMPANIES RECEIVING U.S. PATENTS IN 2008

Corporation	Number of Patents
1. IBM	4,169
2. Samsung Electronics	3,502
3. Canon Kabushiki Kaisha	2,107
4. Microsoft Corp.	2,026
5. Intel Corporation	1,772
6. Toshiba Corp.	1,575
7. Fujitsu Ltd.	1,475
8. Matsushita Electric Industrial Co.	1,469
9. Sony Corp.	1,461
10. Hewlett-Packard	1,422

Source: U.S. Patent and Trademark Office, "Patenting by Organizations 2008."

Patents

A patent is defined as the "exclusive right to make, use, or sell an invention for a specified period…granted by the federal government to the inventor if the device or process is novel, useful, and non-obvious" (Garner 1999, 1147). In essence, a patent is monopoly granted by the government for a finite amount of time, despite the general premise that monopolies are disfavored in law or public policy.

Most patents cover functional discoveries (known as utility patents, which last 20 years) and original nonfunctional ornamental designs (known as design patents, which last 14 years), but the Plant Patent Act of 1930 expanded patent protection to newly "discovered and asexually reproduced any distinct and new variety of plant" as long as the plant is a product of "human ingenuity and research" (Friedman 2004, 428). Patents cannot be renewed. Frequently, patent owners will improve a product and receive a new patent (e.g., if the patent on automobile brakes expired but the patent holder improved the brakes with an antilock braking system) (Emerson 2009). A common example of a utility patent is computer software or a process like pasteurization. Design patents are ornamental or distinctive in nature but do not improve the functionality of the product. Examples of a design patent are the shape of the Coca-Cola bottle or the Volkswagen Beetle. Design patents are similar to trade dress (Stim 2009).

Copyright

A copyright is defined as a "property right in an original work of authorship (such as literary, musical, artistic, photographic, or film work) fixed in any tangible medium of expression, giving the holder the exclusive right to reproduce, adapt, distribute, perform, and display the work" and must be creative (an exercise of human intellect) (Garner 1999). Although not required, owners of the copyright can enhance their legal rights by placing a copyright symbol (©) on the work and registering it with the U.S. Copyright Office (Stim 2009).

The rights attributable to a copyright expanded greatly in 1903 after the U.S. Supreme Court ruled that advertisements were protected under the Copyright Act. Thereafter, the rights applied to movies, piano rolls and phonograph records, radio and television, photocopying machines, music downloaded from the Internet, and computer software (Friedman 2004). In the late 1990s, Congress extended copyright protection to the life of the author plus 70 or 95 years (formally 50 or 75 years) after heavy lobbying by the Walt Disney Company. In 1998, the Digital Millennium Copyright Act (DMCA) was enacted to protect the burgeoning software businesses and to comply with the treaties signed at the World Intellectual Property Organization (WIPO) Geneva Conference in 1996. Specifically, the DMCA criminalized unauthorized pilfering of computer software, manufacture of code-cracking devices, and subterfuge around antipiracy measures and required Internet companies that performed services like music downloading (e.g., Kazaa, Napster, Apple iTunes) to pay licensing fees to record companies (Duboff 2002; Emerson 2009).

Trademark

A trademark is defined as a "word, phrase, logo, or other graphic symbol used by a manufacturer or seller to distinguish its product or products from those of others. The main purpose of a trademark is to guarantee a product's genuineness. In effect, the trademark is the commercial substitute for one's signature. To receive federal protection, a trademark must be (1) distinctive rather than merely descriptive, (2) affixed to a product that is actually sold in the marketplace, and (3) registered with the U.S. Patent and Trademark Office" (Garner 1999, 1500). Once a trademark is registered, it is valid for the life of the use of the trademark, as long as it is renewed every 10 years. Trademarks are classified into five categories regarding their inherent distinctiveness: (1) unique logos or symbols (such as the marks used by furniture makers and silversmiths), (2) created or fanciful marks (such as Exxon or Kodak), (3) common or arbitrary marks (such as Olympic for paints and stains or Target for retail sales), (4) suggestive or descriptive marks (such as Chicken of the Sea tuna or Oatnut bread), and (5) generic or common marks that have lost distinctiveness (such as aspirin or elevator). Generic or common marks do not receive trademark protection. Products of distinctive shape may be protected under a concept called trade dress (such as the packaging of a product or the motif used by national chain stores) (Stim 2009).

In 1905, Congress passed legislation to regulate trademarks based on their power to monitor interstate and foreign commerce. In 1946, Congress approved the Lanham Act to codify existing trademark law and afford further protection to businesses from infringement (Friedman 2004).

Trade Secret

A trade secret is defined as confidential business information that is designed to maintain an advantage over competitors. The information can appear as a formula, pattern, process, compilation, method, or program. As a trade secret, the information derives value because it grants a distinct advantage to the business owner, and the business owner implements reasonable tactics to maintain its secrecy. This is accomplished by restricting access to the information (to documents and /or areas where documents are stored), implementing confidentiality and nondisclosure agreements with employees, and preparing appropriate form agreements (Garner 1999; Duboff 2002; Emerson 2009).

The Consequences of Piracy to Business

The United States is the world's largest exporter of intellectual property, including movies and music (Friedman 2004). Piracy of intellectual property costs businesses and consumers $250 billion and 750,000 jobs each year (U.S. Patent and Trademark Office 2006). Nonmonetary losses to piracy are "fame, prestige, the hope of immortality, therapy and inner satisfaction" (Posner 2009, 390). Piracy or infringement is the illegal reproduction or distribution of intellectual property (not by the exclusive or registered owners) protected by copyright, patent, or trademark law (Garner 1999). Piracy has been especially rampant in the communications, music, pharmaceuticals, and software industries. The important question determined by courts in most infringement actions is who (such as an independent inventor or corporate employee) or what (such as a corporation or organization) has ownership of intellectual property, whether it is an idea, expression, source indicator, or business process. Therefore it is imperative for businesses and government to protect intellectual property and develop appropriate commercial and legal strategies to implement that protection.

Protection of Intellectual Property Rights Internationally

Despite the protections afforded by the Constitution and legislation by Congress, infringement is on the rise, especially outside the United States. U.S. companies have filed infringement cases against China-based companies and seek protection from pirates in Latin America, Russia, and other parts of Asia. Once a patent, copyright, or trademark is registered in the United States, the registrar, in essence, becomes the owner and is granted exclusive rights to use that patent, copyright, or trademark within the United States. The registrar may grant a license or sell its interest to another party, domestic or foreign. With the advent of the global economy, industrialized nations and worldwide organizations have pushed for standardized intellectual property protection applicable to every participating country. The most common method to standardize that protection is through the use of treaties and agreements.

For example, agreements with other nations, such as the North American Free Trade Agreement, passed in 1994, strengthened patent and copyright protection in Mexico. Mexico agreed to strengthen its intellectual property laws and honor pharmaceutical patents for 20 years. Treaties like the Patent Cooperation Treaty and the Paris Convention allow U.S. inventors to file for patent protection in selected industrial nations if the inventor files the proper paperwork and fees within a certain time frame. The standards differ from country to country (Stim 2009). In most countries, intellectual property protection begins when it is registered, not on the date it was created or invented (which is true in the United States). In 2005, Congress considered (but did not enact) legislation that would change the date of protection to the date of registration, as in most international markets.

Many patent holders focus on protecting their rights in the United States and file international patents in the European Union and/or Japan, although the benefit of filing patent applications in China, India, and Russia will outweigh the cost in the near future. If infringed goods enter the United States, the owner can contact customs officials to confiscate and destroy the contraband. Likewise, once registered in a foreign country, U.S. registrars can be sued by the host country for alleged infringements, as a China-based corporation did in February 2006 (Parloff 2006). The hope by business analysts is that this type of litigation will force and encourage host countries to seriously police patent infringement.

Copyright protection is stronger internationally than patents because of various treaties like the Uruguay Round Agreement Act of 1994, the WIPO Geneva Conference of 1996 (which extended the Berne Convention), and the DMCA of 1998 (Emerson 2009). But copyright protection is not international because a country signs one of the treaties or agreements. Experts recommend that companies file for trademark protection as well as patent protection (e.g., Reebok in Uruguay) (Bhatnagar 2006).

An additional fear of U.S.-based companies doing business overseas is fighting so-called third-shift products, which are produced by an authorized manufacturer but produced in excess of the number agreed on in the contract. Often, the excess product is sold on the black market. Courts have a difficult time declaring those products counterfeit, because it is nearly impossible to tell the difference or whether that particular product was within the contract (Parloff 2006).

Legal Relief: Infringement Causes of Action, Injunctions, and Contracts

Today, litigants file two types of lawsuits: (1) an infringement cause of action, which seeks monetary damages and a form of injunctive relief, and (2) a breach of contract action. If someone files an infringement lawsuit, the litigant usually requests the court to issue a restraining order or injunction and the awarding of monetary damages, fines, lost royalties, and/or attorney's fees (Stim 2009).

An injunction is a "court order commanding or preventing an action. To get an injunction, the complainant must show that there is no plain, adequate, and complete remedy at law and that an irreparable injury will result unless the relief is granted" (Garner 1999, 788).

A contract is an "agreement between two or more parties creating obligations that are enforceable or otherwise recognizable at law (a binding contract)" (Garner 1999, 318).

Today, courts interpret contracts narrowly by considering the contractual text and limit most types of extrinsic evidence like the contracting parties' intentions, special meaning of words, and/or trade usage of the industry. The court will regard extrinsic evidence only if the contract is vague or ambiguous (Posner 2009). If a plaintiff proves a breach of contract action, the usual remedy is monetary damages to make the plaintiff whole (returning the plaintiff to his or her precontract status). Specific performance is an unusual remedy in such situations.

If criminal behavior is suspected, it should be reported to the proper prosecution bodies—namely, the federal government or local authorities. The types of criminal charges

EXAMPLES OF LAWSUITS DEALING WITH INTELLECTUAL PROPERTY RIGHTS

1. One of the first intellectual property cases heard by the U.S. Supreme Court dealt with copyright infringement of the publishing rights to its own cases: *Henry Wheaton and Robert Donaldson v. Richard Peters and John Grigg* (1834). Henry Wheaton and Robert Donaldson (plaintiffs), located in Philadelphia, Pennsylvania, were under contract to publish the cases decided by the U.S. Supreme Court, a right that they purchased from a prior publisher. One of the plaintiff's responsibilities was to provide a volume to the secretary of state, located in New York City. Richard Peters and John Grigg (defendants) were sued under the premise that they sold condensed versions of the U.S. Supreme Court reporters in New York City. The plaintiffs sought injunctive relief, but the U.S. Supreme Court ruled that "no reporter of the Supreme Court has, nor can he have, any copyright in the written opinions delivered by the court: and the judges of the court cannot confer on any reporter any such right."

2. Fred Waring, owner and conductor of an orchestra (plaintiff), produced phonograph records of its compositions. WDAS Broadcasting Station Inc. (defendant) broadcasted the records on the radio without a license from the plaintiff. In *Waring v. WDAS Broadcasting Station, Inc.* (1937), the plaintiff sought an injunction from the court to prevent the defendant from playing the records. The trial court granted the injunction, because recording of the plaintiff's music was a "product of novel and artistic creation as to invest him with a property right." The appellate courts affirmed the trial court.

3. Kevin E. George (defendant) was convicted of distributing unauthorized copies of recorded devices and distributing items bearing counterfeit marks, third-degree felonies in Pennsylvania, after two investigators for the Motion Picture Association of America (MPAA) spotted the defendant selling counterfeit videotapes from a vending table on a public sidewalk in Philadelphia. The investigators received training to identify fraudulent packaging, especially "blurry printing on their cases, low-quality cardboard boxes, bogus trademarked studio logos and titles of motion pictures that were currently playing in theaters." The investigators went to the police and reported the defendant, who was subsequently arrested and convicted of the above charges (*Commonwealth v. George* 2005).

4. MercExchange LLC (plaintiff) owned a business method patent for an "electronic market designed to facilitate the sale of goods between private individuals by establishing a central authority to promote trust among participants." Previously, the plaintiff licensed its patent to other companies but was unable to complete an agreement with eBay Inc. or Half.com, an eBay subsidiary (defendants). In its patent infringement action, the plaintiff alleged that the defendants used the patent without permission. A jury found that the plaintiff's

(continued)

(continued)

patent was valid and that the defendants had infringed that patent. The jury awarded monetary damages, but the trial court refused to grant the plaintiff's request for injunctive relief (*Ebay, Inc. et al. v. MercExchange, LLC* 2006).

5. Myriad Genetics (defendant), together with the University of Utah, held patents on two genes that the firm successfully sequenced using a proprietary technology and whose genetic mutations are associated with breast and ovarian cancer. The patent owners claimed that isolating DNA from the body and applying measures to it to make it analyzable in the laboratory made the DNA—or, more specifically, the two genes in question—patentable. Bringing suit against them, however, was the American Civil Liberties Union (ACLU) along with various patients and medical organizations. The ACLU argued that the genes in this case were not the product of genetic engineering but rather components of the human genome—naturally occurring substances—and, as such, were not patentable. It further argued that the existence of the patent barred researchers not affiliated with Myriad from exploring the genes and potentially making new discoveries. In the end, the U.S. district court hearing the case ruled in favor of the ACLU, finding that the patent should never have been granted because one was dealing here with a "law of nature," not a human invention (*ACLU v. Myriad Genetics* 2010).

available to a prosecuting agency include "mail fraud, interstate transportation of stolen property, voracious state common law charges, and violation of the federal Economic Espionage Act" (Emerson 2009, 558).

The statutory criminal offense for criminal infringement involves "either (1) willfully infringing a copyright to obtain a commercial advantage or financial gain...or (2) trafficking in goods or services that bear a counterfeit mark....Under the second category, the statute imposes criminal penalties if the counterfeit mark is (1) identical with, or substantially indistinguishable from, a mark registered on the Principal Register of the U.S. Patent and Trademark Office, and (2) likely to confuse or deceive the public" (Garner 1999, 785).

Although a patent may be registered, companies can still challenge the patent, as Ranbaxy Laboratories Ltd. did to Pfizer's patent on Lipitor. One of Pfizer's two patents was invalidated during the litigation, cutting back Pfizer's protection from June 2011 to March 2010. One strategy to elucidate the status of broad patents is for a registrar to file a declaratory judgment with the court to legally define the status of the patent (Smith 2006b).

Controversial Aspects of Intellectual Property

Public opinion indicates that many people believe that the United States is too litigious and question whether an individual or company can own an idea. This leads to controversy regarding intellectual property laws. In the early part of the 20th century, large corporations that subsisted on their employees' sweat and brains controlled patents (Friedman 2004).

In many cases, the courts favored defendants, until 1982, when a law abolished the Court of Customs and Patent Appeals and gave the new Court of Appeals for the

GOOGLE BOOKS

In October 2004, Google announced a partnership with five major research libraries (Harvard, Stanford, University of Michigan, Oxford, and the New York Public Library) to scan millions of books into a company database and make them accessible via an online search engine. Several other universities joined over the next few years. The Google Books Library Project (books.google.com/googlebooks/library.html) has generated controversy from the beginning. In collaboration with the participating libraries, Google scans books in the public domain (i.e., works whose copyrights have expired) along with copyrighted books. For the latter, Google displays bibliographic information (similar to an old card catalog in a library) and supplies only enough of the book's contents (a "snippet") to enable a user to confirm that this is the volume sought. Google's goal is to create an index of all books in the world that can be accessed electronically. The company also intends to scan out-of-print books, which benefits individuals searching for books that might otherwise be difficult or impossible to find.

Critics complain that Google has usurped the rights of authors and publishers to distribute and profit from their works and that the company supplants the traditional function of the public library as well. Google has responded that much of the controversy is the result of inadequate or inaccurate understandings of the issues involved. Regarding the claim that the company is offering every book in the world free to Internet users, Google notes that only full versions of books that are out of copyright are made available. Books still in copyright are displayed in "limited view," with links to where users can buy or borrow them.

Regarding the claim that Google is generating revenue from advertising on its book search service and denying income to copyright holders, Google argues that the company does not put ads on a book's display page unless the publisher wants them there and has given Google permission to do so. It stipulates that the majority of the revenue, in fact, is given back to the copyright holder. In other words, the company profits from ads only to the extent that its publishing partners do as well.

In 2005, several publishers and organizations took Google to court over these issues, claiming that Google had violated the fair use provision of U.S. copyright law. Google countered that everything it was doing was legal. In 2008, a settlement was reached whereby Google has agreed to compensate authors and publishers in exchange for the right to scan and display copyrighted books. The agreement also gives publishers the right to opt out of the program so that any of their books scanned in participating libraries would not be made available to Google users. In April 2010, a group of organizations representing visual artists (photographers, graphic artists, etc.) sued Google for copyright infringement. Whether this case, too, will be settled or will proceed to trial remains to be seen.

Federal Circuit the exclusive right to hear patent appeals. Today, plaintiff patent owners benefit from greater legal securities as the image of a patent shifted from "a tool of big business; now it was a legal shield to protect the entrepreneur, the risk taker, the start-up company" (Friedman 2004, 427–428). Additionally, patent lawsuits in federal court doubled between 1998 and 2001, and patent applications increased from 200,000 in 1994 to 380,000 in 2004. Currently, the Patent and Trademark Office is attempting to reform the system to quicken the review of 1.2 million backlogged patents (Schmid and Poston 2009).

Many fear a frivolous lawsuit that will cost a defendant time, money, stress, and years of frustration. Today, some corporations' sole purpose for existence consists of buying patents and litigating possible infringements (Slagle 2006). For instance, the Rock and Roll Hall of Fame sued a photographer for infringement because he sold a poster depicting the Rock and Roll Hall of Fame before a "colorful sunset" and labeled "Rock n' Roll Hall of Fame in Cleveland." The court dismissed the case, despite a trademark registration and wide public recognition of the photograph (Duboff 2002).

Conclusion

Although protection of intellectual property is vital to businesses and other organizations (such as universities) both large and small, registration of patents, copyrights, and trademarks places limitations on individual creativity. In ancient times, plagiarism was the sincerest form of flattery; now plagiarism and infringement are synonymous with criminal activity. Realistically, intellectual property protections are necessary to protect hardworking inventors against those who seek to subvert the system while chasing ill-gotten gains.

In a global economy, patents, copyrights, and trademarks have an increased importance for organizations of all types and sizes. Advances in intellectual property and piracy affect every segment of industry; therefore, it is imperative that intellectual property be registered in the places where an organization conducts business or that organizations are prepared to deal with the consequences.

See also **Foreign Direct Investment; Free Trade; Globalization; Corporate Crime (vol. 2); Biotechnology (vol. 4); Genetic Engineering (vol. 4)**

Further Reading

Bhatnagar, Parija, "China: Your Company Name May Not Be Yours." *CNN Money* (March 7, 2006). http://money.cnn.com/2006/03/07/news/international/trademark_squatting

"BlackBerry Maker Put on Patent Defensive Again." *CNN Money* (May 1, 2006). http://money.cnn.com/2006/05/01/technology/rim_visto/index.htm

Commonwealth v. George. 878 A.2d 881 (Pa.Super.). 2005.

Duboff, Leonard D., *The Law (in Plain English) for Photographers*. New York: Allsworth Press, 2002.

Ebay, Inc. et al. v. MercExchange, LLC. 126 S.Ct. 1837. 2006.

Emerson, Robert W., *Business Law,* 5th ed. Hauppauge, NY: Barron's, 2009.

Friedman, Lawrence M., *American Law in the 20th Century.* New Haven, CT: Yale University Press, 2004.

Garner, Bryan A., *Black's Law Dictionary,* 7th ed. St. Paul, MN: West Group, 1999.

Gohring, Nancy, "BlackBerry Numbers Rising." *IDG News Service* (June 30, 2006).

Henry Wheaton and Robert Donaldson v. Richard Peters and John Grigg. 33 U.S. 591, 8 L.Ed. 1055. 1834.

Illinois Tool Works, Inc., et al. v. Independent Ink, Inc. 126 S.Ct. 1281, 164 L.Ed.2d 26. 2006.

Locy, Toni, "High Court Rejects BlackBerry Patent Appeal." January 23, 2006. www.law.com

Parloff, Roger, "China Goes A-Courtin'." *Fortune* (March 7, 2006). http://money.cnn.com/magazines/fortune/fortune_archive/2006/03/20/8371752/index.htm

Parloff, Roger, "Not Exactly Counterfeit." *Fortune* (April 26, 2006). http://money.cnn.com/magazines/fortune/fortune_archive/2006/05/01/8375455/index.htm

Posner, Richard A., *Law and Literature,* 3d ed. Cambridge, MA: Harvard University Press, 2009.

Rysavy, Peter, "Air Pressure: Why IT Must Sort Out App Mobilization Challenges." *InformationWeek* (December 5, 2009). http://www.informationweek.com/news/mobility/business/showArticle.jhtml?articleID = 222000504

Schmid, John, and Ben Poston, "Patent Delays Harmful to U.S. Economy, Commerce Secretary Says." *JS Online* (August 21, 2009). http://www.jsonline.com/business/54199852.html

Schwabach, Aaron, *Intellectual Property: A Reference Handbook.* Santa Barbara, CA: ABC-CLIO, 2007.

Schwartz, John, and Andrew Pollack, "Judge Invalidates Human Gene Patent." *New York Times* (March 29, 2010).

Slagle, Matt, "Forgent's Business Model Takes Litigious Path." Associated Press (March 22, 2006).

Smith, Aaron, "Eli Lilly Hit with $65M Damages." *CNN Money* (May 5, 2006a). http://money.cnn.com/2006/05/05/news/companies/lilly/index.htm

Smith, Aaron, "Pfizer May Lose Billions in Lipitor Sales." *CNN Money* (August 7, 2006b). http://money.cnn.com/2006/08/02/news/companies/lipitor/index.htm

Spencer, Jane, and Jessica E. Vascellaro, "Imagining a Day without BlackBerrys." *Wall Street Journal* (January 25, 2006).

Stim, Richard, *Patent, Copyright and Trademark: An Intellectual Property Desk Reference,* 10th ed. Berkeley, CA: Nolo, 2009.

U.S. Patent and Trademark Office, "Global Anti-Counterfeiting and Piracy Initiative." 2006. http://www.uspto.gov

Waring v. WDAS Broadcasting Station, Inc. 194 A. 631 (Pa.). 1937.

Werner, Erica, "Small-time Inventors Take on Congress, High-Tech Industry over Proposed Patent Law Changes." Associated Press (October 25, 2005).

Wong, Grace, "Judge: No BlackBerry Shutdown Yet." *CNN Money* (February 24, 2006). http://money.cnn.com/2006/02/24/technology/blackberry/index.htm

Yu, Peter K., *Intellectual Property and Information Wealth: Issues and Practices in the Digital Age.* Westport, CT: Praeger, 2007.

INTEREST GROUPS AND LOBBYING

Ronald J. Hrebenar

Virtually any discussion of contemporary American social issues has to be framed within the vast array of interest groups and lobbyists who advocate for or resist the adoption of new policies. Of all the nations in the world, interest groups and lobbyists are more important to the outcomes of social issues in the United States and especially in the contemporary political era. If one just follows the course of U.S. politics by reading the political articles in the *New York Times* or the *Washington Post*, one would quickly notice that almost every social issue is understood by an examination of the powerful interest groups involved in the political battles. The essence of the process of U.S. politics is interest groups and lobbying.

The Foundations of Interest Group Politics in America: James Madison's Warnings

Every society has interests. Even the most ancient or primitive societies had key interests such as religion, agriculture, warriors, artisans, businesses or trades, and government. The 13 American colonies in the late 1780s had various interests—some promoted by groups with substantial political and economic power. James Madison, the father of the U.S. Constitution and author of some of the most important Federalist Papers (written in defense of the proposed Constitution), warned about the "danger of factions." Factions in the 1780s were an early form of interest group, and Madison designed the new federal government created by the Constitution as a large republic in order to reduce the power of these interests in the United States. Interest groups and lobbying cannot be eliminated in a free society without sacrificing liberty, so the best that can be done is to create a governmental structure with checks and balances and divisions of power so that powerful interests are less likely to dominate government and public policy.

The causes of faction are based "in the nature of man," and the "most common and durable source of factions has been the unequal distribution of property," wrote Madison. Property in a free society and economy will always be distributed in unequal amounts and types; thus, factions (or interests) will always be present.

Since, as Madison argued, there can be no cure for the causes of faction, one must focus on methods for reducing the negative impacts of factions (or interests) on the political system. This is also one of Madison's great contributions to the establishment of the U.S. political system: the complex or large republic. "A Republic…promises the cure for which we are seeking." Madison designed a republic, not a democracy. The republic is a representative government, not a government of direct citizen decision making. The representatives would use their wisdom to discover the "true interest of their country."

The dangers that Madison envisioned have become more apparent in recent decades as money has flooded into the political system and interest groups have moved to provide millions of dollars to politicians for their campaigns (Kaiser 2010). The 2008 elections cost over $5 billion. Annually, lobbying in Washington and in state capitals costs over $6 billion, and that is just a portion of the grand total (Center for Responsive Politics 2010).

The Nature of the American Interest Group System

When the French aristocrat Alex de Tocqueville toured the new American nation in the 1830s, he was amazed by the tendency of Americans to organize interest groups to advocate social change. Compared to the politics of "Old Europe," Americans preferred to use political organizations to pursue their social objectives. Modern comparative political science supports that conclusion. Among the peoples of developed nations, Americans belong to more interests groups than any other people and expect these groups to promote their interests and preferences for them. Those in the other developed nations tend to leave such tasks to political parties (Hrebenar 1997).

The *Encyclopedia of Associations* lists over 20,000 interest groups operating in the United States in the early 21st century (Hunt 2004). The primary focus point for interest groups and lobbying is the U.S. national capital, Washington, DC. In the past several decades, many interest groups moved their national headquarters to K Street so that they can be close to the action on Capitol Hill. Over 20,000 lobbyists are registered in Washington, DC, and that figure represents only a part of the total of lobbyists representing all types of interests and issue areas.

As more and more state governments have expanded their budgets and activities in recent decades, the state-level interest group systems have become more professional and powerful. Interest group politics in Sacramento, California, Albany, New York, and Springfield, Illinois, have come to resemble that found in Washington, DC.

Who are these lobbyists? Many of them are lawyer-lobbyists. In the latter half of the last century, Washington law firms discovered a new revenue stream can be generated by adding a lobbying corps to the basic law firm. Lawyers have many of the skills that make for effective lobbyists. They are trained to understand the law and how it is made, interpreted, and implemented. They are also trained to be effective negotiators—and negotiation is a crucial activity for lobbyists trying to persuade others to support the political objectives of their clients. Many lobbyists are former bureaucrats who have served for a number of years in the governmental bureaucracy—often as staff members for the Congress and its specialized committees or as staff members for the various departments or agencies of government. Holding such jobs gives these lobbyists both subject expertise and lots of personal contacts with government decision makers. Former members of Congress are also valued as future lobbyists given their experience in various issue areas, political knowledge, and contacts in government. Finally, some lobbyists emerge from within the ranks of interest groups' employees and work their way up the ranks to jobs in political affairs, governmental relations, or as executive directors—top lobbyists for many interest groups in Washington (Hrebenar and Thomas 2004).

What do lobbyists do? Primarily, lobbyists provide information to governmental decision makers. They act as representatives of the various interests to the representatives in government. The types of information they provide vary depending on the background of the lobbyist, the policy situation, the political environment, and the governmental decision maker they are lobbying. Some lobbyists are the nation's foremost experts in a particular and very specialized field, such as the extraction of oil from shale (a rock). Others can advise on the nature of public opinion regarding a particular bill, and still others can help plan strategy for getting a bill passed in Congress or a regulation approved in the federal bureaucracy. Since lobbyists represent so many different groups involved in a particular policy debate, a huge amount of useful information is available to the decision makers. Some lobbyists act as watchdogs for their interests—monitoring the key sites of government and reporting back to their interests if anything is happening in a department, agency, or house of Congress that may impact upon the interest. Others are pure advocates or contact lobbyists—often assigned to the White House, the Congress, or a particular department of the bureaucracy and having a variety of contacts in these sites they can use to try to effect a particular outcome. Some lobbyists are specialists in putting together coalitions for a particular bill and thus maximizing the power behind their cause by dividing up the work needed to achieve victory.

One of the major changes that has characterized lobbying in recent years has been the growing sophistication of the tools of the trade (Cigler and Loomis 2006). In decades past, lobbying was exclusively a face-to-face communications activity. Now, however, much of the communications is increasingly electronic, with e-mail messages replacing the old standard of sending a letter or a telegram to your congressperson. In the 1960s and 1970s, such communications were usually by fax or telephone; now, the Internet is used to alert the group's membership to ask them to help lobby the decision makers. This type of lobbying, the activation of members to get out the message, is called grassroots lobbying. There are several types of grassroots lobbying: "shotgun grassroots," where the activation of many members of an organization or coalition is the goal and thus, maybe millions of members may communicate their support; and "rifling grassroots," where the activation of some elite members of the organization produces a more personal and more effective type of communications. When grassroots lobbying is perceived to be ineffective because it seems too artificial or characterized by many very similar, if not identical, messages, it is called "Astroturf"—after the plastic grass of the Astrodome in Houston.

Another electronic form of contemporary lobbying is found in the various outlets of mass media. While billboards and lawn and telephone signs used to be an effective form of issue communication in the 1950s and 1960s, now television, especially cable

THE DEBATE OVER HEALTH CARE REFORM UNDER PRESIDENT BARACK OBAMA

There have been a series of great lobbying battles in the first decade of the 21st century, but surely one of the greatest was over the Obama administration's efforts to create a more substantial role for the federal government in managing the nation's huge health care insurance program—a sector that accounts for one-sixth of the nation's gross domestic product each year and continues to grow. While the nation's financial system struggled to recover from its near collapse in late 2008 and early 2009, health insurance companies, hospitals, doctors, pharmaceutical manufacturers, corporations, labor unions, consumer associations, and lawmakers organized for a fight over health care. The administration's success or failure in passing a reform bill was regarded as a defining moment for the Obama presidency, just as it had been in 1993–1994 for the Clinton administration. After months of confusion involving the Democratic-controlled Congress putting forth a variety of different proposals, the Obama administration stepped in with a compromise that managed to get just enough votes in the House and Senate to pass. The measure was signed into law by the president in March 2010.

Opponents such as the American Medical Association, the lead association of the nation's medical doctors, continued to oppose medical insurance reforms—as it had since the 1930s, when President Franklin Roosevelt proposed a national health insurance program to be added to his social security initiative, and then again in the 1940s, when President Harry Truman proposed a similar idea. The health insurance companies, too, in this latest round of debate, hired hundreds of lobbyists to descend upon Congress and advocate against the "socialization of American medical care." On the opposite side, a national health care insurance program, including a "single payer" provision that would have bypassed the private insurance companies that lie at the heart of the U.S. system, had long been on organized labor's political agenda. And, in a major switch from the time of the Clinton debacle of the 1990s, the pharmaceutical manufacturers this time were on the side of reform, because the Obama administration had promised them protections once they agreed to reduce the prices on some drugs covered in the new proposals. Big Pharma (i.e., the pharmaceuticals industry) ran some $100-million worth of TV ads in support of the administration's efforts.

When all of the issue advertising and spending on lobbying was over, a new law on health insurance in the United States was passed—and yet no one was completely happy. Tens of millions of Americans gained better access to health care, but the system of for-profit, private health insurance that makes U.S. health care different from care in every other developed nation, was still intact. Insurance companies, however, were now unable to deny people coverage for preexisting health problems, and they could not so easily terminate coverage for people who developed costly diseases or health conditions. Like many interest group battles before it, in this case, too many compromises on both sides produced a mixed outcome for all.

television, offers interest groups the ability to target very specific groups of people. An interest group can run television ads in just the congressional districts represented by all the wavering members of a specific congressional committee considering a bill of great import to the group. This is what the Health Insurance Association of America did in 1993 with its now famous "Harry and Louise" ads, as the Clinton administration tried to pass a health care reform bill. The ads cast doubt on many parts of the proposed law, which finally died in Congress without an up-or-down vote. Recent decisions by the Supreme Court, including *Citizens United v. Federal Election Commission* (2010), have made such advocacy TV ads a much more readily available tool for interest groups to use in electoral campaigns in support of politicians who favor their cause or against those who oppose it.

Many interests, especially those seeking to challenge the existing social, political, or economic orders in the United States, do not have the resources to engage in multi-million-dollar TV advertising campaigns. These interests have some types of resources that can allow them to participate in the political process—even if they are at a serious disadvantage in terms of money and other resources that their more established opponents have in abundance. These interests are usually called social movements because they lack the organization, formal membership, and resources of more traditional interest groups. This is not to say that they are not important parts of the political system. In some cases, they represent millions of people who support to one degree or another a particular policy outcome such as equality of treatment for gays and lesbians or express the anger and frustration voiced by the Tea Party supporters in 2010's elections. These interests usually try to gain greater public support for their cause by creating free media events that allow them to gain free media coverage for their cause. Thus, the tools of choice are marches, demonstrations, boycotts, and various actions that draw people—and especially the media—to cover them and their cause. Many of the great interest groups of the contemporary United States began as disorganized social movements and after some success evolved into the more conventional form of interest groups employing the conventional strategies and tactics of such groups. Some of the groups that emerged out of these broader movements include the National Organization of Women, the National Association for the Advancement of Colored People, and the Friends of the Earth.

Money: The Mother's Milk of Interest Group Politics and Lobbying

Money is called the "mother's milk of politics" because it can be converted into so many other resources that are valuable to lobbying (Unruh 2008). It can be used to build a powerful organizational structure with a staff of experts; it can be used to hire powerful, knowledgeable leadership; it can be used to access the mass media to communicate a group's position in important issue debates; it can be used to organize a grassroots campaign; it can be used to help finance the political campaigns of politicians favorable to its cause; it can even be used to finance a public relations campaign to change the public's image of the group and thus enhance its persuasiveness in the issue debates.

Powerful interests such as the American Association of Retired Persons (AARP, the huge, 35-million-member lobby of senior citizens) have hundreds of millions of dollars in revenues each year to support lobbying campaigns. Wall Street and the U.S. banking industry poured tens of millions of dollars into both Republican and Democratic party campaigns in recent years trying to gain the access they needed to protect their interests if the financial system collapsed (as it did in 2008) and calls for greater regulation of the financial industry threatened the industry. Supporters and opponents of the Obama administration's health care reform bill of 2010 also spent hundreds of millions of dollars in lobbying the issue as well as tens of millions of dollars in donations to campaigns of members of Congress in 2006 and 2008.

What does money buy for an interest? First and foremost, access. Interests that make big donations to a political campaign or a political party can expect to have access to key political leaders and an opportunity to make their arguments at key times during the debates. Interests that do not "play the money game" will have a far more difficult time gaining access. They may eventually get some access, but how seriously will they be listened to? Do large campaign contributions buy favorable decisions for the rich interest groups? There is considerable debate on this. Some argue that it does and can point to hundreds of examples where the big contributors often get the laws and regulations they want—give or take a few details. Others argue that the politicians they support financially in election campaigns already support these outcomes regardless of the financial contributions. What is clear, in any case, is that money does buy access, and the outcomes in policy frequently follow the preferences of the groups that give the money to the politicians for their campaigns.

Conclusion

In the final analysis, the outcomes of debates over controversial social issues in U.S. politics are closely linked to major interest groups and the skills and persuasiveness of their lobbyists. To understand which issues rise to be discussed and then dealt with by the legislatures and executives across the nation, one must understand the roles played by interest groups, mass movements, and lobbyists; and one must also understand how these powerful organizations impact these outcomes and, ultimately, the future of U.S. society. As political scientist Jeffrey Berry has put it, ours is an "interest group society" (Berry and Wilcox 2008).

See also **Election Campaign Finance**

Further Reading

Berry, Jeffrey, and Clyde Wilcox, *Interest Group Society.* New York: Longman, 2008.

Burbank, Matthew J., Ronald J. Hrebenar, and Robert C. Benedict, *Parties, Interest Groups, and Political Campaigns.* Boulder, CO: Paradigm, 2008.

Center for Responsive Politics, Lobbying Database. 2007. http://opensecrets.org/lobbyists/index.asp

Cigler, Allan, and Burdett A. Loomis, *Interest Group Politics*. Washington, DC: Congressional Quarterly Press, 2006.

Costain, Anne E., and Andrew S. McFarland, *Social Movements and American Political Institutions*. Lanham, MD: Rowman & Littlefield, 1998.

Hrebenar, Ronald, *Interest Group Politics in America*. Armonk, NY: M. E. Sharpe, 1997.

Hrebenar, Ronald, and Bryson B. Morgan, *Lobbying in America: A Reference Handbook*. Santa Barbara, CA: ABC-CLIO, 2009.

Hrebenar, Ronald J., and Clive S. Thomas, "Interest Groups in the States." In *Politics in the American States,* ed. Virginia Gray and Russell L. Hanson. Washington, DC: CQ Press, 2004.

Hunt, Kimberly N., *Encyclopedia of Associations*. Farmington Hills, MI: Gale-Thomson, 2004.

Kaiser, Robert G., *So Damn Much Money: The Triumph of Lobbying and the Corrosion of American Government*. New York: Vintage Books, 2010.

Meyer, David S., *The Politics of Protest: Social Movements in America*. New York: Oxford University Press, 2007.

Unruh, Jessie, "Quotes." 2008. http://www.jesseunruh.com

L

LABOR, ORGANIZED

Robert M. Fearn

Many questions arise when one considers organized labor and collective bargaining. Among them are the following:

- Why do people join unions?
- What can unions do for their members?
- What are the economic and social effects of organized labor?
- How have those effects changed over time?
- What is the future of U.S. organized labor in the new world economy?

One approach to answering these (and similar) questions is, first, to define what unions are and what they are not, and, second, to trace the history of unions in the United States through good times and bad up to the present.

Types of Unions

Although unions are an economic entity, they are or can be much more than that. Indeed, organized labor (or unionism) represents a broad socioeconomic movement that has taken many forms in many different countries. Among these are the following:

- *Uplift unions.* Associations of workers that seek to raise the incomes and/or alter the living conditions of their members (and others) by raising the skills and cultural levels of members and by providing aid to members who have experienced economic reverses. Leadership of these unions is often external

(priests, rabbis, ministers, philanthropic volunteers), as distinguished from rank
and file.

- *Political unions.* Associations of workers that seek to achieve similar objectives
  primarily through political action, often in alliance with a political party or parties. Unions in democratic socialist nations often fall into this category.

- *Revolutionary unions.* Associations that seek the same objectives by overthrow-
  ing the system—that is, by forcibly altering the property right and/or economic-
  political system.

- *Industry unions.* Associations that seek to raise the incomes of their members
  and alter the conditions of employment primarily through collective bargaining. Industry unionists generally accept and seek to work within the existing
  political and economic system.

Although all four types of unions have existed in the United States, industry unions
have been the predominant form.

The Rise and Decline of Unions in the United States

Union membership was relatively low prior to the First World War, but it grew sharply
during that conflict, peaking at 5 to 6 million—including Canadian members of U.S.
international unions. Throughout the 1920s and the early 1930s, union membership declined to about 3 million workers, representing 11–12 percent of nonagricultural employment in the early 1930s. The pattern of unionism in the United States has changed since
1930, both in total membership and as a percentage of nonagricultural employment.
Although the available data involve differences in definitions and contain some gaps
over the years, the general trends are clear. Union membership grew very rapidly during
the late 1930s and the World War II period, both in membership and as a percentage
of employment. In 1945, unions represented over 14 million workers—about 35 percent
of nonagricultural employment. Hence, one-third of U.S. wage and salary workers were
unionized. Unions were heavily concentrated in mining, manufacturing, and construction and were located particularly in the northern and western industrial states. Beginning in the late 1940s and throughout the 1950s, union membership grew more slowly,
and membership began a slow decline as a proportion of employment (or labor force).
Total membership peaked in 1979 at 21 million workers (about 24 percent of nonagricultural employment). Thereafter, membership gradually fell.

Worker Attitudes

One powerful influence in the growth of unions was the attitude of many workers toward collective action, both in the workplace and in other aspects of their lives. Many
immigrant groups saw collective action as necessary in the struggle for dignity and
higher incomes. German, Scandinavian, and Midland English immigrants brought

THINGS MAY NOT BE WHAT THEY SEEM

Seeking to limit union monopoly power via the Taft-Hartley Act of 1947, Congress outlawed the closed shop. Closed shops involve practices or contractual arrangements whereby employees are obtained exclusively through a union hiring hall or a union business agent. Hence, only persons who are union members (or approved by the union) are eligible for employment.

Despite the legislative ban, de facto closed shops still exist. Is that fact evidence that employers are intimidated by union (or union mob) muscle, as some people contend? Does it mean also that the legal authorities are refusing to enforce the law? While the answer to both questions could be yes, there is an alternative explanation.

First, unions in such instances generally guarantee some acceptable level of skill or experience among those referred for employment. And de facto closed shops seem to exist primarily (if not exclusively) in activities involving intermittent employment. Construction, entertainment, and longshoring are good examples. While there may be alternative ways for employers to staff those positions (say, by conducting a new search each time workers are needed or by hiring temps through various agencies), the union hiring hall may be the least expensive way of obtaining qualified workers whenever and wherever needed. Hence, the closed shop may still exist because it serves the interests of the unionists *and* the employers.

with them a strong pride of craftsmanship and allegiance to the working class. Although, to some degree, these attitudes were foreign imports, they also resulted from and were strengthened by social and economic pressures created by the rapid industrialization of the United States in the late 1800s, the growing social divide of the times, and serious concern about the distribution of income among the population. Clearly, pride of craftsmanship was a strong component in the earliest unions, which were usually organized along craft lines: printers, carpenters and joiners, plumbers, machinists, railroad engineers, and so on. Other immigrants, such as the Irish and the Jews, were alienated from their new environment and saw a need for group solidarity and protection against the bosses. No doubt, those attitudes reflected previous experiences with foreign overlords as well as ethnic and religious discrimination. Somewhat later, African Americans and Mexican Americans mirrored those attitudes and joined unions in large numbers.

The Desire for More

"More" was his answer when Samuel Gompers, president of the (craft-oriented) American Federation of Labor (AFL), was asked what organized labor wanted. Clearly, with national income rising, with vast fortunes being earned by the bosses, and with periodic depressions and recessions, labor wanted both a larger share of the economic pie and greater security. Moreover, unions were prepared to use collective bargaining, strikes, and boycotts to achieve what they believed to be a more equitable distribution of income. However, it was not until the 1930s that any widespread unionization occurred beyond the traditional craft unions. At that time, the Congress of Industrial Organizations (CIO) spearheaded union organization by industry rather than by crafts and organized large numbers of semiskilled and low-skilled workers into unions. The success of unions in achieving "more" is discussed subsequently.

Labor Market Monopsony and Feelings of Impotence

Closely related to workers' attitudes and desires (and some political initiatives) were (1) feelings of economic impotence among workers and (2) the existence of labor market monopsony (where one or a few firms provide most of the employment in the area). In such so-called company towns, there was often considerable tension between workers and management. Coal and other mining communities are good examples. Moreover, under such conditions, workers might risk their jobs by complaining. Obviously, workers could use what Freeman (1976) calls "exit voice" to relieve their workplace grievances, but "union voice" (including grievance procedures established in the collective bargaining contract) was an alternative approach that provided workplace dignity without the need to search for a new job.

As automobile transport became cheaper, roads improved, labor markets became more competitive, information concerning alternative employment opportunities increased, and immigrant and other workers became less alienated and part of the burgeoning middle class, the demand for unionism to address labor market problems diminished, but it did not disappear. Workers in large firms continued to support union efforts to standardize wages and process workers' grievances. In response, many firms established open-door policies, ombudsmen, and employee relations offices to encourage communication between the firm and the workers, to provide a better human relations climate, and to maintain a regular check on the fairness (and limit the arbitrariness) of first-line and other supervisors.

The Legal Framework

Despite company towns, strong feelings of alienation and inequity, and the desire for "more," unionization and union activities for many years were sharply limited by law. From the early 1800s, unions and union activities were often treated by the courts under the common law as criminal conspiracies—that is, actions or associations in restraint of trade. After *Commonwealth v. Hunt* (1842), unions per se were no longer illegal, but most of their economic actions were. Indeed, under the Sherman Anti-Trust Act of 1890, treble damages were a possibility on conviction. It is not surprising, therefore, that unionism did not grow rapidly until the legal strictures were temporarily relaxed during World War I and later in the 1930s, when the Wagner Act (the National Labor

Relations Act of 1935) somewhat belatedly encouraged unionization as an offset to the power of businesses in labor markets.

The legal climate changed again after World War II with the passage of the Labor-Management Relations (or Taft-Hartley) Act of 1947 and subsequent rulings by the National Labor Relations Board. The 1950s saw the passage of the Labor-Management Racketeering (or Hobbs) Act of 1951 and major congressional hearings. The latter resulted in the prosecution and disgrace of several top labor leaders. While the growth and decline of unionism were affected by changes in the legislative and regulatory climate, those changes cannot account fully for what occurred during the latter half of the 20th century.

Union Successes and Changing Labor Markets

As an economic entity, unions can be more successful in raising wage levels when the wage increases do not lead to major reductions in the employment of their members. When it is difficult or expensive to substitute machinery or other inputs for labor (as, say, in the case of airline pilots), the ability of unions to raise wages above what might otherwise exist is strengthened. The ability to substitute other inputs for labor, however, varies substantially from industry to industry, and it changes over time with new products and new technology. So does the profitability of the firm(s) and the ability to substitute non-union or foreign labor for U.S. union labor. Hence, the ability of unions to raise wages declines when changes in technology, skill levels, and import/export restrictions make substitutions easier or when firms become less profitable.

It is not surprising, therefore, that Lewis (1963) (and his colleagues and students at the University of Chicago and elsewhere) found very sizeable differences in union wage effects across industries and across time periods. Their studies show effects ranging from 100 percent in 1921–1922 for bituminous coal mining to a zero effect in 1945. Only a few studies, however, showed changes in relative wages greater than 25 percent. Indeed, the average wage effect shown by these studies was approximately 10–15 percent. Many seemingly strong unions had little or no effect on wage levels but were apparently able to provide workers with grievance and other workplace protections. As suggested, these protections may be highly valued by workers. Indeed, according to Lewis, less than 6 percent of the labor force showed union wage effects of 20 percent or more. As suggested, these effects varied among and within industries and over time.

Most of these estimates were made during or prior to the 1960s. During the entire post–World War II period, however, there were massive changes in industrial composition and the U.S. labor market. In particular, manufacturing was affected by (1) a substantial rise in productivity (similar to that experienced earlier in U.S. agriculture), (2) the movement of population and some industry to the less unionized southern states, and (3) the increased ability of Japanese and European firms to export their products to the United States.

Indeed, as a result of these and other factors, manufacturing employment in the United States fell by about 5 million workers during the last three decades, reducing the workforce in manufacturing from about 20 percent of total employment in 1979 to about 11 percent in 2005. In addition to the factors noted previously, the U.S. economy and unions in the United States have been affected by globalization and the emergence of world market conditions that increased further the availability of foreign products. Globalization, of course, affected more than the unionized sector. Indeed, many of the low-skill intensive and often nonunion industries (particularly in the South) were heavily impacted by free trade and the formation of new truly global corporations in both manufacturing and commerce. Included among these were textile, garment, and sewing firms. Mergers created numerous new international corporations with plants around the world. In addition, some U.S. firms simply closed their plants in the United States and even overseas, choosing to become wholesalers who contract with foreign-owned firms to meet the product specifications established by the U.S. firm(s). In addition, the massive transformation of the economy in the late 1980s and 1990s known as the dot.com boom sharply altered job skills, communications, business procedures, and industrial composition.

All of these factors sharply affected the ability of unions to raise or even maintain wage levels in the industries and areas where unions had previously exhibited clout, lowering the extent of unionization and altering the composition of the labor movement. As noted, the largest U.S. unions are now concentrated in public-sector service jobs and in transportation, utilities, and construction—industries where the possibilities for foreign labor substitution are smaller than in, say, manufacturing.

According to Deitz and Orr (2006), job losses in manufacturing "are almost certain to continue"—an assessment that surely applies even more strongly to the 2008–2009 recession and its aftermath. Nonetheless, Deitz and Orr found that, in the early 2000s, high-skilled employment in manufacturing rose substantially in almost all manufacturing industries and in all parts of the country. Such a finding is consistent with the comparative advantage of the United States over many other countries in highly skilled activities. It also reflects the fact that it is often more difficult to substitute other inputs for skilled labor. In a previous age, that was one of the strengths of the craft-oriented unions.

Among the industries that were hard hit by the recent recession is the U.S. auto industry. U.S. carmakers have long struggled with high labor costs—salaries, benefits, health care, and pensions—compared to their nonunionized counterparts, the Japanese automakers. Before the recession, Detroit automakers made agreements with unions to reduce wages while making pension and health care commitments to their workers. Nevertheless, that left carmakers vulnerable to drops in the financial markets, as happened at the end of 2008. The terms of the earlier agreements had to be revisited and additional changes instituted. Most of the auto companies, for example, offered their older workers early retirement packages and made agreements with the United Auto Workers to transfer pension obligations to an independent trust. Massive loans from the government also were solicited. Yet, despite even that, U.S. automakers continued to struggle in the market vis-à-vis the Japanese carmakers. As of mid-2010, there were signs both positive and negative regarding Detroit's overall prospects for success.

Union Leadership

No listing of the factors influencing U.S. unionism would be complete without some mention of the many charismatic and often controversial leaders of the movement. Samuel Gompers of the American Federation of Labor was cited previously. John L. Lewis, initially with the Coal Miner's Union, championed the rise of industrial unionism and led in the formation of the CIO. The Reuther brothers, Walter and Victor, developed the sit-down strike into a formidable weapon and directed the once powerful United Auto Workers Union. George Meany, the longtime president of the combined AFL-CIO, also deserves mention. So does Jimmy Hoffa of the Teamsters Union, who was regularly accused of racketeering and connections to the Mob. That circumstance, among other concerns, led to the passage of the Labor-Management Racketeering Act of 1951. In 2005, Andrew Stern, then president of the Service Employees International Union, led his large union out of the unified AFL-CIO in a dispute over how to reorganize the labor movement to meet the challenges of globalization and changing technology. Each of these individuals contributed to the nature and success of unions in the United States, as did a raft of other leaders.

The Future of Organized Labor in the United States

The ups and downs of unionism combined with the uncertainties of the future make any predictions extremely difficult. All one can reasonably do is outline the major factors that could affect unions and union membership now that membership as a proportion of employment is only about 12 percent and slipping.

Several factors weigh heavily in what may occur in the near future. These factors include (1) globalization, (2) the change in the composition of the labor movement from the manufacturing and mining to the service industries, (3) the growing skill levels of U.S. workers within manufacturing and beyond, and (4) the growth of social discord in both the United States and the newly industrializing nations. Moreover, as in the past, legal-legislative changes could have major impacts.

Clearly, the old feelings of alienation, impotency in the workplace, and even class struggle have risen recently with industrial relocation and new technology. It seems likely that these concerns will continue to be addressed among skilled and professional workers largely by exit voice, rather than by union voice. That certainly was the pattern in the 1990s and the early 2000s. Indeed, exit voice among such workers may entail migration across national boundaries, going where the jobs are. Among lower-skilled and semiskilled workers, however, the emerging world labor market may limit the opportunities for exit voice both within and outside the United States, and that may encourage unionization. Many displaced workers have already found their way into the service industries, now the most heavily unionized sector of the economy. Some of these workers, of course, have left the labor force, have relocated into nonunion jobs, or have been retrained for higher-skilled occupations. Union leaders like Andrew Stern argue that recent events require both the reorganization of existing unions and an emphasis on industrywide (rather than firm-level) bargaining. Whether such changes could or would reinvigorate unions or increase membership, however, is problematical. It is also unknown whether the new immigrants to the United States, legal or illegal, will be as supportive of unions as were the immigrants of the middle to late 1800s and early 1900s.

Alternative approaches to strengthen unions may be tried, particularly the formation of truly international unions to match the new international corporations or the insistence on international labor standards via the courts, the United Nations, and various treaties. These approaches face many obstacles. The first is somewhat daunting since political (rather than business) unionism has been the norm in many other developed nations. Moreover, there are innumerable differences in labor laws and regulatory climates among the nations. Also, there are important questions of national sovereignty. Finally, some nations are rejecting globalization and even capitalism, nationalizing industries and hence limiting the opportunities for collective bargaining on either a firmwide or industrywide basis. Nevertheless, there is some agitation overseas (for example, in China) for independent industry unionism now that there are private employers throughout that nation. Of course, U.S. unions would welcome and support such a development in China and elsewhere.

Finally, to the degree that perceived income differences grow among Americans, there will be stronger demands for government regulation of the labor market via living wage and minimum wage laws, governmentally regulated pension arrangements, and the like. As in the past, organized labor in the United States is likely to support both collective bargaining and governmental initiatives to address the overall distribution of income.

See also **Free Trade; Globalization; Immigrant Workers; Minimum Wage; Outsourcing and Offshoring; Pensions; Unemployment**

Further Reading

Bennett, James T., and Bruce E. Kaufmann, eds., *What Do Unions Do? A Twenty-Year Perspective.* New Brunswick, NJ: Transaction Publishers, 2007.

Briggs, Vernon, *Immigration and American Unionism.* Ithaca, NY: Cornell University Press, 2001.

Brody, David, *Labor Embattled: History, Power, Rights.* Urbana: University of Illinois Press, 2005.

Bureau of Labor Statistics, U.S. Department of Labor. "Union Members—2009." January 22, 2010. http://www.bls.gov/news.release/pdf/union2.pdf

Deitz, Richard, and James Orr, "A Leaner, More Skilled U.S. Manufacturing Work-force." *Current Issues in Economics and Finance* 12 (2006): 1–7.

Dine, Philip M., *State of the Unions: How Labor Can Strengthen the Middle Class, Improve Our Economy, and Regain Political Influence.* New York: McGraw-Hill, 2008.

Early, Steve, *Embedded with Organized Labor: Journalistic Reflections on the Class War at Home.* New York: Monthly Review Press, 2009.

Freeman, Richard, "Individual Mobility and Union Voice in the Labor Market." *American Economic Review* 66 (1976): 361–368.

Lewis, H. Gregg, *Unionism and Relative Wages in the United States.* Chicago: University of Chicago Press, 1963.

Martinez, Rick, "Can Unions Fly High Once More?" *News and Observer* (August 25, 2005): 13A.

Troy, Leo, *Beyond Unions and Collective Bargaining.* Armonk, NY: M. E. Sharpe, 2000.

Weir, Robert E., and James P. Hanlan, eds., *Historical Encyclopedia of American Labor.* Westport, CT: Greenwood Press, 2004.

Yates, Michael D., *Why Unions Matter,* 2d ed. New York: Monthly Review Press, 2009.

M

MARKETING OF ALCOHOL AND TOBACCO

Paul W. Schneider

Alcohol and tobacco have served a variety of functions and played a significant role in the marketplace throughout history. Alcohol has long been used as part of religious customs, as medicine, and as a form of sustenance. Tobacco was used as collateral for loans from France during the American Revolutionary War, as a cure-all, and as a diet aid. However, for the last 200 years or so, alcohol and tobacco have been consumed in a fashion consistent with present-day usage, primarily for pleasure. Regardless of the reason for their use, both substances have been popular throughout most of human history. And both substances and their marketing have become controversial.

Historical Developments

As early as the Civil War (1861–1865), organizations were formed to protest alcohol consumption. Although alcohol remained popular among portions of the population, independent movements calling for voluntary abstinence and eventually the prohibition of alcohol by law emerged.

Eventually, as living conditions improved and humans began to live longer, the hazards of alcohol surfaced. The public took notice and actions were taken. Prohibition, a result of the temperance movement and which made the sale and consumption of alcohol illegal, began on January 16, 1919. It was abolished on May 10, 1924.

To date, the marketing of alcohol remains largely self-regulated, and legal limitations on marketing and sales have been more lenient than those on tobacco. Nonetheless, the knowledge that alcohol can contribute to health problems and beliefs that it is responsible for corrupting the family unit have led to the establishment of dry counties in various states. In existence to this day, a dry county is one that prohibits the sale of alcohol.

It was not until the surgeon general released a report called "Smoking and Health" in 1964 that the hazards of smoking were officially and publicly recognized. Negative press surrounding tobacco surfaced due to the health concerns associated with the product. This caused many of the major tobacco producers of the 1960s to consider changing the names of their companies and diversifying their range of products. In marketing, names are important because they convey information about the company to consumers. The information communicated to consumers influences how the company is perceived and how it is positioned in regard to purchasing habits. Tobacco companies acknowledged the importance of brand names, and a trend started that saw tobacco companies actively change their names and products to avoid negative perceptions.

In the United States in the 1960s, a company that produced only tobacco products or had the word *tobacco* in its name was looked upon unfavorably. As a result, American Tobacco Company became American Brands, and Philip Morris bought part of Miller Brewing Company. R. J. Reynolds Tobacco Company changed its name to R. J. Reynolds Industries and ventured into the aluminum industry. (Reynolds Wrap aluminum foil was long part of the R. J. Reynolds line of products.) The government has regulated the sales and advertising of cigarettes and, since 1966, has forced the industry to place health risk warnings on all packaging. Sales of both alcohol and tobacco to minors are limited; these age limitations vary according to state laws.

The Costs of Marketing Alcohol and Tobacco

In the United States, more than $2 billion is spent each year to promote alcoholic beverages (Center on Alcohol Marketing and Youth n.d.). The alcohol industry claims that

ADVANTAGES OF POINT-OF-PURCHASE ADVERTISING

According to the Point-of-Purchase Advertising Institute, sales of point-of-purchase materials bring in nearly $13 billion annually; this makes the sales of point-of-purchase advertising materials third highest of all media in dollar expenditures. Point-of-purchase advertising consists of:

1. Displays, which can range from countertop to refrigerated dispensers
2. Signs, which serve notice of special pricing or other important information about a product
3. Shelf media, which attach to the front of retail shelving and tell the customer about special offers without taking up valuable retail space
4. New media, which can include video displays, coupon dispensers, interactive displays, and audio devices

advertising only affects brand choice and that the marketing of products is done to establish brand differentiation, or anything that positively distinguishes the identity of a company and its products and/or services to consumers from other companies' products. Popular examples of brand differentiation in the alcohol industry include promotions for Samuel Adams reminding consumers that the company uses more hops for flavor in its beer, and Coors Brewing Company's description of its beer as shipped cold and made with Rocky Mountain spring water.

While alcohol producers claim that advertising only promotes distinguishing characteristics to consumers, alcohol researchers, the U.S. surgeon general, and the National Institute on Alcohol Abuse and Alcoholism disagree. They say that heavy episodic drinking, or binge drinking, is at least partially fueled by commercial messages (Center on Alcohol Marketing and Youth n.d.). Binge drinking is regarded as the consumption of five or more consecutive drinks by a male or four or more consecutive drinks by a female. National studies have concluded that 40 percent of college students are binge drinkers.

Alcohol consumption among college students has been shown to have an elastic demand. This means that as the price of alcohol decreases, consumption increases. Because traditional college students are around the legal drinking age, marketing helps fuel the desire for experimentation. Of course, many influences other than marketing (such as parenting and peer pressure) factor into one's decision to consume alcohol. But given alcohol's accessibility, it is believed that marketing initiatives and promotional measures that constantly bombard people with advertising and discounted prices increase consumption by keeping alcohol financially accessible and on consumers' minds (Kuo et al. 2003). Unfortunately, increased drinking by college students leads to a greater number of accidents. The National Institute on Alcohol Abuse and Alcoholism reports that drinking by college students results in more than 1,800 alcohol-related deaths each year (National Institute on Alcohol Abuse and Alcoholism 2009).

It is projected that more than $243 million was spent in 1999 alone to sponsor public service activities that combat alcohol abuse and related problems. Nearly $11 million is spent annually to educate the public about the harm of tobacco (Corporate Accountability International n.d.). (The industry has a daily marketing budget of about the same amount; Educational Forum on Adolescent Health 2003.) While both the alcohol and tobacco industries have marketing programs that are intended to educate the public about potential risks, the difference is that tobacco education has federal funding, whereas alcohol does not. Alcohol education programs are funded by institutions such as Century Council, the Beer Institute, the National Beer Wholesalers Association, Brewers' Association of America, and the alcohol companies.

Aggressive Marketing of Products

Some organizations and activists believe that the products' aggressive marketing practices have an adverse impact on the long-term behavior of the population. Thus, certain marketing approaches may have a variety of opponents. It is logical to ask why companies in these industries would continue practices that lead to such unfavorable attacks on their businesses.

The answer lies in the nearly 5,000 customers that the tobacco industry loses in the United States on a daily basis (approximately 3,500 quit and 1,200 die) and the estimated 100,000 Americans dying annually from alcohol-related causes (Corporate Accountability International n.d.; Mayo Clinic 2007). In fact, it is projected by the U.S. Office on Smoking and Health that smoking results in more than 5.5 million years of potential life lost nationally each year (Centers for Disease Control 2008). Simply put, in order to replace the revenue from those customers that the industries are losing, new customers must be acquired. This is accomplished through multimillion-dollar marketing campaigns. Campaigns of this magnitude are widespread, encompassing many media outlets. This means that marketing messages about alcohol and tobacco will reach the eyes and ears of youths, regardless of the demographic groups that the messages are geared toward.

Consequently, rules surrounding the marketing of tobacco and alcohol are evolving, and marketing campaigns in nearly all parts of the world are aimed at preventing children from developing these habits. The theory is that preventative measures will translate into an absence of alcohol- and tobacco-related problems and health risks in the future.

Marketing Tactics

When marketing abroad, the alcohol and tobacco industries often attach American themes to their brands. This practice is particularly common in tobacco advertisements; for example, in one ad circulated in the Czech Republic, a pack of Philip Morris cigarettes is seen merging with the New York City skyline, and a Polish Winchester Cigarette advertisement features the Statue of Liberty holding an oversized pack of cigarettes. Others showcase prominent U.S. cities; red, white, and blue color schemes; and scenes that depict an American lifestyle (Essential Action n.d.).

Goldberg and Baumgartner found that the use of American imagery in smoking advertisements works because smoking is seen as an attractive part of the American lifestyle in many countries. Those attracted to the United States and who regard it as a place they would like to live are more likely to smoke. Having decided to smoke because they see it as an important part of the American lifestyle, they are more likely to smoke a U.S. brand of cigarette (Goldberg and Baumgartner n.d.).

R. J. Reynolds found in a 1983 study that marketing using American themes is not successful in the United States. Statements made by study respondents included: "It is too nationalistic," "America is not that great," and "It is not appropriate to sell America when selling cigarettes, or at least not in such a directly nationalistic way" (Essential Action 2006).

Nonetheless, the promotion of the perceived customs and norms of a product's place of origin has surfaced in the domestic advertising of alcoholic beverages. Smirnoff Ice, an alcoholic beverage, employs actors with Russian accents and wearing Russian garb for a television advertising campaign. Beer companies such as Heineken and Becks also proudly promote the heritage of the beer's national origin.

Another method that has been effective among U.S. consumers is what author Edward Abbey calls "industrial recreation" (Marin Institute n.d.). Often referred to as "wreckreation" or "ecotainment," the term refers to the utilization of landscape to promote a product. It is argued that such use of terrain in advertising may change the way that the community uses and experiences public space.

Some new marketing campaigns are prompting questions about whether they are bending the rules of marketing. The prevailing rules of marketing rely primarily on codes that are geared toward traditional media. New technologies that utilize both traditional and nontraditional marketing techniques are complicating efforts to restrict and monitor marketing aimed at susceptible groups. These new technologies allow questionable marketing practices, such as cloaking, to go undetected by policy.

Cloaking, or stealth, is an ethically questionable technique employed online by Web sites to index Web pages within search engines in a fashion that is different from the way the page is indexed to other sources. Basically, the technique of cloaking can be used to trick a search engine. Successful cloaking results in higher rankings of inappropriate matches—for example, a search for a word unrelated to alcohol might bring up the sites of alcohol companies, which may lead the user to browse those sites. The logic here is that the more visitors a Web site receives, the more valuable it becomes. Some Web sites that employ cloaking have considerably different content from what the user intended to find and are often of pornographic nature. As such, some feel that the rules that govern marketing need to be revamped to ensure consistency among standards in relation to newly emerging marketing tactics.

Should the Marketing of Alcohol and Tobacco Be Limited?

Yes

Ninety percent of all smokers begin smoking before age 21, and 60 percent of current smokers picked up the habit before age 14 (U.S. Department of Health and Human Services 1989). The American Public Health Association, citing government research, states that every day "an estimated 3,900 young people under the age of 18 try their first cigarette" (American Public Health Association 2010). Clearly, children are the growth opportunity for the tobacco industry. If people do not start as children, they are significantly less likely ever to use the products. Cartoon characters were banned from tobacco advertising in 1991 after Joe Camel, the famous cartoon representative of the Camel cigarette brand, was shown to be more appealing to children than adults. In 2010, the Food and Drug Administration, which regulates tobacco sales, applied new restrictions to cigarette vending machines and barred tobacco companies from advertising at popular sporting events or offering merchandise such as hats and T-shirts. Stipulations such as these are an attempt to prevent the exposure of children to tobacco marketing and, it is hoped, tobacco products.

Possibly the most disturbing of such accusations is the charge that the marketing and advertising firms working for the tobacco industry employed psychologists to better understand children and how to more effectively target them. One of the revelations of the recent tobacco-related court cases was that tobacco companies asked retail outlets to place tobacco products in proximity to external doors in unlocked cabinets. They told the store owners that they would be reimbursed for stolen products. A few stolen cigarettes today can lead to hundreds of cartons of cigarettes sold 20, 30, and 40 years later. Health departments have been quick to encourage stores to discontinue this practice.

The alcohol industry has not seen the same level of concern over the advertising of alcoholic beverages. For instance, the introduction of spirits advertising on cable television was not opposed in 1996, even though, according to the 1986 Nielsen Report on Television, children watch an average of 28 hours of television per week. Ironically, permission to advertise alcohol on television was granted five years after the banishment of cartoon characters from cigarette advertisements.

Currently, 70 percent of the U.S. population is 21 years of age or older. In accordance with industry codes for beer and distilled spirits, the placement of alcohol-related advertisements is permissible in nearly any piece of media that is not specifically geared toward young children (National Institute on Alcohol Abuse and Alcoholism n.d.). The concern is that the messages of alcohol companies are reaching a vast number of youths through the television programs they watch and the magazines they read in their homes. Some argue that seeing an advertisement for alcohol or tobacco next to an advertisement for a prestigious or widely desirable product may still be harmful because of an unconscious association that may be drawn by the reader (Marin Institute n.d.).

The Federal Trade Commission and the National Academies Press agree that there should be a reduction in the exposure of youth to alcohol advertising (National Center for Chronic Disease Prevention 2006). Research shows that limitations placed on marketing initiatives in the tobacco industry, in addition to federally funded tobacco education programs, have decreased the amount of tobacco usage. This suggests that similar actions regarding alcohol would decrease sales and consumption as well as the occurrence of the third-leading cause of preventable death in alcohol-related fatalities in the United States (Centers for Disease Control and Prevention 2003). Though exposure of alcohol advertising to youths has been shown to have decreased 31 percent between 2001 and 2004, children are still more exposed, per capita, than adults (Center on Alcohol Marketing and Youth 2007).

Organizations such as Mothers Against Drunk Driving and the Center on Alcohol Marketing and Youth feel that the alcohol industry should not be the only supplier of education concerning alcohol consumption. They advocate federal funding for alcohol education and suggest that the alcohol industry no longer be permitted to practice self-regulation, as was done with the tobacco industry. Self-regulation of alcohol marketing means that the industry itself helps set the standards of regulation in regard to advertising.

Opponents of alcohol self-regulation were recently disappointed when the viability of Australia's self-regulation policy, which mirrors that of the United States, was questioned in a series of allegations. Some marketing tactics that were examined were deemed to be sexually explicit or specifically geared toward children. One of the alcohol advertisements that was often singled out featured the phrase "Come out to play" written in ink on the palm of a woman's hand. It was argued that this advertisement was aimed at children.

The criticism did not bring about a substantial change in self-regulation policy, and this lack of action was felt by many alcohol activists to be a slap on the wrist for a major violation against alcohol advertising regulations and a reminder of the alcohol industry's power. The alcohol companies claim no wrongdoing.

No

Alcohol and tobacco companies already face advertising restrictions that are unheard of in other industries. The International Code of Advertising, issued by the International Chamber of Commerce, asserts that "advertising should be legal, decent, honest, truthful, and prepared with a sense of social responsibility to the consumer and society and with proper respect for the rules of fair competition" (International Chamber of Commerce n.d.). Yet tobacco and alcohol must adhere to additional stipulations. Tobacco has been the target of a national campaign called "We Card" that requires cashiers to ask for identification from anyone who appears to be younger than 30 years old, and limitations are placed on point-of-purchase, or on-site, marketing initiatives for alcoholic products.

Many products in the marketplace have associated risks, but alcohol and tobacco are among the few that face marketing regulations because of the detrimental effects on their consumers' health. For example, an estimated 17 percent of children and adolescents in the United States are overweight (Centers for Disease Control and Prevention 2010). Being overweight can lead to numerous health problems, such as type 2 diabetes, hypertension, stroke, heart attack, heart failure, gout, gallstones, and osteoporosis. However, there are no laws limiting fast-food commercials that target youths. A Burger King Whopper with a large fries and a Coke has 1,375 calories, yet there is no surgeon general's warning on fast-food wrappers (Healthy Weight Forum n.d.). Considering the marketing efforts, availability, and low cost of such restaurants, one would think they would require additional marketing rules, just like alcohol and tobacco. Yet even as obesity is being proclaimed a national epidemic, the post-meal cigarette is still getting all the attention.

The self-regulation policy of the alcohol industry receives much criticism, yet it has many positive attributes. For example, an extensive amount of marketing issues can be attended to without involving constitutional issues of government regulation (Federal Trade Commission 2003). The lack of costly deliberation in high courts concerning alcohol marketing issues saves considerable amounts of taxpayer dollars. A 1999 report to Congress noted that most companies in the alcohol industry complied with the codes of self-regulation and that the culture of some companies causes their practices to supersede industry standards (Federal Trade Commission 2003).

Sports Illustrated is a magazine devoted to sports that is enjoyed by both adolescents and adults. The results of an examination of the alcohol and tobacco advertisements in the last issue for July and the first issue for August from 1986, 1996, and 2006 showed the following:

- In 1986, there were nine alcohol advertisements and five tobacco advertisements (*Sports Illustrated* July 28 and August 4, 1986).
- In 1996, there were five alcohol advertisements and three tobacco advertisements (*Sports Illustrated* July 22 and August 5, 1996).
- In 2006, there were four alcohol advertisements, one tobacco advertisement, and one advertisement for Nicorette gum, a nicotine replacement therapy designed to reduce nicotine cravings (*Sports Illustrated* July 31 and August 7, 2006).

This example shows a decrease in the marketing of alcohol and tobacco over the 20-year period. Also note that the 2006 issues included an advertisement for Nicorette, a product used to assist in breaking the smoking addiction. This is just one illustration of the change that has already taken place.

Conclusion

Ultimately, the burden of counteracting the adverse impact of marketing alcohol and tobacco lies with each of us, as does the decision whether to use such substances. Most organizational and legislative movements do not seek to revoke the right of adults to use these legal substances. The provision of all the facts that will allow individuals to make their own informed decisions seems to be the desire of most groups, regardless of their stance on the product.

The marketing issues surrounding alcohol and tobacco focus on who is really making your decisions, you or marketers? Marketers are trained so well in the art of manipulation that most people fall victim to their messages without realizing it. The most prevalent question about the marketing of alcohol and tobacco is whether such advertising leads the average person (or child) to make poor lifestyle choices.

Should restrictions regarding the marketing of harmful products be implemented to save us from ourselves, and, if so, what should be deemed harmful? For example, is eating fast food on a regular basis harmful? The answer is probably dependent on the individual.

Marketing works. It convinces us to buy products that we do not need, cannot afford, and, in some cases, should not use for a variety of reasons. The goal in regard to the marketing of potentially harmful products is to present both the good and bad features and then allow people to decide for themselves.

See also **Marketing to Children; Addiction and Family (vol. 3)**

Further Reading

American Medical Association (Educational Forum on Adolescent Health), "Youth Drinking Patterns and Alcohol Advertising." 2003. http://www.ama-assn.org/ama1/pub/upload/mm/39/proceedingsalcohol.pdf

American Public Health Association, "Tobacco Facts." 2010. http://www.apha.org/programs/resources/tobacco/tobaccofacts.htm

Center on Alcohol Marketing and Youth, "Drowned Out: Alcohol Industry 'Responsibility' Advertising on Television, 2001–2005." June 2007. http://www.camy.org

Center on Alcohol Marketing and Youth, *Fact Sheets.* http://camy.org/factsheets/index.php?FactsheetID=16

Centers for Disease Control and Prevention. Childhood Overweight and Obesity, 2010. http://www.cdc.gov/obesity/childhood/

Centers for Disease Control and Prevention, "Point-of-Purchase Alcohol Marketing and Promotion by Store Type—United States, 2000–2001." *Morbidity and Mortality Weekly Report* 52, no. 14 (2003): 310–313. http://www.cdc.gov/mmwr/preview/mmwrhtml/mm5214a4.htm

Centers for Disease Control and Prevention, "Smoking-Attributable Mortality, 2000–2004." 2008. http://www.cdc.gov/tobacco/data_statistics/mmwrs/byyear/2008/mm5745a3/highlights.htm

Essential Action, Global Partnerships for Tobacco Control, *Marketing Tobacco and the USA.* http://www.takingontobacco.org/photos/usa.html

Federal Trade Commission, *Alcohol Marketing and Advertising: A Report to Congress.* September 2003. http://www.ftc.gov/os/2003/09/alcohol08report.pdf

Goldberg, Marvin E., and Hans Baumgartner, *Cross-Country Attraction as a Motivation for Product Consumption.* http://marketing.byu.edu/htmlpages/ccrs/proceedings99/goldberg.htm

Healthy Weight Forum, *Calorie Counter: Burger King.* http://www.healthy weightforum.org/eng/calorie-counter/burger_king_calories

International Chamber of Commerce, "Frequently Asked Questions." http://www.iccwbo.org/uploadedFiles/ICC/policy/marketing/Statements/338%20FAQs%20ICC%20Advertising%20and%20Marketing%20Code.pdf

Kuo Meichun, Henry Wechsler, Patty Greenberg, and Hang Lee, "The Marketing of Alcohol to College Students: The Role of Low Prices and Special Promotions." *American Journal of Preventive Medicine* 25, no. 3 (2003): 204–211.

Marin Institute, *Alcohol Facts: Marketing to Youth.* http://www.marininstitute.org/alcohol_industry/marketing_to_youth.htm

Mayo Clinic, "MayoClinic.com Offers Online Alcohol Self-Assessment Tool." 2007. http://www.mayoclinic.org/news2007-mchi/4098.html

National Institute on Alcohol Abuse and Alcoholism, "College Drinking: Changing the Culture." 2009. www.collegedrinkingprevention.gov/

National Institute on Alcohol Abuse and Alcoholism, "Environmental and Contextual Considerations." n.d. pubs.niaaa.nih.gov/publications/arh283/155-162.htm

Pennock, Pamela E., *Advertising Sin and Sickness: The Politics of Alcohol and Tobacco Marketing, 1950–1990.* Dekalb, IL: Northern Illinois University Press, 2007.

U.S. Department of Health and Human Services, *Reducing the Health Consequences of Smoking: 25 Years of Progress. A Report of the Surgeon General.* Atlanta: Center for Chronic Disease Prevention and Health Promotion, Office on Smoking and Health, 1989.

MARKETING TO CHILDREN

PHYLIS M. MANSFIELD AND MICHAEL SHALLY-JENSEN

Purple ketchup, blue squeeze butter, and French fries that are flavored with cinnamon or chocolate—these were all products that were developed specifically to be marketed to children. But products marketed directly to children are nothing new. In the 1950s, the products were toys like Silly Putty, Monopoly, and Barbie. Today, those toys still exist, although the new holiday wish list includes items like iPods, cell phones, and video games.

Even the use of celebrity characters as advertising spokespeople is not a recent phenomenon. Today we have SpongeBob SquarePants, Dora the Explorer, and Blue from *Blue's Clues;* in the 1950s, there were Tony the Tiger, Cinderella, and Mickey Mouse.

Every one of us at one time or another has probably nagged a parent until a favorite toy was purchased. However, in today's society, there is growing concern over the increased consumption and spending by children. Some critics believe that companies are too aggressive in targeting children. Marketers respond that they are only providing the product; it is the parent's job to monitor how much the child spends.

But are children today really different from children of past generations? Are marketers today taking unfair advantage of children, or is the growth in children's consumption just a trickle-down effect of a larger consumer culture?

Children as Consumers

Children are becoming consumers at an increasingly younger age. Just a few decades ago, children were considered to be consumers, or brand aware, by the age of 7; now it's more like 3. Not only are they becoming more brand aware at an earlier age, but they are also spending their own money and influencing family spending in a significant way. In the United States, children ages 4 to 12 spend more than $50 billion directly and are estimated to influence more than $500 billion each year in family purchases, from furniture to the family minivan (Dotson and Hyatt 2005). In fact, kids influence about 62 percent of minivan and SUV purchases, which may be why a number of major manufacturers have run ad campaigns featuring animated cartoon characters such as Jimmy Neutron or Shrek inspecting a vehicle and approving its features (see, e.g., Chrysler 2008).

Children Learn to Spend

Older children are turning to making their own money in order to support their spending habits. Over 55 percent of U.S. high school seniors work more than three hours each day, compared to 27 percent of their foreign counterparts. While many parents may feel that teen employment instills a work ethic early in life, it has been shown that grades and participation in school activities suffer when teens work during the school year (Quart 2004). It is difficult to determine which comes first, however: the positive work ethic a child develops as a productive member of society or the consuming culture that tells the teen he or she has to have the latest and coolest brand.

Similar logic has been used by parents to justify their children's use of debit and credit cards. Marketers promote the cards as ways to teach children how to spend money. However, they may also encourage them to spend money they don't have. Children as young as 8 years old have been targeted by marketers with their own credit card. Hello Kitty, a popular children's brand, has licensed its brand name to MasterCard, which markets the service directly to the parents. The card can be used at stores like a regular credit card or at an ATM to withdraw cash. Kids love it because it makes them look cooler than if they were just using cash (Bodnar 2005). Even the youngest consumers are taught to use plastic in their play. One toy company has a toddler's "first purse" play set that comes complete with a debit card and case. And the Hasbro company recently announced a British version of Monopoly that will use a debit card—no cash play money.

Marketers may tell parents that giving a child plastic helps them learn how to spend, but sociology experts tell parents that direct teaching episodes are a better way to teach children how to become good consumers. Some TV networks that target kids and teens have turned to an old-fashioned way to offer these teaching episodes by promoting "co-viewing," where the child and the parent watch TV together. Marketers actually promote

MARKETING FACTS AND FIGURES

- Companies spend about $17 billion annually marketing to children.
- Children aged 2 to 11 see more than 25,000 ads per year on television (a figure that does not include the Internet or other technologies and sources).
- Teens between ages 13 and 17 have on average 145 conversations per week about brands, which is double the same figure for adults (Campaign for a Commercial-Free Childhood n.d.).
- In the decade between the early 1990s and the early 2000s, there was a tenfold increase (1,000 percent) in the number of food products targeted to children and teens (Institute of Medicine 2006).

TABLE 1. Children's Influence on Family Purchases

Mothers Who Said . . .	Percentage
Kids are influential on purchases made in discount stores.	92
Kids are influential in deciding on vacations.	38
Kids are influential in deciding on computers.	33
Kids are influential in deciding on cell phones.	32
Kids are influential in deciding on family car.	28
They have asked kids to go online and research purchases for themselves.	77
They have asked kids to go online and research family purchases.	25

their products—brands and products whose purchase children significantly influence—to both the parent and the child at once. Cartoon Network shows commercials for automobiles, vacation destinations, and sit-down restaurants alongside those for McDonald's, Cheerios, and Mattel. To better understand this interchange of information, Disney ABC Kids Networks Group commissioned a research study of children's influence on purchases in which mothers and children between the ages of 6 and 14 were interviewed about their purchasing behavior. Some of the results are shown in Table 1 (Downey 2006).

Criticism of Children's Marketing

The growth in the spending power and influence of children has prompted criticism of marketers, parents, and legislators. Juliet Schor, an expert in consumerism and family studies, is one of those critics. In *Born to Buy,* she describes how children as consumers are changing: "Kids can recognize logos by eighteen months, and before reaching their second birthday, they're asking for products by brand name" (Schor 2005).

The increase in brand recognition by young children is at least partially due to the impact of television. In the 1950s, families typically had one television per household, and the programs directed at children were mostly Saturday morning cartoons and a few daily morning shows. Today, there is a proliferation of children's programming, some educational, some not so, and most accompanied by commercials. The typical commercial during a children's program is 15 seconds, half the length of a commercial targeted at older consumers. Children's attention spans are shorter, requiring only a brief ad message. The commercials are also more colorful and action oriented.

In addition to the increased number of ads directed at the children's market, there also has been an increase in the number of hours that children spend watching television and a decrease in the amount of parental control over what is viewed. Schor (2005) says that approximately 25 percent of preschool-age children have a TV in their own bedroom, and they watch that TV for a little over two hours each day. It is estimated that American children watch a total of 40,000 television commercials annually.

One research study by doctors at Stanford University found that children's demands for specific toys and foods increased with the time they spent in front of the television.

The third-grade children who were interviewed averaged 11 hours of TV time each week, and another 12 hours spent on video games or computers. The children were able to identify where the ideas for their requests for toys or food items came from—whether it was from the television or their peers (Murphy 2006).

The quest for brand loyalty is moving to increasingly younger television audiences. Marketers once targeted 7- to 12-year-olds. However, companies realized that they need to attract consumers to their brands at an even earlier age. The new target segment is the preschooler—children ages 2 to 5. In fact, the preschooler market has become increasingly competitive, and television has become a primary medium for advertising messages. "It is estimated that a successful preschool TV show generates more than $1 billion in retail sales in any given year across all related categories, including recorded media, in the U.S.," says Simon Waters, vice president of Disney Consumer Products, Disney's global franchise management branch (Facenda 2006).

Moreover, as more and more children at a younger and younger age spend greater amounts of their time social networking via the Internet (e.g., MySpace) or using hand-held devices such as smart phones, the higher is the likelihood that marketers will continue to expand their efforts in these areas in addition to those they already undertake in the television industry.

Social Issues

Although parents are accountable for the consumer behavior of their children, there is still the question of corporate and social responsibility. The number of advertisements for children's products embedded in television programs and the increase of product placements and movie tie-ins have made the parent's job increasingly more difficult. SpongeBob SquarePants has his own toothpaste and toothbrush product line; Dora the Explorer has a lunch box and other products; and every time a children's movie is released, it is now paired with some type of premium at a fast-food restaurant.

But parents have had to contend with spokescharacters like SpongeBob SquarePants for decades (i.e., the Donald Duck lunch boxes of the 1950s). What is it about today's environment that makes it different from that of previous generations? Two factors that have an impact on the consumer behavior of children are time and money. Parents spend less time with their children today than they did in previous decades. Many children living in single-parent or two-income households obtain a large portion of their skills from their peers at day care or at school. And even schools, once a sanctuary from pervasive marketing tactics, have become the new frontier for commercialism. Faced with declining budgets, schools are turning to subsidies from corporations, which are allowed to come into the school with a program, albeit it educational, that is sponsored by their firm. These sponsorships are considered by some to be subtle forms of advertising.

Children are also more active in sports and other extracurricular activities than they were in previous decades. Many parents find themselves shuttling their children from one event to another after school, the children's calendars booked almost as tightly as their own. Parents are also feeling pressure from longer working hours, which leave them less time and energy to spend with their children. Add to that the fact that the square footage of the average home in the United States has increased significantly, which requires more upkeep and maintenance, and parents have more to do during their off hours. We are working more and spending more, yet relaxing less. In fact, U.S. workers spend more hours at work each week and have less vacation time than workers in any other industrialized nation in the world.

Marketers know that parents who spend less time with their children are willing to spend more *on* them, a relationship that has been substantiated by researchers. It is probably no surprise that children are moving from reasonably priced toys to more expensive electronic products at an ever-decreasing age. Younger children are requesting expensive products like Wiis, cell phones, iPods, and laptops—the type of products that used to be reserved for teenagers and adults. Marketers say that the market for electronic products aimed at tweens grew 46 percent in 2004 (Kang 2005).

When Marketing Tactics are Questionable

Marketers can use subtle messages to get to young consumers that parents may find difficult to overrule. When the tobacco companies were required to remove cigarette ads from media and even withdraw their sponsorship of the Winston Cup NASCAR race, they were forced to look for other ways to promote and increase the sales of their products. One such way is through the product itself. R. J. Reynolds, the company that first used Joe Camel in questionable advertising campaigns, went on to market its products to younger smokers in a different way. R. J. Reynolds introduced in 1999 a new line of candy-flavored cigarettes. They came packaged in a shiny tin box and had names like Beach Breezer (watermelon), Bayou Blast (berry), and Kauai Kolada (pineapple and coconut). The cigarettes were flavored with a tiny pellet that was slipped into the filter (Califano and Sullivan 2006). R. J. Reynolds was criticized for marketing its product to children, who are more likely to begin to smoke if the product tastes better. They maintained that they were only marketing the product to the adult who already was a smoker but wanted a change of flavor. It is common knowledge that most adult smokers begin prior to their 18th birthday. Currently, the average age at which young people begin to smoke is 11 (Mansfield, Thoms, and Nixon 2006).

The flavored cigarettes were once advertised heavily in magazines read by young boys and girls; however, pressure from federal legislators made them retract the ads, and in 2006 the company discontinued this line of cigarettes.

When Marketing Tactics are Used for Good

Not all marketing is necessarily evil, however, even when it is directed toward children. Marketing programs throughout the years have helped children to learn basic skills.

Think of McGruff taking "a bite out of crime." Today one area of concern in the United States is the growing epidemic of childhood obesity. In response to this epidemic, several corporations have developed new marketing campaigns to offset the negative effects of their products. Both Coca-Cola and McDonald's launched fitness programs that are presented in schools and encourage healthy food choices and exercise. Fast-food restaurants like Wendy's and McDonald's have added selections like apple slices and mandarin oranges to their children's menus as an alternative to French fries. General Mills now produces its cereals with whole grains. Other companies are reducing the trans fats in their cookies, crackers, and other baked goods. While the trend toward more healthful eating is at least for now being directed at children, it will be interesting to see how many of the products that are typically sold to this target audience will actually change.

ADVOCACY VERSUS BIG BUSINESS

It is perhaps too easily forgotten that popular children's brands, so appealing to kids and parents alike, have profit-driven corporations behind them. In this world where business interests and family needs meet, there has always been a place for watchdog groups that monitor new products, assess the accuracy of claims made on their behalf, and judge their appropriateness for young consumers.

One such group is the Campaign for a Commercial-Free Childhood (CFCC), based in Boston. This nonprofit organization seeks to counter the negative effects of consumer culture on children. Since its founding in 2000, CFCC has successfully mounted campaigns to get the children's publisher Scholastic to stop selling Bratz doll products at school book fairs (the dolls are viewed as being overtly sexual); to cease the airing of commercial radio (BusRadio) on school buses; to end the practice of inserting Happy Meal ads in report card envelopes; and to curtail the use of product placements (e.g., by Cover Girl) in novels intended for girls (Turner 2010).

In 2009, CFCC prodded Disney to stop using the term "educational" in association with its Baby Einstein line of videos for children aged two and younger. The group charged that there was no firm basis to the claim that the videos served an educational purpose, and the American Academy of Pediatrics had previously recommended that children of this age watch no television or videos (Lewin 2010). Unfortunately in this case, CFCC experienced backlash in the wake of its campaign. A Harvard-affiliated children's mental health center that had been sponsoring CFCC and providing it with office space, the Judge Baker's Children's Center, pulled its support and asked CFCC to leave. It was reported that Disney had contacted the center three times to express its displeasure with CFCC. Although the details of those conversations were not made public, it was widely speculated that pressure, possibly legal pressure, was applied by the corporation. In explaining the Judge Baker's decision to oust CFCC, a spokesperson would only allow that the center's board found that "the targeting of individual large corporations [by CFCC]...poses too much risk" (Turner 2010).

The Marketer's Position

The KidPower Conference meets annually to discuss the latest techniques, successes, and failures of marketing to children and teens. Marketers come to learn the latest on how to maximize the appeal of their brand—more specifically, to target certain age groups and create ads that appeal to different ethnic targets. Additionally, there are sessions on how to do social marketing. Social marketing is using traditional advertising and other marketing techniques to change a child's behavior on issues like refusing drugs, exercising more, and becoming more tolerant of others. While the social marketing conference sessions are definitely targeted at improving society, the overwhelming majority of the conference is on how to market products and brands to kids.

Marketers feel that they are just offering a product that is for sale and that ultimately consumer education needs to start at home. Some consumer advocates agree that parents have a significant portion of the responsibility. Jeff Dess, a prevention specialist for schools in Cobb County, Georgia, says, "We need to talk with our kids about these issues and consider changing our own habits" (McAulay 2006). Some ad agency executives are in agreement with Dess's statement and assert that it is parents and other relatives who are working in ad agencies and in corporations who are advertising the products, so they are also concerned about what the children in their lives are exposed to. Ultimately, it is the parent's job to determine what food his or her children eat and what they buy (McAulay 2006).

See also **Marketing of Alcohol and Tobacco; Marketing to Women and Girls**

Further Reading

Bodnar, Janet, "Give Kids Credit? Not So Fast." *Kiplinger's Personal Finance* (March 2005). http://www.kiplinger.com

Calfee, John E., "The Historical Significance of Joe Camel." *Journal of Public Policy and Marketing* 19, no. 2 (2000): 168–182.

Califano, Joseph, and Louis Sullivan, "The Flavor of Marketing to Kids." *Washington Post* (June 29, 2006).

Campaign for a Commercial-Free Childhood, http://www.commercialfreechildhood.org

Cheap-Cigarettes.com, *Camel Cigarettes.* http://www.cheap-cigarettes.com/camel-cigarettes.asp

Chrysler Group LLC., "2008 Chrysler Town and Country" (television commercial). http://www.youtube.com/watch?v=gEo0fPCHkGw

Dotson, Michael J., and Eva M. Hyatt, "Major Influence Factors in Children's Consumer Socialization." *Journal of Consumer Marketing* 22, no. 1 (2005): 35–42.

Downey, Kevin, "What Children Teach Their Parents." *Broadcasting and Cable* (March 2006). http://www.broadcastingcable.com

Facenda, Vanessa, "Targeting Tots." *Retail Merchandiser* (June 2006).

Institute of Medicine, *Food Marketing to Children and Youth.* Washington, DC: National Academies Press, 2006.

Kang, Stephanie, "Babes in iPodland; Children Go from $30 Toys to $300 Electronic Gadgets at Alarmingly Early Ages." *Wall Street Journal* (November 28, 2005).

Lewin, Tamar, "After Victory over Disney, Group Loses Its Lease." *New York Times* (March 9, 2010).

Mansfield, Phylis, Peg Thoms, and Charisse Nixon, "An Exploratory Analysis of the Relationship between Consumer Socialization Agents and Children's Consumption of Tobacco." *Journal of College Teaching and Learning* 3 (January 2006).

McAulay, Jean, "Buy-Buy, Childhood Pervasive Marketing Aimed at Kids Worries Parents and Experts." *Atlanta Journal-Constitution* (February 19, 2006).

Murphy, Dave, "Children's Demands for Toys and Food Increase with TV Time, Researchers Say." *San Francisco Chronicle* (April 5, 2006).

Quart, Alissa, *Branded: The Buying and Selling of Teenagers.* New York: Basic Books, 2004.

Schor, Juliet, *Born to Buy.* New York: Scribner, 2005.

Turner, Maureen, "Angerfixing the Mouse." *Valley Advocate* (Northampton, MA) (March 18, 2010).

MARKETING TO WOMEN AND GIRLS

Phylis M. Mansfield and John D. Crane

Cosmetics, age-defying cream, weight-loss products, and revealing clothing—these are all products almost exclusively marketed to women. The marketing of beauty products to women is not a new practice. Several decades ago, products were marketed to women with the assumption that they were housewives or were looking for a husband. The product being marketed was designed to assist them in either of these endeavors. Betty Crocker made women's lives easier if they were struggling to do the laundry, feed the children, and put a decent dinner on the table by 5:30 p.m., when their husbands came home from work. Other products addressed the woman who was either trying to stay youthful or trying to be attractive in order to get a husband. Even cigarette companies employed tactics targeted toward this group of women. During the mid-1920s, it was unacceptable for women to smoke in public; however, the tobacco companies saw women as a large target segment of the population that was virtually untouched. The American Tobacco Company began a campaign for its brand, Lucky Strike, targeted at women with the slogan, "Reach for a Lucky Instead of a Sweet." It was the first cigarette campaign that featured a picture of a woman in the ad and that began to associate the idea of smoking with having a slim body (*Albert Lasker* n.d.).

The Impact of Social Change

In the 1970s and 1980s, social convention began to change with regard to the role of women, possibly due to the rise in women's participation in the work force. Advertising changed and began portraying women as confident individuals who could effectively balance their personal and private endeavors. One such ad campaign was for the perfume Enjoli, by Revlon. Debuting during the late 1970s, its jingle began, "I can bring home the bacon, fry it up in a pan, and make you never forget you're a man. 'Cause I'm a W-O-M-A-N" (Vranica 2003). In recent years, advertising strategy has reflected the success of women as breadwinners, executives, and business owners. Many products that were traditionally marketed to men, or to the household as a whole, are now marketed to women. Sellers of automobiles and homes and investment banking advertise to women specifically, acknowledging their status in the marketplace. However, despite the movement toward affirming women as self-confident and successful, there is also another trend that appears to discredit their accomplishments and demean them as sexual objects. Marketers present the idea that women must be physically perfect in order to be truly accomplished. This quest for the perfect body has made it now socially acceptable to openly discuss one's latest cosmetic surgery. The negative impact that this pressure from the media has on women may be filtering down to their daughters, even those of a very young age.

What is the Ad Selling?

Those who have browsed the pages of *Cosmopolitan, Vogue,* or *GQ* have most likely perused page after page of half-naked women advertising various beauty products. In some, just a silk scarf is strategically placed across the woman, who is selling a product such as moisturizing lotion, shampoo, or even men's cologne. Airbrushing and other technologies provide the magazine glossies with perfect-looking models, devoid of any blemish or cellulite. There is no doubt that sexy photos of women can help sell products to men, but how do women and girls respond to this marketing technique? Clearly, the photos used in many ads have no connection to the actual use or purpose of the product. For example, diet products and exercise machines should be used only for health-related reasons and should only be used under the direct supervision of a doctor. The ads rarely present this aspect of the product's use and instead focus on the physical attractiveness of the user.

There is a growing concern about the effect this type of advertisement has on women's and girls' self-images. One doesn't have to look far to see the impact that this type of body consciousness has on young women in the movie industry. Tabloids contain story after story discussing how a young star is looking extremely thin after losing weight, some to the point of anorexia. Even a 2006 television advertising campaign for a health insurance company stresses the physical appeal rather than the health-related benefits of physical exercise programs for young girls. HealthMark, a BlueCross BlueShield affiliate, had a young girl playing soccer while talking about how she used to hate to shop for clothes because she was "big." Now she doesn't mind shopping and loves her team picture because she doesn't look "big" anymore (HealthMark 2006). In an effort to diminish the obesity epidemic in the United States among children, the ads promoting increased activity should be applauded. It is questionable, however, whether they should focus more on a child's appearance than the health benefits that result from exercise.

WHAT'S IN A SIZE?

For some time, the clothing industry has not been held to any standardized measurements in the design and creation of women's apparel. It's not a secret between women that finding waist sizes that fit is as much of a gamble as picking a horse based on its name. One of the main reasons for the large discrepancy between designers' sizes is their original consumer segment. All clothing is designed with a specific consumer in mind. In women's fashion, consumers at higher-end stores usually prefer high fashion that typically conforms to the prescribed industry image for body size—which is tall and thin. For example, the women auditioning for the popular television program *America's Next Top Model* need to be at least five feet seven inches tall—and contestants who happen to be six feet tall need to weigh around 135 pounds.

This creates a discrepancy since, in 2010, the average American woman weighed between 142 and 165 pounds and was five feet four inches tall—and therefore is not the target of high-end retailers. Moderate retailers offer the average American woman a wide range of sizes to fit the variations of women's bodies. Recently, the sizes of high-end and moderately priced designers have been growing further apart. High-end retailers have stringent measurements based on industry standards, while those at moderately priced retailers have more flexibility because they target a wider audience and their clothes are not necessarily connected with status. A trend of stores providing so-called vanity sizing has developed. For example, over the past 20 years, the average size 8 dress has increased two inches in waist size. By increasing the waist measurement while keeping the pants size the same, corporations can be more profitable. Women want to feel like the models they see in advertisements and are more likely to shop at a store where size 6 pants fit like a size 10.

"Problem areas" identified by women when looking for clothing and the percentage of women who find a particular area to be problematic include:

- Hips (35 percent)
- Bust (32 percent)
- Waist (32 percent)
- Rear (23 percent)
- Length (20 percent)
- Thighs (17 percent)
- Back (13 percent)

A Cause for Alarm?

Advertisements reflect and shape cultural norms, selling values and concepts that are important to daily living. The trend of using objectified images of the female body in the media is not a new area of research, nor a new area of concern. Consumer activists and some researchers believe that marketers have gone too far in their advertising strategies to women by presenting an unattainable or unhealthy image. One voice of criticism back in

THE FINANCIAL SIDE OF COSMETIC SURGERY

Considering plastic surgery, but don't have the funds to get it? Cosmetic—or elective—plastic surgery is a booming business. Americans spent $10.5 billion on cosmetic procedures in 2009. A number of financial institutions offer financing options for individuals who would like to go under the knife but don't have the funds. According to Helen Colen, "It's exploding; everyone is jumping in." Currently, the cosmetic lending market is approaching the $1 billion mark, but experts expect that figure to triple within the next few years.

The application process is very simple. Patients can have doctors' offices make a phone call to a lending institution and can be approved within an hour. However, not all is as rosy as it seems. Critics have suggested that people are borrowing money they don't have—to get a procedure they don't need. The majority of cosmetic procedures today are performed on individuals who earn between $30,000 and $90,000. People who opt for financial assistance are most likely those who don't have access to the funds.

Here are the average costs for some cosmetic procedures:

- Botox injection: under $500
- Liposuction: $2,000 to $10,000
- Nose job: $3,000 to $12,000
- Face lift: $6,000 to $12,000
- Eyelid tuck: $1,500 to $7,000
- Breast enhancement: $5,000 to $7,000
- Tummy tuck: $5,000 to $9,000

In 2009, Democrats in Congress proposed a tax on cosmetic surgery to help pay down the nation's health care costs as part of an overall health care reform effort, but the measure was later removed from the bill.

Sources: American Society of Plastic Surgeons. http://www.plasticsurgery.org; Plastic Surgery Research. http://www.cosmeticplasticsurgerystatistics.com/costs.html

1963 was that of Betty Friedan, who railed against the "feminine mystique." Friedan reported that, by the end of the 1950s, women who had once wanted careers were now making careers out of having babies. Manufacturers sold bras with false bosoms made of foam rubber for girls as young as 10. Thirty percent of women dyed their hair blonde and dieted so they could shrink to the size of the super-thin models. According to department stores at that time, women had become three to four sizes smaller than they had been in the late 1930s in order to fit into the clothes that were marketed to them (Friedan 2001). Freidan believed that women were being manipulated into becoming the ideal housewife—a Stepford-type housewife—and were feeling a great sense of emptiness in their lives.

The fashion industry may be turning a corner, however. In 2006, the organizers of Madrid's fashion week in Spain banned models who were deemed to be too skinny.

After a model died during a fashion show in South America in August 2006, the subject of extreme dieting became a topic of discussion, resulting in the ban. The typical runway model in the industry is reported to be five feet nine inches tall and weigh 110 pounds, with a BMI (height-to-weight ratio) of 16. She wears a size 2 or 4. The organizers of the Madrid show required the models to have a BMI above 18, which is closer to five feet nine inches tall and a weight of 123 pounds. In contrast, the average American woman is five feet four inches tall, weighs between 142 and 165 pounds, and wears a size 14 (Klonick 2006).

The Emphasis on Beauty

Critics of advertising suggest that the use of nonfunctional aspects in advertising creates an artificial need for many products that do not fulfill a basic physiological need. They believe that the use of perfectly airbrushed models and those with extremely thin bodies suggests to women that they should be just as attractive as the models. This quest for perfect beauty has contributed to the explosive growth of the plastic surgery industry in the United States, where women account for almost 90 percent of all surgeries. In 2008, surgeons performed 12.1 million cosmetic procedures, up 3 percent (even in a recession) from the previous year. Cosmetic surgery is becoming so commonplace that plastic surgeons are seeing increased numbers of men giving it to their girlfriends and wives as Valentine's Day gifts. Experts such as John W. Jacobs, a Manhattan psychiatrist, believe that the gift can be romantic if the recipient longs for it (Kerr 2006).

What is the Effect on Young Girls?

This focus on the emotional and sexual enhancement that products or services offer feeds into the problem of distorted body image and the low-self esteem of many young women. The fascination with the feminine ideal can develop early and can be seen as early as age six, according to data collected for an *Oprah Winfrey Show* a few years ago. "Children are becoming obsessed with external beauty at a much younger age," Winfrey noted, "and the consequences are going to be shattering." One story was about a young toddler, only three years old, who was obsessed with her looks. The young girl demanded lipstick, makeup, and hairspray in order to look beautiful. When refused these items, she looks into the mirror, cries, and says that she doesn't look pretty. The young girl's mother fears what the youngster will be like in another 10 years and worries that her own insecurities have added to the problem ("Healing Mothers" 2006).

A study by the Dove Campaign for Real Beauty found that 57 percent of young girls are currently dieting, fasting, or smoking to lose weight. And almost two-thirds of teens ages 15 to 17 avoid activities because they feel badly about their looks (Etcoff et al. 2004). Girls at younger ages are also feeling the need to diet. One four-year-old girl studied skips breakfast and eats only fruit for lunch because it will make her skinny. While her mother thinks that other children's comments about her daughter being fat are to blame for the young girl's behavior, interviews uncovered other possible reasons. The girl's mother reported that she measures out exact portions of her own food at mealtimes and exercises at least once each day, sometimes twice ("Healing Mothers" 2006). Robin Smith, a psychiatrist, says that mothers unconsciously hand down their insecurities to their children. Parents, as well as peers and the media, shape children's self-image and must work to break the curse that is handed down from generation to generation (Etcoff et al. 2004).

During adolescence, a girl's obsession with her body becomes even more apparent. This is accompanied by increased attention to what her peers think and increased attention to the media and advertising. Not only are younger girls and adolescents using cosmetics and dieting, but they are also turning to plastic surgery at younger ages than ever before. Like their mothers, they are in search of the perfect body, and it shows in the numbers of surgeries done on girls under the age of 18. In 2003, the number of plastic surgeries performed on children under 18 was almost 75,000 in the United States, a 14 percent increase over those performed in 2000. According to the American Society of Plastic Surgeons, the number of breast augmentation surgeries done on girls under 18 tripled in just one year (Kreimer 2004).

This focus on the perfect and slimmest of bodies may also be the root of the increase in cigarette smoking by girls. The number of teenage girls who smoke and abuse prescription drugs has now surpassed that of boys. In 2005, more girls began smoking than did boys (Connolly 2006). One reason for this increase may be body image. These young women have not seen the advertisement for the Lucky Strike cigarettes that urged consumers to "Reach for a Lucky Instead of a Sweet," but they are getting the message that cigarettes can help you stay slim. Girls as young as nine years old have been reported to take up smoking in attempts to lose weight (Greene 1999).

On the Other Hand—The Benefits of Advertising

In today's fast-paced society, marketers play an important role in educating consumers about new products and processes available to them. The average consumer has a plethora of choices available to him or her in an infinite marketplace. If each person had to personally evaluate each product, no one would ever be able to make an informed or timely decision concerning the functionality of a product for a certain purpose.

This is particularly apparent in the cosmetic and beauty industry. Technology is constantly evolving so that new products providing better health rewards without potentially damaging consequences can be created. The marketing of these types of products allows consumers to quickly evaluate the products in a company's product line. This type of marketing strategy only shows the consumer what is available in the marketplace. It does not make consumers purchase the product or buy into the idea of the marketing message; it is purely informative. Marketers assert that they cannot make someone buy a product; they can only influence people. It makes sense to market to women, because 80 percent of discretionary consumer spending in the United States is by women. Women buy 90 percent of all food, 55 percent of all consumer electronics, and over half of all cars sold ("Hello Girls" 2009).

The companies that market beauty and fashion products suggest that the healthy-looking models in beauty advertisements provide good role models for girls and women to aspire to. The products they are advertising provide women the means to achieve whatever level of beauty and healthiness they desire. Therefore, they say, marketers are actually providing a public service to today's busy woman.

The dynamic nature of marketing allows the consumer to make the decision to listen to the message or to move on. Advertisements on television and in magazines clearly give the consumer the opportunity to change the channel or flip the page if he or she does not approve of the message. Ultimately, it is the consumer who chooses to listen to or ignore the message that is presented.

See also **Advertising and the Invasion of Privacy; Marketing to Children; Sex and Advertising; Eating Disorders (vol. 3)**

Further Reading

Albert Lasker Promoted Lucky Strike, n.d. http://users.ap.net/~burntofferings/adslasker.html

American Academy of Facial Plastic and Reconstructive Surgery, http://aafprs.org

Centers for Disease Control, "Body Measurements." http://www.cdc.gov/nchs/fastats/bodymeas.htm

Connolly, Ceci, "Teen Girls Using Pills, Smoking More Than Boys." *Washington Post* (February 9, 2006).

Etcoff, Nancy, Susie Orbach, Jennifer Scott, and Heidi D'Agostino, *The Real Truth about Beauty: A Global Report.* September 2004. http://www.campaignforrealbeauty.com/uploadedfiles/dove_white_paper_final.pdf

Friedan, Betty, *The Feminine Mystique.* New York: W. W. Norton, 2001 [1964].

Greene, Alan, "Preteens Start Smoking to Control Weight." *Pediatrics* (October 1999): 918–924.

Grogan, Sarah, *Body Image.* New York: Routledge, 2007.

"Healing Mothers, Healing Daughters." *Oprah Winfrey Show* (April 28, 2006).

HealthMark advertisement, Broadcast on NBC, May–September 2006.

"Hello Girls: Recession-Hit Companies Target Female Customers." *Economist* (March 12, 2009).

Kerr, Kathleen, "Plastic Surgery Becomes Hot New Gift for Valentines." *Newsday* (February 13, 2006).

Kilbourne, Jean, *Deadly Persuasion: Why Women and Girls Must Fight the Addictive Power of Advertising.* New York: Free Press, 1999.

Klonick, Kate, "New Message to Models: Eat!" *ABC News Internet Ventures* September 15, 2006. http://abcnews.go.com/Entertainment/story?id=2450069&page=1

Kreimer, Susan, "Teens Getting Breast Implants for Graduation." *Women's eNews.* June 6, 2004. http://www.womensenews.org/story/health/040606/teens-getting-breast-implants-graduation

Lamb, Sharon, and Lyn Mikel Brown, *Packaging Girlhood: Rescuing Our Daughters from Marketers' Schemes.* New York: St. Martin's Press, 2006.

Vranica, Suzanne, "Marketing and Media Advertising: Stereotypes of Women Persist in Ads; Bikinis Still Sell the Suds, as Masculine Views Reign; Agency Gender Gap Blamed." *Wall Street Journal* (October 17, 2003)

Wykes, Maggie, and Barry Gunter, *The Media and Body Image.* Thousand Oaks, CA: Sage, 2005.

MINIMUM WAGE

Walter J. Wessels

Minimum wage laws set the minimum hourly wage a worker can be paid. A minimum wage of $7.25, for example, means a worker cannot legally contract with an employer to work for below $7.25 an hour.

The federal minimum wage sets the wage for the whole nation. In 2010, the minimum wage was $7.25. The federal minimum wage for tipped workers is lower than the standard minimum wage, on the assumption that these workers can meet or exceed the minimum wage through tips. On the other hand, many states have a minimum wage that is higher than that mandated at the federal level. Information on the current minimum wage, both federal and state, and who is covered by the law is available at the Bureau of Labor Statistics Web site (www.bls.gov).

Approximately half of those earning the minimum wage (or less) are young workers (below age 25). Most are adults living alone (23 percent) or teenagers living with their parents (41 percent). About 15 percent are adults raising a family. Another way to look at the statistics is to consider that about 10 percent of teenagers earn the minimum wage (or less), and 2 percent of those above age 25 earn the minimum wage or less. Many studies show that increasing the minimum wage has little impact on the poor. One study, for example, found that, if the minimum wage were raised 30 percent, less than 2 percent of those living in poverty would have their wages directly increased (Wilson 2001).

Many economists oppose the minimum wage for two reasons. First, the minimum wage law, in effect, prohibits from working anyone who cannot produce enough value in his or her work to cover the minimum wage. That is, a minimum wage of $8 an hour does not help the person who can produce a value of only $6 an hour. In addition, it does not seem worthwhile to help 10 workers to earn $1 more an hour, for example, if another worker is forced out of a job paying $5 an hour. While there is controversy about whether a small increase in the minimum wage will reduce jobs, there is no doubt that a very high minimum wage will cause substantial job losses. It may be argued that a very high minimum wage is necessary to give workers a living wage, but this would be counterproductive if the worker cannot get hired at all. To a worker put out of a job, a hiring wage is better than a living wage.

The second reason many economists oppose the minimum wage is that there is a more efficient method of helping the working poor without jeopardizing their jobs—the earned income tax credit. If a person is poor, the earned income tax credit supplements his or her wage earnings. For example, a poor person earning $6 an hour might get another $3 an hour from the government. While the current earned income tax credit program it not that generous, it could be changed to be so and to significantly increase the incomes of the poor.

An earned income tax credit has several key advantages over the minimum wage. First, it only goes to the poor, while the minimum wage favors those whom employers want to retain (who are often the better-educated teenagers whose parents who are well off). Second, the minimum wage does impose a cost on society in the form of higher prices and lower profits. Because the poor are a small fraction of minimum-wage workers, and because the earned income tax credit only goes to the poor, for the same social cost, the earned income tax credit can give the poor a much higher wage than a minimum wage having the same social cost. Third, there is a social justice argument. The earned income credit is paid for by taxpayers, not employers. It can be argued that society (mainly taxpayers) benefits from making the poor better off, so it is just that society—not employers—should pay the cost of making the poor better off. The earned income tax credit is more just than the minimum wage because it is paid for by society. There are some who feel that employers should do more for workers. But employers are doing something for workers—they are giving them a job. Blaming employers for not doing more is as unjust as saying the Salvation Army is responsible for poverty because it could do more.

The Minimum Wage and Employment

Does economic theory say that the minimum wage reduces employment? It does say that a large increase in the minimum wage would reduce employment. But what about a small increase similar in magnitude to past increases in the minimum wage? When labor markets are competitive, wages are bid up to the value of what workers produce. Thus, an increase in the minimum wage would push the wages of some workers above the value of what they are producing, and these workers would lose their jobs. On the other hand, when labor markets are not competitive, it is possible that a higher minimum wage would not reduce employment and, in some cases, would actually increase employment.

A minimum wage can increase employment if an employer is a monopsony. A monopsony is a situation where there is only one employer in a labor market. More generally, any employer who has to pay increasingly higher wages as he or she hires more workers (for example, paying $5 to hire the first worker and $6 for the second, and having to raise both of their wages to $7 to get a third) is a monopsony. Because a monopsony faces rising wage costs, the cost of each added worker includes the worker's wage plus the dollar amount the employer has to pay in order to raise the wages of the other workers to the new wage. For example, suppose an employer employs 9 workers at $10 and must pay $11 to hire the 10th worker. The 10th worker costs $11 plus the $9 needed to raise the pay of the first 9 workers from $10 to $11. Thus, the 10th worker costs $20. If the worker produces a value of $15, the monopsony would not hire him or her. However, if there were a minimum wage of $11, the 10th worker would only cost $11 (since the wages of the first 9 workers do not have to be increased, as they are already at $11). In this case, the worker would be hired. A sufficiently high minimum wage (for example, $16) will cause this worker not to be hired and, if even higher, may cause others to lose their jobs. Over some range, a minimum wage causes a monopsony to hire more workers, but at some point, an even higher wage will cause jobs to be lost.

Research has found that restaurants have monopsony power over tipped workers. In the absence of a minimum wage, a restaurant hiring more tipped servers would find, at some point, that each tipped server earns less in tips per hour (as each will serve fewer patrons in an hour when more waiters are hired). As a result, the restaurant will have to raise the hourly cash wage to remain competitive with other employers. Therefore, a restaurant has monopsony power, and a minimum wage has the potential to increase employment of tipped servers. However, it was also found that when the minimum wage for tipped workers was increased too much, employment fell.

What do the data say about the effect of minimum wages on employment? Most studies of teenagers suggest that the minimum wage does reduce employment: every 10 percent increase in the minimum wage reduces teenage employment by 1 to 2 percent. The reason that most research on minimum wages involves teenagers is that they are the only group sizably affected by the minimum wage, which makes its effects more discernable. David Card and Alan Krueger have conducted considerable research that shows that minimum wages do not reduce employment. For example, they concluded that, when the minimum wage was increased in 1990 and 1991, states with a larger fraction of low-wage workers did not suffer a greater loss in jobs (Card and Krueger 1995). However, a study of the 1996–1997 increase in the federal minimum wage did show a greater job loss in jobs in states with larger proportions of low-wage workers (Wessels 2007). Thus, using their methodology, it appears that the minimum wage did reduce employment.

Another Card and Krueger study (1994) compared employment at fast-food restaurants in two adjoining towns—one in New Jersey, where the minimum wage was increased, and the other in Pennsylvania, where the minimum wage was not increased. They found no difference in before-and-after employment trends between the two towns and concluded the minimum wage had no effect.

Yet for the study's results to be valid, both towns must have basically the same business conditions before and after the minimum wage increase. Otherwise, it is possible that the town with the minimum wage increase also had an improvement in business conditions (while the other town did not) that offset the negative effect of the minimum wage on employment. This is why nationwide studies usually are better sources of evidence; the year-to-year variations in local business conditions usually net out when averaged across the nation. The drawback to using nationwide studies is that the business cycle can be a potentially confounding factor. For example, the increase in the federal minimum wage in 1990 occurred during a recession, and it is possible that the negative effects of the minimum wage found then could have actually been caused by the business downturn. However, the minimum wage has been found to reduce employment in many business conditions.

Other Effects of the Minimum Wage

Minimum wages also have other effects. One major effect is that they raise the wages not only of minimum-wage workers but also of those earning more than the minimum wage. Studies have shown that a 10 percent increase in the minimum wage increases the

---

THE LIVING WAGE

Many cities and counties have living wages. The living wage is a minimum wage set above the federal minimum wage level and usually applies only to employers who have a contract with the city or county. It is called a living wage because it is usually set at a level that allows a full-time worker to support a family of four at the poverty line.

Because the institution of a living wage is relatively recent, it is hard to judge whether it decreases employment. The current evidence suggests that the living wage may reduce employment, but this is open to argument. There are three main reasons why one would expect living wage laws to not reduce employment. First, the very passage of these laws has shown that the cities and counties passing them are willing to absorb added cost increases. Second, the type of services cities contract for cannot be supplied by low-wage foreign or out-of-area firms. Thus, there is less competitive pressure on these firms to keep prices and, therefore, costs down. Finally, the third reason is that the living wage laws may not significantly affect the costs of doing business for many of the affected firms. For example, suppose 10 percent of a firm's costs are increased 30 percent by the living wage law; this will increase its total cost by only 3 percent.

If the living wage laws result in affected jobs paying sizably more, then it might be expected that employers over time would fill vacated jobs with better workers (who are more experienced and better educated) than the ones they currently are hiring. Employers may not explicitly set out to hire better workers, but the higher wage will attract better workers to apply, and it will be the better workers whom firms will hire. Thus, while current low-skilled workers may benefit from the law, over time, new low-skilled applicants will not. Instead, they will find fewer jobs open to them.

average wage of all teenagers around 2 percent. This estimate is probably too low; most other studies have found a larger effect.

Another effect of the minimum wage is that it makes employers cut back on other amenities (by cutting fringe benefits, tightening work rules, and reducing on-the-job training). In this way, employers partially offset the effect of higher wages on their cost. The net effect for workers is that the minimum wage may not make them as well off as the increase in wages might indicate. One piece of evidence suggesting that this is the case is the fact that the past increases in the minimum wage have reduced (or had no effect on) the fraction of teenagers who want to work (as measured by their labor force participation rate). If the minimum wage increases the expected value of seeking and finding work, then it should increase the size of the labor force—but it does not.

A common error concerning the minimum wage is the belief that an increase in the minimum wage will be offset by workers becoming more productive and that, as a result, this will keep employment from decreasing. Various reasons have been given for the minimum wage increasing productivity, including the speculation that workers value their higher-paid jobs more or, alternatively, that employers try to offset the higher wage costs. If this were true, the minimum wage would reduce employment far more than it does. For example, suppose a minimum wage increases wages 10 percent and workers become 10 percent more productive. This will offset the effect of minimum wages on cost and leave the price of products unchanged. As goods cost the same amount, employers will produce and sell the same number of goods as before. But workers are 10 percent more productive, so employers would need 10 percent fewer workers to produce the same numbers of goods as before (indeed, that is what being more productive means). In this case, a 10 percent increase in the minimum wage would lead to a 10 percent decrease in employment. This is a far greater cut in employment than most studies find.

Conclusion

It can be argued that the poor would be better off if the political energy that goes into increasing the minimum wage were used instead to develop programs, such as the earned income tax credit, that truly help the poor. The minimum wage, according to much of the research in the field, reduces employment, but not sizably. More troubling, it does not increase the number of people who want to work, which suggests that it creates some offset such that workers on the whole are not better off. Economists like to say that there is no such thing as a free lunch. The minimum wage is definitely not a free lunch. It may have benefits, but it also has significant costs.

See also **Labor, Organized; Unemployment; Social Justice (vol. 2)**

Further Reading

Andersson, Fredrik, *Moving Up or Moving Down: Who Advances in the Low-Wage Market?* New York: Russell Sage Foundation, 2005.

Card, David, and Alan Krueger, "Minimum Wages and Employment: A Case Study of the Fast Food Industry in New Jersey and Pennsylvania." *American Economic Review* 84 (1994): 772–793.

Card, David, and Alan Krueger, *Myth and Measurement: The New Economics of the Minimum Wage.* Princeton, NJ: Princeton University Press, 1995.

Ehrenreich, Barbara, *Nickel and Dimed: On (Not) Getting By in America.* New York: Henry Holt, 2002.

Neumark, David, and William L. Wascher, *Minimum Wages.* Cambridge, MA: MIT Press, 2008.

Pollin, Robert, Mark Brenner, Jeannette Wicks-Lim, and Stephanie Luce, *A Measure of Fairness: The Economics of Living Wages and Minimum Wages in the United States.* Ithaca, NY: ILR Press, 2008.

Wessels, Walter, "Does the Minimum Wage Drive Teenagers Out of the Labor Market?" *Journal of Labor Research* 26 (2005): 169–176.

Wessels, Walter, "A Reexamination of Card and Krueger's State-Level Study of the Minimum Wage." *Journal of Labor Research* 28, no. 1 (2007): 135–146.

Wilson, D. Mark, "Who Is Paid the Minimum Wage and Who Would Be Affected by a $1.50 per Hour Increase?" June 28, 2001. http://www.heritage.org/Research/Reports/2001/06/Who-is-Paid-the-Minimum-Wage

O

OIL ECONOMICS AND BUSINESS

Edward W. Erickson

This is a good-news/bad-news entry. Since the 19th century, there has been both a regular and periodic concern that fossil fuel supplies will be inadequate to support and maintain the world's energy-dependent economy and society. In the 20th century, the most prominent advocate of the theory of impending trouble was the well-respected geologist and geophysicist M. King Hubbert, who predicted in 1956 that U.S. crude oil production would peak between 1965 and 1970. U.S. crude oil production did in fact peak in 1971. Hubbert further predicted in 1974 that global crude oil production would peak in 1995. However, world oil production has not yet peaked.

In the 21st century, there continues to be widespread concern and support for Hubbert's contention that the fossil fuel era would be of very short duration. Some analysts argue that Saudi Arabian oil production may have already peaked and may now be in decline. Saudi Arabia is the largest supplier of crude oil exports to the world market. Others argue that total world oil production, if it has not already peaked, will peak in a few years.

The first piece of good news is that world oil production has not yet peaked and may continue production at current, or higher, levels in the foreseeable future—decades or more. The second piece of good news is that, even if the pessimists are correct, it is likely that there will be cost-effective fossil fuel substitutes for oil that allow continued economic growth and improvement in living standards for the population of the world. There is no question that the fossil fuel content of the geology of the Earth is finite.

What is the bad news? Just as the world is now predominantly a fossil fuel economy, the world is likely to continue to be a predominantly fossil fuel economy for at least the next several decades, if not the balance of the 21st century. And, of course, when fossil fuels are used, they emit greenhouse gases. The 1997 Kyoto Protocol amended the international treaty on climate change to assign mandatory targets for the reduction of greenhouse gas emissions, and the 2009 Copenhagen Accord raised the question of setting more ambitious targets (though little was actually agreed to). If there are adequate fossil fuel resources to maintain or increase our global fossil fuel consumption, then there will be unavoidable tension between maintaining and improving our energy-dependent standard of living for the growing population of the world and curbing greenhouse gas emissions. "Unavoidable tension" is a polite way of saying a political catfight. And this, moreover, is an international political catfight that may take decades to resolve.

The Centrality of Oil

The primary source of energy used by the world economy comes in a variety of forms: petroleum (crude oil); natural gas; coal; and hydro, geothermal, solar, wind, biomass, and nuclear energy. Electricity is a derived form of energy that can be generated by any of the primary energy sources. Many energy sources have multiple uses. For example, wind can power turbines to generate electricity or propel sailing ships. Sunlight can generate electricity photovoltaically or directly provide space heating. Natural gas can be used for space heating and cooling or to generate electricity. Coal can be used for transportation (locomotives and steamships), space heating, or electricity generation. These energy sources compete with each other in the energy market, and this competition determines which source is the most cost effective and technically efficient alternative for each specific use.

There is, however, only one energy source that broadly competes with all other energy sources in all uses. This is petroleum. The competitive centrality of petroleum, in addition to petroleum's predominance as the largest single source of energy for the world economy, is why so much attention is focused on world crude oil supplies. Because of petroleum's worldwide competitive interconnectedness to the markets for all other sources of energy, when the world oil market sneezes, each of the markets for other types of energy at least sniffles.

The Flow of Oil

The standard way that energy economists think about the amount of oil produced and consumed is in barrels per day. There is a good reason for this. Oil is always on the move. It flows in drill pipes from underground geological formations to the surface of the Earth. There it is temporarily deposited in lease tanks before beginning another journey by pipeline to a refinery. A refinery is a vast network of pipes, pressure vessels, and storage tanks through which oil flows as it is converted from crude oil to refined products such as gasoline, jet fuel, and heating oil.

OFFSHORE OIL DRILLING IN THE GULF OF MEXICO

Offshore oil production in the Gulf of Mexico began in the 1930s. In shallow water near to the shore, large wooden platforms were built on wooden pilings and drilling rigs and production facilities operated from these platforms. The platforms were connected to each other and to the shore by a network of docks and walkways.

After World War II, steel platform technology began to advance. This was complemented by advances in drill ship and drilling barge technologies and advances in undersea pipeline-laying techniques and technology. But compared to current industry offshore operations, exploration and production were still limited to relatively shallow water. Steel platforms could be set in 100 feet of water. Using directional drilling, drill bits could be turned (or "whipstocked") so that wells could be completed in water that was 300 feet deep. A deep well was a completion (as it is called) into a reservoir that lay 10,000 feet under the floor of the gulf.

In 2006, the so-called Jack field in the deep waters of the central Gulf of Mexico was flow tested. The discovery well was drilled in 6,000 feet of water. The producing formation lies 25,000 feet under the floor of the Gulf of Mexico. The Jack field is part of a larger geologic formation that is estimated to contain 9–15 billion barrels of oil, a 50 percent increase in U.S. proved reserves. The seismic and geophysical technologies that allowed identification of the Jack field and the drilling and production technologies that allow development of the field are major advances. And in this sense, new technologies create new resources.

Now, of course, in the wake of the 2010 BP–Deepwater Horizon oil spill in a nearby region of the gulf, even greater technological improvements will be needed. Deepwater Horizon was a giant rig capable of operating in waters up to 8,000 feet deep and drilling to a depth of 30,000 feet. It had a massive blowout preventer that was supposed to have guarded against just the kind of uncontrolled gushing of crude that occurred after the rig exploded and collapsed into the sea. Shortly after the accident, President Barack Obama, who weeks before had called for expanding offshore oil and gas drilling, ordered a hold on new drilling and stepped-up safety inspections for existing wells.

Refined products leave the refinery and move to market through pipelines. Sometimes crude oil and refined products also move great distances around the world by ocean tanker. Since time is money, there are large economic incentives to minimize the amount of time that oil spends in storage tanks along its route from geological formation to refined-product customer.

The United States uses about 20 million barrels of oil a day. How much is that? An oil barrel is 42 gallons, so 20 million barrels a day equals 840 million gallons per day. And how much is this? Visualize a red one-gallon gas can used to fill a lawn mower. Start at Miami and line up 42 of these one-gallon cans across the northbound lane of the interstate highway from Miami to Chicago. Repeat that lineup of cans across the interstate all the way to Chicago until the northbound lane is *full of gas cans*. That is 840 million gallons of oil.

Now, blink your eyes, and all the oil cans disappear (i.e., the oil is consumed). Tomorrow, blink your eyes again and all 840 million oil cans—full of oil—reappear. The vast production network of wells, pipelines, tankers, and refineries replaces yesterday's consumption with today's new production.

This is a logistic miracle. It happens every day, day in and day out, 365 days a year. It happens not only in the United States, but all over the world. And world production and consumption is 85 million barrels of oil a day.

The planning and implementation imperatives that this daily feat of logistics imposes upon the oil industry are the practical reasons why industry operators commonly measure production and consumption in millions of barrels a day. Oil, of course, is not the only source of energy. So it is useful to have a measure of energy that allows comparison across the various types of energy. That measure is the British thermal unit, or Btu. Production and consumption statistics are also kept on an annual basis. But beneath the annual numbers, energy is moving in a ceaseless hourly and daily flow.

The Patterns of Energy Consumption

The world used 472 quadrillion Btus of energy in 2006 (and an estimated 508 quadrillion in 2010). A Btu, or British thermal unit, is the heat equal to 1/180 of the heat required to raise the temperature of one pound of water from a temperature of 32 degrees Fahrenheit to 212 degrees Fahrenheit at a constant pressure of one atmosphere. An atmosphere is the air pressure at sea level. A quadrillion is a million billion, or 10^{15}. This is a tremendous amount of energy. The word used to mean a quadrillion Btus is *quad*.

Table 1 shows the types and amounts of each type of energy consumed in the United States in 1985 and in 2009, and the increases (or decreases) in energy consumption over the 1985–2009 interval. Table 2 shows the relative percentage shares of each type of energy for 1985 and 2009 and the 1985–2009 increases (or decreases).

Between 1985 and 2009, U.S. energy consumption increased 27.5 percent, from 76.5 quads to 94.6 quads (Table 1). Fossil fuels supplied 66.1 percent of U.S. energy consumption in 1985 and 78.4 percent in 2009. Fossil fuels also supplied 68.0 percent of the 18.1 quad increase in U.S. energy consumption over the 1985–2009 interval (Tables 1 and 2). Between 1985 and 2009, the total renewable energy consumption in the United States increased 1.6 quads, or 25.8 percent. This net increase reflects a 2.0 quad increase for the combination of biomass, geothermal, solar, and wind forms that is partially offset by a 0.3 quad decrease in U.S. hydropower. In general, although the use of hydropower increased on a worldwide basis and decreased in the United States, the pattern of U.S. energy consumption is similar to the pattern for the world. Over the quarter century from 1985 to 2009, both the United States and the world increased total energy consumption. For both the United States and the world, by far the principal source of total energy

TABLE 1. U.S. Consumption of Energy by Type of Energy (1985 and 2009)

| Type of Energy | Quadrillion Btus Consumed | | | |
	1985	2009	Increase	Percent Increase
Petroleum	30.9	35.3	4.4	14.2
Natural gas	17.7	23.4	5.7	32.2
Coal	17.5	19.8	2.3	13.1
Total fossil	66.1	78.4	12.3	18.6
Hydro	3.0	2.7	−0.3	−10.0
Biomass	3.0	4.0	1.0	33.3
Geothermal	0.2	0.4	0.2	100.0
Solar	NA	0.1	0.1	
Wind	NA	0.7	0.7	
Total renewable	6.2	7.8	1.6	25.8
Nuclear	4.1	8.3	4.2	102.4
U.S. total	76.5	94.6	18.1	23.7

Note: Due to rounding, totals may not add up.
Source: U.S. Energy Administration, *Monthly Energy Review* (April 2010).

consumption was fossil fuel. In relative terms, fossil fuels lost a few percentage points of market share. But for both the United States and the world, increased fossil fuel consumption accounted for roughly 70 percent of the total increase in energy consumption. Use of nuclear power increased in both absolute and relative terms in the United States and worldwide. With the exception of hydropower outside the United States, renewable sources made relatively modest contributions to both absolute and relative energy consumption in the United States and on a worldwide basis.

Oil Production: The Intensive Margin

Economists have long considered two general approaches to increasing or maintaining the production of output: the intensive margin of production and the extensive margin of production. Think of a tomato farmer. If the farmer wants to increase production, one way to accomplish this is by getting more output from her existing fields. This can be achieved by installing irrigation, applying fertilizer, hiring more labor to pick and cultivate more carefully, applying pesticides and herbicides, and the like. These production enhancement techniques are all examples of expanding output at the internal margin of production.

There is also an external margin of production—an alternative way the farmer could expand production. She could plant, cultivate, and harvest additional fields of tomatoes. She could manage the new fields in exactly the same way that she managed her original

TABLE 2. Relative Contributions of Various Types of Energy to Total U.S. Energy Consumption (1985 and 2009)

Type of Energy	Percent Contribution to Total U.S. Consumption		
	1985	2009	1985 to 2009 Increase
Petroleum	40.4	37.3	24.3
Natural gas	23.1	24.7	31.5
Coal	22.9	20.9	12.7
Total fossil	86.4	82.9	68.0
Hydro	3.9	2.9	−1.7
Biomass	3.9	4.2	5.5
Geothermal	0.3	0.4	1.1
Solar		0.1	0.6
Wind		0.7	3.9
Total renewable	8.1	8.2	8.8
Nuclear	5.4	8.8	23.2
U.S. total	100.0	100.0	100.0

Note: Due to rounding, totals may not add up.

Source: U.S. Energy Information Administration, Monthly Energy Review (April 2010).

fields. If she were to follow this approach, the farmer would be expanding output at the external margin of production. Not surprisingly, if there are economic incentives to expand the output of some commodity, there are production responses at both the internal and external margins of production.

Terms of art in the oil and gas industry are *resource* and *proved reserves*. Resources exist in nature. Proved reserves are an artifact of humans. Resources are the total global endowment of fossil fuels that nature has bestowed upon us. Resources exist, whether they have been discovered or not. Proved reserves are the portion of a discovered resource that is recoverable (or producible) under existing technological and economic conditions.

To understand how the concept of the internal margin applies to oil production, it is necessary to review a little petroleum geology. Oil does not occur in huge underground lakes or pools. What is often called a pool of oil actually appears to the naked eye to be solid rock. The oil is contained in the microscopic pore spaces between the tiny grains of sand that make up the rock. Porous rock that contains oil is called reservoir rock. The reservoir rock of the Prudhoe Bay oil field on the North Slope of Alaska could be cut into thin slabs, polished up, and used as the facing on a bank building. Passers-by would be none the wiser.

Geologists speak of source rock, reservoir rock, and caprock. Source rock is the progenitor of fossil fuels. Eons ago in geologic time, plant and animal life lived and died and were deposited as organic material in sedimentary basins. The Earth's crust moved and buckled and bent and folded over upon itself. This process rolled organic sedimentary material deep underground, where, over the course of geologic time, heat and pressure converted the organic sediments to fossil fuels—petroleum, natural gas, and coal.

Fossil fuels are solar fuels. The energy they contain derives from the energy of the sun. But the production process that created them is much more roundabout—millions of years more roundabout—than the process that uses the energy of the sun to warm a solar water heater.

Oil formed in the source rock is pushed by underground pressures through various strata of permeable rock until it is trapped against a layer of impermeable rock—the caprock. The source of the pressure pushing the oil into the ultimate strata of reservoir rock is often water driven by a subterranean aquifer. If no caprock stops its pressure-driven journey, the oil escapes to the surface of the Earth—on land or under the oceans. These are natural oil spills. One of the largest known deposits of oil in the world—the Athabasca Tar Sands in Alberta, Canada—is such a natural oil spill.

Nature abhors a vacuum. Nature also abhors a partial vacuum. Oil in a strata of reservoir rock is under great pressure, trapped between a water drive and the impermeable caprock. It requires tremendous pressure to force oil to flow through solid rock from the source rock to the caprock. When a well pierces the caprock and enters the reservoir rock, a partial vacuum is created. The great pressure differential between atmospheric pressure at the surface of the Earth and the underground reservoir pressure causes the oil to flow to the well bore and then up through the well casing to the wellhead at the surface.

In the 19th century and the first half of the 20th century, successful oil wells were often allowed to erupt as gushers and temporarily spew a fountain of oil from the drilling derrick. This is no longer the case. Reservoir pressure is precious and managed carefully. As natural reservoir pressure dissipates, less and less oil is forced through the reservoir rock to the well bore, and daily production declines.

Not all the oil in place in a reservoir is produced. In the earliest days of the oil industry after Col. Edwin Drake drilled his discovery well in 1859 near Titusville, Pennsylvania, as little as 10 percent of the oil in place was produced before the natural reservoir pressure was exhausted and primary oil production ceased to flow. To offset the loss of production as primary output slowed, secondary production techniques were developed.

There are many different kinds of secondary production technology. The classic secondary production technique is the walking beam pump, which resembles a mechanized sawhorse bobbing up and down. Others include drilling injection wells and pumping water, natural gas, or carbon dioxide into the reservoir to maintain pressure. Secondary recovery shades into tertiary recovery, such as injecting steam to make heavy oil flow more freely or injecting surfactant detergents to maintain reservoir pressure and to wash oil out of tight pore spaces and help it to flow to the well bore. From the inception of production, modern reservoir engineering now uses whatever techniques are cost effective to maintain reservoir pressure, improve flow, and increase the ultimate recovery of oil in place. The result has been a significant increase in the percent of oil in place that is recovered through production. In the 20th century, 10 percent recovery became 30 percent recovery. Now it is often possible to achieve 50 percent or higher ultimate recovery of the oil in place. Higher prices for oil make application of expensive enhanced recovery technologies more cost effective and also encourage the development of new technologies.

A large fraction of the oil discovered from 1859 to the present remains unrecovered and in place in known reservoirs. This includes recent discoveries of shale oil (i.e., oil embedded in shale and only extractable by new technologies that force it out using pressure). At historical and current prices with historical and current technologies, it has not been cost effective to produce it. Most of the oil in place that has not qualified to be designated as proved reserves will likely never be recovered and produced. But if petroleum becomes more scarce relative to our desire to benefit from its use, its price (adjusted for inflation) will rise, perhaps dramatically. If, or when, that occurs, a variety of responses, interactions, and consequences will ensue. One of these responses will be at the intensive margins of production. New discoveries will be developed more intensively, and old oil fields will be intensively reworked.

Fossil Fuel Production: The Extensive Margin

The fossil fuels are all hydrocarbons. Petroleum is the most widely used fossil fuel with the largest market share of any energy source, because transportation is such an important use. Liquid transportation fuels—for example, gasoline and jet fuel diesel—are easier, more convenient, and less costly to store, transport, distribute, and use than solid or gaseous fuels. However, the resource base for petroleum is smaller than that for coal and natural gas.

Engineers and scientists can convert the hydrocarbons in coal into liquid fuels. The Fischer-Tropsche process (named for two German chemists) is the best-known technology. It was used by Germany in World War II and by South Africa during the apartheid embargo. A variation of the backend of the Fischer-Tropsch process can be used to convert natural gas to liquid fuel. Exxon-Mobil is building a big gas-to-liquids (GTL) plant in West Africa. Qatar is building a very large GTL plant in the Persian Gulf to facilitate the marketing of its substantial natural gas reserves. The output of a GTL plant is equivalent to an environmentally friendly diesel fuel. We are on the cusp of extending the commercial production of liquid hydrocarbon fuels to natural gas. Higher oil prices will extend the commercial horizon to coal-based liquid hydrocarbon fuels.

The recent exploration activity focused upon the Lower Tertiary geologic formation in the deepwater Gulf of Mexico is another illustration of the relevance of the extensive margin. Two-thirds of the surface of the Earth is covered by water.

There has been considerable exploration for and production of oil and natural gas on the great deltas of the shallow near-shore outer continental shelf—the North Sea, the Bight of Benin, the Gulf of Mexico, the South China Sea, and so on. Exploration and production in water depths up to 10,000 feet and at geologic horizons 25,000 feet beneath the ocean floor are now possible.

CAN ETHANOL REPLACE GASOLINE?

Ethanol is a type of ethyl alcohol. Ethanol has been used as an additive for gasoline to oxygenate the fuel in order to reduce emissions and pollution. For this purpose, a common blend of ethanol and ordinary gasoline is a fuel called E15. E15 is 85 percent petroleum-based gasoline and 15 percent ethanol. A much more ethanol-intensive blend is E85. E85 is 85 percent ethanol and 15 percent gasoline.

The U.S. automobile industry produces many cars that are ethanol capable and can run on either 100 percent gasoline or fuels such as E15 and E85. E15 ethanol is used as a replacement for the chemical methyl tertiary butyl ether (MTBE) for purposes of oxygenation. E85 ethanol is used primarily as a replacement for gasoline itself. Ethanol contains about 80 percent as many Btus of energy per gallon as does gasoline.

In the United States, most ethanol is made from corn. There are biofuels other than ethanol and biological feedstocks other than corn. The cultivation of alternative biofuel feedstocks—switchgrass, for example—is apt to be less energy intensive than the cultivation of corn. But corn is currently a major U.S. crop. The conversion of corn to ethanol is a market-tested technology. So, for illustrative purposes, the focus here is upon corn-based ethanol.

The U.S. corn harvest averages about 11 billion bushels of corn per year. The principal use of corn is for animal feed. Between 1.5 and 4 billion bushels of corn are exported for this purpose. There are about 81 million acres of cropland planted for U.S. corn production. For the last decade, the average price of corn has been about $2.00 per bushel, although in 2006 corn was $2.50 per bushel. A bushel of corn is 60 pounds of corn.

The United States uses 144 billion gallons of gasoline per year. The conversion process of corn into ethanol yields slightly more than 2.7 gallons of ethanol per bushel of corn. If the entire 11 billion–bushel U.S. corn crop were converted into ethanol, about 20 percent of U.S. gasoline use could be replaced by ethanol.

Such a program would have many major consequences. Consider just two. First, U.S. demand for imported oil would be reduced. Second, the U.S. price of corn would increase dramatically. We would pay for the program at both the gas pump and the grocery store. There is a place for ethanol, but that is likely to be a small market as a substitute for MTBE rather than a broad market as a major replacement for gasoline. Furthermore, early predictions regarding the value of ethanol as a substitute have been revised downward.

Vast new areas about which we now know relatively little have become accessible. Attractive prospects will not be limited to just the near-to-shore relatively shallow waters bordering the continents. New deepwater geologic horizons lie before us. A great adventure will continue. If the last 50 years of history in the Gulf of Mexico tell us anything, the technological limits will not long remain at 10,000 feet of water depth and 25,000 feet beneath the ocean floor—that is, as long as adequate environmental safety measures can be put in place. For liquid hydrocarbon fuels, Hubbert's peak lies before us—perhaps a long way before us.

Price Volatility

Following World War II, oil prices were quite stable for a number of reasons. Prices spiked in the early middle 1970s following the Arab oil embargo. Prices spiked again at the end of the 1970s and in the early 1980s, coincident with the Iranian revolution. In the early 1990s, the first Gulf War was accompanied by another spike in prices. In 2006, due to supply dislocations in Alaska, Venezuela, Nigeria, and Iraq, prices spiked again and reached nearly $80 a barrel. We can learn a number of things from these price spikes.

First, short-term demand for and supply of oil are quite inflexible. Small dislocations on either side of the market can cause big swings in price. Second, volatility is a two-way street. What goes up often comes down. The price bust in the mid-1980s and the soft markets of the late 1990s and early 2000s illustrate such turnarounds. The big downward slide of prices from the 2006 highs punctuates the message. Third, economic recessions are often attributed to oil price spikes, but we should be cautious about such suggestions. In every instance, oil price spikes were accompanied by restrictive monetary policies applied by the sometimes draconian U.S. Federal Reserve restrictions. Fourth, there is upward pressure upon prices due to increasing demand for energy from the growing economies of India and China. This is good news. The world is a much better place with billions of Indians and Chinese participating in dynamic economies that are demanding more energy than it would be were these countries failed societies with stagnant demands.

There is a further general lesson in our experience of price volatility. As prices fluctuate, we adapt. The original Honda Civic and the SUV are classic examples of our response to higher and lower prices. In an important sense, $75 oil and $3 gasoline are a bargain. In terms of what oil (and, potentially, other liquid hydrocarbon fuels) does for us, and what we would have to give up without it, there are no readily available cost-effective substitutes.

In Europe, high fuel taxes cause gasoline prices to be more than $5 a gallon. But even at these prices, motor vehicle use in London has to be restricted in order to reduce congestion. As a hypothetical example, consider the effects of $5-a-gallon gasoline in the United States. If gasoline cost $5 a gallon because of long-term higher crude oil prices, this would be equivalent to a price of $125 a barrel for crude oil. Such prices would cause much pain, but after adjusting and adapting, it is unlikely the economy would suffer long-term collapse. Supply-side initiatives at all dimensions of the intensive and extensive margins, however, would be undertaken with incredible creativity and vigor. Demand-side responses would also be significant. In the short run, high-tech modern versions of the original Honda Civic would be widely adopted. In the long run, land-use patterns and building design and construction would change.

Conclusion

Fossil fuels are the workhorse of the world energy economy. Nuclear power is making a growing contribution to electricity generation. Outside the United States, new hydro facilities have also contributed to increased energy consumption. Nonhydro renewable energy use has grown rapidly from a small base. But these nonhydro renewable sources make a very modest contribution toward meeting increased energy demands or total energy use. It is likely that supplies of fossil fuel resources will be ample to meet growing energy demands for the foreseeable future.

Consumption of fossil fuels generates carbon dioxide. Many environmentalists believe that the greenhouse effect of increased atmospheric concentrations of carbon dioxide is the principal cause of global warming. In *The Skeptical Environmentalist*, Bjorn Lomborg (2001) expresses reservations about the extent of environmental degradation due to human activities and the link between carbon dioxide concentrations and global warming. Nevertheless, serious people consider the links between human activity, fossil fuel use, increased carbon dioxide concentrations, and global warming to be very strong and regard the situation to be very serious. Moreover, in light of the 2010 BP–Deepwater Horizon disaster and other such human-caused events, the problem of preventing oil spills and containing environmental damage associated with spills is regarded as equally serious.

Modern societies and the global economy are built on fossil fuel use. There are now no cost-effective substitutes for fossil fuels. Reducing carbon dioxide emissions significantly will require dramatic changes in the way we organize our activities and live our lives. Many people, especially skeptics, will not make these sacrifices happily. If the skeptics are correct, we will incur great costs for few, if any, benefits. The resolution of these questions will become an increasingly important item on the global political agenda.

See also **Free Trade; Supply Chain Security and Terrorism; Biodiesel (vol. 4); Fossil Fuels (vol. 4); Nuclear Energy (vol. 4); Oil Drilling and the Environment (vol. 4); Solar Energy (vol. 4); Wind Energy (vol. 4)**

Further Reading

Downey, Morgan Patrick, *Oil 101*. New York: Wooden Table Press, 2009.

Grace, Robert, *Oil: An Overview of the Petroleum Industry*. Houston: Gulf Publishing, 2007.

Juhasz, Antonia, *The Tyranny of Oil: The World's Most Powerful Industry—And What We Must Do to Stop It*. New York: Harper, 2009.

Klare, Michael T., *Blood and Oil: The Dangers and Consequences of America's Growing Dependency on Imported Petroleum.* New York: Henry Holt, 2005.

Lomborg, Bjorn, *The Skeptical Environmentalist.* New York: Cambridge University Press, 2001.

Paul, William Henry, *Future Energy: How the New Oil Industry Will Change People, Politics, and Portfolios.* New York: John Wiley, 2007.

Priest, Tyler, *The Offshore Imperative: Shell Oil's Search for Petroleum in Postwar America.* College Station: Texas A&M University Press, 2007.

OUTSOURCING AND OFFSHORING

John Silvia

Behaviors and perceptions sometimes disconnect. This is evident when the words *outsourcing* and *offshoring*—which mean the placement of U.S. jobs in foreign countries—raise the hackles of the public that appears to benefit from the lower consumer prices and mortgage rates occurring as a result of globalization. Consumers economize by buying the least expensive item that they believe meets their needs. Store owners recognize that and ask their suppliers to provide those items at the lowest cost. The wholesalers, in turn, seek out the least expensive producers for the given quality of the good in question. Since the 1960s, the least expensive producer has increasingly been overseas, and U.S. manufacturers have moved abroad. Meanwhile, foreign investors have supplied capital to U.S. capital markets and have helped keep interest rates lower than otherwise possible.

So how does the same globalization phenomenon generate economywide benefits, yet there are still winners and losers on an individual level? How do changes in the domestic economy interact with the patterns of globalization? Finally, why is there a disconnect between economic benefits and public perceptions?

Macro Benefits and Micro Winners and Losers in a Dynamic Economy

Economies grow and change over time. This growth increases the standard of living for a society, but not all participants benefit equally, and there are often losers in the process, as owners of once-valuable resources (e.g., real estate in the old ghost towns of the West and riverfront mills in the industrial Northeast) find that the demand for those resources has declined. Yet the globalization of the U.S. economy has been a long-term trend, as exhibited in Figure 1, which shows combined exports and imports as a percentage of annual national income. Today this measure of globalization stands near 20 percent of the U.S. economy.

The theme underlying any effective Western economic system is that each consumer acts in her or his own interest to minimize costs, while each producer seeks to maximize profit. Consumers maximize their welfare subject to income limitations. Producers, meanwhile, act to offer the least expensive product that will meet the customer's

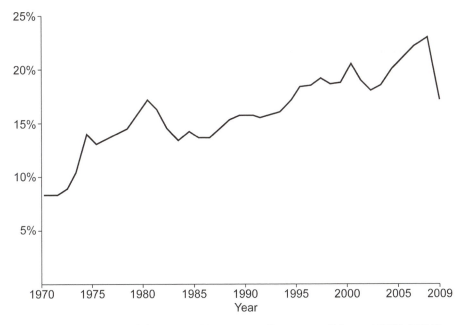

Figure 1. Globalization: U.S. Exports and Imports as a Percentage of Nominal GDP (U.S. Department of Commerce)

needs. The boom in discount and Internet shopping over the past 10 years reflects the consumer's desire to minimize expense of dollars, time, or both. In response, producers have sought to minimize costs in order to maximize profit and thereby have an incentive to seek international sourcing of goods and services that many in the popular press call outsourcing.

Global Labor Market

Trade allows for the division of labor across countries. This division of labor in turn allows for economies of scale and scope and the development of specialized skills. Specialization encourages innovation and promotes dynamism. Economies of scale, scope, and specialization allow production to be more efficient and therefore lower cost. Historically, we have seen the migration of production in the United States in agriculture and textile production. The opening of the Midwest made New England farms high cost and led to a shift of major agricultural production from the Northeast to the Midwest. As for textile production, there has been a migration from England to New England, then to the Southeast, and then on to Mexico and China, and now to Vietnam. Over time, this industry has moved to locations where manufacturers can economize on their biggest cost—labor.

Geographical migration of production has benefited consumers by providing a greater supply of goods and services at a lower price. The lower prices mean that consumers have more real income to be spent elsewhere. In turn, consumers' standard of living has increased.

The shift in the locus of manufacturing production also means that there are gainers and losers in jobs and land values over time. Southern cities and low-skilled workers have benefited, while New England cities and higher-wage union workers have been the losers. The process of production relocation generally benefits society at large, as less expensive goods are produced for all consumers in the nation, while there is also a regional redistribution of jobs and wealth within the economy.

In recent years, there has been a global redistribution of production, with lower-wage manufacturing jobs in textiles and apparel relocating to Asia. Meanwhile, states like North Carolina increased their exports of high-valued manufactures such as chemicals and electronic products. Today, these two sectors, along with vehicles and machinery, comprise the state's top four export industries. The globalization of product markets has led to an expansion of world trade. Durable goods manufacturers, such as construction, farm, and industrial machinery, have seen a global increase in demand for their products. Yet as production has grown, there are many physical as well as practical barriers to labor mobility. Therefore, manufacturers that wish to be close to their customers are finding that they cannot source all production from their U.S. base and, as a result, must outsource production to other countries to remain competitive.

Trade does lead to both losses and gains of jobs—both directly in the affected community and indirectly in the surrounding community. As discussed below, policies encouraging the retraining of workers are more likely to be successful than those increasing the prices to consumers. On net, however, lower consumer prices provided by more efficient global production result in an increase in household purchasing power and a broader variety of goods and services for consumers in general. It is helpful to recall that the United States is the world's largest exporter as well as a major beneficiary of foreign direct investment, which provides jobs in this country. This inflow of foreign capital is seen in the form of a Japanese aircraft manufacturer in North Carolina and a German auto manufacturer in South Carolina.

Unfortunately, those who lose jobs due to trade are not necessarily the same people who get jobs created by trade. Short-term adjustments are painful and represent economic and social challenges. However, our focus should be on the worker, not the job.

Overall, trade has a small net effect on employment, and this trade effect on employment is overwhelmed by the normal massive turnover in the labor market (see Figure 2). Rather than trade, it is population, education and training, labor force participation, institutions, and flexibility of the labor force that determine long-term employment growth. Labor markets evolve over time, and trade is just one of many influences. We do know that trade often leads to structural change in the labor markets with consequential effects on the mix of jobs across industries, the skill levels required, and the ultimate

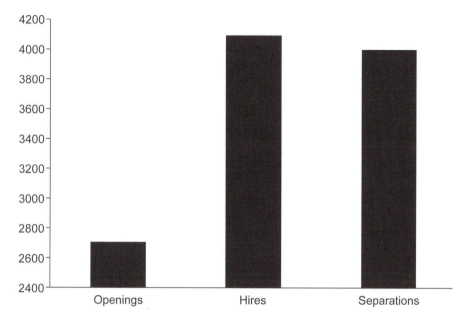

Figure 2. Job Market Dynamics, March 2010 (thousands of jobs) (U.S. Department of Commerce)

locations of job growth. For example, in recent years, lower transaction costs and improvements in international communications have led to a rising global demand for computerization and digitalization of business services, which has boosted the fortunes of U.S.-based software and hardware firms.

Meanwhile, the customer service of many of these software and hardware products and services has increased the global demand for educated English-speaking workers abroad in places such as Ireland and India. This demand for foreign workers is driven by the consumer who wants 24-hour service at the touch of a button. Therefore, companies are more likely to meet that demand at lower wages and benefit costs by hiring first-shift workers in India or Ireland than second- and third-shift workers in the United States.

In contrast, attempts to manipulate the economic theme of markets by tariffs, quotas, or labor regulations may temporarily slow job loss, but at the cost of higher prices to consumers and a misallocation of resources toward inefficient production in the rest of society. In the past, this inefficient production has been seen in subsidies to steel and textile industries and in the tariffs imposed in the 19th century to protect inefficient agriculture. In the end, the steel and textile mills still closed, and many Eastern and Southern farms became suburbs. Government interference in the economic process only increased short-term costs to the rest of the economy through higher prices. Moreover, over the long term, government interference frequently prevented the proper reallocation of resources to more productive uses. Protectionism on trade provoked retaliation from foreign governments and a retreat from competition. As a result, protectionism leads to bloated, inefficient industries that decrease productivity and engender a lower standard of living.

Insourcing Services

Balanced discussions on trade issues are often interrupted by emotional outbursts or political grandstanding. While some manufacturing jobs are disappearing, many higher-paid service positions are being created here as foreigners increase their demand for U.S.-based services. These high-value services provided to users abroad include legal, financial, engineering, architectural, and software development services. This insourcing of professional services to the United States generates a surplus in the service component of our balance of payments accounts. The economic market-based system provides a wider array of goods and services at a lower cost than the alternatives. Greater global competition provides such benefits to society overall. There are costs of globalization that should be addressed, but by means other than preventing trade.

Global Capital Markets: Inflow of Capital to the United States

Another variation on the theme is the pattern of global capital (financial) flows and the globalization of capital markets. In contrast to labor, capital crosses borders fairly easily. In sympathy with labor, the return of capital provides an incentive to allocate capital to its best use. U.S. consumers benefit from an inflow of capital that lowers the price of credit interest rates—relative to what they would be otherwise (this reduces the interest rates on home mortgages, for example).

In addition, global capital markets lead to the development of new financial instruments that provide greater liquidity to international investors. We see this in the development of instruments such as mortgage-backed and asset-backed securities. Globalization of product markets has meant the introduction of new brands and products from foreign countries into the U.S. consumer market in particular. With capital markets, globalization has meant that U.S. financial assets such as mortgage-backed securities are now available for sale across the globe, while foreign investors with excess cash can now direct that cash toward U.S. markets.

Globalization of products leads to an expansion of world trade. The globalization of capital markets is also leading to an expansion of financial markets. For the United States, particularly in nonrecessionary times, this means a broader demand for mortgages, car loans, and business credit, which thereby effectively lowers interest rates for the U.S. consumer. In this case, the consumer comes out the winner from globalization. Consumers find that credit is more readily available at lower interest rates.

Foreign investors benefit by purchasing U.S. financial assets that are perceived to offer higher returns and lower risks than many foreign assets. This is particularly true when you view the benchmark interest rates between countries (Figure 3). Prior to the

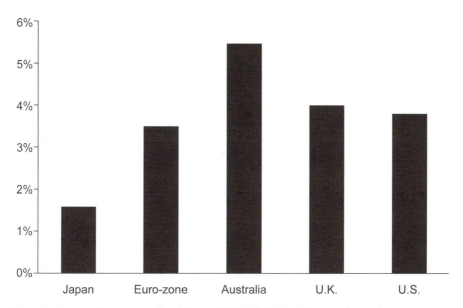

Figure 3. 10-year Government Bond Rates (Q1 2010) (Federal Reserve System)

economic crisis of 2008–2009, which hit the U.S. financial sector particularly hard, the United States led the pack, rating above 5 percent in the years immediately preceding the crisis.

Public policy in the United States has promoted these capital flows by reducing taxes on dividend and capital gains, while also lowering barriers to cross-border investment by foreign investors. This has helped promote capital flows into the United States, even while other nations limit capital flows into or out of their own nations.

Just as trade alters the global distribution of production, capital flows alter the global distribution of financial investment. Over recent years, with the exception of the 2008–2009 economic crisis, the United States has experienced growth of financial instruments and market values. Therefore, the United States benefits from the globalization of financial markets. Global savings migrate to higher return on U.S. investments (Figure 4) and thereby raise output and incomes.

What Should Be Done about Globalization?

Globalization is a product of economic incentives, not the result of some great conspiracy. Households have a limited budget and attempt to save money when they shop. Producers attempt to meet consumer demands by supplying products at a price that meets their budget. Meanwhile, many U.S. firms cannot meet their global demand by production solely in the United States and thereby locate production facilities near their customers. On the financial side, the globalization of capital markets has led to an increase in financial flows to the United States and has thereby increased the

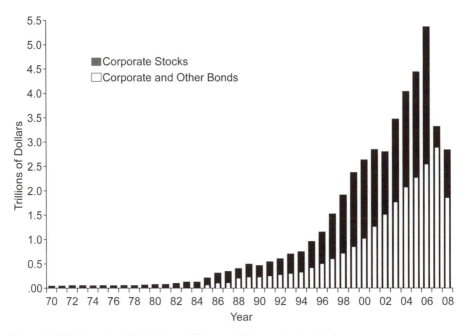

Figure 4. U.S. Securities Held Abroad (Bureau of Economic Analysis)

availability of credit and lowered interest rates. Lower rates mean that more families are able to purchase homes and businesses can finance expansion. This process is unlikely to stop.

Policymakers and voters need to recognize the dislocation costs associated with the global reallocation of production and financial flows along with the benefits that derive from such reallocation. For U.S. workers, the cost disincentives of retaining labor in many facilities in the United States may be too large to retain the old jobs in the old facilities. This may be particularly true for labor-intensive manufacturing and service jobs that require low- or semiskilled workers. In U.S. history, we have seen the migration of jobs before, from the agricultural work forces in rural areas to the manufacturing facilities of the pre–World War II era. Technological and communication changes have made many low-skilled jobs obsolete and therefore not viable economically over the long run. Certainly many workers can no longer build careers upon these jobs. Recall that consumer preferences have also shifted, with more consumer dollars going toward services—for example, eating out as opposed to buying groceries at the store to prepare all the household's meals.

While jobs may go, workers remain, and this should be our focus. Public and private programs need to be directed at worker retraining—not factory retention—in cases where the economics are clear. Labor markets are becoming increasingly flexible so that jobs are more likely to come and go, but the workers remain. Public policy is better served by the improvement of the skills of workers rather than the preservation of specific jobs. Many states have seen the emergence of programs at community colleges with a dedicated focus on worker retraining. Of course, it is incumbent upon the worker to recognize that there is a responsibility to develop those skills and to be willing to move or change jobs more in the future than was necessary in the past.

As for manufacturing, it is important to note that many public policy decisions are aimed at discouraging production in the United States. Whatever their intentions may be, many communities simply do not want a factory in their backyard. As a result, firms are outsourcing production abroad simply because they cannot produce the gasoline, plastics, rubber, metals, textiles, and the like in this country.

On the other hand, large capital inflows into the United States also offer a solution by which incentives can be directed to foreign firms to allocate capital to areas where there is a viable workforce. We have seen this in many states where incentives are offered to locate firms in certain communities.

Offshoring creates value for the U.S. economy by passing on the efficiency that results in lower costs of goods and services to the U.S. consumer. This consumer then takes the extra money saved at the store and spends it elsewhere. U.S. companies benefit by being able to meet consumer demand by supplying the goods or services at a lower cost. Economic resources can be used then for more value-added products and services. Redeployed labor and capital to other manufacturing and service-sector activities will be more productive and have a longer economic life than those production activities and jobs in declining industries. U.S. workers and consumers benefit from specialization. Final assembly can often occur in the United States, while component production takes place around the globe. Production of goods and services is not carried on for its own sake but is undertaken to serve the demands of the consumer. Therefore, the value of any product is determined by consumers and then works its way down into the factors of production. It is impossible to governmentally control trade and consumer choice without distorting economic activity.

When a less costly way to make a good is discovered, the value of all factors used in making that good also changes. The national standard of living cannot rise when states attempt to force up the price of some factors so that the owners of those factors used in production gain an artificial advantage that results in the inefficient allocation of scarce resources in the economy. Globalization reflects the demands of the consumer. Attempts to alter that trend will only diminish the welfare of the average consumer.

See also **Foreign Direct Investment; Free Trade; Globalization**

Further Reading

Burkholder, Nicholas C., *Outsourcing: The Definitive View, Applications and Implications.* Hoboken, NJ: John Wiley, 2006.

Feenstra, Robert C., *Offshoring in the Global Economy: Microeconomic Structures and Macroeconomic Implications.* Cambridge, MA: MIT Press, 2010.

Freeman, Jodi, and Martha Minnow, *Government by Contract: Outsourcing and American Democracy.* Cambridge, MA: Harvard University Press, 2009.

Mol, Michael, *Outsourcing: Design, Process and Performance.* New York: Cambridge University Press, 2007.

Oshri, Ilan, Julia Kotlarsky, and Leslie P. Willcocks, *The Handbook of Global Outsourcing and Offshoring.* New York: Palgrave Macmillan, 2009.

P

PENSIONS

JEANNE M. HOGARTH AND MICHAEL SHALLY-JENSEN

A pension is a regular payment given to retired employees. Pensions are only one part of a retiree's income, however. Other income sources include Social Security, income from personal retirement savings, and earnings. Many older people continue to work during retirement, especially in the early years of retirement. So consumers planning for retirement need to think about all four sources of income.

Pension benefits are usually paid monthly. People use the terms *pension plans* and *retirement plans* to mean essentially the same thing—the term *pension plan* is used here. Pension plans are divided into two broad types: defined benefit and defined contribution plans.

According to a study by the Employee Benefits Research Institute, in 2008, 67 percent of workers age 16 and over worked for an employer that sponsored a retirement or pension plan. Of these, about half (51 percent) participated in their employer's retirement plan. Most (55 percent) were in a defined contribution plan; 33 percent were in a defined benefit plan, and about 10 percent were in both defined contribution and defined benefit plans. In addition, more than half of all workers (55 percent) had either a pension plan or other retirement savings in their own individual retirement account (IRA) or Keogh plans. Data from the Federal Reserve Board's 2007 Survey of Consumer Finances show that 53 percent of workers and retirees have a pension or retirement savings in an IRA or Keogh.

Defined Benefit Plans

Defined benefit plans are an older form of pension plans. Defined benefit plans define the amount of the pension benefit that will be paid to employees at retirement, and then the employer sets aside funds to pay that future benefit.

Suppose Ann is 25 years old. Her boss tells her that she will pay Ann $12,000 a year in retirement when Ann is 65. Ann's boss must set aside enough money now to make those $12,000-a-year payments 40 years from now. Ann's boss will need to estimate what investment return she can earn on the funds and how many payments she will need to make (i.e., how long Ann will be retired).

In some cases, instead of a fixed amount, the pension benefit amount is calculated based on a formula—for example, a combination of worker's earnings and years of work. Suppose the formula for Sam's company pension is 1 percent of the average of his earnings for the last three years times the number of years he has worked for the company. Sam's earnings for the last three years were $40,000, $50,000, and $60,000 (the average is $50,000), and he retired after 30 years of work. The formula is: 1% × 50,000 × 30= $15,000.

Again, Sam's boss must set aside enough money now to make those $15,000-a-year payments 30 years from now. In addition to estimating the investment return she can earn on the funds and how long Sam will be retired, she will need to estimate how long Sam will work for her and what Sam's salary will be in his last 3 years of work.

With a defined benefit plan, employers are responsible—and bear the risk—for having enough money in the fund to be able to pay for the pension. The actual cost of the defined benefits plan to the employer is uncertain. The cost is only an estimate because the formula depends upon a number of variables, such as the average retirement age, the life spans of employees, the returns earned by any of the pension's investments, and any additional taxes.

Up until the 1980s, defined benefit plans were the most common type of pension plan. But these plans lost popularity due to their cost and changes in the laws that cover pensions. Also, as workers changed jobs more often, there was a need to have a pension plan that was more portable and could move with the employee from one employer to another. The need to maintain defined benefit plans contributed to the financial woes of companies such as General Motors during the economic crisis of 2008–2009.

Defined Contribution Plans

In contrast to a defined benefit plan that defines the benefit to be paid in the future in retirement, a defined contribution plan defines the amount an employer will contribute into an account for each employee. Employees may be able to choose how the contributions to their accounts are invested; choices can include mutual funds, stocks or other investments, and securities. The returns on the investments, either gains or losses, are credited to the individual employee's account.

At retirement, the amount of money in the account is used to create the series of payments the retired worker will receive in retirement. With a defined contribution plan, employees—not the employer—bear responsibility for having enough money in the pension account for retirement. If employers contribute enough and make good investment choices, the investments grow and employees will have a large amount in their accounts to use in retirement; if employers make poor choices, employees will not have as much money in retirement.

For example, suppose Ben's employer tells Ben he will put $1,000 per year into a defined contribution plan. At the end of 30 years, Ben's employer will have paid $30,000 into Ben's account. If Ben's employer chooses an investment that pays 2 percent per year, at the end of 30 years, Ben will have $1,217,042 in his account. If Ben takes out $5,000 per month, his money will last about 30 years. On the other hand, if Ben's employer chooses an investment that pays 5 percent, at the end of 30 years, Ben would have $1,993,165—or nearly $776,000 more. He could take out $10,700 a month—more than double—and his money would still last 30 years.

Employers can easily calculate the cost of a defined contribution plan, in contrast to the defined benefit plan. Once employees are vested (eligible to receive money) in the plan, most plans are portable—as workers change jobs, they can take their funds with them or roll them over into an individual retirement account.

Defined contribution plans, since their emergence in the 1980s, have shown themselves to be highly successful retirement tools; indeed, they have become the modern standard for U.S. corporations. At the same time, however, participants in these plans can face risks if they are not careful in monitoring their investments. In some cases, in fact, such as that of the collapse of the investment market in 2008, even monitoring may not help. It is estimated that *trillions* of dollars in savings were lost virtually overnight by owners of retirement accounts (401(k)s, IRAs) when the markets ceased functioning.

Cash Balance Plans

A third type of pension plan—the cash balance plan—is a defined benefit plan, but the benefit that is defined is an account balance, not a monthly benefit. For example, instead of promising workers a pension of $12,000 a year, a cash balance plan would promise a nest egg of $100,000 at retirement. When workers reach retirement, they have a choice of taking a series of monthly payments (an annuity) or taking the entire cash balance as a lump sum. Most traditional defined benefit pension plans do not offer this lump sum payout feature.

How Are Pension Benefits Paid Out?

Most pensions give retirees a choice of how to receive benefits—and how much they receive depends on which option they choose, because some options pay more per month than others. As with the cash balance plan, one option may be to take a lump sum from

STATE PENSIONS AND FISCAL CRISIS

As the economic meltdown of 2008 began to spread throughout the economy, states came to realize that they were extremely vulnerable. Not only did they face some of the largest budget gaps ever (over $300 billion collectively by the end of 2009), but revenues dropped significantly and, to date, remain in a troubled state. Moreover, state pension funds—money set aside for retired teachers, state police, and other government employees—face severe shortages.

According to the Pew Center (2010), there is a $1 trillion gap between what states have promised to pay their retirees and what they actually hold as financial assets. Some researchers, in fact, consider this estimate to be far too low (Biggs 2010). The problem has to do in part with where state pension funds were invested before the recession; in many cases, the funds were tied to high-risk, high-yield hedge funds along with more traditional investments, many of which collapsed or shrank dramatically in the economic downturn. In some cases—as in California, Colorado, and Illinois—governors previously had approved pension increases for state employees or had taken out bonds to cover their states' pensions, expecting that the investment market would increase and the value of their pension funds would rise.

Once the ensuing budget crunch hit home, however, lawmakers were forced to seek alternative solutions. New York, for example, raised its retirement age for new hires from 55 to 62. New Hampshire, Connecticut, and Texas required new workers to contribute more from their paychecks to state pension plans. Oregon and Vermont reorganized their pension investment boards to bring greater expertise to the table. And several states altered the formulas they used to calculate benefits. Even with such efforts, however, experts expect that it could be a decade or two before states start realizing any positive effects emerging directly out of changes to their pension plans.

the plan. Retirees could then invest this amount in an account and then withdraw interest and principal from the account.

Employees may have a choice of how much their monthly benefits will be. Usually, the option that pays the most per month is a single life annuity option. In this payout plan, pension benefits are paid out based on the retiree's life expectancy. Because women tend to live longer than men, the payout for men is usually higher than for women. Another option is a joint and survivor annuity. The benefits are based on the life expectancy of the retiree and the joint beneficiary of the pension—usually the husband or wife of the retiree. The monthly benefits for a joint and survivor annuity are generally lower than the single life annuity option, because the pension plan has to pay out benefits over the combined life expectancy of two people, which is usually a longer period of time.

Some pension plans provide for benefits to be paid out for a guaranteed number of years, regardless of how long the retiree lives. For example, employees may be able to choose a 20-year certain single life annuity. If an employee retired at age 65 and chose this option, he would receive benefits throughout the rest of his life, even if he lived to be 100. If he only lived until age 75, the remaining 10 years of the 20-year certain payouts would go to a designated beneficiary. The payouts for this option depend on the number of years of guaranteed payouts and are generally lower than those for the single life annuity but higher than payouts for the joint and survivor annuity.

Not all pensions adjust to accommodate cost-of-living increases—an important feature to consider in planning for retirement income. Suppose a pension paid out $1,000 a month, with no cost-of-living adjustment. If prices rise 10 percent over five years, it would take $1,100 to buy the same goods and services that once cost $1,000, but the pension stays at $1,000. Retirees would need to have some other source of funds, such as other retirement savings or IRAs, to maintain their purchasing power.

Consumer Protections in Pension Plans

The major federal law that provides consumers rights and consumer protections for their pensions is the Employee Retirement Income Security Act (ERISA). For example, ERISA sets out the maximum vesting period—how long employees need to work for an employer before they have a right to a pension that cannot be taken away. There are two vesting options for pension plans. The first option, called cliff vesting, provides employees with 100 percent of their benefits after five years of service. If an employee leaves after only four years of work, she will have no pension.

The second option provides for graduated vesting; employees earn a right to 20 percent of their benefits after three years, and then increases of 20 percent per year (40 percent after four years, 60 percent after five years, 80 percent after six years), so that after the seventh year, employees have rights to 100 percent of their benefits.

What happens if the company goes out of business—and the pension that workers were counting on goes away? ERISA also created the Pension Benefit Guaranty Corporation (www.pbgc.gov), which ensures pension benefits for workers. The drawback is that the benefit amounts retirees receive from the PBGC may be less than the pension benefits they were expecting—so they have less money in retirement. (And PBGC was itself hit hard by the recession but remains properly funded.)

ERISA also requires that if a retiree chooses a single life annuity option, the spouse must cosign the benefit selection form. This provision came about because many retirees were choosing single life annuity options, which paid more while the retiree was alive but left their spouses with no pension income. In an era when many women were not employed outside the home, this made a lot of sense—without a pension, many widows had to survive only on Social Security.

401(k), 403(b), and 457 Plans

A 401(k), 403(b), or 457 plan is an employer-sponsored retirement plan that allows employees to set aside some of their current earnings as personal savings for retirement.

Employees do not pay taxes on these earnings until they withdraw them in retirement, when their tax rate may be lower. The numbers refer to the sections in the Internal Revenue Service tax code that apply. The 401(k) applies to most workers, while a 403(b) plan covers workers in educational institutions, religious organizations, public schools, and nonprofit organizations; 457 plans cover employees of state and local governments and certain tax-exempt entities.

Neither benefits nor contributions to these plans are defined. Employees choose how much to contribute (up to limits set by the IRS) and how to invest the money. Workers over age 50 can contribute extra money into a catch-up fund for retirement. If employees move to a different job, they can roll over the money into an individual retirement account, or they may be able to move the assets into the new employer's 401(k) plan.

Employers may match worker contributions—an important benefit to think about when one is looking for a job. Consider Matt and John. Both work for Mega Corporation, which provides a match of up to 5 percent in the company 401(k). Both make $40,000 a year. Matt does not participate in Mega's 401(k), so his taxable salary and total compensation are $40,000. John, on the other hand, contributes 5 percent to his 401(k). His pay is reduced by $2,000, so his taxable salary is $38,000 instead of $40,000. But Mega Corp. adds a matching 5 percent—$2,000—to his 401(k) fund. So John's total compensation is his $38,000 pay plus the $2,000 he puts into his 401(k) plan plus Mega's $2,000 contribution to his 401(k)—or a total of $42,000.

Some employers have opt-in 401(k) plans and others have opt-out or automatic enrollment plans. For automatic enrollment plans, employers set an initial contribution rate and investment option. In either case, employees can choose how much to contribute and how to invest the money to tailor it to their specific needs.

IRAs, SEP IRAs, and Keogh Plans

Individual retirement accounts are self-directed retirement accounts—workers choose how much to contribute and how to invest the money. Money contributed to an IRA must come from earnings, although spouses not employed outside the home are allowed to put money into an IRA as well. There are three kinds of IRAs: pretax IRAs, posttax IRAs, and Roth IRAs.

Contributions to a pretax IRA are restricted to people without other pensions and are subject to income limits set by the IRS. Taxes on the money put into the account and taxes on any interest or gains are deferred until retirees withdraw the money.

Almost anyone can set aside money in a posttax IRA, again subject to IRS limits for annual contributions. When retirees withdraw the money, they pay taxes on the earnings but not on the principal.

A Roth IRA is a special kind of posttax IRA; contributions are limited by income, but all withdrawals are tax-free. Money invested in any of theses types of IRAs is usually put into securities, particularly stocks, bonds, and mutual funds.

SEP IRAs, simplified employee pension plans, are usually used by small businesses that want to provide their employees with some retirement funding. Employees set up their own IRAs and employers can contribute to these accounts.

Keogh plans are for self-employed individuals and their employees. These plans receive special tax treatment like a tax deferral on contributions and earnings until workers retire and start receiving benefits.

The Internal Revenue Service has special rules about money in IRAs, which it enumerates in IRS Publication 590 (available at http://www.irs.gov/pub/irs-pdf/p590.pdf). If workers withdraw money before age 59 1/2, they have to pay taxes on that money as well as a 10 percent penalty. Also, workers must start withdrawing funds by age 70 1/2, and there are specific minimum withdrawals required under tax law.

Conclusion

There are more options, and therefore more choices, for retirement planning today than in the past. The days of working without having to worry about retirement are long gone (if, indeed, they ever existed in the first place). Especially as more people change jobs over the course of their careers, taking advantage of options for accumulating funds for retirement becomes even more important.

Many commentators on both sides of the political spectrum welcome the range of retirement options and find that a mix of corporate and individual responsibility is the best means for satisfying the working public's retirement needs. Critics on the right (i.e., conservatives and libertarians) generally prefer that businesses not be unduly burdened with providing for the retirement security of their employees; they emphasize the need to shift pensions in the direction of individual savings and investment accounts. Critics on the left (i.e., liberals and social democrats), on the other hand, tend to prefer that businesses contribute significantly to the retirement security of their employees; they argue that personal retirement accounts are not for everyone. Where the pendulum rests at any given moment depends on many factors, both economic and political.

See also **Executive Pay; Labor, Organized; Social Security**

Further Reading

Biggs, Andrew G., "Comment Re: 'Promises to Keep: State's Face a Looming Pension Crisis'." *Economist* (February 18, 2010).

Blake, David, *Pension Economics.* New York: John Wiley, 2006.

Bucks, Brian K., et al,. "Changes in U.S. Family Finances from 2004 to 2007: Evidence from the Survey of Consumer Finances." *Federal Reserve Bulletin 95* (February 2009): A1–A55.

Employee Benefits Research Institute, *EBRI Databook.* 2009. http://www.ebri.org/publications/books/index.cfm?fa = databook

Gale, William G. et al., eds., *The Evolving Pension System: Trends, Effects, and Proposals for Reform.* Washington, DC: Brookings Institution Press, 2008.

Ghilarducci, Theresa, *When I'm Sixty-Four: The Plot against Pensions and the Plan to Save Them.* Princeton, NJ: Princeton University Press, 2008.

Lowenstein, Roger, *While America Aged: How Pension Debts Ruined General Motors, Stopped the NYC Subways, Bankrupted San Diego, and Loom as the Next Financial Crisis.* New York: Penguin, 2009.

Modigliani, Franco, and Arun Muralidhar, *Rethinking Pension Reform.* Cambridge, England: Cambridge University Press, 2005.

Morris, Charles R., *Apart at the Seams: The Collapse of Private Pension and Health Care Protections.* New York: Century Foundation, 2008.

Orenstein, Mitchell A., ed., *Pensions, Social Security, and the Privatization of Risk.* New York: Columbia University Press, 2009.

Pew Center on the States, "The Trillion Dollar Gap: Underfunded State Retirement Systems and the Roads to Reform." February 2010. http://downloads.pewcenteronthestates.org/The_Trillion_Dollar_Gap_final.pdf

POVERTY AND RACE

James H. Johnson Jr. and Michael Shally-Jensen

Before the 2010 oil spill in the Gulf of Mexico, Hurricane Katrina's devastation of the city of New Orleans and other Gulf Coast communities in 2005 refocused the nation's attention on the relationship between race and poverty. The people most adversely affected by this catastrophic event and its aftermath were overwhelmingly black and overwhelmingly poor. A common reaction to the media's dramatic images of disaster victims in New Orleans, especially those seeking refuge in the attics of flooded homes, building rooftops, and the Superdome, was "I didn't think the problem of race and poverty was still with us."

As this entry shows, the attention to poverty and race brought about by Katrina is yet another phase in the race/poverty discourse in the United States, which has shifted sharply several times over the past few decades. In this entry, we will show how the face of poverty in the United States has changed over the past 40 or 50 years in response to antipoverty policies and structural changes in the economy.

Background and Context

Concerns about America's poor ebbed and flowed throughout the 20th century. After receiving limited public policy attention prior to World War II, concern about the United States' poverty problem abated after the war, and it did not become a priority policy issue again until the early 1960s.

Since the early 1960s, public policies implemented to alleviate poverty in the United States have ranged from the very liberal to the extremely conservative. Reflecting this state of affairs, the absolute and relative size of the poor population in the United States has fluctuated widely over the last 50 years. Table 1 shows the poverty status of the U.S. population for selected years between 1960 and 2008.

The Poor and Efforts to Alleviate Poverty in the United States

Political attitudes toward America's poor were decidedly liberal during the 1960s. In both political and policy circles, the prevailing view was that poverty was a structural problem characterized by racial discrimination and systematic exclusion of racial minorities in all walks of American life. This view led to the first major federal effort after World War II to address the country's poverty problem: the war on poverty and the Great Society programs launched by President Lyndon Johnson.

Before the war on poverty, the U.S. poor totaled 39.8 million, 22.4 percent of the nation's population in 1960 (Table 1). As a consequence of the Johnson administration's antipoverty programs, which sought to redress the systematic inequities in U.S. society, the incidence of poverty was reduced by 36 percent during the 1960s. By 1970, only 25.4 million people (12.6 percent of the U.S. population) were poor.

But the war on poverty was short lived, as the Vietnam War assumed center stage during the early 1970s, resulting in a redirection of federal resources away from efforts to eradicate poverty. Moreover, with the election of President Richard Nixon, attitudes toward the poor became more conservative: the prevailing view held that poverty was a function of human or personal failings rather than a structural problem. As a consequence of these developments, the assault on America's poverty problem was substantially curtailed just as economic stagflation and a deep recession occurred, resulting in an increase—absolute and relative—in the size of the nation's poor population. During the 1970s, the U.S. poor grew from 25.4 million to 29.2 million, increasing from 12.6 percent to 13 percent of the total population by 1980 (Table 1).

Political attitudes toward the poor became even more conservative during the 1980s. Instead of acknowledging the short duration of the nation's official war on poverty, both the Reagan and Bush administrations of the 1980s argued that the nation's persistent

TABLE 1. Poverty Status of the U.S. Population (in thousands),* Selected Years (1960–2008)

Year	All People	Poor People	Percent Poor
1960	179,503	39,851	22.2
1970	202,183	25,272	12.6
1980	225,027	29,272	13.0
1990	248,644	33,585	13.5
2000	278,944	31,581	11.3
2008	301,041	39,829	13.2

*Population figures must be multiplied by 1,000. Thus, 179,503 becomes 1,795,300.
Source: U.S. Census Bureau. "Poverty." Historical tables. http://www.census.gov/hhes/www/poverty/histpov/histpovtb.html

poverty problem, especially the resurgence of growth during the 1970s, was a product of 1960s-era liberal policymaking. In their eyes, the federal welfare program—Aid to Families with Dependent Children (AFDC), in particular—was the culprit.

AFDC, they contended, destroyed the work ethic, bred long-term dependency, and encouraged a range of other antisocial or dysfunctional behaviors, including out-of-wedlock pregnancy, family disruption, and even illegal activities revolving around gangs and drug dealing, especially in the nation's cities. The problem, they asserted, was not material poverty but, rather, moral poverty. They also believed that the antipoverty programs of Johnson's Great Society slowed the economy by sapping taxes from productive investments that would otherwise spur economic growth and job creation.

To combat these problems and behaviors, the Reagan and Bush administrations waged what some characterize as a war on the poor, drastically cutting federal spending on social programs (especially AFDC) and eliminating government regulations viewed as crippling industry and private enterprise. These policies, especially efforts to create a deregulated business environment, drastically altered the structure of economic opportunity for the nation's most disadvantaged citizens, in particular the large number of African Americans concentrated in urban ghettoes.

Specifically, the business policies accelerated the decline of highly unionized, high-wage, central-city manufacturing employment—a process referred to as deindustrialization—and accelerated capital flight away from U.S. cities and toward Third World countries—a process referred to as employment deconcentration—leaving behind a substantial population that became the jobless or underemployed poor. Partly as a function of these business policy impacts and partly as a consequence of cuts in a host of 1960s-era social programs, the poor population continued to increase during the 1980s, reaching 33.5 million, or 13.5 percent of the total U.S. population, by 1990.

During the 1990s, the poor population declined for the first time since the 1960s—from 33.5 million (13.5 percent of the total population) at the beginning of the decade to 31.5 million (11.3 percent of the total population) at the end. It should be noted that this decline occurred despite prognostications that poverty would increase substantially after the enactment of the most sweeping welfare reform legislation since the war on poverty was launched in the mid-1960s—the Personal Responsibility and Work Opportunity Reconciliation Act of 1996 (PRWORA).

In an effort to respond to past criticisms of the social welfare system, especially those advanced by conservative social policy analysts, the 1996 PRWORA sought to reduce dependency by imposing time limits on welfare. Reflecting liberal views about the underlying causes of poverty, it also provided a range of supports designed to encourage and facilitate former welfare recipients' transition to work. Thus, in contrast to the liberal policies of the 1960s and the conservative policies of the 1980s, this legislation was decidedly centrist, as it represented a "carrots" (work incentives and supports) and "sticks" (welfare time limits) approach to poverty alleviation in the United States.

DUELING MEASURES OF POVERTY

Although poverty might seem like a simple concept, it isn't. Measuring poverty requires specific calculations, which means poverty must be precisely defined.

The official definition of poverty used by the U.S. Census Bureau is nearly 50 years old. Developed in 1965, the formulation of the definition involved several steps. First, the spending necessary for a household to consume nutritious yet frugal meals was calculated. This spending was different for households of different sizes. Second, this food spending was multiplied by a factor—roughly three—to equal the spending necessary to afford an adequate amount of all consumer goods and services. This, then, was the poverty threshold. Finally, if a household's income from working was below the poverty threshold for its size, then the household was classified as poor. Each year the poverty thresholds are adjusted upward to account for the general increase in the cost of living.

There are many issues with the official measure of poverty, but two in particular stand out. One is whether simply multiplying food spending by three is adequate to produce an income that would allow one to afford all necessary goods and services. What if prices and costs for some services, like health care, are increasing much faster now than in the past? This might mean the poverty thresholds are too low.

A second issue is whether the values of various kinds of public assistance received by households should be included before it is decided whether a household is poor. For example, many households receive assistance through programs like Food Stamps and Medicaid. Many households also receive direct cash assistance through temporary welfare payments and payments from the government if they are working and their earnings fall below a certain level (the name of this program is the earned income tax credit). If the objective of measuring poverty is to see how many people are poor after government-provided help is accounted for, then the value of these government programs should be included in a household's income.

The U.S. Census Bureau calculates poverty rates based on these two concerns. An alternative poverty rate includes the cost of medical services in the poverty thresholds. When this is done, the poverty rate (percentage of people who are designated poor) increases approximately 1 percent from the official rate. Another alternative poverty rate is calculated after the values of government antipoverty programs in a household's income are included. These poverty rates are approximately four percentage points below the official rate.

The conclusion is that how much poverty exists depends on how poverty is defined and measured.

The successful implementation of the reforms inherent in the 1996 legislation was aided tremendously by the decade-long economic boom, which created a large number of entry-level jobs that matched the skill levels of the long-term welfare-dependent population. But the economic crises of 2008–2009 adversely affected the federal government's effort to move former welfare recipients to the world of work as well as the structure of employment opportunities in the U.S. economy more generally, especially for low-skilled workers. Due to the massive layoffs spawned by corporate scandals and business failures, the U.S. poor population increased by 8.2 million after 2000, bringing the total to 39.8 million in 2008. As a result of this absolute increase, the share of the U.S. population that was poor increased from 11.3 percent in 2000 to 13.2 percent in 2008. (More recent data, although incomplete, looks just as bad or worse.)

Uneven Impacts of Past Poverty Alleviation Programs

Focusing on the period from 1970 to the present (for which there are more complete data available), and notwithstanding the fluctuations in the absolute and relative size of the U.S. poverty population over the last 40 years, there were, according to the Census Bureau, 14.6 million more poor people in the United States in 2008 than there were in 1970 (or about the same number of poor as in 1960). It should be noted that this absolute increase occurred in the midst of a 49 percent increase in the total U.S. population—from 202.2 million in 1970 to 301 million in 2008 (see Table 1). However, compared to the period 1960 to 2000, where there was an even greater relative increase in population (55 percent) together with an absolute *decrease* in the number of poor people (8.3 million), the more recent period (1970 to 2008) looks remarkable for its lackluster results. One could perhaps point to the 1960s social programs at the one end of the scale and the layoffs of the 2000s (capped by the start of the economic crisis of 2008–2009) at the other end, to explain part of this striking difference.

As should be evident from these data, past efforts to alleviate poverty in the United States have been unevenly distributed, resulting in a significant shift in both the demographic composition and the geographical distribution of the poor. Figure 1 provides insight into where significant inroads have been made in the alleviation of poverty and where major challenges remain. Figures 2 through 5 illustrate how the face of poverty in the United States has changed over the last 40 years as a consequence of the uneven distributional impacts of past poverty alleviation efforts.

Between 1970 and 2008, as Figure 1 shows, there was a 14.9 percent decrease in the rate of poverty among senior citizens, an 8.8 percent decrease in the rate of poverty among blacks (as many moved into the middle class), a 6.7 percent decrease in the poverty rate among women-headed households, a 4.2 percent decrease in the poverty rate in the South (as employment increased), and a 1.8 percent decrease in the poverty rate in nonmetropolitan areas. On the other hand, there were increases in the poverty rate in many categories: 3.9 percent among children and youth; 3.5 percent in central cities; 2.7 percent among adults aged 18 to 64; 2.7 percent in noncentral cities; between 2.4 and 2.2 percent in the Midwest, the West, and the Northeast; and smaller but notable increases among whites (1.1 percent), men (0.9 percent), families (0.6 percent), Hispanics (0.5 percent), and women (0.4 percent).

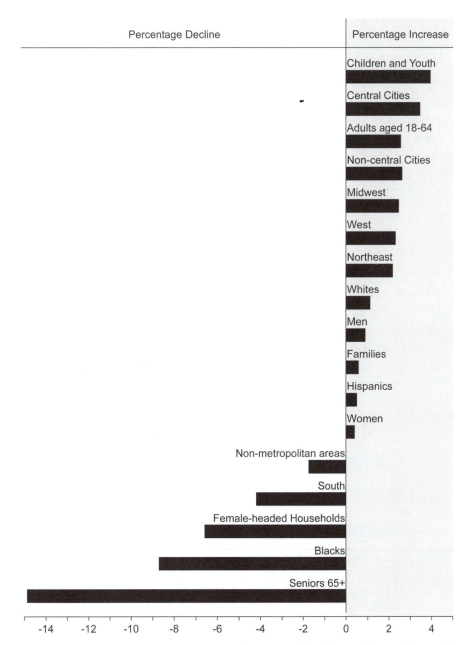

Figure 1. The Changing Profile of the U.S. Poor (1970–2008) (U.S. Census Bureau. "Poverty." Historical Tables. http://www.census.gov/hhes/www/poverty/histpov/histpovtb.html)

Undergirding these statistics are five noteworthy shifts that have transformed the face of poverty in the United States over the last 40 years: shifts in regional distribution and place of residence as well as changes in the age, family status, and racial and ethnic composition of the nation's poor.

As Figure 2 shows, the decline of the South's share of the U.S. poor and the concomitant increase in the West's share is one of these shifts—even while the South remains the region with the highest number of poor. In the early 1970s, close to half of the nation's poor was concentrated in the South. Close to 40 years later, the South's share of U.S. poverty had decreased to 40 percent. Paralleling the South's declining share, the West's share of the nation's poor increased from 16 percent in 1971 to 24 percent in 2003. As shown below, this shift is due in part to the influx of poor Hispanic immigrants into the United States over the last three decades, most of whom settled—at least initially—in the Southwest. Throughout this period, as Figure 2 shows, the Northeast's and Midwest's shares of the nation's poor remained relatively stable—in the 17–20 percent range in both regions.

Changes in the types of communities in which the nation's poor reside constitute a second major shift. As the United States has become more urbanized, so has the poor population. In the early 1970s, as Figure 3 shows, almost half of the nation's poor resided in rural areas. By 2008, only 17 percent resided in such areas. Today, a majority of the U.S. poor lives in metropolitan areas, with significant concentrations both inside and outside central cities.

Over the past 40 years, the age composition of the poor also has changed; this constitutes the third major shift. In general, the shares of the U.S. poor under age 18 and over

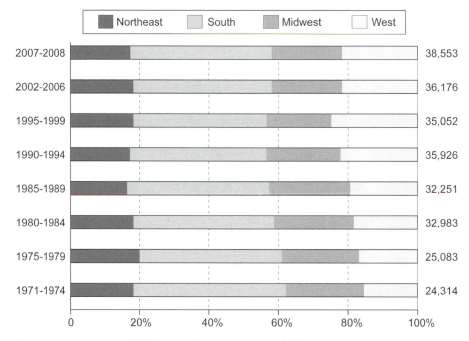

Figure 2. Distribution of U.S. Poor by Region (1971–2008) (U.S. Census Bureau. "Poverty." Historical Tables. http://www.census.gov/hhes/www/poverty/histpov/histpovtb.html)

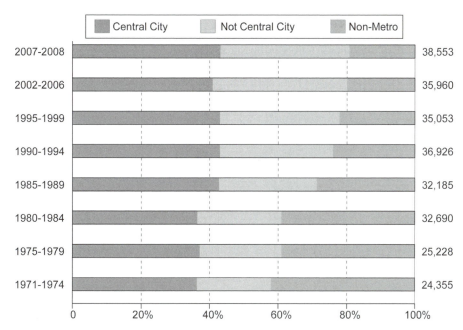

Legend: Central City | Not Central City | Non-Metro

Period	Value
2007-2008	38,553
2002-2006	35,960
1995-1999	35,053
1990-1994	36,926
1985-1989	32,185
1980-1984	32,690
1975-1979	25,228
1971-1974	24,355

Figure 3. Distribution of U.S. Poor by Place of Residence (1970–2008) (U.S. Census Bureau. "Poverty." Historical Tables. http://www.census.gov/hhes/www/poverty/histpov/histpovtb.html)

age 65 decreased, while the number of those in the 18–64 age group increased sharply (see Figure 4). Historically, poverty among working-age individuals (ages 18 to 64) was due primarily to detachment from the labor market (i.e., jobless poverty). However, as the U.S. economy was structurally transformed from goods production to service provision, a growing contingent of the labor force became what is referred to as the working poor. Due to skills deficits or other types of constraints (e.g., lack of affordable child care, inferior public school education, lack of economic opportunities in close proximity, and employer bias), these individuals have been relegated to part-time jobs they do not want—mainly in the service sector of the U.S. economy—or full-time jobs that pay below poverty-level wages, provide few (if any) benefits, and offer no prospects for career mobility (see Table 2). Many of these problems were exacerbated by the recent financial crisis, as figures for the period after 2008 (not published by the Census Bureau at the time of this writing) are likely to show.

The family context in which the poor find themselves is the fourth major shift. Poverty among all families increased slightly—by 0.6 percent—over the last four decades. As can be seen in Figure 5, moreover, poverty has become less concentrated in married-couple families and more concentrated in women-headed families, which accounted for about half of all families in poverty in 2008. This shift has been termed the *feminization of poverty*. Even so, as noted above in the discussion of Figure 1, some progress has been made since 1970 in reducing (by 6.7 percent) the poverty rate within this demographic

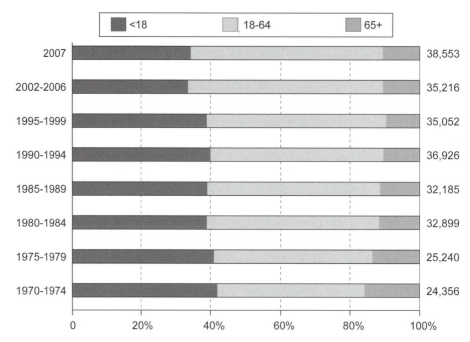

Figure 4. Distribution of U.S. Poor by Age (1970–2007) (U.S. Census Bureau. "Poverty." Historical Tables. http://www.census.gov/hhes/www/poverty/histpov/histpovtb.html)

group. In other words, as the *number* of women-headed households continues to increase and as poverty affecting families in general remains at a relatively high level, the prospect of experiencing poverty remains an issue for these families; and yet, as a group or class, women-headed households have witnessed a decline (6.7 percent) since 1970 in the *rate* at which they experience poverty.

Change in the racial and ethnic composition of the nation's poor population is the fifth major shift. Heightened immigration—legal and illegal—from Mexico, other parts of Latin America, and Southeast Asia is principally responsible for the increasing diversity of the nation's poor. The white share of the U.S. poor declined from nearly 70 percent in 1970 to 42.7 percent in 2008. During this period, the African American share declined from 30 percent to 24 percent. These declines have been offset by increases among the immigrant groups, especially Hispanics. Since the early 1970s, the Hispanic share of the nation's poor has grown from 10 percent to 27.6 percent.

Conclusion

A range of public policies spanning the political ideological spectrum have been implemented to address the poverty problem in the United States since the 1970s. Whether because of these policies or their failure or because of fundamental shifts in the U.S. economy, more Americans live in poverty today than 40 years ago, in both proportional

TABLE 2. Work Status of Poor People Age 16 Years and Older (in thousands),* Selected Years (1980–2008)

Year	Total Number of People Age 16 and Older	Worked		Worked Full-Time	
		Number	Percent	Number	Percent
1980	18,892	7,674	40.6	1,644	8.7
1985	21,243	9,008	42.4	1,972	9.3
1990	21,242	8,716	41.0	2,076	9.8
1995	23,077	9,484	41.1	2,418	10.5
2000	21,080	8,511	40.4	2,439	11.6
2005	25,381	9,340	36.8	2,894	11.4
2008	27,216	10,085	37.1	2,754	10.1

*Population figures must be multiplied by 1,000. Thus, 18,892 becomes 18,892,000.
Source: U.S. Census Bureau, "Poverty." Historical tables. http://www.census.gov/hhes/www/poverty/histpov/histpovtb.html

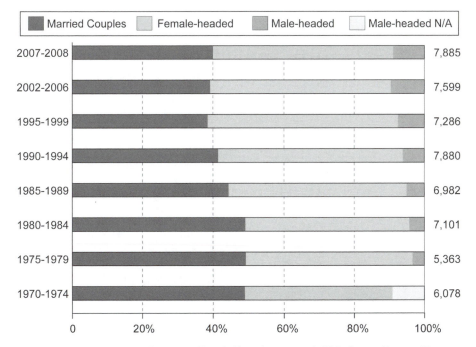

Figure 5. Distribution of U.S. Poor by Family Type (1970–2008) (U.S. Census Bureau. "Poverty." Historical Tables. http://www.census.gov/hhes/www/poverty/histpov/histpovtb.html)

terms (12.6 percent to 13.2 percent) and absolute terms (from 25.3 million to 39.8 million).

While many of the social and economic conditions associated with poverty in the 1970s persist, immigration, combined with regional and global shifts in job growth, changed the face of poverty in the United States in several ways.

- Poverty in the South declined significantly, but there were increases in the other regions as the economy adjusted to globalization.
- Rural poverty declined, while urban poverty grew.
- Poverty among senior citizens and blacks declined, while poverty among both working-age adults and children and youth increased significantly. Today, the working poor account for a higher proportion of Americans in poverty than the jobless poor, and children and youth have suffered the effects along with their parents or guardians.
- Poverty decreased in women-headed, single-parent households even as the number of these families grew, especially among African Americans. At the same time, poverty in families in general increased slightly.

Given the current economic downturn, this picture is likely to get worse before it gets better. If and when the situation does turn around, or perhaps even before that, policymakers would do well to revisit the issue of poverty in the United States and decide what can be done to build on progress that has been achieved to date while also attending to those areas that remain challenges.

See also **Affirmative Action; Consumer Credit and Household Debt; Immigrant Workers; Minimum Wage; Unemployment; Child Care (vol. 3); Homelessness (vol. 3)**

Further Reading

Arrighi, Barbara, and David J. Maume, eds., *Child Poverty in America Today.* Westport, CT: Praeger, 2007.

Chappell, Marisa, *The War on Welfare: Family, Poverty, and Politics in Modern America.* Philadelphia: University of Pennsylvania Press, 2010.

Chih Lin, Ann, and David R. Harris, eds., *The Colors of Poverty: Why Racial and Ethnic Disparities Exist.* New York: Russell Sage Foundation, 2008.

Conley, Dalton, ed., *Wealth and Poverty in America: A Reader.* Malden, MA: Blackwell, 2003.

Epstein, William M., *Good Citizenship and the War on Poverty.* University Park: Pennsylvania State University Press, 2010.

Goode, Judith, and Jeff Maskovsky, eds., *New Poverty Studies: The Ethnography of Power, Politics, and Impoverished People in the United States.* New York: New York University Press, 2001.

Henry, C. Michael, ed., *Race, Poverty, and Domestic Policy.* New Haven, CT: Yale University Press, 2004.

Lang, Kevin, *Poverty and Discrimination.* Princeton, NJ: Princeton University Press, 2007.

Lindsey, Duncan, *Child Poverty and Inequality: Securing a Better Future for America's Children.* New York: Oxford University Press, 2009.

Newman, Katherine S., *The Missing Class: Portraits of the Near Poor in America.* Boston: Beacon Press, 2007.

Patterson, James T., *America's Struggle against Poverty: 1900–1985.* New York: Basic Books, 1986.

Royce, Edward Cary, *Poverty and Power: The Problem of Structural Inequality*. Lanham, MD: Rowman & Littlefield, 2009.

Schram, Sanford F., Joe Soss, and Richard C. Fording, eds., *Race and the Politics of Welfare Reform*. Ann Arbor: University of Michigan Press, 2003.

Wilson, William Julius, *More than Just Race: Being Black and Poor in the Inner City*. New York: W. W. Norton, 2009.

PRESCRIPTION DRUG COSTS

Brandon Kramer and Michael Shally-Jensen

Few issues have created such controversy as the rising cost of prescription medicine. News reports often quote examples of patients, especially seniors, who cannot afford their medications. The pharmaceutical industry and advocacy groups maintain very different positions as to why prescription drug costs are so high in the United States compared to other countries. This entry examines the costs and related issues from both the industry and consumer advocate perspectives.

Research and Development

Industry Standpoint

Pharmaceutical companies contend that searching for new drugs, or the next cure, can be a costly venture. It may take hundreds and possibly thousands of "concepts" (experimental compounds) to create one drug that makes it to market. Cost estimates of researching both successes and failures range from $500 million to $800 million. An estimate released in a study by economists at Tufts University stated that, on average, it takes almost 15 years to bring a new drug compound to the market. Only 1 compound out of 5,000 ever makes it to market. Only 30 percent of drugs that make it to market will ever recoup their research and development costs (Clayton 2008). The cost and risk involved are very high. This is one way the industry justifies the high cost of medicine.

The U.S. Food and Drug Administration (FDA) maintains a strict and lengthy process to approve a medication for use. After filing a patent for a new compound, the drug manufacturer has approximately 20 years to research, receive FDA approval, and market the new drug. This process often leaves only five or six years to profit from the extensive research before generic manufacturers can challenge the patent. Therefore, a company can be limited in the time it has to recover its investment.

The pharmaceutical industry defends its position on research and development costs by demonstrating that all top companies in a variety of industries are research and development–intensive. The pharmaceutical industry relies on new drugs to keep an income stream from which it can continue to search for new drug compounds. Pharmaceutical companies invested roughly $50.3 billion in research and development in 2008, which is roughly a 51 percent increase since 2003 (Archstone Consulting and Burns 2009).

U.S. FOOD AND DRUG ADMINISTRATION DRUG REVIEW STEPS

1. The sponsor holds preclinical (animal) testing.
2. An investigational new drug application outlines what the sponsor of a new drug proposes for human testing in clinical trials.
3. The sponsor holds phase 1 studies (typically involving 20 to 80 people).
4. The sponsor holds phase 2 studies (typically involving a few dozen to about 300 people).
5. The sponsor holds phase 3 studies (typically involving several hundred to about 3,000 people).
6. The pre–new drug application (NDA) period begins, just before a NDA is submitted. This is a common time for the FDA and drug sponsors to meet.
7. The submission of an NDA follows, which is the formal step asking the FDA to consider a drug for marketing approval.
8. After an NDA is received, the FDA has 60 days to decide whether to file it so it can be reviewed.
9. If the FDA files the NDA, an FDA review team is assigned to evaluate the sponsor's research on the drug's safety and effectiveness.
10. The FDA reviews information that goes on a drug's professional labeling (information on how to use the drug).
11. The FDA inspects the facilities where the drug will be manufactured as part of the approval process.
12. FDA reviewers will approve the application or find it either approvable or not approvable.

The U.S. government offers some help (mainly through research grants from the National Institutes of Health, or NIH), but in terms of overall development, the industry maintains that it bears most of the burden. The industry maintains that roughly 91 percent of all drugs brought to market have been fully funded by the industry, with no help from the NIH (GlaxoSmithKline 2005).

Consumer Advocate Standpoint

Consumer advocate groups contend that the numbers pharmaceutical companies present regarding the cost of research are overstated. Public Citizen, for example, released a report showing how the $500 million figure that the industry uses as a benchmark for new drug development is wrought with flaws and overestimates. The report showed that the $500 million figure is suspect and more likely a mathematical estimation. The true cost of researching and developing new medications, the report states, is significantly less—between $70 million and $110 million (Public Citizen 2001).

Anti-industry groups also illustrate that the pharmaceutical companies receive certain advantages—tax breaks, for example—for doing the research and development. These government tax breaks could lower a pharmaceutical firm's tax burden considerably. The amount of tax incentives companies receive is a closely guarded secret within the industry. One such tax break involved incentives for pharmaceutical companies that built manufacturing facilities in U.S. territories. Many major manufacturers opened facilities in Puerto Rico to take advantage of this opportunity. Under this incentive plan, the industry's average tax rate was believed to be around 26 percent, as compared to roughly 33 percent for all other major U.S. industries (Greider 2003). Advocates for lower drug prices cite examples such as these to show that pharmaceutical companies do receive some benefit for the heavy investment in research and development.

Consumer groups also dispute claims that the pharmaceutical industry pays for most of the research involving new cures. The advocate groups believe that the National Institutes of Health often conducts the most basic and risky research and that the pharmaceutical companies begin their research only after an opportunity arises based on discoveries made through government research efforts. In recent years, in fact, there has been increased spending by pharmaceutical companies on the development of so-called me too drugs, or medications that do not differ in any fundamental way from medications already on the market but rather offer minor differences in terms of dosing, price, or similar aspects. These drugs are patently less expensive to produce.

New Medicine or Old Technology

Industry Standpoint

Recent television advertisements quote lines such as, "Today's medicines, financing tomorrow's miracles." This sums the industry view that, to discover new treatment, the cost of medication must remain at its current level. The industry invests heavily in research and development and needs to have adequate income to fund these ventures. New treatments for every disease, from AIDS to cancer, are being researched.

The principal industry trade group, Pharmaceutical Research and Manufacturers of America, or PhRMA, believes that these new cures are not only improving patient lives but are, in the long run, reducing the overall cost of health care. One study showed that treating patients with the latest medicines actually reduced their nondrug medical spending—for example, spending on hospitalization. The study showed that, for every extra dollar spent on new medicine, a corresponding decrease of $7.20 could be found in other health care costs (PhRMA 2005). Thus, the industry believes that it is not only funding future cures through revenues from its products but also helping to reduce the overall costs of health care by means of these new treatments.

Consumer Advocate Standpoint

Consumer groups respond to the pharmaceutical companies' suggestion that they are searching for the next cure by showing that many of the drug companies' newest products are me-too versions of existing drugs rather than new chemical entities. The new drugs may offer extended release (XR), controlled release properties to existing drugs (CR), or a combination of two readily available drugs in one pill. This allows for patent extension and continued profits from a drug that is about to become generically available. The producer simply changes the pill to make it time released or endow it with other properties and does clinical research showing the benefits of doing so. The FDA is more likely to approve the XR or CR version, which then becomes a market drug with extended patent protection. Advocacy groups see a serious decline in the number of compounds being studied to treat or cure new diseases or new ways to treat existing conditions. In fact, most widely advertised products are often product line extensions based on existing chemical entities. The industry is providing fewer new drug entities and increasing its output of current brand extensions. In fact, according to one report, only 15 percent of new drugs developed between 1989 and 2002 were made of new chemical compounds, and over half of the new drugs brought to market were product line extensions (Public Citizen 2001).

Marketing and Administration Costs

Industry Standpoint

Many believe that perhaps the reason drug costs are so high is that pharmaceutical companies spend a lot of money on product promotion. Pharmaceutical companies refute this argument by stating that they spend far more on research and development than on marketing. The companies maintain that they are not as heavily involved in advertising, for example, as consumer-oriented companies such as Coca-Cola are.

To help get their messages to patients, pharmaceutical companies have, however, launched direct-to-consumer (DTC) campaigns aimed at helping the consumer/patient appreciate whether a drug may be right for him or her. This information is then to be discussed between the patient and the physician to determine whether the drug is appropriate. The cost of DTC is relatively low compared to other industry advertising of products. One industry estimate shows that only 2 percent of U.S. drug costs are attributed to DTC advertising (Greider 2003).

The majority of all sales expenditures for marketing are for the salespersons each company employs. They act as consultants on particular disease states and promote medications using clinical data to demonstrate why their products are superior. The sales representative is trained as an expert and is versed in the latest clinical research, bringing the newest information to physicians to help them treat their patients. It is the strong belief of the pharmaceutical companies that the most effective way to keep physicians abreast of the latest clinical data is through this type of selling (McKinnell 2005). The physicians simply do not have time to keep up with every new publication and study.

Consumer Advocate Standpoint

Responding to the industry view regarding marketing expenditures, advocates point to some interesting information. One study found, for example, that eight of nine pharmaceutical companies studied spent twice as much on marketing, advertising, and administration as on research and development (Families USA 2002). Such high expenditures fuel the argument that research and development into new cures might not need to suffer if price controls were to be implemented.

Administrative costs tend to garner attention when the top officers of a pharmaceutical company have their salaries and bonuses published annually by the Securities and Exchange Commission. These generous salary packages are one of the areas that advocacy groups point to as needing reform if the cost of prescription medications is to go down. Even in the wake of the economic crisis of 2008–2009, the major drug companies remained hugely profitable. Net incomes for these companies are reported to be several times the median for Fortune 500 companies (Angell 2010). Too much of that profit, say consumer advocates, goes into marketing products, paying salaries and bonuses, and providing "educational services" for physicians.

The latter is something unique to the field of medicine. Most states require doctors to take what are called continuing medical education (CME) courses to maintain their licenses. The idea is that doctors must stay abreast of developments in their field, and CME courses are a means of ensuring that. Unlike professionals in other fields, however, who either pay for their own continuing education or receive offsets from the companies for which they work, CME courses are typically paid for by drug companies as a way of bringing a physician on board. In addition, academic researchers and doctors are courted using meals, payments for conferences and speaking engagements, offers of substantial research grants, assistance with publication, and so on in an effort to bring or keep them on board with respect to the company's research interests. Besides posing questions about conflicts of interest, consumer advocates note that the practice adds considerably to pharmaceutical companies' overall costs (Angell 2010).

GENERIC DRUG PRICE COMPARISON

Drug	United States	Canada
Amiodarone	$41.89	$134.90
Verapamil	$43.97	$93.95
Diltiazem	$127.99	$145.00
Warfarin	$20.69	$24.90
Lisinopril 20 mg	$16.19	$97.90

Note: One-month supply shipping charges from Canada not included.
Source: U.S. Food and Drug Administration 2004.

Importation

Industry Standpoint

One of the hottest issues in pharmaceuticals is the possibility of seniors seeking cheaper medications from other countries such as Canada. To afford their medications, many people feel forced to bring cheaper medicines into the United States from other countries.

The pharmaceutical industry maintains that drug importation is illegal and is in violation of the Federal Food, Drug, and Cosmetic Act. The industry cautions against the importation of prescription drugs by consumers. Drugs manufactured outside the United States are not subject to the same FDA safety regulations. Therefore, there are no assurances that medications acquired from foreign pharmacies are chemical equivalents of U.S. medications. Sometimes the medications received from foreign pharmacies may be counterfeit. Because the FDA does not regulate these medications, there is no recourse for the patients who have been wronged by such a transaction. The online foreign pharmacies often have waivers that must be acknowledged by patients, stating that they have no recourse if they receive noncomparable medications through the transaction.

Not only can importation be unsafe, but the foreign medications are not always cheaper than U.S. medications. In general, generic medications are cheaper from U.S. than from foreign pharmacies.

Consumer Advocate Standpoint

The problem is obvious to consumer advocate groups, who cite numerous examples of seniors organizing bus trips and traveling hours to Canada or Mexico to buy their prescriptions. To consumer advocates, this practice shows that there is a major problem with the price of U.S. prescription medicines.

There is a certain trade-off that exists when a patient must look to other means to acquire his or her prescription medicines. Often, a patient may simply be unable to afford those prescriptions, and the only alternative other than importation is to not purchase, and therefore not take, the medicine that has been prescribed. This practice is, of course, very dangerous—and costly. One estimate is that $100 billion per year is spent on hospitalizations that could have been avoided had the patient properly taken his or her medication ("Potential Encapsulated" 2010). And, indeed, most patients recognize the danger; hence the interest in foreign pharmacies.

Another concern is that the FDA process for inspecting drugs is imperfect. The prescription drug Vioxx, for example, was associated with serious and sometimes fatal cardiac events in a small population of patients. Vioxx was an FDA-approved drug and had met all the requirements to be marketed. Some groups believe, in fact, that the FDA process is industry-friendly and that pressure from a company will hasten a product's approval. This makes the industry's argument against importation somewhat suspect. Political resistance to importation in the United States is intense. European countries, such as Germany and England, do allow drug importation. In the United Kingdom, at least eight prescriptions under the National Health Service are filled by imports from countries such as France and Spain, where drug prices are cheaper. The practice has been estimated to save the government $130 million a year (Public Citizen 2001).

Though generic drugs may be somewhat cheaper in other countries, such as Canada, advocate groups point to the fact that, in many cases, branded prescription drugs (newer medicine that is still under patent protection) are significantly cheaper.

Price Controls

Industry Standpoint

Why do branded medicines cost more in the United States? Government-imposed price controls are one option to help control the cost of medication. Canada has imposed a countrywide price for each medication. Under this system, the price of medications is specifically regulated. The belief is that more patients have access to the best medications.

The pharmaceutical industry maintains that government restrictions would severely limit the research and development potential. One study shows that the United States accounts for roughly 70 percent of the world's new medical therapies (Clayton 2008). The industry points to the low percentages of innovation and new drug introductions in countries subject to price controls. From an industry standpoint, price controls are not the solution to improving access to the newest medications. The industry points out that prices are lower in countries with socialized medicine, a type of system repeatedly rejected by Americans.

BRANDED PRICE COMPARISON OF DRUGS IN THE UNITED STATES AND CANADA

Price of Drug	United States	Canada
Plavix	$397	$213
Lipitor	$214	$162
Actos	$542	$377
Zocor	$423	$231
Celexa	$281	$138

Note: Prices include medication and shipping for a three-month supply.
Source: International Medication n.d.

The industry believes that using medications is actually cost-effective for the consumer, because it prevents costly surgeries or other hospital care caused by a preventable event. For instance, paying for a high blood pressure medication is cost-effective when compared to paying for hospitalization following a heart attack caused by uncontrolled high blood pressure.

Consumer Advocate Standpoint

Advocate groups argue for price controls by showing the effectiveness that the U.S. government has in negotiating prices for medications for its veterans and military personnel. The government set a price for branded and generic drugs that companies must meet. This allows for every veteran and active soldier to have access to necessary medication. Advocates believe that the government can go one step further and institute this type of system for the country's seniors so that they, too, can have access to necessary medicine.

In comparison to other developed countries, consumer advocates show that the United States pays more for prescription drugs than any other country. In the United Kingdom, patients pay roughly 69 percent of the cost patients pay in the United States. The difference is the same for patients in Switzerland. Germans pay 65 percent, Swedes pays 64 percent, the French pay 55 percent, and Italians pay 53 percent (Public Citizen 2001).

Advocates point to the success of Canada's Patented Medicine Prices Review Board, which puts a ceiling on prices for all drugs. Many of the drugs purchased in Canada are purchased by the government. This allows access for low-income and elderly patients. This system is very similar to how the United States purchases medications for military personnel, but Canada implements controls on a much wider scale.

As for the argument that price controls stifle innovation, a recent study found that European pharmaceutical companies are just as innovative, or perhaps even more so, than their U.S. counterparts, despite the existence of price controls. In addition, some countries, such as the United Kingdom and Germany, encourage comparative-effectiveness reviews, whereby cost-benefit analyses are applied to rival drugs to determine which perform best. The market values of the drugs—that is, their prices—are then adjusted accordingly ("Reds under Our Meds" 2009). Supporters of the idea say that, if anything, it *encourages* innovation.

Profits

Industry Standpoint

The pharmaceutical industry is currently extremely profitable. The industry maintains that the high profitability is necessary to attract new investment for further research and development. For the year 2008, as with previous years, *Fortune* magazine ranked industries in terms of their profitability. The pharmaceutical industry ranks third on the list behind network/communications equipment and Internet services/retailing (CN-NMoney 2009). This represents a climb from the fifth spot just two years before.

The pharmaceutical industry, besides suggesting that profits are plowed back into research and development, cites examples of charity toward individuals in need of medication. It estimates that, in 2003, it distributed approximately $16 billion worth of free samples to U.S. physicians' offices (Greider 2003). This provided patients access to the newest treatments for all types of illness.

The industry further demonstrates acts of giving in Third World nations, where patients have no possible means of paying for such medication. In these cases, the industry freely dispenses the necessary medications to those in need. Instances of giving in times of disaster can also be found. Emergency shipments of medications have been sent to victims of the recent tsunami as well as to U.S. hurricane disaster victims.

The industry trade group PhRMA has presented figures that show that the cost of medicine is in line with the increases in overall health care spending. Pharmaceuticals accounted for only 11 cents of every health care dollar spent. In fact, PhRMA suggests that the overall cost of prescription drugs has remained roughly 10 percent of overall health care costs for the past 40 years (Clayton 2008).

Consumer Advocate Standpoint

Consumer advocates believe that pharmaceutical profits are a clear example of the excess that exists in the industry. The pharmaceutical industry consistently ranks among the top in terms of profitability. For a 10-year period ending in 2001, the industry was the most profitable in the United States and, on average, was five and a half times more profitable than the average of other Fortune 500 companies (McKinnell 2005).

The industry spends a tremendous amount of money to protect its interests as well. For instance, the industry in 2002 had approximately 675 lobbyists in Washington, DC, to promote industry-friendly legislation. This amounts to seven lobbyists for every U.S. senator (Public Citizen 2003).

Although the industry may at times be charitable, such charity, particularly in the case of U.S. patients receiving free samples from their doctors, is surely, say consumer advocates, a form of marketing or public relations. The motives of the industry in providing a small sample of what normally turns out to be a longer course of drugs, are hardly pure; in fact, calling it charity rubs many the wrong way.

Advocacy groups are, moreover, quick to identify what they feel is a much larger issue. The rate at which prescription costs have risen in the past two decades is alarming. Costs began to increase significantly in the 1980s, but, between 1995 and 2005, the rate of increase averaged 10 percent per year, becoming a much larger component of overall health care costs and greatly exceeding the rate of inflation (Congressional Budget Office 2008). Fortunately, there are indications that the rate has begun to decelerate in recent years, perhaps owing to technological advances.

Conclusion

The issue of prescription drug costs in the United States remains very complicated. In many cases, the information supporting either side can be confusing. For every study that promotes an industry stance, a consumer advocate group has information that argues just the opposite. The government is little help when trying to find answers to the problem of high medication costs. Both sides of the argument frequently cite studies from the National Institutes of Health to support their own viewpoints. Regardless, it is imperative that patients always have access to all medications. Pharmaceutical companies have various discount programs designed to assist financially struggling patients receive medicine at reduced cost. Some companies even give medications at no cost to patients who can prove that their situation leaves no way of paying for the medicine. Although these programs can be complicated and time consuming, they can help alleviate the burden of prescription drug costs until definitive research can be conducted to find permanent solutions to this problem.

See also **Health Care; Interest Groups and Lobbying; Off-Label Drug Use (vol. 4); Vaccines (vol. 4)**

Further Reading

Angell, Marcia, "Big Pharma, Bad Medicine: How Corporate Dollars Corrupt Research and Education." *Boston Review* 35 (May/June 2010): 7–10.

Angell, Marcia, *The Truth about the Drug Companies: How They Deceive Us and What To Do about It.* New York: Random House, 2004.

Archstone Consulting, and Lawton R. Burns, *The Biopharmaceutical Sector's Impact on the U.S. Economy: Analysis at the National, State, and Local Levels.* Stamford, CT: Archstone Consulting, 2009.

Avorn, Jerry, *Powerful Medicines: The Benefits, Risks, and Costs of Prescription Drugs.* New York: Vintage, 2005.

Clayton, Anne, *Insight into a Career in Pharmaceutical Sales,* 10th ed. Deerfield, IL: Pharmaceuticalsales.com Inc., 2008.

CNNMoney, "Fortune 500: Our Annual Ranking of America's Largest Corporations." May 4, 2009. http://money.cnn.com/magazines/fortune/fortune500/2009/performers/industries/profits/

Congressional Budget Office, *Technological Change and the Growth of Health Care Spending.* Washington, DC: CBO, 2008.

Engelhardt, H. Tristram Jr., and Jeremy R. Garrett, eds., *Innovation and the Pharmaceutical Industry: Critical Reflections on the Virtues of Profit.* Salem, MA: M&M Scrivener Press, 2008.

Families USA, *Profiting from Pain: Where Prescription Drug Dollars Go.* 2002. http://www.familiesusa.org/assets/pdfs/PPreort89a5.pdf

Finkelstein, Stan N., *Reasonable Rx: Solving the Drug Price Crisis.* Upper Saddle River, NJ: FT Press/Pearson Education, 2008.

GlaxoSmithKline, *The Value of Medicines: Beyond the Basics.* Brentford, Middlesex, England: GlaxoSmithKline, 2005.

Greider, Katharine, *The Big Fix: How the Pharmaceutical Industry Rips Off American Consumers.* New York: Public Affairs, 2003.

International Medication Program Price List, n.d. http://www.wecaremedicalmall.com/prices.htm

McKinnell, Hank, *A Call to Action: Taking Back Healthcare for Future Generations.* New York: McGraw-Hill, 2005.

PhRMA, *What Goes into the Cost of Prescription Drugs?* 2005. http://www.phrma.org/files/Cost_of_Prescription_Drugs.pdf

"Potential Encapsulated: Medicines That Can Talk to Doctors." *Economist* (January 14, 2010). http://www.economist.com/business-finance/displaystory.cfm?story_id = E1_TVNSGSPD

Public Citizen, *Rx R&D Myths: The Case against the Drug Industry's R&D "Scare Card."* 2001. http://www.citizen.org/documents/ACFDC.PDF

Public Citizen, *2002 Drug Industry Profits: Hefty Pharmaceutical Company Margins Dwarf Other Industries.* 2003. http://www.citizen.org/documents/Pharma_Report.pdf

"Reds under Our Meds: Could Health-Care Reform in America Stop Innovation in Pharmaceuticals?" *Economist* (August 27, 2009). http://www.economist.com/research/articlesBySubject/displaystory.cfm?subjectid = 531766&story_id = E1_TQPNSPPV

U.S. Food and Drug Administration, *U.S./Canadian Price Comparisons October 2004.* http://www.fda.gov

U.S. Food and Drug Administration, *From Test Tube to Patient: The FDA's Drug Review Process: Ensuring Drugs Are Safe and Effective.* n.d. http://www.fda.gov/fdac/special/testtubetopatient/drugreview.html

S

SEX AND ADVERTISING

Mary Beth Pinto and John D. Crane

Jean Kilbourne contends, "These days, graphic sexual images seem more extreme, more pervasive, and more perverse than ever before. Images that used to belong to the world of pornography are now commonplace in family magazines and newspapers, in TV commercials, on billboards, and online" (Kilbourne 2005).

Consider the words from "Poker Face," a popular song by Lady Gaga that topped the pop charts internationally in 2009 and won the 2010 Grammy Award for best dance recording:

> Russian Roulette is not the same without a gun
> And baby when it's love if it's not rough it isn't fun

Some might say that the lyrics sound more like a whispered conversation in a sex club or a scene from an X-rated movie than part of the opening verse of an award-winning pop song. U.S. culture is awash in sexually explicit content, and the music industry is just one example. All forms of the media are caught up in the sex craze. We live in what appears to be a sex-obsessed society, with rude language, nudity, and eroticism all around us. What was once the unexpected (in terms of acceptable content or language) has become the expected, and the expected has now become the norm. It is no longer necessary to read men's magazines like *Penthouse* or *Maxim* to see sexual imagery. Just surf the Web, turn on the TV, go to the movie theater, take a look at what teens are wearing, watch commercials, and look at print advertising.

Although the emergence of sex in advertising is not new, some of the controversies regarding it are. There are two basic issues surrounding sex in advertising: Does sex appeal work? In other words, does it really sell products and services? And has the use of sex in advertising gone too far? Should organizations limit their use of sexual images to sell their products and services, even if it does work? This chapter will explore both of these controversies.

Does Sex Appeal Work?

Yes

The use of sex appeal is not a new phenomenon in marketing. The blatantly sexual images depicted on walls in ancient Pompeii suggest that sex was used in public places to advertise various products ranging from food to baths to prostitution. (This is reminiscent of the explicit catalogs of "services available" that are distributed by hand and found in display cases along the streets of Las Vegas every night.) In ancient times, these public advertisements were not limited to "sin cities" like Pompeii, nor to just "sin services."

As early as Victorian 1850, marketers were using the opposite sex as eye-catching images to promote their products and services. According to Goodrum and Dalrymple (1990), "Full female nudity was introduced with a photograph...to illustrate a Woodbury Soap ad in 1936." Prior to that time, advertisers used sexual innuendo in copy by barely hinting at sexual images. Take, for instance, an advertisement for Iron Clad Hosiery from 1927. An attractive woman dressed in what today would be considered not very revealing undergarments seems to be caressing her "Iron Clad" ankle with an air of sensuality that is barely perceptible. The image is accompanied by the slogan, "The kind of beauty that thrills." In addition, the print in the ad notes the "mysterious quality which glorifies the wearer's own shapeliness and grace" that the hosiery offers. The image is less sexually suggestive than the copy of the advertisement (Goodrum and Dalrymple 1990).

Sexual appeal has been defined as "the degree of nudity or sexual explicitness found in visual, audio, and/or verbal elements of advertisements" (Gould 1994; Reichert and Carpenter 2004). It has long been accepted that sex appeals have stopping power, encouraging readers and viewers to stop, look, and listen. The "wow" factor of sexual appeals attracts attention to promotional messages, encouraging readers to notice specific messages out of the media clutter or barrage of stimuli to which they are exposed.

Nowhere has the stopping power of sex been used with more success than in the retailing industry. Consider Abercrombie and Fitch and its former quarterly publication called by many a "magalog." Although the company contended the publication was a catalog to showcase and sell its merchandise, most of the models in the magazine were nude or nearly nude. It should have made even the casual viewer wonder, "How can a retailer expect to sell clothes from a catalog when none of the models are wearing any?" The company and its magazine sparked public outcry with its depiction of teenage boys and

ABERCROMBIE AND FITCH

Picture a long, slender figure in the background of a very dark room. As you look, you notice that what you see is a male body with no clothing on. You begin to wonder, "Did I pick up the wrong magazine?" Trying not to draw attention to yourself, you slowly peer over the cover page and notice that indeed you are looking at a catalog—a clothing catalog, yet no one has clothes on.

The depiction is one that many young people have seen in the Abercrombie and Fitch quarterly catalog. Since the catalog's debut in 1997, its content has drawn regular protests. Items such as thongs for children with the words "eye candy" on them are just the beginning. In an effort to curb public criticism, the store placed the catalog in plastic bags and only distributed them through their online shop to consumers age 18 and older. Although their efforts were applauded, they decided in the winter of 2003 to pull the catalog from circulation.

Abercrombie and Fitch's financial state has been in jeopardy for some time. Market positioning and segmentation issues have plagued the company because of its racy appeal. Although racy appeal is commonplace in today's culture, the decline in profits for Abercrombie and Fitch brings about the question, Is it the racy content that the consumer is avoiding or the products themselves?

Sources: "Abercrombie to Kill Catalog after Protests over Racy Content." *Wall Street Journal* (December 10, 2003); DeMarco, Donna. "Abercrombie & Fitch Pulls Children's Thong." *Knight Ridder Tribune Business News* (May 23, 2002).

girls scantily clothed (if at all) in very suggestive poses. According to critics, "Not only did the magazine target teens, it did so in a sexual way…evident in the way the individual images in the magazine were staged" (Spurgin 2006).

No

Sexual imagery can also create problems and be counterproductive for marketers. It is widely accepted that sex appeal attracts attention, but studies show that it rarely encourages actual purchase behavior. Specifically, sexual images attract consumers to the ad but do not enhance the profitability of the brand or product. In some cases, sexual appeal has been shown to distract the audience from the main message of the marketer and interfere with comprehension, especially when there is complex information to be processed.

If marketers are going to use sexual images in ads, it is imperative that they know their audience, because several variables have been shown to play a role in the effectiveness of sexual appeals. For example, sex appeal seems to work differently for men and women and affect message comprehension and recall. Studies show that men often become so aroused by nudity used in ads that they have a hard time remembering components of the actual message or what the ad was about (Schiffman and Kanuk 2007). Women tend to be attracted to ads that use elements of fantasy, love, and romance, whereas men are more attracted to appeals that use nudity (Anne 1971). In addition, age seems to be related to whether a viewer responds favorably or unfavorably to sexual appeals (Maciejwski 2004). Younger audiences are usually less offended by sexual images, although this too may differ by gender. In a study of college-age consumers, researchers found that men and women differ significantly in their assessments of sexual appeals. Advertisers must take care when using sexual imagery (especially featuring women) in ads targeted to female college-age consumers (Maciejwski 2004). What one person finds erotic, another person may find offensive.

The bottom line for marketers is synergy. Sex ads do not work for all products. Sexually oriented appeals may be a poor promotional choice if the product, the ad, the target audience, and the sexual images themselves don't all fit and complement each other (i.e., when the sexual images are unrelated to product claims, such as scantily clad women selling products for a hardware store).

Has the Use of Sex in Advertising Gone Too Far?

Most people agree that "the sexual ads that have drawn the most protest are those that exploit women as sex objects and those that use underage models in suggestive ways" (Duncan 2002). With the use of sexually oriented advertising comes scrutiny and protests by parents, legislators, and consumer activists—just to name a few groups. Consider the public furor over the FCUK brand from French Connection or the Janet Jackson and Justin Timberlake incident during the half-time show at the 2004 Super Bowl, when Jackson's breast was exposed to viewers. This so-called wardrobe malfunction resulted in months of debate about American core values and the role of the Federal Trade Commission (which is only one of several federal agencies that has jurisdiction over the monitoring of one or more aspects of advertising and marketing communication in the United States) in regulating live television programs (Elliot 2005). In the wake of this incident, a time delay has been placed on all live television programs.

People still talk about the Calvin Klein controversy of the mid-1990s, when the designer used young-looking models (albeit over 18) to star in his controversial jean ads. While many critics rated these ads as outright "kiddie porn," others contended that any PR is good PR (Lippe 1995). Some commentators compared these ads to the bare-bottomed toddler girl in the classic Coppertone ads, which are now viewed in a different way due to the current spotlight on pedophilia. The question remains: Was Klein just a wise businessman capitalizing on America's craving for sex? Are sexual images in advertising today just good marketing? On one side of the argument is the belief that "the chief aim of marketing is to sell more things, to more people more often for more money" (Danziger 2002). The bottom line is profit, and, therefore, the sole obligation of

FCUK

"FCUK like a bunny." Wait, was that... oh no, it's just a T-shirt from French Connection UK, circa 2001. After the creation of the acronym FCUK, French Connection came under a plethora of scrutiny. The parallels between their acronym and a word many find offensive is easily seen, but the use of this type of "gonzo" marketing tool is becoming more common. FCUK was heavily criticized publicly for the use of its label, and company profits eventually fell.

The negative reaction of public watchdog groups influenced consumers not to buy FCUK's products. However, governmental agencies did not see anything wrong with the label FCUK. In 2005, the United Kingdom patent office upheld the use of the French Connection acronym with arguments by lawyers that it is "completely mainstream." Although French Connection moved on to other advertising campaigns after discontinuing the FCUK campaign in 2006, it seems that this type of explicit language is commonly accepted as a functional aspect of culture.

Sources: Adapted from Lea, Robert. "Under-Pressure FCUK Kisses Ad Man Goodbye." *Knight Ridder Tribune Business News* (July 7, 2006); Rossiter, James. "Patent Office Decides that FCUK Doesn't Spell Trouble." *Knight Ridder Tribune Business News* (December 21, 2005).

the firm is to do whatever is necessary, within legal parameters, to maximize return on shareholder equity.

So, if sex sells more products, then sex in advertising is good for business. It sure has been good for a coffee stand in Seattle, Washington (Brady 1995). The owner has developed a special niche for his retail store, and business couldn't be better. He uses gorgeous women barely dressed in bras and panties to lean out the window to take orders and deliver coffee and sweet treats. According to the owner, anything is fair game as long as his employees' breasts and buttocks are covered so they aren't breaking the law. The business owners report few complaints other than long drive-through lines.

The alternative point of view says that organizations must look beyond the specific profit interests of the firm and consider their greater social responsibility. Is sex in advertising going against moral and ethical standards? Is it exploiting women? Has it turned "sex into a dirty joke" (Kilbourne 2005)? Are sexually oriented ads just outright distasteful and wrong? Or do they just reflect a culture in which "the heat level has risen, the whole stimulation level is up" (Brady 1995)? An additional concern is that the more sexual images that are used in the media and advertising, the more acceptable the extent of the sexuality that will become in future advertising. In other words, sexual images are now an expectation in the advertising of clothing, perfume, body lotions, and hair products. The laws regarding sexual harassment indicate that acceptable behavior should be defined by what a "reasonable woman" would consider acceptable behavior. As we become socialized toward sexual innuendo and images, reasonable women will become more and more accepting of lewd behavior and images. This may up the ante for advertisers who feel continuously pressured to increase the "wow" factor and therefore increase the amount of sexual imagery they use.

As stated above, the unexpected in terms of sex appeal in advertising has become the expected, and now it has also become the norm. But the larger question is: Does that make it right? What are these graphic images teaching our youths? "That women are sexually desirable only if they are young, thin, carefully polished and groomed, made up, depilated, sprayed and scented" (Kilbourne 2005). At the opposite end of this spectrum, however, are new approaches to advertising, including the Dove theme suggesting that all women, regardless of their body type, are beautiful and desirable. Many advertisers are now using larger women as models. It has yet to be seen whether this is an improvement or simply an extension of the use of sexual imagery. In other words, if large and less traditionally attractive women are also presented as sexual objects, some might say that we are going backward instead of forward.

The women's movement has spent decades fighting for an equal place at the table (i.e., equal pay for equal work, fair treatment, and the elimination of the glass ceiling). Has the women's rights movement been a waste of time if we are still reducing women to nothing more than sex objects? We are teaching our youths (both boys and girls) to devalue the mental and spiritual aspects of a woman and focus exclusively on the physical.

For thousands of years, advertisers have used women as eye-catching images in their ads. At the start of the 21st century, this strategy continues full speed ahead. By modern standards, the images are raunchier, more explicit, and more widely employed. As a society, we get to decide where to draw the line. Therein lies another controversy—in a complex culture, which ones of us will make the decision? Will we turn off the TV, decide not to buy a product, or refuse to shop at a retail store that uses sexually explicit images in its advertisements? Regardless of our opinions about the use of sex in advertising, we ought to be concerned that private companies and their advertising agencies appear to be making those decisions now. We need to ponder the long-term effects on our culture.

See also **Marketing to Women and Girls; Obscenity and Indecency (vol. 3); Internet (vol. 4)**

Further Reading

Anne, C., "Sexual Promotion Can Motivate, Distract, Alienate, or Liberate." *Advertising and Sales Promotion* 19, no. 10 (1971): 52.

Associated Press, "Coffee Shops Show a Little Skin to Compete." *KOMO-TV- Seattle, Washington-News* (January 9, 2007). http://www.komotv.com/news/5402241.html

Brady, James, "Fueling, Feeling the Heat." *Advertising Age* (September 4, 1995): 1, 34.

Danziger, Pamela N., *Why People Buy Things They Don't Need.* New York: Paramount Market Publishing, 2002.

Duncan, Tom, *IMC: Using Advertising and Promotion to Build Brands.* New York: Irwin/McGrawHill, 2001.

Elliot, Stuart, "Emphasizing Taste, and Not Just in Beer, at Super Bowl." *New York Times* (January 26, 2005).

Goodrum, Charles, and Helen Dalrymple, *Advertising in America: The First 200 Years.* New York: Harry N. Abrams, 1990.

Gould, Stephen, "Sexuality and Ethics in Advertising: A Research Agenda and Policy Guideline Perspective." *Journal of Advertising* 23, no. 3 (1994): 73–81.

Kilbourne, Jean, "What Else Does Sex Sell?" *International Journal of Advertising* 24, no. 1 (2005): 119–122.

Lippe, Dan, "Readers Rate Klein 'Porn' Campaign." *Advertising Age* (September 4, 1995): 34.

Maciejwski, Jeffrey J., "Is the Use of Sexual and Fear Appeals Ethical? A Moral Evaluation by Generation Y College Students." *Journal of Current Issues and Research in Advertising* 26, no. 2 (2004): 97–105.

Reichert, Tom, *The Erotic History of Advertising.* Amherst, NY: Prometheus Books, 2003.

Reichert, T., and C. Carpenter, "An Update on Sex in Magazine Advertising: 1983 to 2003." *Journalism and Mass Communication Quarterly* 81, no. 4 (2004): 823–837.

Rutherford, Paul, *A World Made Sexy: Freud to Madonna.* Toronto: University of Toronto Press, 2007.

Schiffman, Leon G., and Leslie Lazar Kanuk, *Consumer Behavior,* 9th ed. Upper Saddle River, NJ: Pearson Education, 2007.

Spurgin, Earl W., "What Was Wrong with Abercrombie and Fitch's 'Magalog'?" *Business and Society Review* 111, no. 4 (2006): 387–408.

SOCIAL SECURITY

Lois A. Vitt

The American dream is about freedom and financial security. But it is possible to lose everything. One day a person has a job, a family, and a house. Then there is a layoff, an accident, an illness, or the death of a breadwinner. One misfortune piles upon another. As late as the 1930s (and even in the 1940s), a person with no income or savings and no children to take him or her in risked going to the "poorhouse."

By the time Social Security became law in 1935, every state except New Mexico had poorhouses. Sometimes called almshouses or poor farms, their existence is a little known fact in U.S. history today. Yet there were thousands of such places across the country, and becoming an inmate at a taxpayer-funded, county-run poorhouse was a fate to be dreaded (Altman 2005).

In the 1920s, the federal government sent volunteers to examine more than 2,000 poorhouses. The report came back that conditions were shameful (Gunderson and Julin 2002). A report by the New York State Commission on Old Age Security found that "sick people are thrown together with the well…people of culture and refinement with the crude and ignorant and feeble-minded" (Altman 2005).

Then came the added toll from the nation's Great Depression. The stock market crash of Black Tuesday—October 24, 1929—shook America's very foundations. Banks failed, savings were wiped out overnight, homes and farms were lost in foreclosures. Twenty-five percent of all workers and 37 percent of all non–farm workers were unemployed. Financial gloom was everywhere, and people starved (Smiley 2010). Even with so much human misery in full view, passing the law that established Social Security was not an easy task.

Controversy surrounded the Social Security Act even as President Franklin D. Roosevelt signed it into law in 1935. Social security had been the product of several years of bitter controversy, negotiation, lobbying, and compromise. The debate had been widespread: from the Congress, big business, and the press to the workplaces and streets of America. One side believed, among other things, that the program was a "communist" one, and government could not be trusted to pay benefits properly, if at all. Supporters keenly felt the desperate need to protect older workers and their families against grinding poverty that had already struck millions of Americans upon retirement and was awaiting millions more (Landis 1997).

A New Kind of Insurance Program

President Roosevelt envisioned Social Security as a new kind of government program, uniquely suited to its mission of promoting both the work ethic and the dignity of older individuals and their families. It was established as *social insurance*, not public assistance, even though that is the way it was depicted by its detractors. The program was planned to provide a reliable retirement income to people at age 65. They would get no handout. Instead, workers would be required to contribute to their future retirement out of their current income and, by doing so, would earn the right to their Social Security pension.

On August 14, 1935, the day President Roosevelt signed the Social Security program into law, he explained his reasons for proposing it this way:

> Today a hope of many years' standing is fulfilled.…We can never insure one hundred per cent of the population against one hundred per cent of the hazards and vicissitudes of life, but we have tried to frame a law which will give some measure of protection to the average citizen and to his family against the loss of a job and against poverty-ridden old age. (Landis 1997)

Many people think of Social Security as merely a retirement program, but from the beginning it has been much more than that. In 1935, the insured events were retirement or death of workers, but they were expanded later to include the total disability of workers as well.

It is a comprehensive insurance program that provides protection for workers and also for their dependent family members. As with any type of insurance, Social Security buys working taxpayers protection against loss—specifically the loss of income in the following categories:

- **Retirement benefits**—for workers who retire from the workforce and have reached an eligible age (currently 62 years old for reduced benefits and 67 years old for full benefits).
- **Family benefits**—for family members who are dependents of workers who have become totally disabled or retire.
- **Survivors benefits**—for surviving family members of workers who die. Benefits are similar to life insurance.
- **Disability coverage**—for workers who become totally disabled and can no longer work even though they have not reached retirement age (Landis 1997).

Social Security is funded through dedicated payroll deductions under the Federal Insurance Contributions Act (FICA). These payments are formally deposited in trust funds to be paid out to workers when they reach retirement age or become disabled and can no longer work. The payroll tax rate is split between employee and employer, currently 6.2 percent of earnings for employees, and 6.2 percent for employers. The rate for individuals who are self-employed is 12.4 percent. These rates apply to wages up to and including an annual income (from wages) of $106,800. For income above that amount, there is no Social Security tax to pay.

In general, workers must make payroll contributions for 10 years or more to become eligible for a Social Security pension when they retire. Spouses are also covered, even if they have never worked. Benefits are based on a worker's average wage, calculated on the 35 years of highest earnings. When high-income earners retire, they receive higher monthly benefits, but not proportionately so. The idea is that benefits should be proportionately more for those with lower earnings than for those with higher earnings. The benefit formula under the Social Security system is weighted in favor of lower-income groups (Myers 2003).

How Social Security Has Performed

Social Security accomplished what President Roosevelt and supporters of the program hoped it would do, but not overnight. The first monthly benefit check was issued by Social Security to retired legal secretary Ida May Fuller, who received $22.54 in January 1940. In 1950, benefits were raised for the first time. In 1972, Congress enacted a law that allowed for cost-of-living adjustments to help the elderly cope with annual increases in the rate of inflation.

Before Social Security, the poverty rate among older adults was three times that of the general population. Economists estimate that, without Social Security, the elderly poverty rate would have been 40 percent rather than the 9.4 percent it was in 2008. The current average monthly payment is $1,094 (Carr 2010).

The program significantly affects the lives of a majority of Americans. According to AARP, some of the basics reported as of July 2010 include the following:

- Monthly benefits are paid to about 54 million Americans.
- For 25 years, Social Security has received more in payments than it has paid out. It now has a $2.5 trillion reserve fund invested in government bonds.
- In 2010, the recession and high unemployment brought in fewer payments than anticipated, and Social Security has been drawing on its reserves.
- The Congressional Budget Office estimates that the reserve fund and payroll taxes will cover full payment of benefits for another 33 years.

Income security for the retired is not the only benefit successfully provided by Social Security; it also supports families struck by the death or disability of a breadwinner. Much like any private insurance, the Social Security program philosophy was to collect payments from workers and then pay a defined amount back to them (or their family) when certain events occur.

Social Security and the World Trade Center Disaster

In her book *The Battle for Social Security,* Nancy Altman tells the story of how Social Security employees worked to assist the survivors in the chaotic aftermath of the September 11 attacks on the World Trade Center. The story can serve as a case study of how the Social Security insurance system assists those eligible to receive family and survivors benefits under the program.

Two days after the attacks on the World Trade Center, the Social Security Administration went into action to identify and contact the family members of workers who perished in the attack. The task was to meet with employers and family members to help them secure the financial protection their loved ones had earned for them.

Altman writes that the Social Security Administration was among the first insurers to meet with employers and victims' family members. Its employees worked with the New York City Police Department, the New York City Fire Department, and the Port Authority to find the families of every firefighter and police officer who had died. They were present at the family assistance centers and set up a Web page to inform family members how to apply for benefits. By September 16, every major network affiliate in New York carried public information spots about Social Security.

Employees from the Social Security Administration distributed fact sheets to advocacy organizations and established lines of communication with local hospitals, unions, and other local organizations. They worked 15-hour days, seven days a week, to get benefits to spouses and dependent children as quickly as possible. They knew that they were throwing an economic lifeline to the families when they needed help the most. On October 3, Social Security checks were mailed and electronically transferred to thousands of members of families who lost loved ones on September 11, 2001 (Altman 2005).

The Politics of Social Security Today

The struggle that surrounded President Roosevelt's efforts to pass the Social Security Act in 1935 as well as the process of enacting amendments that improved the program over the past 75 years still rages today. As before, much of the battle involves passionate emotions and clashing values about who we are and want to be as Americans:[1]

1. Are we a society where individuals look after themselves and are responsible for their choices and financial security no matter what might be happening in the business and financial sectors and the general economy?

    Or are we a society that can be independent and responsible for our own well-being while also contributing resources and sharing risks that can offset personal financial ruin during times of economic upheaval in the general economy?

2. Do we trust the unregulated business and financial communities to provide stable employment, disability coverage, and retirement pensions that will assure for us later-life financial security?

    Or can we support policymakers who will strengthen the Social Security program and continue to oversee both our own contributions and, more importantly, those of the nation's employers on behalf of working Americans?

The Controversies

Politicians and the media frequently warn that Social Security is headed for bankruptcy. Not true. The Social Security program is not a cause of the federal government's current deficit and debt concerns. In fact, the program has been running surpluses since 1984 (Gregory 2010). The federal General Fund experienced an annual surplus of $86 billion in 2000, meaning that taxpayers contributed more in all federal taxes than was spent in all federal programs and operations. However, that surplus fell year by year after 2000 because of tax cuts, funding for wars, and other government spending to a deficit of $1.55 trillion in 2009 (Congressional Budget Office 2010a).

By contrast, the Social Security program has amassed a trust fund reserve now amounting to $2.5 trillion (Board of Trustees 2009; Congressional Budget Office 2010a). In addition, the trust fund has been lending funds to the government that it would otherwise have had to borrow from national and international public markets. Moreover, Social Security trust fund reserves are expected to increase to $3.2 trillion by 2015 and to $3.8 trillion by 2020 (Congressional Budget Office 2010b) *unless* the decrease in contributions due to unemployment continues to erode the reserves required to meet the growing surge of individuals who are reaching retirement age or are becoming disabled. Because the law requires 75-year solvency for the Social Security trust funds, and since numbers can be used to project future circumstances in different ways, no one can ascertain with any certainty what will happen over a 75-year period of time.

To summarize the important fiscal realities today, the Social Security reserve is being built primarily with:

1. FICA taxes paid at the rate of 6.2 percent of earnings by lower- and middle-income workers up to a maximum wage level of $106,800, plus matching FICA tax payments by employers at 6.2 percent of earnings. These contributions currently total 12.4 percent.
2. Interest paid on FICA taxes borrowed from the Social Security trust fund over the past 25 years to help finance the rest of government (Sloan 2009).

The long-term costs and paid-out benefits of the Social Security program are projected to rise with the increasing number of retirees from the baby boom generation during the coming years. This means that, in order to preserve the long-term viability of Social Security, certain actions must be taken by Congress. Suggested changes have included (a) increasing the maximum wage level on which FICA taxes are now paid; (b) increasing the age at which workers are eligible to receive retirement benefits from age 67 to (say) age 70; and (c) means-test the benefits so that only the poor receive benefits.

Arguments against these three proposed fixes are these: (a) at 12.4 percent, increasing the maximum wages to (say) $170,000 would be a large tax increase on an already ailing middle class; (b) increasing the age at which Social Security benefits may be obtained could be wrong-headed for anyone engaged in an occupation that involves physical activity; and (c) means-testing the benefits would be a terrible mistake that would violate the social compact that everyone pays Social Security taxes and everyone receives their benefits (Sloan 2009).

In the past decade, Republicans, along with a few Democrats, have campaigned for a radical restructuring of Social Security—namely, permitting workers to divert part of their payroll taxes from Social Security into *personal retirement accounts,* which could be invested in the stock market. The earnings on these accounts would replace a portion of Social Security benefits. This push to privatize has been a major conflict over Social Security.

Supporters of privatization argue that Social Security must be overhauled because its rate of return is dismal. In response, experts point out that comparing the rate of return on Social Security with that of an investment portfolio is "comparing apples and oranges" (Diamond n.d.). Social Security is not a portfolio, they say; it is insurance, which provides benefits in the event that a particular problem (e.g., disability) or condition (e.g., retirement) occurs. The opponents of privatization maintain that claiming Social Security's return is dismal is as meaningless as claiming that the return you get on your fire insurance premiums is dismal.

The heart of the battle over privatization may be more about profits for the financial markets and financial businesses than about individual freedom and collective responsibility. These values have an honored place in U.S. tradition and easily tap into the emotions of U.S. voters. One side sees a society in which individuals are responsible for their lives and are free to make their own financial decisions (Suellentrop 2005). On the other side, a deeply held value embodied in Social Security is that real freedom requires a nation to protect the well-being of its members against harm. Risks of unemployment, disability, changes in the general economy, and in the practices of businesses (e.g., outsourcing employment) are to be shared and insured against to the extent possible.

Conclusion: Speaking Out, Speaking Up

The bottom line is that many older workers who felt reasonably well positioned for retirement a few years ago now need Social Security more than ever. Middle-aged individuals who may have time to recover savings and home equity are needed more than ever to contribute to the future viability of the program. Employers' matching contributions are also required more than ever to sustain the Social Security system. Each of these social groups must also demonstrate to the nation's young adults that they will have a realistic plan for future benefits (Sloan 2009).

This is no time to overlook, dismiss, or ignore the continued performance of the nation's Social Security program, the social compact that helped to lift generations of older adults out of poverty and helped to close the nation's poorhouses. Failing to understand the real economics of the Social Security program can bring back the poorhouse for individuals who suffer through financial ruin that is not their fault—sudden unemployment, loss of pensions or savings or home. Doing nothing is not an answer either.

Worse, believing that "Social Security will not be there for me when I grow older," an opinion heard more and more frequently these days from younger Americans, might guarantee the untimely demise of this invaluable program, since one's voice to save it will not have been heard.

See also **Income Tax, Personal; Pensions**

Note

1. For this section and parts of the one below, the author wishes to acknowledge Arthur Benavie for his essay "Social Security, Medicare, and Medicaid" (published in M. Walden and P. Thoms, eds., *Battleground: Business,* Greenwood Press, 2007), which I have drawn upon here.

Further Reading

Altman, Nancy J., *The Battle for Social Security: From FDR's Vision to Bush's Gamble.* Hoboken, NJ: John Wiley, 2005.

Benavie, Arthur, *Social Security under the Gun: What Every Informed Citizen Needs to Know about Pension Reform.* New York: Palgrave Macmillan, 2006.

Board of Trustees, *Annual Report of the Board of Trustees of the Federal Old-Age and Survivors Insurance and Federal Disability Insurance Trust Funds.* Washington, DC: Social Security Administration, 2009. http://www.ssa.gov/OACT/TR/2009/index.html

Carr, Deborah, "Golden Years? Poverty among Older Americans." *Contexts* (Winter 2010). http://www.context.org

Congressional Budget Office, *Budget and Economic Outlook: Historical Budget Data.* Washington, DC: The Office, January 2010a.

Congressional Budget Office, *Combined OASDI Trust Funds March 2010 Baseline.* Washington, DC: The Office, March 2010b.

DeWitt, Larry, Daniel Béland, and Edward D. Berkowitz, *Social Security: A Documentary History.* Washington, DC: CQ Press, 2008.

Diamond, Peter A., ed., *Issues in Privatizing Social Security: Report of an Expert Panel of the National Academy of Social Insurance.* Cambridge: MIT Press, n.d.

Gregory, Janice M., *Testimony before the National Commission on Fiscal Responsibility and Reform on June 30, 2010.* Washington, DC: National Academy of Social Insurance, 2010.

Gunderson, Dan, and Chris Julin, "Poor Conditions at Poorhouses." Minnesota Public Radio, July 29, 2002. http://news.minnesota.publicradio.org/features/200207/29_gundersond_poor farm-m/

Landis, Andy, *Social Security: The Inside Story.* Menlo Park, CA: Crisp Publications, 1997.

Livingstone, Steven Greene, *Social Security: A Reference Handbook.* Santa Barbara, CA: ABC-CLIO, 2008.

Myers, Robert J., "The Social Security Program of the United States." In *Encyclopedia of Retirement and Finance,* ed. Lois A. Vitt. Westport, CT: Greenwood Press, 2003.

Rogne, Leah, et al., eds., *Social Insurance and Social Justice: Social Security, Medicare, and the Campaign against Entitlements.* New York: Springer, 2009.

Sloan, Allan, "A Flimsy Trust: Why Social Security Needs Some Major Repairs." *Washington Post* (August 2, 2009). http://www.washingtonpost.com/wp-dyn/content/article/2009/07/31/AR2009073104214_pf.html

Smiley, Gene, "The Great Depression." In *The Concise Encyclopedia of Economics,* 2d ed., ed. David Henderson. Indianapolis: Liberty Fund, 2010.

Suellentrop, Chris, "George W. Bush. Philosopher King." *Slate* (January 17, 2005). http://www.slate.com

Vitt, Lois A., "Evaluating Program Outcomes in Financial Education." Unpublished manuscript, 2010.

Weinstein, Deborah, *The Recession Generation: Preventing Long-term Damage from Child Poverty and Young Adult Joblessness.* Washington, DC: Coalition on Human Needs, 2010.

SUPPLY CHAIN SECURITY AND TERRORISM

Peter B. Southard

The supply chain of any product consists of all the businesses involved in moving that product from the raw material stage into the hands of the final consumer. In addition to the various manufacturers, suppliers, and retailers, it also includes transportation, storage, and distribution firms as well as the indirect resources such as finance, accounting, and information systems. All these companies—as well as the customer—are linked together to fulfill a customer's order.

One of the major themes dominating the recent thoughts of both supply chain managers and their suppliers has been the growing trend toward outsourcing and the use of international suppliers for raw materials, parts, and components. A second theme that has been dominating the thoughts of the same group as well as those of countries around the globe has been that of security from terrorist acts by individuals and groups. Unfortunately, the two themes are becoming more and more interrelated. This interrelationship has been underscored by the publicity surrounding the management and security control of ocean ports within the United States. A recent article in *CIO Magazine* suggested that the U.S. government will soon be requiring much more information on incoming foreign goods from firms that do business internationally. Specifically, the firms will need to provide information regarding not only the content of shipments prior to their arrival ashore but also the history of that content, points of origin, and routes of passage as well as who, specifically, has handled any shipments arriving in the United States from overseas. These requirements will undoubtedly increase the total costs of that material to the firm and also, since there is only a single true source of funds in any supply chain, to that source: the customer. Those costs are not just monetary in nature. They also include other aspects of a firm's competitive advantage and the customer's requirements, such as speed of delivery, flexibility, and reliability. These last costs can be significant when viewed in context with other recent business trends.

The move toward leaner production systems, such as those of Dell and Hewlett-Packard, where inventory levels are kept at a minimum, has meant lower costs with greater selection to the consumer. What it has also meant, however, is a supply chain that is much more vulnerable to interruption, because even a short delay in the shipment of components or raw materials could mean the shutdown of an entire production facility.

These supply chain challenges are not limited to the links of seagoing ports. The other three major modes of transport—air, truck, and rail—and their distribution and transfer centers are all experiencing the same pressures. A recent article in *Air Transport World* describes the preliminary measures and costs being felt by European air freight companies. They include the millions of euros being spent for the new equipment and organizational changes needed to meet the new industry requirements. U.S. trucking and rail associations are also exerting efforts and have developed an Anti-Terrorist Action Plan. Every mode of transport and every transfer point involved in the supply chain is coming under scrutiny. At this point, however, no mode is receiving focused direction from the government in terms of concrete requirements or policies, which means that all security initiatives are either in the pilot study phase, sitting on a shelf, or awaiting development.

CURRENT INITIATIVES

Customs-Trade Partnership against Terrorism (C-TPAT)

This is probably the best-known and most widely used antiterrorist security initiative. It is a voluntary program, begun in November 2001, between private global organizations and the U.S. government. It is administered through the Department of Homeland Security by U.S. Customs and Border Protection. Currently, the program offers expedited customs handling for participants. In return, the participants provide customs with information that indicates the company has performed security risk analysis on itself and its trading partners as well as ongoing best practices security measures. There are currently over 7,400 private participants. Further information can be obtained through the U.S. Customs and Border Protection Web site (www.cbp.gov).

International Ship and Port Facility (ISPS) Security Code and the Maritime Transportation Security Act of 2002 (MTSA)

The Maritime Transportation Security Act of 2002 (MTSA) is the U.S. response to the International Ship and Port Facility (ISPS) Code. ISPS is a 2002 code set out by the international maritime community delineating security requirements to be followed by all interested parties, including governments, shipping companies, and port authorities. MTSA is the U.S. version that was passed in 2004. Both have three levels of security based on the perceived security threat. Information is available at the Web sites of the International Maritime Organization (www.imo.org) and the U.S. Coast Guard (www.uscg.mil).

Automated Commercial Environment and Advance Trade Data Initiative

The Automated Commercial Environment is another U.S. Customs initiative. It is a trade processing system designed to provide the backbone of an enterprise resource planning system for Customs that will enable it to monitor its own processes and transactions. Its impact here is that it will also be used to analyze such things as risk factors in targeting containers for inspection. As an additional module, Customs has also been looking at the Advance Trade Data Initiative, which will be the data collection interface with importers. It will require importers to submit information regarding all shipments, such as the purchase order, ports through which the shipment has passed, final destination, and even where on the ship a particular container is located. This program may eventually become a requirement of C-TPAT.

CommerceGuard and RFID

CommerceGuard is a technology for securing cargo containers and is jointly held by GE Security, Mitsubishi Corporation, Samsung C&T Corporation, and Siemens Building Technologies. It consists of a relatively small device that magnetically clamps across the door of a cargo container and monitors both the door and the contents. It can record when and how many times the door was opened, temperature changes inside the container, and other information, as programmed. Visit www.commerceguard. com for additional information. Radio frequency identification (RFID) is a method of

(continued)

(*continued*)
identifying unique items using radio waves. Although it is not a new technology, it gained attention recently when Wal-Mart required many of its vendors to apply RFID tags to their goods. Different RFID technology can be used in varying applications, including determining and recording the temperature, light, and sound environment through which the RFID tags (and the goods to which they are attached) have passed. Various associations and committees are in the process of establishing standards for this technology.

The basic conflict faced by U.S. businesses is the security of goods entering the borders of the United States versus the cost of that security. The ramifications are twofold. First are the implications for competition: If a company can move its goods through security points and inspections faster and at a lower cost, then it has a competitive advantage. Second is the additional cost to the final consumer, who will ultimately bear the burden of the heightened security requirements.

This entry discusses the challenges associated with developing the necessary supply chain skills and infrastructure that will likely be needed in the future to minimize those costs. Specifically, it looks at new heightened security requirements from the perspective of their effect on the two major components of supply chain management: the supply chain strategy and the supply chain structure, which includes the drivers of supply chain performance. These four drivers are facilities, inventory, transportation, and information. Finally, it will look at tactics to facilitate that security.

Supply Chain Strategy

Hau Lee of Stanford University has developed a highly regarded framework for the strategic design of supply chains based on the variability, or risk, in both the demand for a product and the supply of raw materials, parts, and components to produce that product. As the variability of either dimension increases, the cost of designing and operating a supply chain increases, as does the complexity of managing it. Past terrorist attacks and threats have led to an emphasis on increased security, which, if randomly applied to incoming shipments, will increase the variability in acquiring upstream materials from suppliers. This variability may take the form of longer times waiting for inspections, the amount of time required for more thorough inspections, or even the availability of goods from certain points of origin.

The strategic design of the supply chain, based on demand variability, is to provide either efficiency through low cost or responsiveness through speed and flexibility. Either choice is affected by the time and cost created by added security.

The lowest-cost and least flexible chain is termed an efficient supply chain. At the opposite end of the spectrum is the agile supply chain. More and more, the two trends of increasing competition and a more demanding consumer are forcing companies to move their supply chains toward the agile. By definition, this supply chain strategy requires shorter lead times, higher customer service levels, greater flexibility, and the ability to handle supply uncertainty. All of this agility, of course, comes at a cost; companies employing this strategy employ more expensive modes of transportation and maintain excess capacity to handle both supply and demand variation. While meeting the new specter of international terrorism will impose added costs, those on the agile end of the supply chain spectrum are more adapted to handle the variation.

Where the costs will have the most effect will be on the efficient supply chain. These supply chains operate on the basis of lowest cost created by very stable and predictable supply and demand. Staples such as food items and standardized commodities that operate on a very low margin fall into this category. Even a minimal increase in the cost of goods sold is felt immediately. Added variability in this supply chain strategy would be quickly translated into higher costs. The focus at both ends of the spectrum, then, will be to reduce the variability on either side of the supply chain in order to create and maintain a competitive advantage.

Finally, any supply chain strategy must include a contingency plan. The value of such a contingency plan was well illustrated by Dell during the West Coast dock strike of 2002. While other computer manufacturers were scrambling to find alternative sources for components that were being manufactured on the Pacific Rim or sitting idle during the 10-day strike while their parts sat on idle ships, Dell was able to continue operating with just 72 hours of inventory. Dell did all this without a single delay in customer orders. It was able to do so because it had previously developed an internal management team designed to handle such situations, close ties to various suppliers, and access to alternative transportation sources.

A firm's strategy determines how the supply chain must be structured in order to achieve that strategy. The strategy selected will necessarily have a major impact on the cost of securing that supply chain.

Supply Chain Structure and Drivers

The drivers of supply chain performance are facilities, inventory, transportation, and information. How these are organized and positioned within the supply chain establishes the structure of the supply chain. An agile supply chain will generally have more decentralized facilities and a distributed, standardized inventory in order to provide the most flexibility and to be located as close to the customer as possible. It will use faster transportation, which will result in higher costs per item. Information systems must be more robust and complex. What this means in terms of security is a more complex system to oversee and protect.

Facilities are the physical locations (land and buildings) where products are created, manufactured, assembled, or stored. The more agile the supply chain is, the more facilities will be involved. The impact here will be both on the facilities themselves as well as the equipment necessary to meet the new security requirements. Part of this will likely be in the form of special radio frequency identification (RFID) tags or other similar electronic monitoring devices such as GE's CommerceGuard, which are attached to the products or the containers in which the products are stored. This means that specialized equipment will need to be present in the facilities to read the product devices, which becomes part of the facility cost. Other facility costs will be those necessary to secure the physical property itself, such as fencing, security personnel, and alarm systems.

Inventory consists of all raw materials, work in process, finished goods, and supplies held. There are four costs associated with inventory: holding or carrying cost, setup or changeover costs, ordering costs (which includes shipping), and the cost of stock-outs (not having the product when the customer demands it). The strategy and structure of the supply chain affect these costs. Reducing inventory reduces the holding costs but increases ordering costs (since more frequent orders are needed to meet the same demand) and vice versa. The more facilities the chain employs, the more inventory is needed to stock each location, increasing both holding and ordering.

Security against terrorism will mean that the stores of inventory being held will need to be more closely guarded and monitored, increasing the holding costs. As closer monitoring, tagging, and information requirements for each shipment increase, so do the ordering costs. RFID tags or other identification methods will be added to the cost, as will the labor and equipment needed to apply and read them.

Although the cost of shipping is usually accounted for under inventory costs, there are several decisions involved with this driver. These include the mode of transportation (air, truck, rail, or water), routing, and the network design (e.g., use of direct shipping, warehouses, cross-docking, or postponement). Since every additional link in the supply chain may mean an added security step or check, companies may be inclined to move more toward direct shipping, bypassing the intermediaries of warehouses, distributors, or even retailers. It may also mean an increasing use of third-party logistics companies so that a firm may hand off the responsibility for the security of a shipment to a company that specializes in logistics and is able to use economies of scale to absorb the additional costs of security.

Every security initiative under consideration at the current time will involve, at the very least, an increased requirement for information on the contents and history of all shipments entering or traversing the United States, whether this data will need to be supplied to U.S. Customs or another agency. These increased information requirements necessitate the need for new methods for collecting the data, more complex software to receive and organize it, and the hardware and peripherals on which to operate it. While the cost of RFID tags and the associated reader equipment is coming down, they still present a formidable outlay of capital, especially for smaller companies.

In addition, many of the initiatives under consideration involve the use of some type of tracking device attached to or inserted in each shipment. Some even call for identification of each item in that shipment. In either event, this would require reading equipment as well as software that will provide an interface between the equipment and the company's internal information system.

All this information will not only need to be maintained by the company, but it will also have to be forwarded to the appropriate government (and possibly industry) body in the format dictated by that group. Unfortunately, that standard has yet to be established.

Tactics

Tactics to address the impact of added security on the supply chain focus on the strategy and drivers. Strategically, firms must understand that regardless of whether they consider their products to be functional or innovative, their supply chains will need to maintain a higher degree of flexibility to remain competitive. In the paranoid environment in which businesses now operate, it takes little to disrupt a supply chain. A terrorist attack is not even needed. Take, for example, the closing of Port Hueneme in Ventura County, California. This major port was closed for hours because dock workers found a threatening sentence scrawled on the interior bulkhead of a ship coming in from Guatemala. Since this is one of the largest ports in the United States in terms of fresh produce imports, such a shutdown had the potential to create major problems. The case of the Alameda Corridor illustrates that it is not just facilities themselves that pose a risk in the supply

THE ALAMEDA CORRIDOR

The Alameda Corridor is a 20-mile multirail right-of-way that connects the ports of Los Angeles and Long Beach to the rest of the nation's rail lines. It was completed in 2002 at a cost of $2.4 billion. What is its significance for security in the supply chain? Consider this. Together, those two seaports handle more cargo traffic than any other port in the United States. Over one-third of all traffic entering or exiting those ports does so through the Alameda corridor. The heart of the throughway is a 10-mile-long trench that is 33 feet deep and 50 feet wide, which might appear to be an easier target than the 7,500 acres that the Port of Los Angeles occupies. Also consider the fact that most of the other two-thirds of that cargo traffic is carried in 6.3 million containers per year on the highways in the Los Angeles area, most of which travels on a single freeway: the 710, Long Beach Freeway. A terrorist attack would not necessarily need to pinpoint a port. Crippling access to any point of aggregation for shipments to and from U.S. businesses would effectively serve to close the port and seriously affect the economy. For more information on this vital artery in the U.S supply chain, access the Alameda Corridor Transportation Authority Web site (www.acta.org).

chain. Firms must be prepared for such events with alternative supply chain tactics that include having excess capacity in the drivers.

The drivers themselves must be more flexible and robust. Companies must have alternative transportation partners and modes, alternative facilities in terms of distribution or aggregation points, and alternative sources of inventory in terms of suppliers.

The form of the method will be in two areas: prevention and disaster recovery. Prevention will likely take the form of increased information requirements from companies about their shipments, increased inspections, and increased physical security requirements, such as monitoring and safety equipment. Exactly what prevention measure will be required will depend on the level of risk the company is willing, or able, to accept. How much it is willing to risk will be a corporate decision. How much it is able to risk will likely be a government or industry decision implemented by standards and regulations. Disaster recovery tactics will need to include preplanning efforts, a predesignated and well-trained team, and flexibility and alternative driver capabilities.

The added prevention measures and maintaining this flexibility in terms of alternate sources of strategies and drivers will cost money. Companies will tend to avoid costs for threats that have not yet materialized, because the added cost will, in the short run, put them at a competitive disadvantage. As Dell proved, however, in the dock strike of 2002, such upfront costs should be considered an investment that will pay dividends at a later time.

Somehow, these costs will filter down to consumers. It is the price to be paid for maintaining the amount and breadth of products that U.S. consumers have come to expect.

Conclusion

What is the final balance between security against terrorism and the price of that security? It is likely that the level of security will eventually be established by either government mandate or, even more likely, voluntary industry standards. That level will be a determining factor in the cost to us, the consumers. It may also mean that smaller companies—those without the capital resources necessary to acquire and maintain the needed equipment and procedures—may lose their ability to operate in a global environment unless they are partnered with a larger company that has that capability. But what that level may finally be, if indeed it ever is final, is now unknown. What is known, however, is that one business axiom will still hold true. Whichever companies manage to achieve that level at the lowest cost will create a competitive advantage. Early adopters and experimenters may be able to develop a sustainable advantage if their lower costs enable them to increase their market share sufficiently.

See also **Outsourcing and Offshoring; Aging Infrastructure (vol. 4); Airport and Aviation Security (vol. 4)**

Further Reading

Cook, Thomas A., *Managing Global Supply Chains.* Boca Raton, FL: Auerbach Publications, 2008.

Lee, Hau, and Chung-Yee Lee, eds., *Building Supply-Chain Excellence in Emerging Economies.* New York: Springer, 2007.

McNichols, Michael, *Maritime Security: An Introduction.* Burlington, MA: Butterworth-Heinemann, 2007.

Ritter, Luke, et al., *Securing Global Transportation Networks.* New York: McGraw-Hill, 2007.

Sweet, Kathleen M., *Transportation and Cargo Security: Threats and Solutions.* Upper Saddle River, NJ: Prentice Hall, 2005.

Thomas, Andrew R., *Supply Chain Security.* Santa Barbara, CA: Praeger, 2010.

SUSTAINABILITY

Robin Morris Collin

Sustainability literally means the capacity to endure. In 1987, the World Commission on Environment and Development, also known as the Brundtland Commission, applied the term to development—officially, *sustainable development*—as that which "meets the needs of the present without compromising the ability of future generations to meet their own needs." That definition was written into the Swiss federal constitution and is similar to the *seventh generation* philosophy articulated in the Iroquois Confederacy. It mandated that chiefs of that Native American nation must look seven generations into the future to consider the effects of their actions on their descendants before making a move.

The 1999 book *Natural Capitalism* recommends including four types of capital in any model for sustainable development: financial capital, manufacturing capital, natural capital, and human capital. Since then, many organizations added specific criteria as guidelines, including social criteria, environmental criteria, and financial criteria.

Sustainable Development

The concept of sustainable development hinges on ideas that support any practice placing equal emphasis on environment, economics, and equity rather than on economic interests alone. It is controversial, because it limits human activities in light of their environmental and equitable impacts on all affected communities.

Sustainable development assumes continuous economic growth without irreparably or irreversibly damaging the environment. Human population growth is difficult for this model, because it requires placing economic value on lives in the future. Some environmentalists challenge the assumption of growth at all. The fundamental battleground for this emerging controversy is one of values. The continued prioritization of economic growth over environmental protection, combined with population increases, may have irreparable impacts on the environment. British Petroleum's Deepwater Horizon gushing offshore oil rig is one example of unsustainable economic development. The idea of sustainable development is a fundamentally different model of growth from the business model of colonial and industrial progress. It stresses equality in the distribution of benefits. This egalitarian model of development recognizes the economic burdens on society created by the oppressive policies associated with industrial capitalism and sovereign powers.

Additionally, the sustainable model requires governments to place constraints on developments, including constructing roads, bridges, and dams. It also focuses on new manufacturing methods. Sustainable development requires commitment to the principles and practices of clean production and manufacturing techniques rather than continued reliance on fossil fuels or other dirty energies to propel manufacturing.

Shifting models of development give rise to controversies that may involve problems of unequal opportunity for women and subordinated ethnic groups and the environmental impacts of the industrial use of natural resources. These controversies stem from the development policies and practices of an earlier age that did not require accountability for the social or environmental consequences of development. The changed model has been hardest to accept in the United States.

Global Background

In 1987, Gro Harlem Brundtland, then prime minister of Norway, authored a report for the World Commission on Environment and Development called "Our Common Future." In it, she described a concept of sustainable development as "development that meets the needs of the present without compromising the ability of future generations to meet their own needs." This has become the defining statement about sustainable human development. Sustainability focuses on fairness to future generations by ensuring that the ecosystems on which all life depend are not lost or degraded, and poverty is eradicated. Sustainable development seeks these goals of environmental protection and ending poverty by implementing several key concepts in development policies and practices.

The United Nations Conferences on Environment and Development have become the forums in which these key concepts have been turned into implementable policy statements. The agreements and statements resulting from these conferences are often identified by their host city. Perhaps the most famous of these conferences was the Earth Summit held in Rio de Janeiro in 1992. At this conference, the nations of the world, including the United States, agreed to implement seven key concepts to ensure sustainable development in a declaration called the Rio Declaration, and they wrote out a work plan called Agenda 21, which remains the source of much international controversy to this day. The seven key principles emerging from the Earth Summit and found in the Rio Declaration and Agenda 21 are:

1. Integrated decision making (three Es: environment, social equity, and economics)

2. Polluter pays
3. Sustainable consumption and production
4. Precautionary principle
5. Intergenerational equity
6. Public participation
7. Differentiated responsibilities and leadership

Another conference based upon this same United Nations Conferences on Environment and Development plan was held in Kyoto, Japan, in 1997, resulting in the Kyoto Protocol on climate change and the limits on emissions of greenhouse gases. Although a signatory to the protocol, the United States has not moved forward with ratification of the protocol even though it is the world's largest producer of carbon dioxide, because it disagrees with the exemptions given to developing economies like China and India.

The Copenhagen Accord, set in writing in December 2009, focused on planetary warming and cooling as a global issue requiring nations to work together to investigate ways of sustaining life on Earth. While setting emissions limits was central to the Copenhagen talks, no commitments resulted. Some news analyses of the Copenhagen gathering considered the accord a failure resulting from global recession and conservative domestic pressure in the United States and China. Despite financial woes, the voluntary-compliance Accord included a pledge by the United States to provide $30 billion to the developing world during 2010–2013, increasing to $100 billion per year by 2020.

Controversies for Businesses and Industries

Sustainable development often means designing pollution and waste out of the manufacturing cycle (industrial ecology) and thinking about a product in terms of its total life span, beyond its point of sale (also known as product life cycle management). Additionally, clean production may require a substantial investment in new technology and plants that is prohibitive to small business enterprises. These requirements challenge businesses and industries in virtually all sectors of an economy to change what they are doing and how they are doing it. What makes the task of change even harder is the fact that many established businesses and industries have been subsidized directly or indirectly through tax benefits conferred by national governments, which enhances the reluctance of businesses to change. But some businesses have pioneered change by embracing concepts of a restorative economy and natural capitalism.

Businesses that have taken short-term transitional losses to eliminate waste and toxins in their products and production methods have been rewarded in long-term economic gains and have created measurable improvements in their environmental impacts. These businesses have embraced the linkage between environment and economy, but they have not necessarily incorporated communities and their well-being into this new model.

Environmentalists

Environmentalists have documented the scope of environmental degradation all eco-systems are suffering as the result of human activities. The news they deliver is sobering. Human activity is threatening to cause the collapse of the living systems on which all life on our planet depends. This leads some environmentalists to advocate protection of the environment above all other concerns, including economic concerns and the needs of human communities. Trying to determine the causes for this dangerous state of the environment leads some environmentalists to identify population growth as the most substantial factor. Others point to the use of fossil fuels to propel our activities. Still others identify overconsumption of resources as the basis for this state of environmental degradation.

Environmentalists employing such data and using this type of formula often find themselves in conflict with business and industry as they press urgently for changes in manufacturing processes. Mainstream environmentalists tend to be from relatively priv-ileged backgrounds in terms of wealth and educational opportunities. They frequently find themselves in conflict with communities and developing countries for their stands about population control and their relative indifference about the plight of the poor, who bear the costs of unsustainable practices more than any other class.

Communities

Communities and their physical and economic well-being are often excluded from deci-sion making concerning economic opportunities and environmental consequences with which they must live. This exclusion can arise from structural separation between dif-ferent administrative branches of government or from the separation between different levels of government. It can also arise from cultural and social forces that operate to exclude poor people or people stigmatized by historical discrimination. Exclusion of community interests and participation affects the viability and efficiency of efforts to protect the environment and to develop a community economically in several ways. People driven by insecurity regarding their basic living conditions are likely to accept employment opportunities regardless of the consequences to human and environmental health. This eliminates labor as an agent of change toward sustainable production tech-nologies and allows continued pollution and waste to be externalized into the environ-ment with long-term disastrous consequences for human health.

Moreover, people faced with exposure and hunger will also contribute to environ-mental degradation to meet basic life needs. Whether in a developed or a developing country, poverty and the inability to meet basic needs for food, shelter, and care make some human communities even more vulnerable to environmentally degraded condi-tions of work, living, recreation, and education.

Conflicts arise as these communities strive to participate in environmental deci-sion making and decisions concerning the use of natural resources. These communities

INDUSTRIAL ECOLOGY

Industrial ecology is the shifting of industrial process from open-loop systems, in which resources and capital investments move through the system to become waste, to a closed-loop system where wastes become inputs for new processes. Robert Frosch and Nicholas Gallopoulos first proposed the idea of industrial ecology in an article published in *Scientific American* in 1989. They asked, "Why would not our industrial system behave like an ecosystem, where the wastes of a species may be resource to another species? Why would not the outputs of an industry be the inputs of another, thus reducing use of raw materials, pollution, and saving on waste treatment?" The idea of industrial ecology is to model this human-made system on the performance of those based on natural capital that do not have waste in them. The term *industrial ecology* was defined as a systematic analysis of industrial operations by including factors like technology, environment, natural resources, biomedical aspects, institutional and legal matters, as well as socioeconomic aspects.

Industrial ecology conceptualizes industrial systems like a factory or industrial plant as a human-made ecosystem based on human investments of infrastructural capital rather than reliant on natural capital. Along with more general energy conservation and material conservation goals, and redefining commodity markets and product stewardship relations strictly as a service economy, industrial ecology is one of the four objectives of natural capitalism. This strategy discourages forms of amoral purchasing arising from ignorance of what goes on at a distance and implies a political economy that values natural capital highly and relies on more instructional capital to design and maintain each unique industrial ecology.

are often not welcomed into dialogue at a meaningful and early stage and are forced to seize opportunities to participate in controversial ways. In the United States, the environmental justice movement has pioneered processes of public participation designed to ensure community involvement with environmental decision making. Internationally, the United Nations has developed the Aarhus Convention to assure such participation. Banks and other international lenders are beginning to require such community participation in development projects. For example, the World Bank now requires community participation and accountability to communities in its lending programs under the Equator Principles. Additionally, ethnically stigmatized groups, women, and those disadvantaged by informal social forces are striving to use these methods and others to participate in environmental and economic decision making. In the United States, these efforts are being developed through the environmental justice movement. Internationally, the United Nations supports efforts to build strong nongovernmental organizations through which these and other community interests can be effectively championed. The United Nations activities are being developed through the Civil Society initiatives.

Conclusion

There is a strong international and national push for a new kind of environmentalism that includes sustainable development. Like all the environmental policies before it, sustainable development policies will need to have accurate, timely, and continuous data of all environmental impacts to be truly effective. So far, knowledge needs about environmental impacts generate strong political controversies. In the United States, most of the industry information is self-reported, the environmental laws are weakly enforced, and environmental governmental agencies are new. Sustainability will be controversial because it will open old controversies like right-to-know laws, corporate audit and anti-disclosure laws, citizen monitoring of environmental decisions, the precautionary principle, true cost accounting, unequal enforcement of environmental laws, and cumulative impacts.

The concept of sustainability has captured the environmental imagination of a broad range of stakeholders. No one group is against it, in principle. It is the application of the principle that fires up underlying value differences and old and continuing controversies. In many ways, the strong growth of the principles of sustainability represents exasperation with older, incomplete environmental policies. These policies now seem piecemeal, ineffective in individual application, and an impediment to collaboration with other agencies and environmental stakeholders. The new processes of policies of sustainability could be radically different than environmental decision making is now. Communities are demanding sustainability, some even adopting the Kyoto Protocol despite the United States' not signing it. They want to be an integral part of the process, especially as they learn about the land, air, and water around them. As environmental literacy spreads, so too will all the unresolved environmental controversy. It is these controversies that lay the groundwork for the functional advancement of U.S. environmental policy. Sustainability will require complete inclusion of all environmental impacts—past, present, and future.

See also **Cumulative Emissions (vol. 4); Environmental Impact Statements (vol. 4); Solar Energy (vol. 4); Wind Energy (vol. 4)**

Further Reading

Bernard, Ted, *Hope and Hard Times: Communities, Collaboration, and Sustainability.* Gabriola Island, BC, Canada: New Society, 2010.

Collin, Robin Morris, and Robert William Collin, *Encyclopedia of Sustainability.* Westport, CT: Greenwood Press, 2009.

Dernbach, John C., ed., *Agenda for a Sustainable America.* Washington, DC: Environmental Law Institute, 2009.

Frosch, Robert, and Nicholas E. Gallapoulos, "Strategies for Manufacturing." *Scientific American* 261, no. 3 (1989): 144–152.

Harris, Jonathan M., *A Survey of Sustainable Development: Social and Economic Dimensions.* Washington, DC: Island Press, 2001.

Maser, Chris, *Ecological Diversity in Sustainable Development: The Vital and Forgotten Dimension.* New York: Lewis, 1999.

Mazmanian, Daniel A., and Michael E. Kraft, eds., *Towards Sustainable Communities,* 2d ed. Cambridge, MA: MIT Press, 2009.

Rao, P. K., *Sustainable Development.* Oxford, England: Blackwell, 2000.

Riddell, Robert, *Sustainable Urban Planning: Tipping the Balance.* Oxford, England: Blackwell, 2004.

T

TRADE DEFICITS (AND SURPLUSES)

Raymond Owens

Trade is the basis of much of the economic activity we see around us. Most of our day-to-day activities involve trade. Examples abound—trading cash for food at the grocery store and trading our time and effort (working) for income. The government regularly accounts for the result of all this trading with quarterly readings on the pace of economic activity in the United States. In those reports, one category of trade is singled out. Trade with foreigners is highlighted and measured separately.

What Is So Special about Foreign Trade?

Essentially, we trade because doing so makes us better off. One of the first lessons we learn in economics is that we are not all equally proficient at the same things. For example, one person may be a better cook and another a better carpenter. Individually, one would be ill fed but well housed and the other well fed but ill housed. By trading services, each could—in theory, at least—be both well housed and well fed. The added benefits from trading make both better off.

So trading is good, because people engage in it only when it makes them better off. And we recognize the benefits of trade and economic activity within our borders. Every third month, when the latest report on the gross domestic product (GDP) of the U.S. economy is released, the nightly news blares the rate of growth over the airwaves. Politicians take credit or pass blame. Stock traders rejoice or moan. Bond traders take notice. A big increase in GDP suggests that production and trade among

Americans has increased, translating into stronger economic growth and cause for celebration.

But a big increase in trade with foreign interests is often met with far less enthusiasm. On the face of it, the reason is not apparent. As noted above, we only trade with others—domestic or foreign—if it makes us better off. This activity gives U.S. consumers more products from which to choose and products that are, in some cases, less expensive. The same is true for foreign buyers of U.S. goods and services. An increase in trade with foreign interests should be good news. So why not view it that way? Well, probably because if we buy more things from foreigners than we sell to them (as is usually the case), our measured economic activity tends to shrink. And lower measured economic activity in the U.S. economy is generally frowned upon.

In contrast, if we as a nation trade more with foreigners by selling them more than we buy from them, then more trade with foreigners is viewed as good because it raises measured economic activity in the United States.

So we generally view trade with other Americans as nearly always good but trade with foreigners as only good if we sell more to them than we buy from them. In other words, trade is not always viewed as good, even though both parties voluntarily engage in it, which presumably makes each better off.

Deficits, Surpluses, and Balance

As mentioned earlier, a lot of trade takes place each day, both among domestic residents and with foreigners. On the foreign trade front, domestic residents typically both trade their dollars for foreign goods and services (buy) and receive dollars from foreigners for U.S.-made goods and services (sell). If we buy more than we sell, we are said to have a trade deficit. If selling outweighs buying, a trade (or current account) surplus emerges. When buying and selling perfectly match one another, the result is balanced trade.

If voluntary trade makes parties better off, why separate foreign trade in the economic accounting, and why distinguish between deficits, surpluses, and balance? In a nutshell, trade with foreign interests is often viewed as having a dark side, in that sending more dollars abroad than we receive (a deficit) means some of our domestic consumer demands are met by foreign firms, which causes a drag on demand facing U.S. firms and reduces the demand for workers in the United States. Of course, consumers are made better off in that they have a broader array of goods from which to select. This benefit to consumers is widely recognized but typically is not publicized as a precisely measured benefit. Far more publicity is garnered by the estimated size and presumed costs imposed on U.S. citizens from trade deficits. A second concern is how long the U.S. economy can sustain trade deficits. Under the assumption that deficits create a drag on the economy, how much of a drag is required to slow the economy substantially? Let's address each of these questions in turn.

How Big Are Trade Deficits?

The U.S. trade balance is measured as the net difference between the dollar value of the goods and services we buy from abroad (imports) compared to the dollar value of goods and services we sell abroad (exports). In late 2009, exports were averaging almost $135 billion per month, seasonally adjusted. Imports at that time were over $165 billion a month.

As shown in Figure 1, it is clear that the value of both imports and exports is typically rising over time, recessionary periods excluded. This is not surprising given the diverse nature of goods produced in the United States, the prominence of the currency, and the well-developed infrastructure, which makes the physical transportation of goods (and services) relatively easy. But with the value of imports rising faster than exports, the U.S. trade sector is increasingly in deficit, to the tune of about $33 billion per month, or roughly $375 billion per year, according the most recent reports.

The United States has experienced trade deficits in recent decades, as shown in Figure 2. These deficits grew relatively large in 2006, reaching around 6 percent of the nation's economy as measured by GDP. However, with the sharp recession in 2008 and early 2009, the trade deficit moderated to about 3 percent of GDP. Even with this moderation, the current deficit remains sizeable and—if sustained or enlarged—is cause for concern. The mid-decade bulge partly reflected soaring prices of imported oil, and the moderation partly resulted from sharp declines in oil prices. With future oil prices uncertain, further improvement—or deterioration—in the deficit might be in the cards. Of course, the persistence of a negative trade balance has spurred discussion

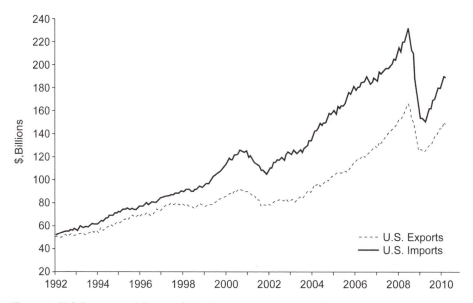

Figure 1. U.S. Imports and Exports (U.S. Commerce Department/Haver Analytics)

Figure 2. U.S. Trade Balance (U.S. Commerce Department/Haver Analytics)

over the drag these large trade deficits could potentially exert on the U.S. economy and the long-term consequences of this drag.

In part, deficits' impact on the economy depends on their causes. Since exports and imports—the two components of the trade balance—are measured in U.S. dollars, changes in the value of the dollar compared to the value of other currencies can affect the deficit's size. As of mid-2010, the dollar's value had strengthened compared to the values of the currencies of the United States' major trading partners. This made the price of U.S.-produced goods relatively less attractive than the prices of foreign goods. Initially, an increasing value of the dollar can potentially compress the measured trade gap, as foreigners pay more for U.S. goods and U.S. consumers pay less for foreign goods. This can occur especially when the volumes of the goods traded change little. Over time, however, the less attractive prices of U.S. goods would be expected to cool demand for our products, constraining U.S. export volume and possibly widening the trade gap.

Another reason the U.S. trade deficit may widen is that, as the United States emerges from recession, stronger demand for imported goods typically emerges. As incomes in the United States strengthen, consumers respond by ramping up spending, including spending on foreign-produced goods. Typically, this strength is not matched by foreign demand for U.S. goods—pushing the deficit deeper into negative territory.

Has Domestic Economic Activity Been Harmed by Trade Deficits?

It is difficult to assess whether trade deficits have affected the U.S. economy in a precise fashion (recall the earlier discussion of the arithmetic of consumer benefits, for example). However, data from U.S. labor markets and trade accounts do not make a compelling case for a strong near-term relationship between a rise in deficits and a drag on U.S. economic activity—at least through the labor market channel. Since the early 1990s, for example, the trade deficit has generally grown markedly but has not trimmed domestic production enough to persistently raise the unemployment rate. As shown in Figure 3, there have been fluctuations in the unemployment rate since 1992, but the periods of large increases have been tied to recessions that were largely independent of foreign trade. In the early 1990s, a recession occurred after the real estate and stock markets unwound following run-ups in activity in each. In the early 2000s, a recession followed a reversal of the sharp increases in stock market prices in the preceding years. Most recently—in 2008 and early 2009—a deep recession occurred in the wake of an episode of home overbuilding and the attending difficulties in financial markets. Domestic demand for foreign goods softened more than demand for U.S. goods overseas. The trade deficit lessened, but again, because of the broader weakness in domestic economic conditions, unemployment soared.

In fact, the recent recessionary period aside, the unemployment rate has mostly trended lower throughout the period, with the tightest labor markets often occurring during times when trade deficits were on the rise. From this perspective, it is not at all obvious that running a trade deficit has led to a pronounced loss of jobs and higher unemployment in the overall economy.

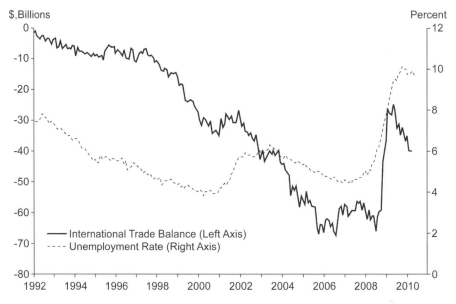

Figure 3. U.S. Trade Balance and Unemployment Rate (U.S. Commerce Department/Haver Analytics)

This is not to suggest, however, that trade deficits have had no impact on jobs in the United States. With the expanded global market in recent years, not only have global trade volumes increased, but the location of global production has been more dynamic. That is, firms have increasingly shifted their production among countries in an ongoing effort to contain costs and to match the location of production to that of emerging market demand. Through these channels, individual job categories in the United States have been affected. Jobs have declined in industries like textiles, for example, but have risen in other categories. This is textbook comparative advantage at work—with foreign producers making more of the world's fabric, U.S. producers can develop more pharmaceuticals.

What Do Trade Balance Figures Tell Us?

Broadly speaking, trade balance figures tell us very little, really. While trade figures imply that the United States consumes more foreign goods than it ships abroad, this interpretation is not particularly important, on balance. First, with well-functioning international financial markets, trade between nations has many implications that influence both the benefits and costs of the trade activity. The measures of trade flows (as imperfect as they are) are just one part of the story. Also important are the financial flows that result from the trade transactions.

When a domestic purchaser buys a good or service produced abroad, the purchase is an import. In this setting, the disposition of the dollars received by the foreign producer is important in determining the impact of the transaction on the U.S. economy. A foreign producer has several options with the acquired dollars: hold them (an interest-free loan to the U.S. government); exchange them for U.S. dollars on the foreign exchange markets (adding to the supply of dollars and pressuring the dollar lower); or invest them in dollar-denominated assets like a U.S. Treasury security or a factory in the United States.

In the first instance, we would like the foreign supplier to stuff its mattress with—or, better yet, burn—the dollars it receives. This way, we would get the goods or services from the supplier and would provide in exchange only paper bills (which cost our country little to print). By either destroying or otherwise not spending the dollar bills, foreign claims to U.S. goods or assets are relinquished. But this is not likely to occur very frequently, because trading of this type is not in spirit mutually beneficial to both parties. More likely, the foreign holders of dollars will delay spending or investing those dollars—while they hold the dollars, they earn no interest on them—effectively providing an interest-free loan to the United States.

In the second case, dollars received by foreign producers are exchanged for their home currency. With a trade surplus (from their perspective, since if we have a deficit, they must have a surplus), they receive a greater amount of dollars than we receive of their currency. To equate the currency amounts on the foreign exchange market, the value of the dollar must fall relative to the value of the foreign currency. This makes goods and services priced in dollars more affordable, driving up the quantity of those goods demanded on international markets. But a falling dollar may jeopardize inflows of foreign capital into the United States and make dollar-denominated investments less attractive—but that's another story.

In the third instance, the foreign producer accumulates dollars to purchase assets valued in U.S. dollars. Toyota, Honda, and many foreign-based computer firms have large production facilities in the United States, for example, though most are invested in financial instruments. This is good, because these businesses create investment, tax revenues, and jobs here. But foreign investment in the United States leaves some uncomfortable. In the late 1980s, Japanese firms were purchasing farmland in the United States, which led to debate about the impact on the U.S. economy. More recently, some concerns continue to be voiced about who receives the profits on the investments. With global stock markets, we need not be too concerned. If a U.S. citizen wants the profits from a large foreign corporation, then stock in that company—and a share in its profits—is available for purchase.

In addition, in today's world economy, firms in the United States sometimes have operations overseas. Imagine that a furniture producer in the United States decides to open a factory in China. To open the plant, the U.S. firm buys enough Chinese yuan (the Chinese currency) to enable it to build the plant. But the output is shipped to the United States (a foreign import that tends to add to our trade deficit) and the profits are dollars, part of which the firm retains in the United States and part of which are converted to yuan to cover the continuing operating expenses of the plant. In this case, the trade gap has widened, but the Chinese have not substantially increased their claims to U.S. assets in the future.

Is this kind of activity important? In a word, yes. If we receive goods today and exchange only paper dollars, that's one thing. But if those paper dollars can potentially be redeemed for goods or factories or real estate in the United States at some future date, then that's another story, and we are a debtor nation, meaning we owe more money to foreigners than they owe us.

Much of the money we owe to foreigners is in the form of Treasury securities. The foreigners bought them, and we will have to redeem them one day. But is being a debtor nation necessarily so bad? As with many other aspects of trade and international finance, the answer is not crystal clear. One way to gauge the United States' net position as a debtor nation is simply to look at the income the nation earns on assets owned abroad compared to the payments made to foreign entities that own assets in the United States. Figure 4 shows that U.S. payments to foreigners soared in recent years, before pulling back with the 2008–2009 recession. But the chart also shows that, over the period, payments from foreigners have kept pace. In fact, the chart suggests relatively little reason to lie awake at night worrying about our status as a debtor nation.

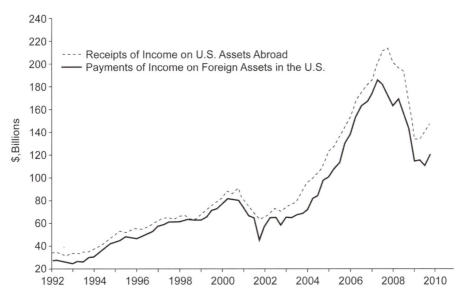

Figure 4. U.S. International Financial Payments. (U.S. Commerce Department/Haver Analytics)

What about Future Generations?

Much of the discussion here has focused on the near-term implications of the U.S. trade position. But critics point out that the impacts of today's trade actions may affect future generations. The argument is that trade deficits occur when society consumes more than it produces. This behavior, if left unchecked, will eventually leave the nation with large unpaid bills for the goods and services consumed. This is like dining out excessively on a credit card. These critics correctly note that to eventually pay off the debt, the country will have to sell off some assets, leaving the next generation with fewer assets and potentially reducing its ability to produce goods and services.

This argument is plausible and probably correct if sizeable trade deficits persist over a long period. But it is far from a foregone conclusion. For one thing, the trade deficit may fluctuate as energy prices rise and fall and the dollar rises and falls in value. But there is another consideration. Just as running up a credit card balance sometimes makes sense, so does running a trade deficit. Imagine that some large nations are ramping up production but still have a lot of underutilized capacity. For a time, the goods produced in these nations may be a bargain. In this case, taking advantage of the sale prices may be worth reducing one's asset holdings temporarily. Later, when assets are cheaper relative to consumer goods, the logical choice could be to accumulate capital goods relative to consumer goods.

Conclusion

This entry began by asking what all the fuss concerning foreign trade is about. If trade with your neighbor is good, then isn't trade with your neighboring nation also good?

The answer to this and other trade-related questions—unfortunately—is not clear-cut. While most agree that trade with other nations has many substantial benefits for the United States, measuring these benefits is difficult. In addition, many people are comfortable with trade as long as the value of exports exceeds that of imports—a trade surplus.

But aside from a surplus, the U.S. trade position with other nations often elicits mixed feelings. These feelings turn to concern as the trade balance moves deeper into deficit territory. Such movements have occurred in recent years, aside from the recent recession-related compression. But the general widening of the trade deficit has not resulted in especially troubling effects on the U.S. economy. Economic growth in the United States has fluctuated widely along with domestic housing activity in recent years, and labor markets have reflected those fluctuations. However, during some of this period, relatively long periods of solid economic growth and tight labor market conditions have occurred while trade deficits grew. There are no compelling signals yet that trade deficits are costing Americans jobs in the aggregate. In fact, labor markets were arguably becoming too tight in late 2007, as labor cost pressures emerged and complaints of a worker shortage were being heard.

In addition, concerns that trade deficits lead to outsized foreign ownership of U.S. assets and debt may also be a bit overblown. More of our assets are in foreign hands, but so too are we holding many foreign assets. On balance, earnings from those assets are about matching the interest and payments we make to foreign holders of U.S. assets.

In fact, as long as foreign interests want to hold more U.S. dollars, we can buy goods from abroad and foreign interests can get the dollars they want to hold. We want their goods, and they want our dollars. Their use of those dollars can have somewhat differing impacts on our economy, but no uniformly bad impacts appear to be occurring. We need to remember that consumers reap large benefits when they buy goods and services from foreign firms. But we can also increase trade deficits when our dollars flow to companies located abroad that are owned by U.S. parent firms. Such arrangements can offer these firms flexibility and profitability while containing the outflow of dollars that concerns some.

The bottom line may be that it does not matter so much with whom we trade. The real issue may be whether the United States is consuming more than it is producing. If we, as a society, persistently consume more than we produce, we will eventually have to draw down our accumulated wealth to pay for the excess consumption. Whether we transfer that wealth to another nation or to someone in our nation, the bottom line is that future generations will have a lower stock of capital, and that could, under some circumstances, constrain their ability to produce goods and services in the future. But this is not to suggest we are at or near that point. It is not obvious that we are consuming substantial amounts of our capital base or seed corn. In addition, eating some seed corn today may be reasonable if some categories of goods and services currently are a bargain that is not expected to persist. So one possibility is to refocus the discussion to worry more about whether we, as a society, are properly balancing our consumption and savings and worry less about where production is located.

See also **Debt, Deficits, and the Economy; Dumping of Imports; Foreign Direct Investment; Free Trade**

Further Reading

Cline, William R., *The United States as a Debtor Nation.* Washington, DC: Institute for International Economics, 2005.

Dunway, Steven Vincent, *Global Imbalances and the Financial Crisis.* Washington, DC: Council on Foreign Relations, 2009.

Eisner, Robert, *The Great Deficit Scares: The Federal Budget, Trade, and Social Security.* New York: Twentieth Century Foundation, 1997.

Little, Jane Sneddon, ed., *Global Imbalances and the Evolving World Economy.* Boston: Federal Reserve Bank of Boston, 2008.

Preeg, Ernest H., *The Trade Deficit, the Dollar, and the National Interest.* Indianapolis: Hudson Institute, 2000.

U

UNEMPLOYMENT

Geoffrey Gilbert

When there are not enough jobs for everyone wanting to work in a particular city, region, or industry, economists look for the underlying causes, which can include technological change, rising resource costs, stiffer competition from imports, or a fundamental change in consumer preferences. Any of these may explain a localized gap between jobs offered and jobs wanted. At the national or macroeconomic level, however, unemployment generally cannot be traced to any single cause; rather, it is a feature of the business cycle. Every economy is subject to cyclical expansions and contractions. The U.S. economy, for example, has experienced 11 recessions since World War II, with the national unemployment rate topping 10 percent during 2 of them. (By comparison, at the depths of the Great Depression, unemployment reached 25 percent.) Unemployment takes an economic toll in terms of foregone output—goods and services that could have been produced if all available workers had held jobs. It also entails serious social costs for those out of work and for their families. Government can ease the financial burden of joblessness through such programs as unemployment insurance, job retraining, and tax credits for companies that hire new workers.

Four Types of Unemployment

Economists have described four different types or categories of unemployment. *Frictional* unemployment refers to the normal job switching that occurs in a market economy; at any given moment, there are bound to be some workers who are temporarily between jobs. *Seasonal* unemployment refers to those who are out of work because of normal seasonal variations in employment. This can be seen in resort communities, where, for example, jobs may be plentiful during the winter in a ski town or during the summer in a seaside town but scarce during the rest of the year. Certain industries, like agriculture and construction, also exhibit high seasonal unemployment rates. *Structural* unemployment occurs when jobs disappear due to changes in the structure of the economy, as, for example, when companies move their operations overseas in order to lower their wage costs. Finally, *cyclical* unemployment is the type that rises and falls according to the overall condition of the national economy.

When the U.S. Bureau of Labor Statistics (BLS) announces the latest unemployment rate on the first Friday of each month, it does not distinguish among these four types. One may safely assume, however, that any large movements in the official unemployment rate are mainly due to the ups and downs of cyclical unemployment. The unemployment rate is inversely related to the national output rate, but it does not track it precisely. Unemployment is a so-called lagging indicator, meaning that when the economy starts to shrink, or go into a recession, it may take several months before the unemployment rate begins to rise, and when the economy hits bottom and starts to make a recovery, it may take some time before the unemployment rate begins to fall in response.

How Unemployment Is Measured

The BLS estimates the number of people unemployed in the United States by sampling the population rather than attempting to actually count every person who is looking for work and not finding it. The sample consists of 60,000 randomly selected households, representing about 110,000 individuals. Each month, trained interviewers check up on these households—some by phone and some in person—to determine their work activity in the previous month. Every individual who is 16 years of age or older is potentially a participant in the civilian labor force. Many, however, do not participate, including those who are retired, on active duty in the armed forces, in school full-time, totally disabled, institutionalized, or, for a variety of other reasons, not looking for employment. These individuals are not counted as part of the labor force. Only those who have jobs or are available for work and actively trying to find it get counted in the labor force, as defined by the BLS. The official unemployment rate is computed by dividing the number of people who are jobless but actively looking for work by the total number who are in the labor force. This fraction is then multiplied by 100 so that the unemployment rate can be expressed as a percentage.

An important group of people excluded from the labor force are those known as "discouraged workers." These are individuals who tell the interviewer that they want work, are available for work, have looked for work during the previous year, but are not *currently* looking for a job. They have become discouraged because they feel they have the wrong skills, are too young or too old, are likely to experience hiring discrimination, or just do not fit the jobs that currently exist. Beyond this group of workers, who are discouraged for job-related reasons, there is an even larger group of workers called "other marginally attached," who say they are not job searching because of health problems, child care issues, or difficulties arranging transportation. These individuals say they want work and have looked for a job in the past year, but they have not looked in the past four weeks.

The most comprehensive measure of unemployment goes beyond what has just been described to include individuals who work part-time because they are unable to get the additional hours of work they would like. Under the standard BLS definition, a person who works for pay as little as 1 hour per week is categorized as employed, even though *under*employed would be a more accurate term if the worker would prefer to be working 10, 20, or 40 hours a week. Millions of workers in the United States can be described as holding their jobs "part-time for economic reasons," not by choice. When we take into account all the forms of subemployment outlined above, we get a much higher number than the conventional, and most widely publicized, unemployment rate. In April 2010, for example, the standard unemployment rate was 9.9 percent, while the broadest, most encompassing measure of underemployment stood at 17.1 percent. Both numbers were swollen by what some called the Great Recession of 2008–2010, yet even when the economy is in a healthier state, the gap persists. In April 2000, for example, the official unemployment rate was 3.8 percent, while the broader gauge of labor-force underutilization reached 6.9 percent.

The Uneven Impact of Unemployment

Americans experience unemployment in different ways and at different rates, depending on their age, gender, education level, and race or ethnicity. The monthly BLS unemployment report sheds light on all of these differences. For the month of April 2010, the unemployment rate for teenaged workers, ages 16 to 19, was a whopping 25.4 percent. This implied that for every four teenagers who were counted in the labor force (meaning they were either employed or looking for a job), only three were able to find work. For adults age 20 and older, unemployment was far lower, at a little over 9 percent.

Gender disparities in unemployment are much smaller than disparities by age. For most of the 2000–2010 decade, there was no consistent difference between men's and women's jobless rates. That changed near the end of the decade, however, as the economy fell into recession. More jobs were lost in male-dominated occupations, like construction and manufacturing, than in the rest of the economy, causing men's unemployment to rise faster than women's. In April 2010, the rate for all men age 16 and older stood at 10.8 percent, compared to 8.8 percent for women. If teenaged workers were excluded, the rates were 10.1 and 8.2 percent for men and women, respectively.

Education strongly influences one's chances of being unemployed. More highly educated Americans experience less joblessness than those with fewer educational credentials. The April 2010 figures were illustrative. Among workers aged 25 or older, those lacking a high school diploma had a 14.7 percent unemployment rate. The comparable rates for those with a high school diploma but no college, those with some college or an associate's degree, and those with a bachelor's degree or higher were 10.6 percent, 8.3 percent, and 4.9 percent, respectively. The advantage enjoyed by those with more education can also be seen in their higher rates of participation in paid work. Fewer than half the individuals who lacked a high school education participated in the labor force in April 2010. Those with more education had higher participation rates. College graduates, for example, participated at a 77.3 percent rate.

Race and ethnicity also affect one's likelihood of being unemployed. Historically, African Americans have been jobless at higher rates than whites or Hispanics. In April 2010, the black unemployment rate stood at 16.5 percent, compared to 12.5 percent for Hispanics, 9.0 percent for whites, and 6.8 percent for Asians. When high-unemployment categories overlap, the resulting unemployment rates can be extraordinarily high. In December 2009, for example, the unemployment rate for black teenagers (ages 16 to 19) reached an astonishing 48 percent. (For white teens, the rate was a little under 24 percent.)

Short- and Long-Term Unemployment

The longer a person remains without work, the deeper the impact on finances, family well-being, sense of self-worth, and even health. Some workers are out of a job so briefly they do not even bother to file for unemployment compensation. At the other extreme, some workers spend long months and even years looking in vain for work. Workers who lose their jobs in middle age can be especially devastated, since they often shoulder heavy financial responsibilities and do not have time to start a new career in the working years they have left.

During the recession of 2008–2010, observers noted a considerable increase in the amount of time workers typically spent unemployed. So not only were there an unusually large number of people out of work—even for a recession—but they were staying unemployed much longer than usual. Data from the BLS showed that, in April 2010, more than three-fifths of the unemployed had been out of work for 15 weeks or more, and fully 46 percent met the definition of "long-term unemployed" by being out of work for more than six months. The median period spent unemployed was about 22 weeks, meaning that as many people were unemployed *longer* than 22 weeks as were unemployed for *less* than that length of time. In historical data going back to 1967, there is nothing comparable to this figure; only once previously had the median length of unemployment even reached 12 weeks (in March 1983).

The social consequences of unemployment are manifold. The unemployed face a greater risk of clinical depression, hospitalization, and other adverse effects, as studies have shown in the United States and abroad. The damage can be straightforwardly physical: a study conducted under the auspices of the Harvard School of Public Health showed that even short periods of unemployment lead to more diagnoses of high blood pressure, heart disease, and diabetes (Strully 2009). A Swedish study found that individuals experiencing unemployment face higher mortality risk, partly due to increased rates of suicide (Gerdtham and Johannesson 2003). It has also been shown that domestic violence, divorce, and child abuse increase when fathers are unemployed (Schiller 2008, 91). Given the well-established physical and mental health consequences of unemployment, it should hardly come as a surprise that unemployment has also been linked, in a British study, to lower levels of happiness. Somewhat less expected were the findings that unemployment produces less unhappiness among the young, among those who have been unemployed for longer periods of time, and in those regions where the overall unemployment rates are high (Clark and Oswald 1994).

"Natural" Unemployment, the Phillips Curve, and Okun's Law

At various times from the 1960s onward, economists in the United States have offered opinions about the rate of unemployment that should be considered normal or "natural." If the actual unemployment rate fell below this natural level, it would signal an overheated economy likely to be experiencing inflation. If it rose above the natural level, it would signal slack in the system, suggesting that the economy was performing below its potential. The cumbersome, technical term for the natural rate of unemployment is *nonaccelerating inflation rate of unemployment,* or NAIRU. Economists have tried to determine what the natural rate of unemployment would be in a given economy. For the United States, some thought 4 percent, some 5 percent, some even thought 6 percent unemployment might be the natural level. To date, no consensus has emerged, and in fact the search for the true NAIRU appears, for now, to have been suspended.

Implicit in discussions of NAIRU was the assumption that for any given economy there was a stable relationship between unemployment rates and inflation rates. Empirical research in the 1950s and 1960s appeared to support this notion. Soon economics students were finding something new in their principles textbooks—the Phillips Curve, which graphed an inverse relationship between the inflation rate and the unemployment rate. The Phillips Curve seemed to offer policymakers the possibility of choosing from a variety of inflation–unemployment combinations. If they wanted to lower the unemployment rate, the cost would be higher inflation; if they wanted to lower inflation, the cost would be higher unemployment.

In the same era that produced NAIRU and the Phillips Curve, another empirical relationship involving unemployment was put forth: Okun's Law. Named for the economist Arthur Okun, this law posited a stable inverse relationship between changes in the unemployment rate and the economy's real growth rate. Growth in this case referred to increases in the real, inflation-adjusted gross domestic product, or GDP. Okun's Law builds on the obvious fact that, if national output is to be increased, more labor will have to be employed, and that will reduce unemployment. A widely accepted version of Okun's Law states that, for every 2 percent growth in GDP above its long-term trend rate, unemployment falls by 1 percent. For example, if the long-term GDP growth trend is 3 percent and GDP actually grows by 5 percent, the unemployment rate would be expected to fall by 1 percent. (In this example, therefore, if unemployment had previously been 6 percent, it would fall to 5 percent.) As with the Phillips Curve, Okun's Law has fallen into disfavor among most economists; neither appears to have strong enough empirical underpinnings to be relied upon as a macro policy tool.

Unemployment Insurance

When workers lose their jobs not through any fault of their own but because their industry—or the entire economy—is going through a cyclical downturn, most people believe they need and deserve some kind of temporary financial assistance from the government. Such was not always the case. Historically, state assistance to the unemployed could not be legislated as long as the public viewed joblessness as a matter of individual responsibility. During the periodic depressions that characterized the 19th century, even private charity for the unemployed was sometimes decried as "pauperizing"—that is, liable to turn temporary hardship into permanent dependency. But gradually opinion shifted toward a more positive view of public responsibility to aid the jobless, whether in the form of emergency public relief programs during times of mass unemployment or through employment bureaus operated by cities and states on a model borrowed from Great Britain. (Such bureaus could be found in more than half the states by 1915, according to Roy Lubove 1968.)

Compulsory unemployment compensation plans began to be introduced into state legislatures during the 1920s, but only Wisconsin enacted a program before Congress passed the Social Security Act of 1935. Under that landmark law, all states must operate unemployment insurance (UI) programs. The features that are common to all state programs are: UI applicants must have some work experience; they must have lost their jobs through no fault of their own; and they must be ready and willing to work. Benefit levels vary widely and generally make up only a fraction of the worker's normal wage income. The benefits paid during the standard 26-week period of eligibility are financed out of state payroll taxes. In times of unusual economic distress, Congress can authorize a 13-week extension of UI benefits, in which case the funding is shared by the states and the federal government.

The common view that almost any unemployed person can collect unemployment benefits is far from true. Of those counted as unemployed by the BLS at any given time, only about one-third are able to receive unemployment compensation. The jobless who are just entering the labor force—college graduates, for example—or who are reentering the labor force after a period spent out of work are ineligible to receive UI benefits. Also ineligible are those who have been dismissed for cause from their jobs.

Unemployment and Poverty

The correlation between unemployment and poverty in the United States is not hard to understand. When the economy goes into a recession and jobs are lost or hours are cut, families that had been managing to stay just above the poverty line can easily drop below it. When the economy recovers and laid-off workers go back to work, many families have a chance to earn their way out of poverty. A graph showing the trend lines for unemployment and poverty in the United States from 1960 to 2004 strongly confirms the correlation between these two rates (Schiller 2008, 99). The data since 2004 offer further confirmation. Poverty rates stayed in the 12 percent range from 2004 to 2007, while the unemployment rate trended downward from 5.6 to 4.4 percent. But in 2008, as the recession got under way, the poverty rate shot up to 13.2 percent—its highest level in more than a decade—while the unemployment rate also rose significantly. Poverty statistics are never released in as timely a fashion as the monthly unemployment statistics, but it is a safe bet that, when the poverty rates for 2009 and 2010 are released, they will mirror the dramatic increases seen in the U.S. unemployment rate during the recession.

The Political Economy of Unemployment

People have very different takes on what, if anything, should be done about unemployment and the hardships it produces. Those on the conservative end of the spectrum have long argued that unemployment is an inevitable feature of the dynamic capitalist economy. The 20th century's most outspoken advocate of free enterprise, Milton Friedman, asserted in *Capitalism and Freedom* (1962) that severe unemployment was almost always the result of government ineptitude, not ordinary business cycles. He also blamed some unemployment on minimum wage laws, which, therefore, he wanted to see abolished. At the other (left) end of the political spectrum, radical thinkers from Marx onward have depicted unemployment as both a systemic and a necessary feature of capitalism. Periodic bouts of mass unemployment, in their view, serve to weaken labor unions, restrain wages, and bolster corporate profits. In Marx's view, capitalist crises could be expected to not only continue but grow in intensity, cutting into production and expanding the "reserve army of the unemployed," until at last the working classes threw off their shackles and seized control of the system.

The centrist view of unemployment since the Great Depression has been to see the macro economy as subject to periodic (though not worsening) downturns, which the government can moderate but not eliminate. Unemployment is therefore accepted as a fact of the modern mixed economy. By a proper use of fiscal and monetary tools, economic fluctuations can be held within acceptable bounds, and unemployment insurance—part of a broader safety net—can keep the consequences for individual workers tolerable. It would be hard to find a prominent conservative or libertarian thinker today who would advocate abolishing the UI system that Americans have had since 1935. Debate about how best to help the unemployed centers instead on where the benefit levels should be set and how long the unemployed should be able to collect their benefits. If benefit levels are set too low, the safety net will not meet the basic test of adequacy. There may be another problem as well: low benefit levels will tend to cause the unemployed to shorten their job searches and accept the first job that comes along, even if it does not make appropriate use of their human capital. The end result is inefficiency in the economy. If benefit levels are set too high, it allows workers to extend their job searches beyond what would otherwise be the case. This, too, can be a source of economic inefficiency and waste.

See also **Consumer Credit and Household Debt; Labor, Organized; Minimum Wage; Poverty and Race**

Further Reading

Clark, Andrew E., and Andrew J. Oswald, "Unhappiness and Unemployment." *Economic Journal* 104, no. 424 (May 1994), 648–659.

Friedman, Milton, *Capitalism and Freedom.* Chicago: University of Chicago Press, 1962.

Gerdtham, Ulf-G., and Magnus Johannesson, "A Note on the Effect of Unemployment on Mortality." *Journal of Health Economics* 22, no. 3 (May 2003), 505–518.

Lubove, Roy, *The Struggle for Social Security, 1900–1935.* Cambridge, MA: Harvard University Press, 1968.

Schiller, Bradley, *The Economics of Poverty and Discrimination,* 10th ed. Upper Saddle River, NJ: Pearson Prentice Hall, 2008.

Sharp, Ansel, Charles Register, and Paul Grimes, *Economics of Social Issues,* 19th ed. New York: McGraw-Hill/Irwin, 2009.

Strully, Kate W., "Job Loss and Health in the U.S. Labor Market." *Demography* 46, no. 2 (May 2009), 221–246.

"Symposium: The Natural Rate of Unemployment." *Journal of Economic Perspectives* 11, no. 1 (1997): 3–108.

U.S. Department of Labor, Bureau of Labor Statistics, "How the Government Measures Unemployment." http://www.bls.gov/cps/cps_htgm.htm#where

U.S. Department of Labor, Bureau of Labor Statistics, "Economic News Release: The Employment Situation—April 2010." http://www.bls.gov/news.release/empsit.nr0.htm

W

WAR AND THE ECONOMY

Lee A. Craig

The link between war and the economy is an ancient one. More than 2,000 years ago, Cicero observed, "*Nervo belli, pecuniam infinitam*"—the sinews of war are money in abundance (Cicero 2003)—and war has often been viewed as an avenue to economic prosperity. A leading economic history textbook has a chapter entitled "The 'Prosperity' of Wartime" (Hughes and Cain 2010), and World War II has become the standard explanation for the end of the Great Depression: "It has long been an article of faith that the Second World War brought an end to the long depression of the thirties" (Smiley 1994). In his Pulitzer Prize–winning history of the era, David M. Kennedy notes that "the war compelled government spending on an unexampled scale, capital was unshackled, and the economy energized." He concludes: "Ordinary Americans…had never had it so good" (Kennedy 1999). In the run-up the to the U.S. invasion of Iraq in 2003, Senator Robert Byrd accused President George W. Bush of using the war as a means of addressing "weaknesses in the economy [and] jobs that are being lost" (Nyden 2002).

Despite the unambiguous tone of these observations, opinions on war's impact on the economy are hardly unanimous. The great Austrian economist Ludwig von Mises attacked the very notion of wartime prosperity: "War prosperity is like the prosperity that an earthquake or a plague brings" (Higgs 1992). While economists, historians, and politicians debate the point, generals seem less divided. Douglas MacArthur emphasized war's "utter destruction," and William Tecumseh Sherman famously said of war that "it is all hell" (MacArthur 1951). Tellingly, neither emphasized war's prosperity.

What is the supposed link between war and economic prosperity? How might a war lead to prosperity? Why did Mises equate wartime prosperity with that of a natural disaster?

Grasping the Problem

Calculating the cost of war presents economists and historians with a challenge. There are the direct costs—largely government expenditures on material, which are easy enough to track—and there are also indirect costs, which, although just as important in an economic sense, are less easily quantified. Take, for example, the lost economic production that results from a war-related death. We do not know exactly how much output the dead individual would have contributed to the economy over the course of his or her life; neither do we know exactly what the present market value of that worker's future output would be. After all, the value of a dollar today is not the same as the value of a dollar 10 or 20 years from now. However, because the fact that a topic is difficult does not mean we should avoid it. Economists regularly estimate the future productivity of individuals—for example, those injured or killed in automobile accidents—and they calculate the value today of future income streams, which also happens to be the foundation of the thriving business in annuities. If one applies these techniques to the estimation of the direct and indirect costs of war, some interesting figures emerge.

For example, during the Civil War, the United States government directly spent $1.8 billion, while the Confederate states spent $1.0 billion (in 1860 dollars). Estimates of the indirect costs of the war are in the neighborhood of $1.6 billion for the United States and $2.3 billion for the Confederacy (Goldin 1973). Thus, the combined costs of the war were $6.7 billion ($3.4 billion for the North and $3.3 billion in the South). With a total U.S. population of roughly 35 million, it follows that the war cost about $50 per person per year, during its four years.

To put these figures into perspective, consider that the cost of purchasing the freedom of the entire slave stock in 1860 would have been $2.7 billion, or about 40 percent of the war's actual cost. Financed by the issue of 30-year U.S. treasury bonds at 6 percent interest, this option would have cost the northern population $9.66 in taxes per person per year. Indeed, depending on which groups were taxed to pay off the bonds, the payments would have been considerably less than this. Given that annual income per person at the time was around $200 dollars, the tax rate would have been less than 5 percent—a fraction of the current average federal income tax rate today. Perhaps somewhat paradoxically, these figures seem to confirm Ulysses S. Grant's observation that "There never was a time when, in my opinion, some way could not be found to prevent the drawing of the sword" (West Point Graduates against the War n.d.).

Of course, calculations such as these distort the fact that the fundamental economic condition of war is not its average cost or benefit but rather its distributional effect, or, as one economic historian put it: "The economic benefits of the Civil War were bestowed upon those who were able to take advantage of the changes it generated [not the least of whom were the emancipated slaves], while its costs were most heavily born by those who suffered and died on its fields of glory" (Craig 1996).

What Is War Prosperity?

The standard economic indicator for the performance of any economy is gross domestic product (GDP)—"the total value of all final goods and services produced for the marketplace during a given year within a nation's borders" (Lieberman and Hall 2005). It follows from this definition that GDP is the sum of various types of expenditures on goods and services, including private personal consumption expenditures, investment, expenditures on exports minus those on imports, and government expenditures. In any economy at any point in time, it is possible—perhaps even likely—that there are some productive resources (e.g., land, labor, or capital) that are unemployed or at least underemployed. As war approaches or is unleashed, governments employ their coercive powers to facilitate military operations. Men are conscripted to fight, capital is directed toward the production of war materiel, and so forth. Thus, government expenditures tend to increase, sometimes dramatically, during wartime, and since those expenditures are mathematically a component of the GDP, it typically increases during war.

To see this phenomenon in practice, consider Figure 1. It shows an index of real (i.e., inflation-adjusted) GDP for the U.S. economy before, during, and after U.S. involvement

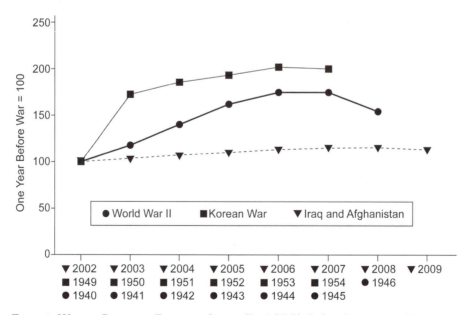

Figure 1. Wartime Prosperity: Economic Output (Real GDP): Before, During, and After World War II, the Korean War, and the Wars in the Middle East (Author's Calculation from U.S. Department of Commerce, www.commerce.gov and www.bea.gov)

in three wars: World War II (1941–1945), the Korean War (1950–1953), and the recent and ongoing wars in the Middle East. Using the year before the United States entered each war as the base year, in which GDP = 100, the figure illustrates how the economy expanded during the war years and how it leveled off as the war ended. Clearly, from this indicator, one would be justified in referring to the prosperity associated with these wars.

If government spending during wartime leads to prosperity, then shouldn't government spending during peacetime lead to prosperity? In other words, why isn't more government spending always a good thing? To answer these questions, we must consider where the government obtains the money it spends during wartime or peacetime. Governments obtain funds from three sources. They can raise the money via taxation; they can borrow the money, which is just future taxation; and they can print more money, which just leads to inflation and is a form of taxation. (Since printing money depreciates the value of money, inflation is a form of taxation on those holding money.) So, in the end, all government spending is financed one way or the other through taxation. Typically, governments turn to some combination of all three revenue sources, especially during wartime.

Once we recognize that government spending is just taxation, then we can see why it does not in general lead to prosperity. If governments fight wars with tax dollars, and if they obtain the tax dollars from consumers, then it follows that a dollar of taxation going to government spending and increasing GDP will simply be taken from a dollar of private personal consumer spending, which would in turn decrease GDP.

It does not always work like this, dollar for dollar, for at least two reasons. First, with respect to borrowing, recall that GDP represents the value of current expenditures. Government borrowing is future taxation, and the decrease in consumer spending might not show up immediately. Thus, GDP goes up today and is reduced at some time in the future. This is just robbing Peter tomorrow to pay Paul today. As a general policy, government borrowing might or might not be good for the economy—depending on how the borrowed funds are expended—but the exigencies of war are such that governments often do not worry about the future consequences of borrowing.

Second, war changes the economy in other ways that would offset the decrease in consumption resulting from taxation. For example, one of the most common forms of taxation during war is the conscription or drafting of soldiers who pay the tax with their labor. Historically, soldiers were not paid a market wage, which is why conscription is a regular companion of war. The difference between what conscripted soldiers are paid and what they would have to be paid in order to get them to volunteer represents a measure of the soldiers' tax burden. When a soldier goes to war, he (historically, conscripts tend to be men) leaves the civilian labor force, which tends to reduce his family's consumption, but often women (and children and the elderly), who might otherwise have been employed in nonmarket pursuits, replace men in the labor force. Thus, economic activity, as measured in GDP, would now include the government spending on the soldier and the consumption generated by the women who replaced soldiers in the labor force. Rosie the Riveter, of World War II fame, is the classic example of this phenomenon. Since Rosie's prewar nonmarket activity in the household was not counted as a component of GDP—riveting is; preparing dinner, changing diapers, and cleaning the house are not—when her work is added to the government's increased wartime spending, GDP increases, just as it did during World War II.

This, then, is wartime prosperity. Unemployed or underemployed resources, or resources formerly employed in nonmarket activity, are put to work by government's wartime spending—usually spurred by increased borrowing—as companies obtain government contracts and individuals who formerly did not contribute to GDP now do so (like Rosie the Riveter); and many who did contribute to GDP in the private sector are now contributing in the government sector, albeit as conscripted soldiers. Prosperity, at least as measured by GDP, follows. Why, then, have some of the leading figures in economics and economic history questioned the concept of wartime prosperity?

Is War a Human-Made Disaster?

The comparison of war to a natural disaster is common, because both seem to create prosperity. It is not uncommon for certain types of economic activity to pick up following a natural disaster. For example, in the wake of a hurricane, roofing contractors expect to see an increase in the demand for their services, as they are called upon to repair damage to homes resulting from falling trees. Indeed, consider the whole series of related economic activities. A tree service might be called to remove the tree, the family might stay in a hotel until the roof is repaired, painters might repair internal water damage, and so forth. None of these particular expenditures would have been made by the family in the absence of the hurricane. Multiplying these and other costs incurred from damage by the number of households affected by the hurricane would yield an aggregate measure of the value of services rendered following the storm. Thus, one might conclude that the storm itself yielded the resulting prosperity.

The fundamental problem with this observation is that it assumes that the families would have neither spent nor saved the monies they expended as a direct result of the storm. Perhaps they would have purchased a new automobile, a purchase that will now be postponed. Perhaps they would have stayed in a hotel on vacation, a trip that will now be canceled. In these cases, all the hurricane did was redirect the families' spending from something they had planned or hoped to purchase (i.e., a new car or a vacation) to something they would not have wanted in the absence of the storm (i.e., a new roof and a stay at the hotel down the road).

What if a family had merely taken money out of the bank to pay for the new roof and hotel visit—money that they were, in fact, saving for a rainy day? They could still purchase the car and vacation with other funds. Would these monies not be better spent on a new roof than just sitting in the bank? The answer is no, because the bank does not just sit on the money that is deposited there; it turns around and loans that money for productive economic activity. If people take loanable funds out of banks to pay for new roofs that they would not have needed in the absence of a hurricane—that is, if they reduce the supply of loanable funds—then the banks increase their interest rates in order to induce other people to make new deposits. This increase in interest rates in turn reduces the number of loans taken.

Why not just borrow the money from the bank? Because as people borrow money to repair the storm damage, they increase the demand for loanable funds, which in turn increases interest rates and reduces the number of loans taken. Thus, as a result of the hurricane, economic activity is redirected—from new cars and vacations to new roofs—and less economic activity occurs as upward pressure is placed on interest rates. Neither of these effects is good for the economy.

War has the same two negative effects on the economy. The opportunity cost of war is never zero. A dollar spent on a weapon, a shell, or a uniform is a dollar extracted through taxation or borrowed, which again is merely future taxation, and therefore not spent on some other activity. If consumers were better off purchasing a shell rather than an automobile, they would demand shells during peacetime rather than cars or houses or education for their children. So the forced substitution of war production for private consumption cannot be understood generally as making people better off.

As for borrowing, recall that one of the most common of war's effects on the economy is an increase in the demand for credit, as countries borrow to finance the construction of their war machines. This increases the demand for credit, which increases interest rates, which tends to drive down or crowd out private investment. So we again see governments' wartime expenditures simply replacing private expenditures. Since people generally prefer to borrow money for a home, automobile, or education rather than a plane that might get shot down over enemy territory, it is difficult to argue that the increase in government spending improves people's financial situations.

As for printing money and generating inflation to finance the war, if this were good for the economy (and it is not), then we would expect to see governments doing this during peacetime as well. Although in recent decades there has been some peacetime high inflation, it is not perceived to be a positive factor for the economy, and anything more than a little inflation is generally greeted unfavorably by lenders and consumers (and voters; woe to the president running for reelection during periods of rampant inflation, such as Jimmy Carter).

Of course, war, just like a natural disaster, redirects economic activity. Suppliers of weapons and uniforms will see an increase in the demand for their products relative to other goods and services—just as roofers see an increase in the demand for their services after hurricanes. Those who see their taxes increase, now and in the future, are among the groups whose resources are directed toward military suppliers, but the group most likely to bear a disproportionate share of the tax burden is the soldiers who pay with their labor, especially those who ultimately pay with their lives. The death of soldier is a tragedy to his or her family. For the economy, it represents the loss of all of his or her future economic output.

What does this tell us about the persistent metaphor of wartime prosperity? The main thing is that the manner in which standard economic measures of well-being, such as GDP, are constructed biases them upward during wartime. The substitution of market for nonmarket activity increases GDP, but it does not mean people are necessarily better off. In addition, the substitution of spending today in return for consumption tomorrow might be good public policy, but it should not be confused with prosperity in any conventional sense of the word.

Measuring Wartime Prosperity

Are people better off economically as a result of wars? How do we calculate economic well-being? The great Scottish philosopher and economist Adam Smith had an answer. According to Smith, "Consumption is the sole end and purpose of all production" (Smith 1976). Typically, personal consumption expenditures are the largest component of a country's total economic output, as measured by gross domestic product. So, looking at what happens to consumption expenditures during wartime is a good place to begin in answering questions about the link between wars and economic prosperity.

Table 1 contains an index of personal consumption expenditures, adjusted for inflation, between 1939 and 1945—the years coinciding with World War II (although the United States did not formally enter the war until after the attack on Pearl Harbor in December 1941, war production had begun to accelerate in 1939). The figures in column 1 are based on U.S. Commerce Department data and show a 23.4 percent increase during the war. This would correspond with an average annual compounded rate of growth

TABLE 1. Estimates of Real Personal Consumption Expenditures (1939–1945)

Year	Base Measure	Inflation-Adjusted
1939	100.0	100.0
1940	104.6	104.2
1941	110.5	108.7
1942	109.8	104.2
1943	112.4	101.9
1944	115.9	102.0
1945	123.4	106.8

Source: Higgs, Robert. "Wartime Prosperity? A Reassessment of the U.S. Economy in the 1940s." *Journal of Economic History* 52 (1992): 41–60.

of 3.6 percent, which was quite robust at the time, considering that, during the previous decade, the country had weathered the Great Depression. When comparing the war years to the Great Depression, it is not surprising that many U.S. citizens remembered the war as an era of economic prosperity, at least those citizens who were not in Bastogne or on Guadalcanal.

However, the measurement of consumption expenditures is not without controversy. For one thing, there was tremendous inflation during the war—inflation that was accompanied by government-mandated price controls. Thus, the official prices used to adjust for this inflation do not necessarily account for the true inflation rate as reflected in, for example, black-market or illegal prices. The figures in column 2 of the table, which adjust personal consumption expenditures during the war, were calculated using an alternative set of inflation-adjusted prices. Here we see that consumption increased by only 6.8 percent over the course of the war, a rate of growth that did not even keep up with population growth. Thus, during the so-called wartime prosperity, real average consumption per person actually fell. This is not what one typically associates with prosperity. As is often the case in economics, the devil is in the details, and the details are in the numbers.

Winners and Losers

From the discussion above, it appears that rather than enriching an economy, war simply changes it, and the changes are a function of the size of the war relative to the size of the economy. At the peak of government military spending during World War II, in 1944, national defense spending was 41 percent of GDP. Currently, with two campaigns active in the Middle East, the defense share is 8 percent of GDP. This explains the more dramatic curvature of the World War II data relative to the Middle East wars shown in Figure 1.

But, holding other things constant, the key to understanding the impact of war on the economy is appreciating that war represents a net transfer of resources from taxpayers (including soldiers) to suppliers of war materiel (companies), and from borrowers (again, future taxpayers) to holders of savings (buyers of government bonds). Of course, in war, other things are not constant. In particular, the discussion to this point has said nothing about winners and losers. The destruction wrought by war can nearly completely devastate an area. After the destruction of Carthage in 146 B.C., the Romans supposedly sowed salt in the earth so that the Carthaginians would never rise again. Byzantium never recovered from the Fourth Crusade. Hiroshima was turned into ash. Neither the Carthaginians nor the Byzantines nor the Japanese spoke of wartime prosperity.

There is one way in which the economy can emerge a winner from war. This is if war is engaged in to remove a threat to the country and make the economy more secure. Households and businesses will be more reluctant to make important and needed investments in the economy if they fear the country will not exist, or at least will be severely damaged, in the future. In this case, a war to remove the threat and increase the likelihood of a peaceful future can ultimately improve long-term economic prosperity. The cold war's triumph of capitalism over communism offers a good recent example of this type of benefit, perhaps justifying, in economic terms at least, the war's tremendous cost in lives and treasure.

Ultimately, however, war is more than an economic activity. Clemenceau's admonition that war is too important to be left to generals applies here; it is too important to be left to economists as well. For those who see war as the alternative to annihilation, a blip in real GDP in one direction or the other is of little importance. Winning at almost any cost is what matters. Ask the Carthaginians.

See also **Debt, Deficits, and the Economy**

Further Reading

Atack, Jeremy, and Peter Passell, *A New Economic View of American History,* 2d ed. New York: W. W. Norton, 1994.

Cicero (Marcus Tullius), *The Fifth Philippic.* Cambridge, England: Cambridge University Press, 2003.

Craig, Lee A., "Industry, Agriculture, and the Economy during the Civil War." In *The American Civil War: A Handbook of Literature and Research,* ed. Steven E. Woodworth. Westport, CT: Greenwood Press, 1996.

Goldin, Claudia, "The Economics of Emancipation." *Journal of Economic History* 33 (1973): 66–85.

Goldin, Claudia, and Frank D. Lewis, "The Economic Cost of the American Civil War: Estimates and Implications." *Journal of Economic History* 35 (1975): 304–309.

Higgs, Robert, "Wartime Prosperity? A Reassessment of the U.S Economy in the 1940s." *Journal of Economic History* 52 (1992): 41–60.

Hughes, Jonathan, and Louis P. Cain, *American Economic History,* 8th ed. Upper Saddle River, NJ: Prentice Hall, 2010.

Kennedy, David M., *Freedom from Fear: The American People in Depression and War, 1929–1945.* New York: Oxford University Press, 1999.

Lewis, Lloyd, *Sherman: Fighting Prophet.* Lincoln: University of Nebraska Press, 1993 [1932].

Lieberman, Marc, and Robert E. Hall, *Introduction to Economics,* 2d ed. Mason, OH: South-Western, 2005.

MacArthur, Douglas, *Farewell Address to Congress.* 1951. http://www.americanrhetoric.com/speeches/douglasmacarthurfarewelladdress

Nyden, Paul J., "Bush's War Plans Are a Cover-up, Senator Byrd Says." *Charleston Gazette* (September 21, 2002). http://www.dupagepeacethroughjustice.org/byrd.html

Smiley, Gene, *The American Economy in the Twentieth Century.* Cincinnati: South-Western, 1994.

Smith, Adam, *An Inquiry into the Nature and Causes of the Wealth of Nations,* Vol. 2. Indianapolis: Liberty Classics, 1976 [1776].

West Point Graduates against the War, *Wise Words from Old Grads* (n.d.). http://www.westpointgradsagainstthewar.org/wise_words_from_old_grads.htm

Bibliography

Business and Economic Policy and Law

Angell, Marcia, *The Truth about the Drug Companies: How They Deceive Us and What to Do about It.* New York: Random House, 2004.

Avorn, Jerry, *Powerful Medicines: The Benefits, Risks, and Costs of Prescription Drugs.* New York: Vintage, 2005.

Bacon, David, *Illegal People: How Globalization Creates Migration and Criminalizes Immigrants.* Boston: Beacon Press, 2008.

Bagdikian, Ben, *The New Media Monopoly.* Boston: Beacon Press, 2004.

Berry, Jeffrey, and Clyde Wilcox, *Interest Group Society.* New York: Longman, 2008.

Boortz, Neal, and John Linder, *FairTax, the Truth: Answering the Critics.* New York: Harper, 2008.

Borjas, George J., *Heaven's Door: Immigration Policy and the American Economy.* Princeton, NJ: Princeton University Press, 2001.

Burbank, Matthew J., Ronald J. Hrebenar, and Robert C. Benedict, *Parties, Interest Groups, and Political Campaigns.* Boulder, CO: Paradigm, 2008.

Burkholder, Nicholas C., *Outsourcing: The Definitive View, Applications and Implications.* Hoboken, NJ: John Wiley, 2006.

Chester, Jeff, *Digital Destiny: New Media and the Future of Democracy.* New York: New Press, 2007.

Cigler, Allan, and Burdett A. Loomis, *Interest Group Politics.* Washington, DC: Congressional Quarterly Press, 2006.

Croteau, David, and William Hoynes, *The Business of Media: Corporate Media and the Public Interest,* 2d ed. Thousand Oaks, CA: Pine Forge Press, 2006.

Diamond, John W., and George R. Zodrow, *Fundamental Tax Reform: Issues, Choices, and Implications.* Cambridge, MA: MIT Press, 2008.

Ehrenberg, Ronald G., and Robert S. Smith, *Modern Labor Economics: Theory and Public Policy.* Boston: Pearson Addison-Wesley, 2006.

Emerson, Robert W., *Business Law,* 5th ed. Hauppauge, NY: Barron's, 2009.

Feenstra, Robert C., *Offshoring in the Global Economy: Microeconomic Structures and Macroeconomic Implications.* Cambridge, MA: MIT Press, 2010.

Finkelstein, Stan N., *Reasonable Rx: Solving the Drug Price Crisis.* Upper Saddle River, NJ: FT Press/Pearson Education, 2008.

Freeman, Jodi, and Martha Minnow, *Government by Contract: Outsourcing and American Democracy.* Cambridge, MA: Harvard University Press, 2009.

Greenwald, Howard P., *Health Care in the United States: Organization, Management, Policy.* San Francisco: Jossey-Bass, 2010.

Hrebenar, Ronald, and Bryson B. Morgan, *Lobbying in America: A Reference Handbook.* Santa Barbara, CA: ABC-CLIO, 2009.

Hyman, David N., *Public Finance: A Contemporary Application of Theory to Policy,* 10th ed. Mason, OH: South-Western College Publishing, 2010.

Johnston, Mark C., *Free Lunch: How the Wealthiest Americans Enrich Themselves at Government Expense.* New York: Portfolio, 2007.

Kaiser, Robert G., *So Damn Much Money: The Triumph of Lobbying and the Corrosion of American Government.* New York: Vintage Books, 2010.

Kronenfeld, Jennie Jacobs, *Expansion of Publicly Funded Health Insurance in the United States: The Children's Health Insurance Program and Its Implications.* Lanham, MD: Lexington Books, 2006.

Kronenfeld, Jennie Jacobs, and Michael Kronenfeld, *Health Care Reform in America.* Santa Barbara, CA: ABC-CLIO, 2004.

Marmor, Theodore H., *The Politics of Medicare,* 2d ed. New York: Aldine De Gruyer, 2000.

McKinnell, Hank, *A Call to Action: Taking Back Healthcare for Future Generations.* New York: McGraw-Hill, 2005.

Mol, Michael, *Outsourcing: Design, Process and Performance.* New York: Cambridge University Press, 2007.

Oshri, Ilan, Julia Kotlarsky, and Leslie P. Willcocks, *The Handbook of Global Outsourcing and Offshoring.* New York: Palgrave Macmillan, 2009.

Pasour, E. C., Jr., and Randal R. Rucker, *Plowshares and Pork Barrels: The Political Economy of Agriculture.* Oakland, CA: Independent Institute, 2005.

Peterson, E. Wesley F., *A Billion Dollars a Day: The Economics and Politics of Agricultural Subsidies.* Malden, MA: Wiley-Blackwell, 2009.

Quadagno, Jill, *One Nation Uninsured: Why The U.S. Has No National Health Insurance.* New York: Oxford University Press, 2005.

Schwabach, Aaron, *Intellectual Property: A Reference Handbook.* Santa Barbara, CA: ABC-CLIO, 2007.

Slemrod, Joel, and Jon Bakija, *Taxing Ourselves: A Citizen's Guide to the Debate over Taxes.* Cambridge, MA: MIT Press, 2008.

Sorkin, Andrew Ross, *Too Big to Fail: The Inside Story of How Wall Street and Washington Fought to Save the Financial System from Crisis—and Lost.* New York: Viking, 2009.

Steuerle, C. Eugene, *Contemporary U.S. Tax Policy,* 2d ed. Washington, DC: Urban Institute, 2008.

Stout, Robert Joe, *Why Immigrants Come to America: Braceros, Indocumentados, and the Migra.* Westport, CT: Praeger, 2008.

Utter, Glenn H., and Ruth Ann Strickland, *Campaign and Election Reform,* 2d ed. Santa Barbara, CA: ABC-CLIO, 2008.

White, Lawrence J., *The S&L Debacle: Public Policy Lessons for Bank and Thrift Regulation.* New York: Oxford University Press, 1991.

Yu, Peter K., *Intellectual Property and Information Wealth: Issues and Practices in the Digital Age.* Westport, CT: Praeger, 2007.

Employment and Unemployment

Anderson, Terry H., *The Pursuit of Fairness: A History of Affirmative Action.* New York: Oxford University Press, 2004.

Andersson, Fredrik, *Moving Up or Moving Down: Who Advances in the Low-Wage Market?* New York: Russell Sage Foundation, 2005.

Barreto, Manuela, et al., eds., *The Glass Ceiling in the 21st Century: Understanding Barriers to Gender Equality.* Washington, DC: American Psychological Association, 2009.

Bell, Ella L. J., and Stella M. Nkomo, *Our Separate Ways: Black and White Women and the Struggle for Professional Identity.* Cambridge, MA: Harvard Business School Press, 2003.

Bennett, James T., and Bruce E. Kaufmann, eds., *What Do Unions Do? A Twenty-Year Perspective.* New Brunswick, NJ: Transaction Publishers, 2007.

Briggs, Vernon, *Immigration and American Unionism.* Ithaca, NY: Cornell University Press, 2001.

Brody, David, *Labor Embattled: History, Power, Rights.* Urbana: University of Illinois Press, 2005.

Card, David, and Alan Krueger, *Myth and Measurement: The New Economics of the Minimum Wage.* Princeton, NJ: Princeton University Press, 1995.

Chappell, Marisa, *The War on Welfare: Family, Poverty, and Politics in Modern America.* Philadelphia: University of Pennsylvania Press, 2010.

Chih Lin, Ann, and David R. Harris, eds., *The Colors of Poverty: Why Racial and Ethnic Disparities Exist.* New York: Russell Sage Foundation, 2008.

Conley, Dalton, ed., *Wealth and Poverty in America: A Reader.* Malden, MA: Blackwell, 2003.

Dine, Philip M., *State of the Unions: How Labor Can Strengthen the Middle Class, Improve Our Economy, and Regain Political Influence.* New York: McGraw-Hill, 2008.

Dobbin, Frank, *Inventing Equal Opportunity.* Princeton, NJ: Princeton University Press, 2009.

Early, Steve, *Embedded with Organized Labor: Journalistic Reflections on the Class War at Home.* New York: Monthly Review Press, 2009.

Ehrenreich, Barbara, *Nickel and Dimed: On (Not) Getting By in America.* New York: Henry Holt, 2002.

Epstein, William M., *Good Citizenship and the War on Poverty.* University Park: Pennsylvania State University Press, 2010.

Goode, Judith, and Jeff Maskovsky, eds., *New Poverty Studies: The Ethnography of Power, Politics, and Impoverished People in the United States.* New York: New York University Press, 2001.

Henry, C. Michael, ed., *Race, Poverty, and Domestic Policy.* New Haven, CT: Yale University Press, 2004.

Karsten, Margaret Foegen, *Gender, Race, and Ethnicity in the Workplace: Issues and Challenges for Today's Organizations*. Westport, CT: Praeger, 2006.

Katznelson, Ira, *When Affirmative Action Was White: An Untold History of Racial Inequality in Twentieth-Century America*. New York: W. W. Norton, 2005.

Kellough, J. Edward, *Understanding Affirmative Action: Politics, Discrimination, and the Search for Justice*. Washington, DC: Georgetown University Press, 2006.

Lang, Kevin, *Poverty and Discrimination*. Princeton, NJ: Princeton University Press, 2007.

Neumark, David, and William L. Wascher, *Minimum Wages*. Cambridge, MA: MIT Press, 2008.

Newman, Katherine S., *The Missing Class: Portraits of the Near Poor in America*. Boston: Beacon Press, 2007.

Pollin, Robert, et al., *A Measure of Fairness: The Economics of Living Wages and Minimum Wages in the United States*. Ithaca, NY: ILR Press, 2008.

Schiller, Bradley, *The Economics of Poverty and Discrimination*, 10th ed. Upper Saddle River, NJ: Pearson Prentice Hall, 2008.

Troy, Leo, *Beyond Unions and Collective Bargaining*. Armonk, NY: M. E. Sharpe, 2000.

Wilson, William Julius, *More than Just Race: Being Black and Poor in the Inner City*. New York: W. W. Norton, 2009.

Yates, Michael D., *Why Unions Matter*, 2d ed. New York: Monthly Review Press, 2009.

Financial Matters

Balsam, Steven, *An Introduction to Executive Compensation*. Burlington, MA: Academic Press, 2002.

Black, William K., *The Best Way to Rob a Bank Is to Own One: How Corporate Executives and Politicians Looted the S&L Industry*. Austin: University of Texas Press, 2005.

Blake, David, *Pension Economics*. New York: John Wiley, 2006.

Calavita, Kitty, Henry N. Pontell, and Robert H. Tillman, *Big Money Crime: Fraud and Politics in the Savings and Loan Crisis*. Berkeley: University of California Press, 1997.

Cecchetti, Stephen G., *Money, Banking, and Financial Markets*, 2d ed. Boston: McGraw-Hill Irwin, 2007.

Committee on Governmental Affairs, *The Role of Professional Firms in the U.S. Tax Shelter Industry*. Washington, DC: U.S. Government Printing Office, 2005.

Crystal, Graef S., *In Search of Excess: The Overcompensation of American Executives*. New York: W. W. Norton.

Edwards, Chris, and Daniel J. Mitchell, *Global Tax Revolution: The Rise of Tax Competition and the Battle to Defend It*. Washington, DC: Cato Institute, 2008.

Friedman, Milton, and Anna Jacobson Schwartz, *A Monetary History of the United States, 1867–1960*. Princeton, NJ Princeton University Press, 1963.

Frontline: Breaking the Bank. Documentary. Michael Kirk, dir. Boston: WGBH/Frontline, 2009.

Gale, William G., et al., eds., *The Evolving Pension System: Trends, Effects, and Proposals for Reform*. Washington, DC: Brookings Institution Press, 2008.

Ghilarducci, Theresa, *When I'm Sixty-Four: The Plot against Pensions and the Plan to Save Them*. Princeton, NJ: Princeton University Press, 2008.

Hyman, David N., *Public Finance: A Contemporary Application of Theory to Policy,* 6th ed. Orlando: Dryden Press, 1999.

Kay, Ira T., and Steven Van Putten, *Myths and Realities of Executive Pay.* New York: Cambridge University Press, 2007.

Lewis, Michael, *The Big Short: Inside the Doomsday Machine.* New York: W. W. Norton, 2010.

Lowenstein, Roger, *While America Aged: How Pension Debts Ruined General Motors, Stopped the NYC Subways, Bankrupted San Diego, and Loom as the Next Financial Crisis.* New York: Penguin, 2009.

Meltzer, Allan H., *A History of the Federal Reserve.* Vol. 1, *1913–1951.* Chicago: University of Chicago Press, 2003.

Modigliani, Franco, and Arun Muralidhar, *Rethinking Pension Reform.* Cambridge, England: Cambridge University Press, 2005.

Morris, Charles R., *Apart at the Seams: The Collapse of Private Pension and Health Care Protections.* New York: Century Foundation, 2008.

Orenstein, Mitchell A., ed., *Pensions, Social Security, and the Privatization of Risk.* New York: Columbia University Press, 2009.

Ritholtz, Barry, *Bailout Nation: How Greed and Easy Money Corrupted Wall Street and Shook the World Economy.* Hoboken, NJ: John Wiley, 2009.

Shaviro, Daniel N., *Corporate Tax Shelters in a Global Economy.* Washington, DC: AEI Press, 2004.

Slemrod, Joel, *Taxing Ourselves: A Citizen's Guide to the Debate over Taxes,* 4th ed. Cambridge, MA: MIT Press, 2008.

Smith, Hedrick, *Tax Me If You Can.* Documentary. Boston: PBS (a Frontline coproduction with Hendrick Smith Productions), 2004.

Stern, Gary H., and Ron J. Feldman, *Too Big to Fail: The Hazards of Bank Bailouts.* Washington, DC: Brookings Institution Press, 2004.

Summers, Lawrence H., *Tackling the Growth of Corporate Tax Shelters.* Washington, DC: Office of Public Affairs, Department of the Treasury, 2000.

White, Lawrence J., *The S&L Debacle: Public Policy Lessons for Bank and Thrift Regulation.* New York: Oxford University Press, 1991.

Marketing

Berger, Arthur, *Ads, Fads, and Consumer Culture,* 3d ed. Lanham, MD: Rowman & Littlefield, 2007.

Campaign for a Commercial-Free Childhood. http://www.commercialfreechildhood.org

Consumers against Supermarket Privacy Invasion and Numbering. http://www.nocards.org

Danziger, Pamela N., *Why People Buy Things They Don't Need.* New York: Paramount Market Publishing, 2002.

Goodrum, Charles, and Helen Dalrymple, *Advertising in America: The First 200 Years.* New York: Harry N. Abrams, 1990.

Grogan, Sarah, *Body Image.* New York: Routledge, 2007.

Kilbourne, Jean, *Deadly Persuasion: Why Women and Girls Must Fight the Addictive Power of Advertising.* New York: Free Press, 1999.

Kirkpatrick, Jerry, *In Defense of Advertising: Arguments from Reason, Ethical Egoism, and Laissez-Faire Capitalism.* Claremont, CA: TLJ Books, 2007.

Pennock, Pamela E., *Advertising Sin and Sickness: The Politics of Alcohol and Tobacco Marketing, 1950–1990.* Dekalb: Northern Illinois University Press, 2007.

Quart, Alissa, *Branded: The Buying and Selling of Teenagers.* New York: Basic Books, 2004.

Reichert, Tom, *The Erotic History of Advertising.* Amherst, NY: Prometheus Books, 2003.

Ries, Al, and Laura Ries, *The Rise of PR and the Fall of Advertising.* New York: Collins, 2002.

Rutherford, Paul, *A World Made Sexy: Freud to Madonna.* Toronto: University of Toronto Press, 2007.

Schor, Juliet, *Born to Buy.* New York: Scribner, 2005.

Schwartz, Barry, *The Paradox of Choice: Why More Is Less.* New York: HarperCollins, 2004.

Stanford, Eleanor, *Advertising: Introducing Issues with Opposing Viewpoints.* San Diego: Greenhaven Press, 2007.

Wilkins, Lee, and Clifford G. Christians, eds., *The Handbook of Mass Media Ethics.* New York: Routledge, 2009.

Wykes, Maggie, and Barry Gunter, *The Media and Body Image.* Thousand Oaks, CA: Sage, 2005.

Trade Issues, Globalization, and the General Economy

Aronowitz, Stanley, and Heather Gautney, eds., *Implicating Empire: Globalization and Resistance in the 21st Century World Order.* New York: Basic Books, 2003.

Atack, Jeremy, and Peter Passell, *A New Economic View of American History,* 2d ed. New York: W. W. Norton, 1994.

Bhagwati, Jagdish, *Free Trade Today.* Princeton, NJ: Princeton University Press, 2002.

Cline, William R., *The United States as a Debtor Nation.* Washington, DC: Institute for International Economics, 2005.

Cook, Thomas A., *Managing Global Supply Chains.* Boca Raton, FL: Auerbach Publications, 2008.

Crystal, Jonathan, *Unwanted Company: Foreign Investment in American Industries.* Ithaca, NY: Cornell University Press, 2003.

De Rivero, Oswaldo, *The Myth of Development: The Non-Viable Economies of the 21st Century.* New York: Zed Books, 2001.

Downey, Morgan Patrick, *Oil 101.* New York: Wooden Table Press, 2009.

Dunway, Steven Vincent, *Global Imbalances and the Financial Crisis.* Washington, DC: Council on Foreign Relations, 2009.

Easterly, William, *The White Man's Burden: Why the West's Efforts to Aid the Rest Have Done So Much Ill and So Little Good.* New York: Penguin, 2006.

Eisner, Robert, *The Great Deficit Scares: The Federal Budget, Trade, and Social Security.* New York: Twentieth Century Foundation, 1997.

Gálvez-Muñoz, Lina, and Geoffrey G. Jones, eds., *Foreign Multinationals in the United States: Management and Performance.* New York: Routledge, 2001.

Gordon, John Steele., *Hamilton's Blessing: The Extraordinary Life and Times of Our National Debt.* New York: Walker, 2010.

Grace, Robert, *Oil: An Overview of the Petroleum Industry*. Houston: Gulf Publishing, 2007.

Hilton, Matthew, *Prosperity for All: Consumer Activism in an Era of Globalization*. Ithaca, NY: Cornell University Press, 2009.

Hufbauer, Gary Clyde, et al., *U.S.-China Trade Disputes: Rising Tide, Rising Stakes*. Washington, DC: Institute for International Economics, 2006.

Hughes, Jonathan, and Louis P. Cain, *American Economic History*, 8th ed. Upper Saddle River, NJ: Prentice Hall, 2010.

Irwin, Douglas A., *Free Trade under Fire*, 3d ed. Princeton, NJ: Princeton University Press, 2009.

Juhasz, Antonia, *The Tyranny of Oil: The World's Most Powerful Industry—And What We Must Do to Stop It*. New York: Harper, 2009.

Kelly, Robert E., *The National Debt of the United States, 1914–2008*. Jefferson, NC: McFarland, 2008.

Kennedy, David M., *Freedom from Fear: The American People in Depression and War, 1929–1945*. New York: Oxford University Press, 1999.

Klare, Michael T., *Blood and Oil: The Dangers and Consequences of America's Growing Dependency on Imported Petroleum*. New York: Henry Holt, 2005.

Landes, David S., *The Wealth and Poverty of Nations: Why Some Are So Rich and Some So Poor*. New York: W. W. Norton, 1999.

Lindsey, Brik, and Daniel Ikenson, *Anti-Dumping Exposed: The Devilish Details of Unfair Trade Law*. Washington, DC: CATO Institute, 2003.

Little, Jane Sneddon, ed., *Global Imbalances and the Evolving World Economy*. Boston: Federal Reserve Bank of Boston, 2008.

Manula, Marko, Guten Tag, *Y'all: Globalization and the South Carolina Piedmont, 1950–2000*. Athens: University of Georgia Press, 2009.

Maynard, Micheline, *The End of Detroit: How the Big Three Lost Their Grip on the American Car Market*. New York: Broadway Books, 2004.

Maynard, Micheline, *The Selling of the American Economy: How Foreign-Owned Companies Are Remaking the American Dream*. New York: Broadway Books, 2009.

McNichols, Michael, *Maritime Security: An Introduction*. Burlington, MA: Butterworth-Heinemann, 2007.

Morgan, Iwan W., *The Age of Deficits: Presidents and Unbalanced Budgets from Jimmy Carter to George W. Bush*. Lawrence: University Press of Kansas, 2009.

Paul, William Henry, *Future Energy: How the New Oil Industry Will Change People, Politics, and Portfolios*. New York: John Wiley, 2007.

Preeg, Ernest H., *The Trade Deficit, the Dollar, and the National Interest*. Indianapolis: Hudson Institute, 2000.

Priest, Tyler, *The Offshore Imperative: Shell Oil's Search for Petroleum in Postwar America*. College Station: Texas A&M University Press, 2007.

Ritter, Luke, et al., *Securing Global Transportation Networks*. New York: McGraw-Hill, 2007.

Roberts, Russell D., *The Choice: A Fable of Free Trade and Protectionism*. Upper Saddle River, NJ: Pearson Prentice Hall, 2007.

Saul, John Ralston, *The Collapse of Globalism and the Reinvention of the World*. Toronto: Viking, 2005.

Smiley, Gene, *The American Economy in the Twentieth Century*. Cincinnati: South-Western, 1994.

Stiglitz, Joseph, *Globalization and Its Discontents*. New York: W. W. Norton, 2003.

Stiglitz, Joseph, *Making Globalization Work*. New York: W. W. Norton, 2007.

Sweet, Kathleen M., *Transportation and Cargo Security: Threats and Solutions*. Upper Saddle River, NJ: Prentice Hall, 2005.

Thomas, Andrew R., *Supply Chain Security*. Santa Barbara, CA: Praeger, 2010.

U.S. Tariff Commission, *Information Concerning Dumping and Unfair Competition in the United States and Canada's Anti-Dumping Law*. Washington, DC: U.S. Tariff Commission, 2009.

Wilkins, Mira, *A History of Foreign Investment in the United States, 1914–1945*. Cambridge, MA: Harvard University Press, 2004.

Wright, Robert E., *One Nation under Debt: Hamilton, Jefferson, and the History of What We Owe*. New York: McGraw-Hill, 2008.

Yarrow, Andrew L., *Forgive Us Our Debts: The Intergenerational Dangers of Fiscal Irresponsibility*. New Haven, CT: Yale University Press, 2008.

About the Editor and Contributors

Editor

Michael Shally-Jensen is former editor-in-chief of the *Encyclopedia Americana*, executive editor of the *Encyclopedia of American Studies*, and editor of numerous other books and reference publications. He received his PhD in cultural anthropology from Princeton University, having specialized in aspects of American culture and society. He lives in Amherst, Massachusetts.

Contributors

Carl R. Anderson is vice president of finance at High Pressure Equipment Company and an adjunct faculty member at Edinboro University of Pennsylvania. His areas of expertise are financial and cost management.

Anita C. Butera is an assistant professor of criminal justice at Marist College in Poughkeepsie, New York. She holds a PhD in sociology from American University and a JD from State University of New York–Buffalo.

Jason A. Checque practices law in Erie, Pennsylvania. He received an MBA from the Black School of Business, Penn State Erie, The Behrend College, and a law degree from Duquesne University School of Law.

Robin Morris Collin is professor of law and director of the certificate program in sustainability and law at Willamette University College of Law in Salem, Oregon. She is coauthor, with Robert William Collin, of *The Encyclopedia of Sustainability* (Greenwood Press, 2009), among other publications.

Lee A. Craig is an alumni distinguished undergraduate professor of economics at North Carolina State University, where he has taught for almost two decades. A noted economic historian, Craig has written on such diverse topics as the history of public pensions, the impact of mechanical refrigeration on nutrition, and the European economy.

John D. Crane is a psychological and marketing researcher at the Pennsylvania State University, with expertise in the effects of marketing endeavors on vulnerable populations and cultural socialization influences on individuals' behavior. He trained as an insurance management officer at Bankers Life and Casualty Company.

Peter H. Denton is associate professor of history at the Royal Military College of Canada (Kingston, Ontario), instructor in technical communications and ethics at Red River College (Winnipeg, Manitoba), and a minister in the United Church of Canada. His research applies the philosophy of technology to contemporary global issues, including environmental sustainability, social responsibility, and warfare.

Ashutosh Deshmukh is a professor of accounting and management information systems at the Black School of Business, Penn State Erie, The Behrend College. He specializes in accounting information systems and auditing and has published extensively in these areas.

Edward W. Erickson is a professor emeritus of economics at North Carolina State University, where he taught for over 35 years. Predating the energy crises of the 1970s, he earned a PhD from Vanderbilt University and wrote his dissertation on the oil market. He then became an internationally recognized expert on energy and oil and published and consulted on these topics throughout his career.

Keith C. Farrell is the accounting manager at Reed Manufacturing Company in Erie, Pennsylvania. His areas of expertise are financial accounting, cost management, and corporate taxation.

Robert M. Fearn is a professor emeritus of economics at North Carolina State University. He has focused his teaching, research, and writing on the operation of labor markets. Prior to his academic career, he worked as a specialist on the former Soviet Union's economy for the U.S. Central Intelligence Agency.

Geoffrey Gilbert is professor of economics and Lloyd Wright Professor in Conservative Studies at Hobart and William Smith Colleges in Geneva, New York. His research focuses on the economics of population and world poverty issues. Recent publications include *World Population* (2006) and *World Poverty* (2004), both from ABC-CLIO.

Thomas Grennes is a professor of economics at North Carolina State University, where he has taught for 40 years. His research specialties are international trade and monetary economics. He has published books and academic articles and has been a guest lecturer in Eastern Europe.

Scott E. Hein is Robert C. Brown Professor of Finance at the Rawls College of Business Administration, Texas Tech University. He also serves as the faculty director of the Texas Tech School of Banking. Among his numerous publications is *The Stock Market* (Greenwood Press, 2006), coauthored with Rik W. Hafer.

Jeanne M. Hogarth is program manager in the Division of Consumer and Community Affairs at the Federal Reserve Board. She has had a long career in education, including as a high school teacher and an associate professor at Cornell University. She has published widely on consumer economics and personal finance.

Ronald J. Hrebenar is professor of political science at the University of Utah. His research focuses on interest groups, lobbying, political parties, and elections in the United States, Japan, and Europe. Among his recent books are *Lobbying in America* (ABC-CLIO, 2009) and *Parties, Interest Groups and Political Campaigns* (2008), coauthored with Matthew J. Burbank and Robert C. Benedict.

David N. Hyman has been a professor of economics at North Carolina State University for over 35 years. He earned his PhD from Princeton University. He is the author of several popular college-level economics textbooks and served on the staff of the President's Council of Economic Advisors during the Reagan administration.

James H. Johnson Jr. is the William R. Kenan Jr. Distinguished Professor of Entrepreneurship and director of the Urban Investment Strategies Center at the University of North Carolina at Chapel Hill. His PhD is from Michigan State University, and his research interests include community economic development and the effects of demographic change on the workplace. Johnson is frequently quoted in the national media, including *USA Today* and National Public Radio.

Brandon Kramer is a territory manager in the pharmaceuticals industry. His areas of expertise are health care management and pharmaceutical sales.

Jennie Jacobs Kronenfeld is professor of sociology at Arizona State University, Tempe. She has published over 100 articles in medical sociology, public health, and health care policy. She has authored, coauthored, and edited over 20 books on a wide variety of topics related to health and social policy, professional development, health policy concerns, and research in the sociology of health care.

William M. Kunz is associate professor in the Department of Interdisciplinary Arts and Sciences at the University of Washington at Tacoma. He has also worked as a vice president and senior producer at Turner Broadcasting and as a producer with

ABC Sports and NBC Sports. Among his publications is *Culture Conglomerates: Consolidation in the Motion Picture and Television Industries* (2006).

Kenneth Louie is an associate professor of economics and chair of the international business program at the Black School of Business, Penn State Erie, The Behrend College. His areas of expertise are international economics and the economics of labor markets.

Robert D. Manning is a research fellow at the Filene Research Institute, past director of the Center for Consumer Financial Services at Rochester Institute of Technology, and founder of the Responsible Debt Relief Institute. Author of the widely acclaimed *Credit Card Nation* (2000), which received the 2001 Robert Ezra Park Award for Outstanding Contribution to Sociological Practice, Manning is a specialist in consumer finance, financial education, retail banking deregulation, race and ethnic studies, and globalization.

Phylis M. Mansfield is an associate professor of marketing at the Black School of Business, Penn State Erie, The Behrend College. She is the author of several book chapters and articles on consumer complaint resolution, service quality, and social issues and ethics in marketing. In addition, she has 20 years of corporate marketing experience.

Elizabeth A. Nowicki is currently a visiting associate professor of law at Boston University and a member of the Tulane Law School faculty. She has written on securities law topics and on topics related to corporate governance and directors' liability. Her areas of interest include corporate law, mergers and acquisitions, securities regulation, publicly held businesses, and corporate finance.

Raymond Owens is a research economist at the Federal Reserve Bank of Richmond. He holds academic degrees from Virginia Tech, and he tracks the national and regional economies for the bank. A frequent public speaker, Owens has also written papers on credit issues, real estate markets, and economic development incentives.

Diane H. Parente is associate professor of management at the Black School of Business, Penn State Erie, The Behrend College. She is a second-career academic and the author of numerous articles, mostly concerning interdisciplinary solutions to business issues. She is a frequent speaker on strategy, online education, and project management.

E. C. Pasour Jr. is a professor emeritus of agricultural and resource economics at North Carolina State University. With a PhD from Michigan State University, Pasour is the author of two books and numerous articles, primarily on the agricultural economy and market economics.

Mary Beth Pinto is an associate professor of marketing and director of the Center for Credit and Consumer Research at the Black School of Business, Penn State Erie, The Behrend College. She is the author of numerous articles on consumer behavior, health care marketing, and advertising.

Paul W. Schneider holds an MBA from Penn State Erie, The Behrend College. He has numerous regional publications and professional organization memberships and specializes in communications.

John J. Seater is professor of economics at North Carolina State University. He has also worked at the Federal Reserve Bank of Philadelphia. His teaching and research are in the areas of macroeconomics and monetary economics, and his journal publications include articles on impacts of budget deficits, movements in interest rates, and the response of household spending to changes in income.

John Silvia is chief economist for Wachovia Corporation. He holds a PhD from Northeastern University, and, prior to joining Wachovia, he worked for Kemper Funds and in positions at the U.S. Congress. Silvia sits on several boards and advisory groups, including the Economic Development Board for the State of North Carolina and the National Association of Business Economics, and has been president of the Charlotte Economics Club.

Peter B. Southard is an assistant professor of management at the Black School of Business, Penn State Erie, The Behrend College. His expertise is in supply chain management, operations planning and control systems, and information systems. His management experience includes banking and at the U.S. Department of Agriculture.

Ruth Ann Strickland is a professor of political science at Appalachian State University, Boone, North Carolina. Her areas of interest include U.S. government, public policy, the judicial process, and administrative law. She is the author of five books, including *Campaign and Election Reform* (ABC-CLIO, 2008), with Glenn H. Utter.

William M. Sturkey holds a master's degree in African American studies from the University of Wisconsin–Madison and is currently a PhD student in history. His area of expertise is the post–World War II history of African Americans.

Lois A. Vitt is the founding director of the Institute for Socio-Financial Studies, Charlottesville, Virginia. She is a sociologist who has conducted research on consumer decision making, financial literacy education, consumer health finances, the finances of retirement and aging, and financial instruments and organizations. Among her publications is the two-volume *Encyclopedia of Retirement and Finance* (Greenwood Press, 2003).

Michael L. Walden is a William Neal Reynolds Distinguished Professor in the Department of Agricultural and Resource Economics at North Carolina State University. Holder of a PhD from Cornell University, Walden's career spans 30 years and includes publication of seven books and hundreds of articles as well as service on dozens of commissions and study groups. Additionally, Walden writes a regular newspaper column and produces daily radio programs, for which he has won national awards.

Walter J. Wessels is a professor of economics at North Carolina State University. A nationally recognized expert on the labor market, his PhD is from the University of Chicago, and he has been teaching for over 30 years. His recent research and publications have dealt with the impact of unions and consequences for raising the minimum wage.

Index